Praise for *On Royalty*

"Best known for his confrontational interviews on current-affairs program *Newsnight*, Paxman keeps his scabrous side firmly in check, taking a relaxed, even humorous approach here . . . The author casts his net wide as he sets about his task, demonstrating a vast knowledge of all things royal as he darts back and forth in time, linking various events from the past to those of the present . . . A witty, edifying treatise."

—*Kirkus Reviews*

"As Paxman seeks to fathom the mesmeric hold of monarchy—particularly British—on our imaginations, his remarkable access lets him spy closeup on today's royals . . . Paxman proves a vastly knowledgeable and tartly entertaining guide to a magical realm that is stranger than fiction."

—*Publishers Weekly*

"A thoroughly enjoyable book . . . [Paxman] certainly has some stories to tell, and even readers who have read all the latest books on the House of Windsor will find themselves eagerly turning the pages . . . We expect to be both informed and entertained and are not disappointed."

—*Library Journal*

"Fascinating, well-researched, often amusing." —*Nashville Tennessean*

"A nuanced, if at times acerbic, look at the institution of monarchy."

—*Sunday Express* (UK)

"Clever, cogent, and entertaining . . . This is a perfect Survival Guide for Royalty . . . Paxman's book is stuffed with witty anecdotes and is beautifully written. It also contains a serious message for all those interested in the fate of our own Royal Family."

—Mark Bolland, *Mail on Sunday* (UK)

"Jeremy Paxman's study of the British monarchy is hugely entertaining, and the view through the Windsors' keyhole is irresistible."

—Rachel Redford, *The Observer* (UK)

"If these are indeed the last days of the monarchy as we have known it, Paxman has produced a highly entertaining book that will help to explain to future generations why Good Queen Bess was so loved while her heir remained unpopular." —Billy Bragg, *The Guardian* (UK)

"If Jeremy Paxman were not a highly successful television journalist he could have made a living as a writer . . . [On Royalty] is action-packed and entertaining . . . The Palace will be quietly pleased with this honest, amusing book."
—ANNE CHISHOLM, *The Sunday Telegraph* (UK)

"Paxo has great fun with these figures, in a pugnacious and abrasive attack. Yet there is also a thread of humanity running through his account—a certain sympathy for those victims of pomp and circumstance."
—NICK GROOM, *Arts and Book Review* (UK)

"An anecdote-strewn study of the changing role of kingship. The *Newsnight* Torquemada explains his own conversaion from republican to fan of hereditary Highness. Many interviews, much absurdity, great fun."
—JOHN WALSH, "Ten Best Autumn Reads," *The Independent*

"Paxman's book is everything that royalty is not allowed to be—witty, stylish, intelligent, pugnacious and political."
—IAIN FINLAYSON, *The Times* (UK)

"Brilliant, wide-ranging . . . Paxman bracingly points out the virtues of patriotism and the richness of our heritage."
—ROGER LEWIS, *The Express* (UK)

"[Paxman's] withering wit is offset by an openmindedness that other commentators would do well to mimic . . . [His] accessible approach offers the author freedom to uncover fascinating little corners of history."
—PAUL CONNOLLY, *The Evening Standard* (UK)

"On Royalty is an absorbing, well-researched book, part serious enquiry, part rollicking anecdote. The absurdities of royal figures make wonderful copy and Jeremy Paxman has taken full advantage of it . . . His observations on the nature of royalty, the evolution of monarchy and its changing role from warrior king to constitutional queen are acute and widely researched."
—SARAH BRADFORD, *The Evening Standard*, (UK)

"An entertaining historical primer for new readers wondering what the fuss is about and it is glued together with tart dexterity."
—PETER PRESTON, *The Observer* (UK)

On Royalty

By the same author

ON ROYALTY

A Very Polite Inquiry Into Some Strangely Related Families

JEREMY PAXMAN

PublicAffairs
New York

First published in 2006 in the UK by the Penguin Group, Viking.
www.penguin.com
First published in 2007 in the United States by PublicAffairs™,
a member of the Perseus Books Group; paperback edition published in 2008.

Printed in the United States of America.

PublicAffairs books are available at special discounts for bulk purchases in the U.S. by corporations, institutions, and other organizations. For more information, please contact the Special Markets Department at the Perseus Books Group, 2300 Chestnut Street, Suite 200, Philadelphia, PA 19103, or call (800) 810-4145, ext. 5000, or e-mail special.markets@perseusbooks.com.

Grateful acknowledgement is made for permission to reprint extracts from the following works: *The Apple Cart* by George Bernard Shaw, reprinted by kind permission of the Society of Authors, on behalf of the Estate of Bernard Shaw. *And They Call It Cricket* by John Osborne, copyright the Arvon Foundation. *Elizabeth* by Sarah Bradford, copyright Sarah Bradford 1996 and 2002, reprinted by kind permission of Gillon Aitken Associates. *Great Contemporaries* by Winston S. Churchill, reproduced by kind permission of Curtis Brown Ltd, on behalf of the Estate of Winston Churchill. Every effort has been made to contact copyright holders, but the author and publisher would be happy to correct any error of omission or commission at the earliest opportunity.

Set in Monotype Bembo
Typeset by Rowland Phototypesetting Ltd, Bury St Edmunds, Suffolk

Library of Congress Cataloging-in-Publication Data
Paxman, Jeremy, 1950-
On royalty : a very polite inquiry into some strangely related families / Jeremy
Paxman. — 1st ed.
p. cm.
Includes bibliographical references and index.
HC ISBN: 978-1-58648-491-0
PB ISBN: 978-1-58648-574-0
1. Monarchy—Great Britain—History. 2. Great Britain—Kings and rulers—Biography. I. Title.
DA28.1.P38 2007
941.009'9—dc22

2007007133

British HC ISBN: 978-0-670-91662-7
British PB ISBN: 978-0-670-91679-5

Contents

Preface

As citizens of a nation which calls itself the world's greatest democracy, what other response can Americans have to an institution as primitive as monarchy than to sneer at it slightly and wonder at the anachronism of it all? It's as American as apple paella. The United States got rid of royalty when the country was invented. Come to that, abolishing kings and queens, and their privileged, parasitic relatives was one of the reasons the country came into being.

Well, maybe it's time to rethink a prejudice or two.

I confess I was happy enough in my (I thought) educated conviction which said that kings and queens represented an antique way of organising the world, up there with rain dances and human sacrifice.

And yet many of the most stable twenty-first century societies in the West are monarchies. Maybe it's time to wonder why.

It is not, after all, as if kings and queens in western societies, from Scandinavia to Spain, have any real power. If you want to see a real king at work, you need to watch an American president: his powers are modelled on those of an eighteenth century English king.

But the modern British monarchy has no real power at all. This seems to me to have a number of advantages. Firstly, it keeps the ultimate expression of nationhood—the right to claim to be the embodiment of the nation—out of the hands of those who seek it merely to satisfy their political ambition. The absence of real power means that momentous decisions—like going to war—are merely made by some here-today, gone-tomorrow politician, and not by some booby who claims to personify a people. As Winston Churchill put it, 'a great battle is lost: parliament turns out the government. A great battle is won—crowds cheer the Queen.'

It may not fit with the received wisdom about monarchies. But the fact that these kings and queens have so little autonomy can actually empower their people. Any monarch who begins to harbour delusions about their importance has only got to look at their predecessors. Although monarchy rests upon the idiotic proposition that someone can be born for a role, in fact, the people and their politicians have seen to it that the crown has been passed from one claimant to another like some gilded football.

The British monarchy is pretty much the Gold Standard in these matters, and the long reign of Elizabeth an example to others. Not merely has she managed to spend half a century at the head of people whose society has changed enormously, but she has managed to retain a constant level of support. You will find it hard to discover a single example of her saying anything controversial. But that is the genius of monarchy. It leaves the business of solemn pledges and implausible promises to the tacky world of politics.

In subtle ways, too it is as responsive to public opinion as a bunker-mentality presidency, whose occupant, knowing he has only eight years before his inevitable removal, needs only listen to public opinion for the first four, or, at best, six. To a perpetual monarchy, on the other hand, the public mood is a matter of perpetual concern. When monarchies have lost their sense of this—in seventeenth century England, eighteenth century France, or twentieth century Russia—their subjects will despatch them. This makes monarchies unusual barometers of public mood and fashion. They may not set the pace. But they don't want to be entirely left behind. It's oddly comforting to know that Queen Elizabeth has an iPod, even though we might instinctively envisage her winding up a gramophone.

So this book is an investigation into an institution that has survived, like a threatened species, a safari in search of an elderly but still exotic creature, a lion whose territory is diminished but who would look much less impressive in a zoo.

Would America be better if it had retained a monarchy?

Faced by the rival dynastic succession battles of the Bushes and the Clintons, it is sometimes claimed that American has reinvented a royalty of sorts. It is an exaggeration: what it has is a breed of professional politicians. America has defined itself in part by the way that it filled the vacuum created by throwing off the monarchial yoke. The monarch, in absentia, is as crucial to the identity of America as she is, in person, to the idea of Britain. Perhaps that is why she remains such a figure of fascination.

Introduction

All kings is mostly rapscallions.

Mark Twain, *Huckleberry Finn*, 1884

You come down to breakfast and look out of the window. A man is sitting on the front lawn in a deckchair. He is eating a sandwich. It is a warm summer's morning and he is dressed in dark-blue cotton trousers and a short-sleeved check shirt. He is wearing a straw hat. He brings out another sandwich from the packet on the bench beside him, takes a bite, and chews. Then he clamps a pair of binoculars to his eyes and stares in at you through the window.

The Prince of Wales either doesn't notice or has simply become accustomed to being stared at, because he continues to scatter over his breakfast the seeds and grains which his staff have laid out in front of him. In a couple of hours' time, he is due to open the Sandringham Flower Show, and today the gardens of the house are open to the public. Being a spectacle is part of what he's for.

At the flower show he will admire the flower arrangements, smile appreciatively at collections of giant onions, and make enthusiastic comments about the home-made lemon curd. Last night he had sat in the front row for a performance of Handel's *Samson* by an enthusiastic young opera company in the Palladian splendour of Houghton Hall, the nearby pile rebuilt by Britain's first prime minister, Sir Robert Walpole. He had been placed in the most conspicuous seat in the room, which ruled out any possibility of nodding off. The opera is followed by half an hour in which the entire cast and backstage staff are introduced to him. Tomorrow night, it will be a piano concert, this time in a local church, to be followed by a dinner at which he will be seated next to a Japanese patron, whose command of English appears to be confined to 'Aaaah, zo!' And this is what passes for pleasure. The next day, there will be a trip to Derby to present new colours to an army battalion.

Being in this company is a strange experience. I had arrived at Sandringham, the royal family's house in Norfolk, the previous afternoon to be greeted in the drawing room by plates of little egg-and-cress sandwiches, cream-and-strawberry-jam scones, fruit-cake and a choice of three types of tea. My fellow guests – three writers, a theatre director, a couple of actors, a painter and a few other arty types – were mostly as unknown to each other as they were to our host. But house-parties are an aristocratic convention, quite distinct from the sort of occasion the rest of us might enjoy, when good friends get together for the weekend. A house-party hosted by royalty is stranger still. Friendship implies equality, and a king can have no equals. Instead what they have is status, which is another thing altogether, in which things are turned inside-out and while you know hardly anyone personally, everyone assumes they know you. You will always be the last to arrive anywhere, which means that everyone else has been standing around twiddling their thumbs for an hour or more. There will be drivers standing by to take you at the appointed minute on high-speed dashes to your next engagement. The car will disgorge you at the precisely appointed time of arrival and if you are lucky there will merely be a host to greet you. If you are unfortunate, there will be a receiving line of mayors and aldermen, chief constables, bishops, hospital matrons, district surveyors and local business-people, all of whom must have their hands shaken and their words listened to, and with whom photographs will be taken. This is the eternal, infernal reality. You begin to see why a prince needs valets, as each day may involve five or six changes of dress. For the rest of us, a valet is a challenge.

'My name's John, and I shall be looking after you, sir,' he had said when I found my way upstairs. 'What time would you like your tea or coffee in the morning, sir? And where will you be sleeping tonight, sir?' the valet asked.

'About eight, I suppose,' I replied, 'and I rather thought I'd sleep in the bed there,' I said facetiously, pointing to the bed made up at the side of the room.

'*This*, sir,' the valet said, in a long-suffering sort of way, 'is your dressing room. Your bedroom is over there.'

Being invited to stay with royalty brings problems you had never imagined could exist, like confusing a dressing room, which has wardrobes, bed, washbasin and bedside table, with a bedroom, which has wardrobes, bed, washbasin and bedsides tables. It's obvious, when you think about it. The bedroom is bigger.

Shown to my room, I discovered to my horror that my suitcase had not merely been delivered. It had been unpacked: a row of Marks and Spencer underpants lay in a drawer, jackets hung in a cupboard. But where was the dinner jacket we had all been told we should have to wear that evening? I searched the wardrobe. I checked the empty suitcase. No sign. I was certain I had packed one. I must have forgotten it. A bath had been run, so I climbed in to it, while devising a strategy. Surely I could borrow a dinner jacket from one of the staff? Fine, until I realized that the staff didn't wear dinner jackets. They wore dark-blue uniforms with a crown on the lapels.

I emerged from the bath, and my worries vanished. Magically, the dinner suit had reappeared. There it was, hanging on the back of the chair in the dressing room, an evening shirt laid out, unbuttoned, a pair of socks folded back for instant access. The jacket looked a good deal better than it had done when I last saw it. In the time I had been in the bath, it had been taken away, sponged down and pressed.

I dressed slowly, had the usual tussle with the bow-tie and then noticed that one of the buttons on the front of my shirt was loose. Smart people wear studs rather than buttons, don't they? On the writing desk in the dressing room was an enormous pair of scissors. I began to cut off the buttons. As I was wearing the shirt at the time this was not as easy as I'd expected. I did not draw blood, but the shirt emerged from the operation looking like something created by Jean-Paul Gaultier.

Downstairs the guests were gathering for dinner in the saloon, a gloomy panelled room in which the pieces of a jigsaw are always laid out on a green-baize-covered side-table. This one looks impossible – the pieces are all dark green or black and there is no accompanying box-top to show even which way up the final picture should be. By the time we all leave, three days later, the collective brainpower has managed to assemble about twenty pieces, and even then we have no idea what they are supposed to represent.

And then the prince appears. He is, of course, perfectly turned out: who would not be with two valets and two assistant valets? And his shirt is running not with studs but buttons and his tie is as compactly tied as one of those clip-on devices favoured by cocktail pianists and head waiters. He is affable and smiling and quietly spoken. But the men bow their heads and many of the women drop into curtseys. How can anyone have a normal conversation when you suddenly find yourself inserting the word 'sir' into every second sentence, sinkingly aware that while the words falling from your lips may not be sycophantic they are – which is just as bad – of such staggering, predictable dullness that anyone with worse manners would have glanced across the room and found an urgent telephone call to take. Later in the stay, when someone gets up from their seat to fetch another cup of tea, he begs her, 'Oh don't go! It's happened all the time, from school onwards, people moving away from me, because they don't want to be seen as sucking up.' There's an anguished tone to the outburst which suggests it's the product of painful experience.

Sandringham, with its sixty acres of grounds, hedges with set-square corners, lustrous lawns and raked gravel drives, has been loaned to the prince for three days, so that he can open the flower show and entertain friends. The estate was bought for the future King Edward VII to raise pheasants and children. Here he rebuilt the house in red brick, installed gas lighting and flushing lavatories, and expressed his devotion to shooting by having the clocks running half an hour ahead of standard time, to maximize the winter hours available for killing things. His enthusiasm for eating was shown in the set of jockeys' weighing-in scales inside the front door, to check that guests left more portly than they had been when they arrived. On days when he was shooting, the king would breakfast, at breakneck speed, on bacon and eggs, haddock, chicken and buttered toast. This was followed by hot soup (turtle being a favourite) between drives, and then a large lunch. In the afternoon there was tea (poached eggs, *petits fours*, preserved ginger, rolls, scones, hot tea-cakes, sweet cakes and his favourite Scottish shortbread) in the saloon at the end of the day's sport. After a bath and having dressed there would be dinner of at least twelve courses.[1]

To judge from what his Highgrove chef gives his guests, Prince Charles also enjoys good food. When guests were invited to Sandringham by his mother, they expected to be served tinned tomato soup and were rarely disappointed. Socially ambitious (usually socialist) politicians have been turning their noses up at the modesty of the royal way of life for decades. When invited to stay at Balmoral, for example, they arrived expecting banquets and discovered instead they were expected to attend an endless series of barbecues, with Prince Philip grilling the chops and sausages. Prince Charles appreciates food more than his parents do, but it is in a faddish manner and he has trained himself to manage without much lunch because, apart from anything else, if he got much fatter it would mean remaking so many uniforms.

But to the visitor life in a royal household seems what it is – another world. Here, you are awoken by a valet or a maid with a cup of tea and the newspapers (not for the prince, who has learned from experience that reading them will merely make his blood boil, and prefers to listen to the radio). The curtains are thrown back, clothes are chosen and laid out for you. The pyjamas you wore will be taken away and returned washed and ironed, with the two buttons which have been missing for at least a year replaced. A well-known actor invited to stay at Sandringham recently after a heavy filming schedule which involved a lot of horse-riding discovered that his underpants were in a frightful state. He took them off, rolled them into a ball, climbed on to a chair and hid them on top of the wardrobe. The following evening he returned to his room to find them washed, ironed and folded.

There is a loaded sideboard at breakfast, with napkins the size of some people's tablecloths. A picnic lunch does not mean sausage rolls on a soggy tartan rug but a laid table in a log cabin somewhere on the estate, where the butlers serving you have dressed down to tweed jackets and ties. These men have been brought over from his house at Highgrove. But each of the residences has its own complement of workers: the grounds of Sandringham alone provide work for eight gardeners, ten gamekeepers, a kennel-man, estate managers and numerous farm staff. The indoor staff is supplemented, when the queen is in residence, with cooks, butlers, valets, pages, footmen, a Travelling Yeoman (in charge of the luggage arrangements), maids, police officers and staff ranging from her private secretary to the assistant private secretary's secretary.

In its essentials it is an antique way of life, fitted to the period in history when a citizen of London, Vienna, Paris or Moscow belonged to a nation which identified itself by its monarchy. It does not suit the spirit of our times, which is one of the reasons why the twentieth century was a catastrophe for royalty. It began badly enough when, in July 1900, King Umberto I of Italy was rewarded for acknowledging the cheers of the crowd at Monza with assassination by an anarchist. His son, Vittorio Emmanuele III ('Emperor of Ethiopia' and 'King of Albania'), declaimed loudly about the thousand-year history of the House of Savoy and then scuttled from the throne in July 1946. In 1908, King Carlos of Portugal was assassinated: two years later the monarchy was abolished. In 1913 the King of Greece was murdered. (Later monarchs endured periods of exile, until finally, after coup and counter-coup King Constantine found refuge in north London in the late 1960s.) The First World War was triggered when the chauffeur driving the heir to the throne of Austria-Hungary took a wrong turn in Sarajevo and was unfortunate enough to have to reverse the royal car slowly past a nationalist carrying a Browning semi-automatic pistol. As Leonard Woolf observed, it is inconceivable that Europe would have consumed itself if the person assassinated had been the son of a miner or prime minister. But what began as 'an attempt to make the world safe for kings and archdukes' ended in 'a holocaust of emperors, kings, princes, archdukes and hereditary grand dukes'.[2]

The most infamous destruction was in Russia, where the tsar and his family were murdered in a basement. Almost all these killings and extirpations were presented as nasty necessities in the building of democracy. But they demonstrably failed to do so. In the years which followed the end of their monarchies, the peoples of Russia, Spain, Italy, Germany, Austria, Hungary, Romania, Bulgaria, Greece – most of the population of Europe – found themselves living under dictatorship. Better the crown is worn by a dullard than by someone who thinks he has a mission. As the editor of the left-wing *New Statesman*, Kingsley Martin, pointed out, we should note the warnings from history: 'if we drop the trappings of monarchy in the gutter . . . Germany has taught us [that] some guttersnipe . . . may pick them up'.[3] It may be the sort of admonition which belongs with Hilaire Belloc's advice to 'always keep a hold of nurse, for fear of finding something worse'. But he has a point.

Reflecting on his own ejection from power, the English-educated King Farouk of Egypt famously predicted that by the end of the twentieth century there would be only five monarchies left in the world: the kings of hearts, diamonds, clubs and spades and the King of England. The remark has the whiff of cigary worldliness about it that enabled Farouk to pretend that his own overthrow was the result of irresistible forces of history. In fact his departure from Cairo to the fleshpots of Monaco had as much to do with the fact that he was a pampered, kleptomaniac lard mountain:[4] it was enough to look at his fat face and elaborately waxed moustache to want to punch his nose. But his moustache was sharper than his mind. He was right about the British monarchy, which survived into the twenty-first century because, by *force majeure* and good sense, its shape and powers had been trimmed and trimmed again, having learned the lesson of the great republican Thomas Paine that kings are deposed in the hearts of their subjects long before they are got rid of by legislative decree.[5]

But kings and queens survive elsewhere in Europe. The Netherlands persists happily with a characteristically Dutch arrangement which is half republican and half royalist, in which monarchs treat their role as just another job, from which they can retire when they get tired. Denmark, Norway and Sweden have never been republics and show no sign of becoming disenchanted with their royal families. There is no head of steam to replace the newly restored Spanish monarchy with something more modern, and in Belgium the monarchy is one of the very few institutions which hold an intrinsically incoherent state together.

The figures who sit upon these thrones do not enjoy their privileges because of anything they have done. They do not have to be clever or talented. They do not need ambition: not for them the slog up from insignificance to eminence. It is enough for them simply to be there. They are like a church spire you see across a river valley, the expression of age-old beliefs. When Prince Charles takes the throne, he will do so as the incarnation of something very close to a religion, which certainly defies rational explanation. Of course, he is looked after comfortably, never having to put his hand into his pocket for the right change, never having to drive himself unless he chooses to do so. The stories about his having the toothpaste squeezed on to his brush may be apocryphal, but that they could have been entertained at all says something. In exchange for his comforts, as a once wild animal in a zoo gets used to its mealtimes, he must be gawped at by people eating sandwiches on his front lawn.

Psychiatrists' consulting rooms see a steady procession of people who imagine they have been in conversation with, been visited by or even been intimate with her Majesty Queen Elizabeth II, by the grace of God monarch of the United Kingdom of Great Britain and Northern Ireland, sovereign of Australia, New Zealand, Canada, Jamaica, Barbados, Fiji, the Bahamas, Grenada, Papua New Guinea, the Solomon Islands, Tuvalu, St Lucia, St Vincent and the Grenadines, Belize, Antigua and Barbuda, St Christopher and Nevis, head of the Commonwealth and the Church of

England's Defender of the Faith. The delusion is so commonplace that one bishop, with much experience of working with the mentally ill, has been driven to wonder what on earth they can have delusions about in republics.

And it is not confined to the sick. In the 1970s, an entire book was devoted to the fact that Queen Elizabeth II stalks the dreams of so many of her subjects. The author discovered that in most of their visions her subjects imagined that the queen spent much of her day drinking tea. She was almost always wearing her crown, whether she happened just to have dropped into the local pub or was ambling around Leicester Square. She even wore it while driving long-distance lorries between Edinburgh and London. Yet she was informal in her conversation. 'I was in Canada,' one dreamer admitted, 'and I bumped into the Queen at Niagara Falls. "Betty!", I yelled. "What on earth are you doing here?" '[6] Another accosted the queen at a Buckingham Palace garden party, complaining that she could not get a cup of tea. 'Minutes later she [the queen] appeared in jeans and gumboots, pulling a gigantic trolley, piled high with green cups, the kind you can buy at Woolworths for a few pence.'[7] Others dreamed of falling in love with the queen's children, about being surrounded by hordes of royal corgis, that she had moved into their house and begun darning their socks, that they had rescued her from drowning, that the queen's mother was taking part in a professional wrestling match, or that they had bumped into her out shopping and had to lend her money because she had 'forgotten the Privy Purse'. Some dreamed of previous monarchs, notably Queen Victoria, who in one dream was inexplicably sitting in the corner of the room playing the bagpipes. Mrs Willis of Hereford had dreamed that Queen Victoria had accosted her mother with the memorable invitation, 'Emily, I am *so* pleased to see you . . . What would you like? A cup of tea or a haddock?'

A vast acreage of print has been devoted to the analysis of dreams. Some of it even makes apparent sense. It is noticeable that many of those who seem to dream most about the monarchy are those least likely to have anything to do with it, but perhaps it is just that those closest to the throne are far too discreet to talk about what happens in their sleep. Many of the dreams seem to suggest thwarted wishes, others that the queen has recognized a talent which the dreary friends and colleagues of our waking lives have failed to notice. Certainly they all suggest that the queen signifies something more than the local newsagent. She is usually friendly, and simultaneously both more and less imposing than other authority figures, such as the teacher we remember from our schooldays. Who knows how many of us have had a member of the royal family play around in our unconscious dressed as a clown, a gravedigger or a fishmonger? Just because one does not recall dreaming of the queen does not mean one has not done so, merely that one has not remembered. Even the writer Martin Amis, who claimed to be utterly uninterested in the royal family, once claimed that he had recently had a sex dream about the Duchess of York, Sarah Ferguson. 'You may be touched – and surprised – to learn that I found Fergie to be both a considerate and an inventive lover,' he told the world.[8] This book is an attempt to understand how it is that the kings and queens of Britain and some of the other monarchies of Europe have come to exercise the hold they have upon our imaginations.

We do not, on the other hand, speak of the hold they have upon power, because the notable characteristic of the royal families of Europe is that they have so very little of anything remotely resembling true power. Increasingly, they tend towards the condition of pipsqueak principalities like Liechtenstein and Monaco – fancy-dress fodder for magazines which survive by telling us things we did not need to know about people we have hardly heard of. At Sandringham I asked Prince Charles what he thought was the function of monarchy, and he replied in a world-weary way, 'I think we're a soap opera.'

This is a characteristically Eeyorish thing for him to say, which one can perhaps understand from a man saddled with the tedium of spending most of his adult life waiting for a death in the family before he can take on the only role for which he has been told he is fitted. But it falls far short of a complete explanation. No soap opera lasts for ever, which is the central conceit of monarchy, and those television series which survive any length of time do so only by introducing fresh characters and inventing increasingly preposterous plot-lines. Apart from the occasional marriage, monarchies are stuck with a familiar cast, and the activities we see them perform – the opening of another bypass or hospital wing, the reciting of turgid speeches compiled by unimaginative functionaries, the formal glad-handing of civic worthies – are anything but glamorous. It is hard enough to stay awake. Apart from the very occasional coronation, royal wedding or state funeral, the public lives of kings and queens are of ineffable dullness.

For me – as for most reasonably modern, reasonably well-educated people, I suspect – the kings and queens of modern Europe have never been objects of awestruck fascination. The complicated bloodlines which have given them their eminence are slightly absurd things, anyway: if you go back far enough, just about anyone with European ancestry is descended from royalty. Calvin Coolidge could trace his descent from Charlemagne, and a mere twenty-two generations separated Walt Disney from Edward I. The powers they have are few enough: for intrinsic interest, give us an absolute monarch any day, even if the only places you can find such people nowadays are corrupt kingdoms in vast expanses of sand or obscure African statelets like Swaziland. For those who live in constitutional monarchies, the king or queen is just a fact of life, like the weather: occasionally you enjoy it, but most of the time you just put up with it. Come to think of it, they are a good deal less interesting than the weather, for the simple reason that predictability is of their essence.

I have vague memories of being taken out, at the age of four or five, 'to see the queen' as she visited the naval dockyard where my father's ship was then based. I seem to recall my mother walking me across the village green, to watch a car pass slowly – but not slowly enough – and a hand waving from it. But I cannot be sure. For most of the citizens of the countries over which the handful of surviving kings and queens preside that is probably their closest experience of royalty. The intriguing question is why the citizens should turn out to gaze upon such a spectral figure at all.

I certainly recall the widow of George VI visiting my school on its centenary. My sister recently found a pile of old 8 millimetre film at the back of a cupboard, which showed the queen mother emerging from a helicopter in a pink coat and hat and then being led by the headmaster through crowds of cheering boys and matrons and masters' wives in their best outfits, her arm rising and falling in that effortless royal wave which no other mortal employs. The film had a slightly surreal quality to it: it had been used twice, so the pink hat and coat had been superimposed on pictures of a school sports day, with King George VI's widow waving from the middle of a long-jump pit before being obliterated by a leaping child.

Otherwise, my life has been almost blamelessly royal-free, which is the way I and many other products of post-war Britain have liked it. Any of us could have made the case for abolishing the monarchy from the age of thirteen or fourteen, and, although other targets of teenage truculence fade away, republicanism has often tended to remain an item of faith: any system which puts an unelected person at the head of the country affronts the suffrage, legitimizes the idea that advancement is by breeding rather than effort, and ensures that the country marches into the future looking backwards into its past.

And yet those in whom the spirit of the guillotine lives on would have to admit that republicanism has always been a minority taste in modern Britain. It has a whiff of earnest priggishness about it which has never won over the general public. When the liberal-minded *Independent* newspaper was founded in the 1980s it attempted to ignore royal stories, on the ground that they were an irrelevance. The ban finally withered away to nothingness when Princess Diana's car was written off in a Paris underpass, and it became clear that, whatever else they might or might not be, the lives and deaths of members of the royal family were matters of genuine public interest. The grief which swept the country developed from shock, through mourning, into a teary-eyed hysteria which astonished almost the whole of the ruling class and revealed something remarkable about the intensity of public feeling for these remote beings.

The funeral of Princess Diana demonstrated – and the funeral of Queen Elizabeth the Queen Mother confirmed – how great a hold the royal family has upon public sympathy, particularly it seems among poorer people, older people and those who do not have a university education. The monarchical memorabilia industry directs the marketing of its souvenir mugs, 'miraculously lifelike' dolls, commemorative teaspoons and the rest of its absurdly expensive knick-knacks at the readers of middlebrow newspapers. They do not advertise in the *London Review of Books* – they know that intellectuals hold to the motto of that great vegetarian George Bernard Shaw, that 'kings are not born: they are made by artificial hallucination'.[9] Monarchy is mumbo-jumbo. Yet mumbo-jumbo is the language of magic. I was in Sri Lanka when Lady Diana Spencer married Prince Charles in July 1981. The sight of hundreds of Asian faces pressed against the shop and hotel windows, straining to see the grainy broadcast pictures from another continent, was evidence enough of the mesmeric hold of royalty on the minds of the deprived. A privileged young woman in a bridal dress – sewn, we were told by the doting commentator, with ten thousand mother-of-pearl sequins – her face hidden behind a veil and trailing twenty-five yards of fabric behind her, was the material of which dreams were made.

Most of us grow out of such stuff. But in 2004, long after we had all learned that fairytales do not end with people living happily ever after, a minor epidemic of similar fantasies swept Europe. 'Sometimes I wake up and wonder where I am,' gushed the part-time waitress and single mother marrying Crown Prince Haakon in Oslo. 'I guess you could say it's a modern fairytale,' said Tasmania's Mary Elizabeth Donaldson, of her engagement to Crown Prince Frederick in Copenhagen. In the spirit of hidden identities they were reported to have met when he had introduced himself to her in a bar in Sydney with the words, 'Hi, I'm Fred from Denmark.' When Crown Prince Felipe married in the May rain in Madrid, *Hello!* breathlessly reported, 'He was the Prince who insisted he would marry only for love. She was the talented journalist and newsreader who fell for his sensitivity and intelligence.' But only one style of language is appropriate for these occasions, and even this divorced career woman married her 'dream prince' in a 'fairytale' gown of off-white silk, topped by a platinum and diamond tiara.[10] To the delight of the newspapers, Prince William, heir to the British throne, was being seen with Kate Middleton, whose family ran a mail-order business supplying, among other delights, polyester 'princess' dresses for little girls.

A belief in kings and queens is the adult equivalent of the little girls' belief in fairytale princesses. It has no logic to it, and yet you cannot stop the universal hallucination any more than you can stop little girls wanting to be princesses when they grow up. As recently as 1962 Harold Nicolson could write of the 'fabulous respect for royalty', which 'survives in its glamour and a certain sanctity; it is considered irreverent and almost blasphemous to make jokes in public about the royal family; and we are all conscious, when in the presence of the Sovereign, of a certain tension which is akin to awe'.[11] Nicolson's observations belong to the era when military service had only just ceased to be compulsory and cinema audiences rose to their feet for the national anthem: the social revolution which overtook Britain in the 1960s swept away traditional deference. The first attempts to satirize the monarchy were met with the argument that such attacks were unfair, because 'they can't hit back'. Within thirty years, lampooning the first family on television and in newspapers was commonplace. And yet a curious thing happened. Holding the individuals up to public ridicule did nothing to undermine fascination with monarchy: the more they were told that their kings, queens and princes had feet of clay, the more the public seemed to want to believe that they wore glass slippers. The gross embarrassments of royal children and their unsuitable spouses did nothing to slake the thirst for fantasy. There is a frequently quoted figure that, across the world, 2.5 billion people watched the funeral of Diana, Princess of Wales.[12] Even if it is an exaggeration, and the total was a mere 1 billion, it still represented at the time the largest number of human beings ever to witness the same event simultaneously – just as her wedding had at the time been the most watched event in history. Forty million people bought copies of Elton John's 'Candle in the Wind 1997', £100 million was donated to a memorial fund, and two men killed themselves out of grief.[13] Royalty is somehow the property of its subjects. Another of Harold Nicolson's observations of four decades ago remains true. 'The fact that the glamour of royalty survives as a feeling rather than as a thought, as a sentimental emotion rather than as a logical concept, does not diminish its efficacy . . . it remains potent, widespread and beloved.'[14]

At one point in my journalistic career at the BBC, the organization became convinced that its supreme test would come with the death of King George VI's widow, the mother of Queen Elizabeth II. The conviction reflected its recognition of the emotional power of monarchy. But how to articulate it? Although its news division was largely staffed by the sort of clever young people who affect disdain for monarchy, for many years in the 1980s and 1990s it forced them to give up a Saturday or Sunday afternoon every six months, to practise what would happen when the sad day dawned. Long sets of guidelines were produced and laminated in plastic. Elaborate chains of editorial command were established in which people identified only by impenetrable acronyms would refer the news up, down and sideways to confirm that it was true that a very old lady had indeed done what all old people do sooner or later. A cupboard was organized, filled with identical grey suits, white shirts and black ties (or, as one of the endless memos instructed, 'in the case of female presenters, black shawls').

Each programme was required to practise how it would cope with the news. Reporters would be dispatched to empty corridors and car-park basements, pretending to be at the gates of Buckingham Palace, St James's Palace or Clarence House, where the old lady was then living. Young researchers would be sent to sit in corners of the canteen, where they played the part of one of the Great and Good about to pay homage. 'Are you there, Archbishop?' began one radio dummy-run.

They were a nightmare. You might think that, confronted with a news story, a news organization would immediately check its accuracy, and then broadcast what it had established. But the BBC had devised a formula under which its programmes ignored the first reports and continued to discuss the latest obscure political development in the Balkans or the European Union's Common Fisheries Policy, while, behind the scenes, producers frantically made preparations for breaking the news to the public. A caption would then be displayed, which told the audience to 'stand by for an important announcement'. The moment this notice appeared, the presenter on duty was to sprint from the studio, scuttle up several flights, open the sacred cupboard with the key (which was carried on his person at all times), take out one of the suits and then sprint back down the corridor, descend six floors and career back down to the studio, where, breathless, he was to wait for the caption to be removed. Finally – and there was to be not the slightest deviation from the prescribed words – he would say, 'It is with deep regret that the BBC announces the death of her Majesty Queen Elizabeth the Queen Mother.' Solemn music would then be played, accompanied by pictures of the royal standard flying at half-mast. The BBC's competitors, meanwhile, would presumably have broadcast whatever details they had been able to gather – where she had been when she died, cause of death, reaction of family and statesmen, and so on. The BBC would add such details only after the martial music and long sequences of chocolate-box pictures charting the life and times of the late Elizabeth Bowes-Lyon.

The lumbering, tortuous protocol reflected the organization's uncertainty about its own role: was its job to tell the nation the news (if indeed – as some wondered – the death of an exceptionally old lady was really news at all) or was it somehow to act as part of the Establishment, and to become Chief Mourner? In the rehearsals with which I was involved we never, ever, got it right. On one occasion we had been 'on the air' for the best part of three hours before we discovered that, had we been doing the thing for real, all that the waiting nation would have seen was a caption telling it to stand by for an important announcement. It seemed fatuous conducting interviews with authorities on the House of Windsor in which we discussed the state of the queen mother's recent health: there had been a number of incidents in which fish-bones had become stuck in the royal throat – was it a problem with a particular species of fish? In fact, of course, there was plenty of worthwhile discussion to be had about the queen mother. Some of it was constitutional – the role she had played in restoring the monarchy when her shy and stuttering husband took the throne after the Abdication Crisis caused by Edward VIII; some of it personal – such as her role during the Second World War; and some of it plain scurrilous, involving tales of gin-drinking, horse-racing and an alleged partiality for deeply reactionary politics. But these things would either never have been asked or were deemed too cheeky to be shared with the public before it had first been lulled into a sense of appropriate awe.

Just as the best-laid military plans do not survive the first encounter with the enemy, the strategy was made redundant by the utterly unexpected and hideously dramatic death of Diana, Princess of Wales. This was so far outside the scope of the plastic templates that the organization did what it ought to have planned to do in the first place, treated the public as though they were adults and told them what it could establish, as soon as it could do so accurately. When, one Easter weekend, the queen mother did succumb to mortality at the age of 101, the BBC was caught flat-footed and interrupted normal programmes to transmit the information by a newsreader who was wearing – some newspapers were outraged to report the next day – a *burgundy* tie. *The Times* disclosed that the royal family was 'unhappy' and 'upset', the *Daily Mail* that the queen mother's grandson, Prince Charles, who had been travelling back from Switzerland and had not seen the coverage, nonetheless thought it 'lamentable'.

About a year before Diana died, I had received from her an invitation to lunch. I immediately suspected a hoax. I had never met her, had, as far as I could see, absolutely nothing in common with her, and had never expressed any interest in meeting her. But when I called her private secretary, the invitation turned out to be genuine. I suggested a restaurant. He replied that it would be a lot easier if I went to see her at Kensington Palace. So, on the appointed day I was waved through the barriers and ushered up a flight of stairs into the princess's apartment. I had no idea what to expect. I was aware of her story – who could not be? – but knew little or nothing of who she was, except that almost the only qualification she had earned from an expensive education was a certificate for the best-kept something-or-other. I remembered because it had been a question in a quiz, which someone had answered with the word 'virginity'. I think the right answer might have been guinea-pig.

And then suddenly the most famous young woman in the world appeared at the top of the stairs. She was wearing a pale-blue two-piece suit and was much taller than I had expected.

'Jeremy, so nice of you to come,' she said in a voice as smooth as cream. 'Just the two of us. Can you cope?' A thousand male fantasies flashed through my mind. I said I'd try.

We had a drink (wine for me, water for her) while she asked vague questions about journalism, and then we went through to her dining room to eat. As the two liveried butlers performed an elaborate demonstration of synchronized lid-lifting, I began to realize that the lunch had no agenda. She just wanted someone to talk to, and, unlike other lonely people, was in the happy position of being able to invite anyone she liked and being reasonably confident that they would turn up. So I asked her about herself, her life and the news of the day. She seemed to answer everything entirely directly, even if some of her ideas were distinctly odd – an American airliner which had crashed off Long Island was, she said, 'definitely hit by a missile – that's what my sources say'. About her children, she was very straightforward. Was William looking forward to being king? 'Well, he often says he really doesn't want to do it, but then Harry says, well, if you don't want the job, I'll have it.'

On the way out, I told her how strange the palace seemed – remarkably quiet, yet only a hundred yards or so away from the bustle of Kensington High Street. It felt a bit like a prison, I said. 'No, more like an up-market *Coronation Street*,' she said. 'As we go out, you'll see all the curtains twitching.' The soap-opera theme again. Still, it seems a bit claustrophobic, I said. 'Sometimes,' she said, 'I put on my jeans and a baseball cap and sneak out into the High Street, and sometimes the newspaper vendor will spot me and say "What you been up to now, Di?" But they're terrifically friendly, and if someone starts bothering me I just go into W. H. Smith's, and the staff there are very nice, and they hide me.'

It didn't sound much of a life, but she seemed reconciled to it. As we walked out to my shabby car I fancied I saw a curtain twitch and thought how awful it must be to live a life in which just about anything you did might earn a disloyal neighbour or employee a hundred pounds or so if they told a newspaper about it.

The meeting was never repeated: we were hardly kindred spirits, and she doubtless had dozens of other people she wanted to have lunch with. A year later, she was dead. I was as shocked as anyone. But the controversies which followed – the newspaper outrage at why the sugary tributes of the Prime Minister about 'the People's Princess' were not reflected in royal circles, why the royal standard at Buckingham Palace was not being flown at half-mast (and the response, which was that it was flown only when the king or queen was in residence) – left me cold. When Winston Churchill died, hundreds of thousands had turned out to see his coffin drawn through the streets of London. Now vast crowds were drawn to another funeral. But Churchill had led the country in its darkest hours and had embodied the determination of a people not to succumb to tyranny. What could be said to be Diana's achievement? Churchill had done something. Diana had merely been something.

Of course, people had strong feelings about her, because the separation between Diana and Prince Charles had been so very public. But for a marriage between famous people to fall apart is hardly unusual: among film and music stars the rarity is the marriage which stays intact. When such relationships explode we just shrug our shoulders. But when Charles and Diana split up, it polarized people passionately. You were either in the prince's party – 'He was made to marry a woman he did not love by the forces of the state, and stuck with it until she became utterly impossible.' Or you were with the princess – 'She was an innocent young girl taken up by a much older man, used, betrayed and then spat out.'

Like all good propaganda, each version contained a germ of truth. But why did people hold their positions so fiercely? Why did people say – and seem to mean – 'I can never forgive him/her'? Some of it, perhaps, was common humanity; anyone would sympathize with 'those poor boys', the princes, especially when their mother met her tragic death. But there was a passion to the partisanship which gave it the character of that most intense of conflicts, the civil war. The only plausible explanation for people caring so fervently, it seemed to me, was that they felt the man and woman involved *belonged* to them in some way. What extraordinary alchemy had transfigured this otherwise remote relationship between ordinary people and a uniquely privileged couple?

The obsequies which followed the death of the queen mother were another example. The poor newsreader on duty at the BBC on the afternoon that Buckingham Palace announced she had died in her sleep was visibly nervous. His hands shook. His voice croaked. What was it about this particular event which had reduced him to such anxiety, when the normal fare of news – war, disaster, the consequences of human heroism, folly and malevolence – never ruffled his composure? When the coffin was placed on public display in Westminster Hall the pressure to see the thing was so intense that lines of people waited in the cold for hours upon end, often right through the night. They snaked down the banks of the River Thames, hundreds of thousands of people of both sexes, of all ages, of varied racial backgrounds and of mixed social classes. On the day of the funeral, 1 million people watched the coffin borne on a gun carriage through the streets. Millions more, in shops, offices and factories across the country, observed a two-minute silence as the ceremony began. What did all this signify? Why had they come? The metropolitan media, much of which had predicted minimal interest in the last rites of a very old lady, had seriously misjudged the public mood.

What was it they had failed to detect or understand? Some

commentators in liberal newspapers like the *Guardian* attempted to explain away the crowds by suggesting they were the dupes of an Establishment which knew that if it deployed enough pomp, muffled drums and splendid uniforms it could milk a bereavement to enlist support for a redundant institution. But the polite and good-humoured crowds waiting to file past the coffin did not sound as if that was what had brought them out. Some talked about being there simply because they wanted to be present at an historical event. But most seemed merely to say they were 'paying their respects'. Pressed any further and they spoke of the queen mother almost as if she was a member of their family, their own grandmother perhaps, or a slightly distant, rather grand great-aunt. How had they come to have this relationship with a woman they had never met?

A few years ago, Buckingham Palace advisers decided that the queen really ought to see a little of the working lives of her subjects. Days were organized in which she would be taken on tours to meet people who taught in schools, traded shares or nursed in hospitals. One of the days was to be spent discovering how broadcasting worked. Like all organizations destined to receive a royal visit, the broadcasters were reduced to much anxiety. Walls were painted, people were selected to be presented, 'spontaneous' demonstrations of technology were rehearsed. And in the evening, to say thank you, about three hundred of us would be invited to a reception at Buckingham Palace.

I had decided not to go. And then curiosity, the interest shown by my children and an uncomfortable sense that I was being a prig made me change my mind. It was definitely not one of Buckingham Palace's grandest occasions – warm white wine and the occasional plate of Twiglets scattered here and there. The media crowd would certainly not later accuse the royal household of profligacy. We milled about in some of the enormous state rooms talking to one another and vaguely speculating why any of us was there. I began to wonder whether the queen herself was even present, and sought out a courtier.

'Is the queen here?' I asked.

'Oh, very much so,' she said.

'Well, where is she?'

'She's in thet room over there,' came the cut-glass reply.

Now impulsiveness, braggadocio or the effect of the warm white wine took over.

'I'd like to speak to her,' I said.

'Oh! But you're not on the lest. If you'd been on the lest, you'd have been told as you cem in.'

'Well, I'd like to talk to her.'

'She's in the room over there.'

I cut through the crowd, my resolution wavering with each step. Why did I want to talk to her? What on earth would I say? Why should she want to speak to me? How had I got myself into this mess?

The side-room was packed. I gave a slight sigh of relief on discovering that there was no sign of the queen and struck up a conversation with a former colleague.

'So, the queen's not here, then?'

'Yes she is. She's over there.' And then I realized how remarkably short she was, as the shoulders of the men and women around her parted for an instant, and there she was, smiling in that interested yet impersonal way she has. She was working her way down a long line of people, shaking hands and exchanging pleasantries with those on The List.

'I'd been hoping to have a word with her,' I said.

'I'd go over and do so, then. She's awfully nice,' said the man from Channel Four.

'No,' I said, looking for an excuse, 'it's a very long line and I've got to get back to work soon.'

The truth was that I had been overcome by nerves. What Nicolson had described four decades ago as 'a certain tension which is akin to awe' fitted the mood well enough. A similar feeling overtook me at one point during the research for this book, inside Buckingham Palace. I had gone there to see the State Opening of parliament from, as it were, the other side. After the ceremonial, the carriages returned to the inner courtyard of the palace. I was standing, feeling rather scruffy amid the scarlet tunics, boots and spurs, at the edge of the steps. As she got out of the carriage, the queen heaved a sigh, obviously relieved that the formalities were over. She turned and began to talk animatedly with the Crown Equerry, the splendidly spurred official in charge of her transport. One of the horses drawing her carriage had kicked out and, from what I could hear, she was talking about what had excited it. I thought how much she reminded me of my elderly mother, with her knowledge of, and enthusiasm for, horses. Then, suddenly, the queen shot a look across at me. Probably she was just noticing – as everyone close to her says she notices – something out of the ordinary. For an instant we had eye contact and I thought with utter horror, 'Oh no! She's going to talk to me!' I wanted the ground to swallow me, anything to avoid finding something to say to this particular little old lady. And then, to my relief, the queen's gaze shifted, she turned to gather up her retinue, and they followed her up the steps and into the palace.

Why should one individual have this capacity to strike awe? I have interviewed presidents and prime ministers, murderers and generals – even, once, a living god (the Dalai Lama, who turned out to be surprisingly partial to the smell of bacon sandwiches). What was it about this diminutive grandmother that induced paralysing tension? 'Majesty' is one of those words made almost meaningless through overuse. It is part of the explanation, perhaps. The uniqueness of a king or queen has something to do with it – there is only one of them. But I was a republican, with a full set of coherent, democratic prejudices about the world. What were we doing with this family at the head of a twenty-first-century state? And what must it be like to be one of them?

1. First, Find a Throne

Even on the most exalted throne in the world we are only sitting on our own bottom.

Montaigne, *Essays*, 1580

On 16 August 1923 the London *Evening News* carried the front-page headline 'A CROWN AWAITS AN ENGLISHMAN'. 'Wanted, a King: English country gentleman preferred,' the copy began. 'Apply to the Government of Albania.' Like many newspaper stories, the report was an elaborate piece of embroidery woven on a very small patch of cloth. But it was not a joke. Other countries might have revived their monarchies in the twentieth century. But Albania is the most recent European state to have invented one. The newspaper was anxious to convince sceptical readers. 'It is true. The romantic and picturesque country in the Balkans is a monarchy without a monarch, and its people have an ardent desire to be ruled by an Englishman.' The newspaper warned its readers that applicants for the job would have to be 'country gentlemen', because Albanians detested politicians. In addition to the obvious appeal of being king, the paper reported, the country had its own attractions, not the least of which was that it could offer some of the finest shooting in Europe, including snipe, duck, geese, bears, wolves and wild pigs. The currency, according to an unnamed informant, was entirely gold. 'There are no banks in Albania,' said the source, 'and the government money, I believe, is kept in a tin box. That is their Treasury.'

It was enticing enough. Over seventy people applied for the job, although most came not from landed estates but from suburbs of London. One letter sent to the Albanian Prime Minister was from a ballet teacher, who felt that her ability to soar in the air entitled her to be Queen of the Sons of the Eagle. Other candidates for the job included a British Conservative MP and an American tin-plate tycoon.

The first question to be settled in any inquiry into how monarchies work is how does a king or queen find a throne in the first place? It is generally assumed that the hereditary principle is basic to monarchy, although Edward Gibbon believed that the Antonine period of the Roman empire – when the emperors adopted the young men they thought should succeed them – was 'possibly the only period in history in which the happiness of a great people was the sole object of government'.[1] Most monarchies depend upon the three principles of heredity, consecration and acclamation by the powers in the land. In most European monarchies, the crown was passed from father to son or daughter, but in other traditions – Arab dynasties, for example – the successor can be chosen from among the royal family. Poland was so taken with the idea of acclamation that it invented a most enlightened arrangement by which when a king died the Primate of Poland assumed the title of *Interrex*, while the nobility went about the business of voting for a new king. The person they chose was obliged to swear an oath that he would not marry, divorce, levy taxes or make war without permission and would not attempt to engineer his succession.[2] No room for any nonsense about Divine Right. Unfortunately, as Voltaire commented disdainfully, the system suffered from the significant disadvantage that 'the throne is almost always up for sale, and since there is rarely a Pole rich enough to buy it, it has often been sold to foreigners'.[3] When Poland was partitioned at the end of the eighteenth century, the system perished.

Voltaire was dead and heroically memorialized by the French revolution when the people of Sweden found themselves looking for a new king. They settled upon one of Napoleon's marshals, Jean-Baptiste Bernadotte, who neither spoke Swedish nor was a Lutheran, to become their prince royal. His dynasty, now widely considered to have the dullest, stuffiest court in Europe, still rules Sweden. A century later, when seceding from Sweden in 1905, the Norwegians preferred monarchy to a republican system, so borrowed a Danish prince and created a dynasty. Even at the fag-end of the twentieth century a faith in royalty survived in the Baltic: in 1994 the Royalist Party of Estonia, which held 10 per cent of the seats in that country's parliament, invited Queen Elizabeth's youngest son, Prince Edward, Earl of Wessex, to come and be their king. A Buckingham Palace spokesman described the suggestion as 'a charming but unlikely idea'.[4]

As the Ottoman empire fell apart, thrones became available all over the place. The kingship of Greece was hawked around Europe and finally offered to Prince George of Denmark, who was less than keen until his uncle, the Danish king, threatened to have his father shot. Most famously, there was the example of Bulgaria, which had an urgent need of a king, after the abdication of Alexander I in 1886. Prime Minister Stambolov ('the Bismarck of Bulgaria') sent envoys across the continent in search of a young, wealthy, militarily competent and powerfully connected candidate. The emissaries were, apparently, under the impression that an invitation to become king of Bulgaria would be irresistible. It was not. A grand duke in Russia declined the post. Valdemar of Denmark wasn't keen. A prince in Romania ruled the thing out at once. Then, in a Viennese beer garden, they encountered an Austrian major who, having listened to their tale, 'sprang to his feet and slapped his deerskin riding breeches of spotless white in pure amazement and joy. "Why," he cried, "I know the very man you want; and by a strange coincidence he is here on this very spot. He is Ferdinand of Saxe-Coburg and Gotha, grandson of Louis Philippe of France, and cousin of every crowned head in Europe. He is a prime favourite of both the Emperor of Austria and the Tsar of Russia. And, my boys, don't say I told you so, but he is as rich as Croesus."'[5] The cartoon major took them to a nearby billiard hall and introduced them to the twenty-six-year-old Ferdinand, dressed as a very junior officer in the Austrian army. After dithering for a while he accepted the job with the words, 'I regard it as my sacred duty to set foot at the earliest possible moment on the soil of my new country.'[6]

Albania's choice fell upon an extraordinary Englishman named Aubrey Herbert, without whose efforts the country might never have come into existence. As the Ottoman empire rotted away, the great powers had planned to carve up the territory – known, if it was known at all, for mountains, bandits and 'honorary men' (women who had refused their father's choice of husband, and therefore had to spend the rest of their lives as males), between Serbia and Greece. Aubrey Herbert, squire of Pixton Park and later MP for South Somerset, had become devoted to the place after hiring an Albanian manservant. Kiazim endeared himself to his master with the request that if he forgot any of his duties, Herbert was, please, 'to stab him'.[7] Now, as the great powers discussed the division of the remnants of the Turkish empire, Herbert repaid this obsessional loyalty by a tireless campaign for an independent Albania. He was persuasive.

The Albanians never forgot their debt to this remarkable man, who was the model for Sandy Arbuthnot in John Buchan's yarn *Greenmantle*. Buchan describes him as riding 'through Yemen, which no white man ever did before. The Arabs let him pass, for they thought him stark mad and argued that the hand of Allah was heavy enough on him without their efforts. He's blood brother to every kind of Albanian bandit.'[8] In real life, Herbert had been almost blind from childhood, with piebald hair. He made himself fluent in Albanian, Turkish, Arabic and four other languages and was every bit as colourful as his fictional counterpart. When the First World War broke out, he became an officer in the Irish Guards simply by buying a uniform, sewing on a second lieutenant's pips, and turning up at the docks when the regiment embarked for France in 1914. At Gallipoli it was Herbert who negotiated a truce with the Turks to allow for the burial of the dead.

The First World War had set royal cousin against royal cousin and, by its end, the modern world looked the sort of place in which monarchy had no role. But the new nation of Albania stood aside from the great melting of the crowns. In 1913 it had offered its throne to the man who had done so much to promote the cause of independence. Herbert seemed well qualified for the task, not least because, as an Englishman, he belonged to a nation with no strategic interests in the Balkans. He knew it would be a difficult and dangerous task, given the Albanians' habit of settling disagreements about the weather with the help of a knife or revolver. But there was another consideration. As he wrote to his brother, 'Of course with me, money is the trouble. The Albanians have never paid any taxes, and even if they do, poor lambs, they can't pay much.' Later he added, 'If I had fifty thousand a year, I think I should take Albania.'[9]

Herbert reflected that, in the circumstances, 'I don't think they are likely to get a good Prince. Any prince would be an ass to take it on if he knew the difficulties and more of an ass if he didn't.'[10] Eventually the Albanians found their ass in Prince Wilhelm of Wied, a tiny state on the Rhine. Although Wilhelm's candidacy was supported by Austria, he was not himself particularly wild for the job, and the Kaiser's advice was much the same as that of the British Foreign Secretary: those who wish to keep their sanity avoid the Balkans. But, just as little girls dream of becoming a princess, so princesses dream of being a queen. His wife was keen. The prince's aunt, the Queen of Romania, published a newspaper article promoting the couple's claim under the title 'Fairyland wants its prince'. In 1914, it got him, and the princess became a queen. But fairyland turned out to have primitive customs (the prince was taken for a weakling because he helped his wife out of their carriage) and ferocious politics. Within weeks, the new king had been obliged to set up field guns in the grounds of his palace and blast away at one of his ministers' residences next door. Six months later the couple fled the country, leaving behind six separate governments, each claiming to be the legitimate representatives of the people of Albania.

In the aftermath of the First World War, Albania decided to try once more. In 1923 representatives again approached Aubrey Herbert, undeterred by his habit of dressing like a tramp. Perhaps in time they might have persuaded him to change his mind. Certainly, he thought hard about the proposition, as he put it in what he charmingly believed to be a coded letter, that 'The A's (private) have invited me to be No. 1 big man.'[11] He was tempted, but reluctant, for much the same reasons as before. But less than a month after the *Evening News* announcement the matter became academic. For Herbert had taken the advice of his former tutor at Oxford, who told him that his blindness could be cured by having his teeth removed. He died of the resulting blood poisoning. For several years Albanians are said to have honoured his memory by referring to kind people as 'Herberts'.

All sorts of candidates were then approached, some of them by people who had simply invented for themselves the role of intermediary. The 8th Duke of Atholl, who was (as is his successor) entitled to his own private army of Highlanders, was sounded out, but declined. The shipping magnate Lord Inchcape was asked whether he'd like to drop into Albania next time he was 'cruising in the Mediterranean'. Failing that, could he 'suggest the name of some wealthy Englishman or American with administrative power who would care to take up the cudgels on Albania's behalf, thereby securing an honourable position as Albania's king'? Inchcape replied in two sentences that he had 'received your letter of 29th ulto . . . but it is not my line'.[12] The former England cricket captain, C. B. Fry, was sounded out by a supposed Albanian bishop (Fry thought he bore an uncanny resemblance to the great bearded Victorian batsman W. G. Grace), to see whether he would like the post. Fry's friend Ranjitsinhji eventually advised against the job, on the grounds that 'living in a lonely castle on an island and perhaps [getting] a bullet in the ribs'[13] was not sufficient inducement. Fry took his friend's advice. For Albania, this was to have catastrophic strategic consequences, Fry later reflected, because, had he accepted, he would have introduced the country to cricket, and it would then have been impossible for Mussolini to invade the country, for fear of bringing down the wrath of the Royal Navy.

As it was, in 1928 the throne fell into the hands of Ahmed Zogu, or Ahmed Bey Zogoli, a warrior from the Gheg clan in the north of the country. His rise to kingship had the characteristic of most such ascents, that is to say, an insatiable urge to power. He was

Minister of the Interior at twenty-four, Prime Minister at twenty-seven, President at twenty-nine. Somewhere along the way he is said to have been engaged by *The Times* as its correspondent. Now, armed with the slogan 'we are a primitive and backward people', the liberal use of threats against possible opponents, and the payment of large bribes to potential supporters, he orchestrated a popular campaign to have himself declared king. Rumours of a coup reached the *Times* newsdesk in London, which demanded to know why its local correspondent had failed to file on the story. The reply was said to have read, 'All is quiet in Albania. I am king. Zog.'

He was thirty-two and lord of whatever he could survey in his primitive, backward country. He waxed his moustache into fine points and dressed in a military uniform adorned with stars, chains and gold braid. (On holiday he preferred to dress in blazer and white trousers 'like an Englishman at Henley'.) Wreathed in permanent clouds of cigarette smoke, he was attended, in Albanian tradition, by his several unmarried sisters. These were described by one visitor as 'sloe-eyed, raven-haired and sharing a rather oriental cast of countenance'.[14] They were to be seen marching about Tirana at the head of contingents of the Albanian Women's Association, wearing First World War steel helmets, dark-blue waisted tunics with Sam Browne belts, and khaki riding breeches, each of them carrying a drawn sword.

Enjoyable though it was, Zog found that being king did not meet all his needs. As for all kings, there was the obvious problem that none of his countrymen was quite on the same level. One evening, a group of British businessmen visiting Tirana were surprised by a knock on the door of the hotel room in which they sat playing poker. A messenger explained that their blinds were up and the king had been watching them through binoculars from the palace: would they like to bring the cards over and cut him in? Later, Zog developed the habit of ringing around the hotels of the capital, on the off-chance there might be someone staying with whom he could have a conversation.

Then there was the question of a queen. Emissaries were

dispatched across Europe, equipped with the vital statistics of various Hollywood starlets the king had seen in magazine photographs. In Budapest they found a candidate. She was a Hungarian countess, Geraldine (her mother Gladys was American), twenty years his junior. The family fortune not being all it once was, she was now selling postcards at the museum. Once she had been carted off to Tirana, Zog eyed her up appreciatively and decreed that their wedding was to be the most spectacular event in Albanian history. And so it probably was. The streets were strewn with flowers and the guests festooned with furs, jewels and clanking swords. A gasping witness to the profusion of archimandrites, imams, mountain chiefs in breeches and cloaks from green to vermilion and women in fox-furs and tiaras reached for the inevitable comparison. It 'might have been lifted from the fanciful pages of some fairy book'.[15] Hitler gave the couple a supercharged scarlet Mercedes-Benz as a wedding gift.

Foreign journalists who struggled through the mountains to interview this latest adornment to monarchy were often bowled over. 'Fire away with your indiscreet questions,' he boomed.[16] The correspondent from the *Daily Express* was impressed. After an interview in 1930 he declared, 'Zog I, King of the Albanians, is a great young man of remarkable intelligence. I predict that much will be heard of him, and that he will achieve renown as one of Europe's most able statesmen.'[17] Like many a journalistic prophecy, this turned out to be somewhat wide of the mark. A year after his wedding, instead of leading his primitive and backward people in resistance to an Italian invasion, King Zog ran away into exile.

Unless you are lucky enough to get the call from a country like Albania which is looking for a king, the most important ingredient of monarchy is that you are born to the job. So the first challenge is to have chosen the right parents: the institution depends upon the proposition that those set in authority should have done nothing to earn their position. Wise governments set out to demonstrate by good deeds and compassionate words that they enhance the societies they head. But in a herediary system no amount of deeds or words can bring to the throne someone who has sprung from the wrong loins.

The surest way to establish the superiority of your parentage is to assert that your ancestors were gods. Not many people can match that. When the anthropologist Arthur Hocart came to consider the subject of kingship in the 1920s he concluded that 'the earliest known religion is a belief in the divinity of kings'.[18] Perhaps there were never gods without kings or kings without gods; we do not know. But, when history begins, there are kings. The Jews talked of the 'spirit of the Lord' coming upon their rulers, the Hittites referred to the king as the sun. From Peru to Japan there was a belief that the king was descended from the sun. Chinese emperors were referred to as 'Son of Heaven'. In ancient Egypt the pharaoh's placenta was worshipped in its own right. From Mexico to the South Seas they thought the king's body so sacred that it should not be contaminated by contact with the ground. In some Polynesian societies it was thought that if the king's feet touched the earth it would become holy, which would presumably turn walking into a form of hop-scotch for everyone else. European medieval literature is full of stories of lost or stolen royal princes who establish their claim to the throne by demonstrating that they have on their right shoulder, or on their chest, a skin-blemish in the shape of a cross. Even the Stuart dynasty in Britain had supporters who claimed that its kings were descended from the Virgin Mary.

Nowadays, apart from the Duke of Edinburgh, who sent a photograph of himself to the Iounhanan people of Vanuatu and was rewarded by their deciding that he must be some form of god, royalty must be content with more modest claims. But the urge to credit them with supernatural attributes is profound, and it is important to recognize that it comes not from the kings themselves but from their subjects. When Tiberius was made emperor of Rome in AD 14, he asked his people to recognize that 'I am mortal, that my functions are human functions, and that I hold it sufficient if I fill the foremost place among you.'[19] But the need to explain away why someone else should be set above them was so strong that the senators could not accept such modesty. 'The gods', they told him, 'have made you arbiter of all things; all that we lay claim to is the glory of obedience.'[20] This compulsion to deify – or at least to beatify – royalty is unstoppable. How else can we explain the enormous impromptu shrines thrown up outside Kensington and Buckingham Palaces when Princess Diana, the commoner who had become royal, died in a Paris car crash? The labels attached to the bunches of flowers carried messages like 'A New Angel in Heaven', 'Princess of Love' and, most explicitly, 'Born a Lady. Became a Princess. Died a Saint'. A year after her death, the writer Paul Johnson, who admitted that he prayed *for* and *to* her, claimed that she had 'done more to promote Christian values in this country than all the efforts of our state Church in half a century'. She had undergone 'a demotic canonisation' of the kind which occurred in Europe before the Catholic Church seized control of the process in the twelfth century.[21]

Most European kings and queens have comforted themselves with the belief that while they may not *be* gods, they have God behind them. King James I of England went as far as telling his son, the future Charles I, that he was to worship God for two reasons: 'first, for that he made you a man; and next, for that he made you a little God to sit on his Throne and rule over other men'.[22] Well into the twentieth century there were European rulers who believed that they had been appointed by God and were answerable only to him. Even Winston Churchill could find it in him to forgive Germany's leader in the First World War, Kaiser Wilhelm II, because he had been brought up to believe that he was fulfilling some divine mission.[23] When the King of Spain's decidedly sensible sister, the Infanta Eulalia, visited the German court, she became convinced that 'Kaiser Bill' 'believes that God directs every incident of the life of the world, [and] he believes that he has been divinely appointed to rule over Germany'. He therefore thought that the only person to whom he was responsible was God, and went 'chiefly to prayer for direction'.[24] She had been even more stunned when visiting the Russian court by the realization that until 1905 the tsar had claimed the right to govern not merely the bodies but the souls of his people: those who deserted his Orthodox Church ended up by being banished to Siberia.

But divine appointment is unfortunately not an option available to many. The more obvious routes to a crown are to make love or war: to ensure that at least your children will sit on the throne by marrying a king or queen, or to invade territory and establish a dynasty. The latter route has a long history, as testified to by the Crusader dynasty of the so-called Kings of Jerusalem and Napoleon's habit of adorning his marshals with duchies and princedoms. But in more modern times there are few happy examples. Zog might have been warned by the miserable example of the Emperor Maximilian in Mexico ('Poor Old Montezuma' to his family), who had been installed in the 1860s at the insistence of Napoleon III after his troops staged a coup d'état because France was owed money by the government. The man chosen for the role of emperor was Maximilian, younger brother of the Emperor Franz-Josef of Austria. He was not initially enthusiastic. But his wife Charlotte was smitten with the idea. Maximilian arrived in Mexico in 1864 clad in the full-dress uniform of a Mexican general and sporting the insignia of the newly invented Order of the Grand Cross of Guadeloupe, while Charlotte wore a diamond crown. Although he came to love the country, it was a regime conceived in French imperial ambition, which could survive only with French military support. Soon wags in Paris began to refer to Maximilian as the 'archdupe'.[25] When civil war began, the French government withdrew its troops and advised Maximilian to cut and run too. The story had an inevitable end, with the poor man subjected to a show trial and put before a firing squad on 19 June 1867. His wife had trailed around the courts of Europe pleading for aid – including bursting in on the Pope as he finished his breakfast and plunging her fingers into his hot chocolate, because, she thought, it was the only food she might find that was not poisoned.* She ended her days confined to an old castle where she reportedly

*'Nothing is spared me in this life,' he exclaimed. 'Now a woman has to go mad in the Vatican.'

whiled away the hours talking to a life-sized doll dressed in imperial robes, and receiving visitors in a room full of empty chairs with imaginary occupants. She died the year before Zog was crowned.

Had Maximilian enjoyed the military support which the French had promised him perhaps his dynasty would have survived, even with the zealously anti-monarchical United States on Mexico's doorstep. Maximilian attempted too much, too fast: when Wilhelm I became the first emperor of Germany a few years later, he did so after defeating Napoleon III's forces in the Franco-Prussian War, but also after centuries of gradual accretion of power by his Hohenzollern clan, who had risen from obscure knighthood at the time of the Crusades to kingship in Prussia in 1700. Certainly, the aspiring king can have no better guarantee than possession of a fearsome army. The present Thai royal family was put on the throne in the eighteenth century by one of the generals who expelled Burmese invaders. The three-hundred-year Chinese Ming dynasty was founded by the martial genius who drove the Mongols out of China and was replaced by the uprising which brought to power the Manchurian Qing dynasty.

The less dangerous route to a throne is be politically convenient. Most English and British kings were expected to provide some evidence that they had some sort of 'blood' claim to the crown. But the British, being a highly pragmatic and hypocritical people, were ready, when it was convenient, to interpret these claims very loosely. Henry VII brought the greatest of British ruling houses, the Tudors, to the throne after defeating the Plantagenet Richard III at the battle of Bosworth Field in 1485. But his claim to the throne was based upon double bastardy – on his remarkable mother's side in descent from an illegitimate son of John of Gaunt, and on his father's side from a relationship between the widowed Katherine of France and a Welsh squire. But the Tudors were not good breeders, and the dynasty came to an end when Elizabeth I died childless. The House of Stuart, which followed, could claim descent from Henry VII. But the secret of James I's success was to have been invited by the English to make the familiar journey south taken by so many Scots setting out to better themselves. By the time the last Stuart monarch, Anne, died without leaving an heir (despite conscientiously conceiving some eighteen children), heredity had become secondary to acclamation, bloodlines subsidiary to political congeniality. There were said to be no fewer than fifty-seven people with a better claim to the throne than George, Elector of Hanover, who was invited by government ministers to be her successor. His greatest asset was that he was not a Roman Catholic.

It takes only half an hour by speedboat to get from Corfu harbour to Albania. The strait separating the two countries is so narrow that it has regularly been swum by those desperate enough to want to escape Europe's most backward state. Out past the ornate Greek villas and the house where Prince Philip was born on a kitchen table and you arrive at the quayside in Saranda where open sewers discharge on to the beach and children swim in the sea around a couple of vessels which look as if they have been moored at the quayside for years. The five- or six-hour onward journey takes you through arid mountains where families sell their daughters in marriage and across untilled valleys where the collective farms have vanished and half their members have become illegal immigrants someplace more prosperous. The fields are strewn with hundreds of thousands of enormous concrete mushrooms decreed by the late dictator, Enver Hoxha – Norman Wisdom fan and creator of the world's first atheistic state – to resist an invasion which never came and was never going to come. At the roadside, three-legged dogs doze in the sun, while a double amputee sits in a pothole with outstretched hands as half the stolen cars in Europe career around him. Finally, out in the suburbs of the capital, Tirana, between street vendors selling hub-caps and watermelons, you arrive at the villa of the man who thinks he's king. A couple of flags bearing the black Albanian double-headed eagle hang limply above the walls.

Two security men with pistols on their hips open the gate a few inches and run a metal detector over you before demanding that you take your pen to pieces to prove it is not a gun. A female secretary and a couple of retainers arrive to walk you up the short drive to the villa where Zog's son Leka, King of the Albanians, receives visitors. There is ferocious barking from inside. The door opens. After the sunlight outside, it so dark within that you blink for a moment or two, until an enormous scarecrow of a man emerges from the gloom. He is six feet seven inches tall and wears a short-sleeved pale-blue safari suit. The grey hair on top of his beaky, bespectacled head is cropped close, as if a US Marine Corps barber had been set loose on him. His face has the consistency of wax. There is an immense gold watch on his spindly left wrist and in his right hand he holds a half-smoked Rothmans. The air is rank with stale cigarette smoke. He greets you in flawless English. (As well he might, having left his native land within a week of being born, and not returning for sixty years.)

The House of Zog may have sat upon the throne of Albania for a total of eleven glorious years. But it is characteristic of many born into dynasties – however short lived – that they cannot easily get the thought out of their heads that their countries will always 'belong' to them. The nightclubs and country estates of Europe are splattered with pretenders to thrones which no longer exist, everywhere from Romania to Portugal. What is it that keeps the dream alive?

King Leka ushers me towards one of the long, low brown-leather sofas, and I am about to sit down when two growling boxer dogs appear. One snarls viciously.

Lovely dogs, boxers, I say, trying to break the ice, such a fierce bark and yet they're so soft.

'Not necessarily,' he replies. 'They killed a couple of people who climbed over the fence when we were living in South Africa.' I withdraw my hand, slowly, and the king goes on, mildly puzzled: 'They attack in pairs, you know. One goes high and one goes low – they seem to decide it instinctively – and once they've clamped on you, they use their body weight to drag you down.' He pauses reflectively. 'Never known why one chooses to go for the throat and the other for the lower body.'

Three or four more of the dogs emerge from the shadows. I sit very quietly while the king stubs out his cigarette and lights another. The rest of the conversation is periodically drowned out when one or other of his pack of dogs bares its teeth and growls.

Leka first returned to Albania in the early 1990s when the Communist regime collapsed. That is, if you can 'return' to a country you have lived in only for the first couple of days of your life. After his father's dash into exile there had been refuge in Paris, and when that city fell to the Nazis, there was England where what the Foreign Office called 'King Zog's Circus' was installed first at the Ritz Hotel in London and then at Lord Parmoor's estate in the Chilterns. Here Hitler's Mercedes could be seen tootling along the lanes through the local beechwoods. Local rumour had it that at least one of the baths in Parmoor House had been filled with gold bars and that the king passed his time in marathon poker parties in which vast sums changed hands. English visitors were mildly astonished to discover that the cup of tea they were being offered was in fact neat scotch. When Aubrey Herbert's son called at the house he decided that Zog was 'frankly a cad', an impression that was not improved by hearing Zog's sisters – who wrongly assumed he did not speak Albanian – 'openly speculating on his sexual potentialities'.[26]

At the end of the war, disappearing in a cloud of unpaid bills, the King and Queen of the Albanians and their court were welcomed to Egypt by King Farouk.[27] But when the Egyptian authorities mooted the subject of income tax, Zog declared that 'Kings never pay taxes,' and decamped for the south of France, where the now sickly man insisted upon maintaining a formal court in which people walked backwards out of his presence, bowing. He died there in April 1961.

Leka now succeeded to the throne. But a king without a country is prone to money problems, and although the Spanish dictator General Franco was willing to provide accommodation, there remained the problem of how to make ends meet. Leka had been trained at the British officer academy at Sandhurst, but there was the obvious difficulty that the sole purpose of the Albanian army was to prevent imperialists and their royalist running-dogs from infiltrating the country. Friends like the Shah of Iran, the CIA and

President Richard Nixon were all said to have helped out. But then Leka was arrested in Thailand and charged with arms dealing. A little while later, when the Spanish authorities discovered an arsenal of guns in his compound in Madrid, the restored Bourbon monarchy understood the limits of royal solidarity and asked him to decamp. Leka headed for Africa. When he landed in Gabon he saw off the troops who surrounded his plane by appearing in the doorway cradling a bazooka. He found a readier welcome first from the illegal white-minority regime of Rhodesia, and then in Johannesburg. But when majority rule came to South Africa, the police began to pay closer attention to the king: a raid on his house in the suburbs was reported to have uncovered grenade launchers, anti-personnel mines, assault rifles and 14,000 rounds of ammunition. Conveniently enough, soon afterwards came the call to return to Albania.

Leka claims to have spent his exile plotting the downfall of Albania's Communist regime. There were periodic very grand proclamations in which, using the royal 'we', he called on the people of Albania to rise up. There was said to have been a leaflet drop from a passing balloon. There was a shambolic incident in which a group of men were supposed to have landed somewhere on the coastline and to have been – as a communiqué from the only pure Communist government in the world put it – 'totally liquidated'. None of this will he talk about with any openness, except to say that in September 1979, 'We very nearly did it.' But when I ask him about 'it', he comes over all coy, smiles and says, 'I must keep some things back, you know.'

He is also rather shy on the subject of how he managed to keep his 'court' above water. His villa may be at the side of a thundering highway, with power-lines hanging over the roof, but there is, to judge from the various people coming and going – the gaggle at the gate, someone he introduces as 'general', a man who sits at the side of the room looking gloomy, another in cook's whites – quite a household to support. When his father died he inherited liability for thirty people, which his mother met at first by selling her engagement ring. Later, there were business ventures in Saudi

Arabia, and he became personal friends with the royal family (Prince Faisal was his godfather), generally an association in which few palms remain ungreased. He describes his income as having come from 'commodities', which covers more or less anything. Certainly, his Albanian homecoming was not made easier by his insistence that eleven container-loads of arms were merely his personal collection.

A popular vote, in which the 'king' campaigned in army fatigues, surrounded by goons in dark glasses, showed, according to official figures, that about one-third of the people were prepared to see the monarchy restored. Leka claimed the results were rigged. I wondered how much the latest routinely corrupt government tried to restrict his activities in Albania, to which he replied darkly, 'They'd be foolish to deny the people. This is an armed country, you know.'

But the intriguing thing is why he should ever have bothered to return to Albania. It is not as if there is some ancient weight of destiny sitting on his shoulders. As a model of government in Europe, monarchy had been on the way out long before Zog seized the throne. Why bother to return, to live in the hope of the throne when you could have a perfectly tolerable life somewhere else? King Constantine of Greece survived life in Hampstead without too much hardship, after all.

'It's my duty,' says the cadaverous figure on the sofa.

But why? I ask.

'Why does a soldier go into battle?' he asks in reply.

Training, I suppose, I say, and loyalty to his comrades.

'You've answered your question,' he says.

At this pregnant moment the lights go out. One of the boxer dogs suddenly leaps into the air as if it has bitten into a live electric cable, bounces off the sofa and then shoots under the coffee table, where it crouches, shaking. The king sits on in silence.

A woman in jeans and white shirt enters the room.

'May I present my wife,' he says, and adds, 'Queen Susan.'

She is an attractive, open-faced woman, who looks to be in her early sixties. But Queen Susan? It is not that queens don't wear jeans and shirts and confess to being fans of Jeffrey Archer. It's that it is a little like being introduced to Queen Kylie or Queen Sharon. Queen Susan, it turns out, is the daughter of an Australian sheep farmer. Surely someone from such a young country has better things to do than to sit around waiting and hoping for the chance to restore a medieval system of government to a corner of the Balkans? But she is equally determined.

'I've had so many people ask "why are you throwing your life away?"' She sucks on a cigarette held in her teeth. 'But I don't feel I've wasted my life at all.'

Plenty of people would be glad to be rid of the role, I say.

She draws on the cigarette again (when she dies, a few months later, an obituary comments that 'The royal couple enjoyed a close personal relationship. They both had a keen liking for smoking').[28] 'It's a sense I can make a difference.'

And your son? Is he as committed to turning the country back into a monarchy?

'Oh yes, thank God. More so, in fact.'

Loyalty is part of the deal in marriage and there are millions of wives of car salesmen, headmasters or deep-sea divers showing similar readiness to put up with things for the sake of a lifetime relationship. Being 'queen' – even without a country – is some compensation, perhaps. But people who do other jobs have some choice in the matter. So of course does a deposed king: he could decide to make a career in the real world. There are hordes of Hohenzollerns, Habsburgs, Romanovs and members of other redundant dynasties managing the family estates, running hedge funds or working in international organizations of one kind or another. They may be ready to use their titles to get a table in a restaurant, but otherwise they've mostly got over it.

King Leka, though, claims that the option of living life as a private individual was never open to him.

'It's my duty,' he says, 'I have no choice.'

Yes you do, I say. If you really want to exercise power in Albania, you could go to the inconvenience of putting yourself up for election. King Simeon – grandson of Ferdinand – who reigned as a child-king in 1940s Bulgaria, returned to his country after the collapse of Communism, stood for election as a politician and became prime minister as Mr Simeon Saxe-Coburg-Gotha.

'That is not an option that is open to me,' he says. 'My oath won't allow me. I am the King of the Albanians.'

In that case, I am tempted to say, why don't you swear another oath? But this sort of argument is futile. Albania's royal family may be pipsqueaks by historical standards. But the man has lived all his life believing he will one day return to the country and reintroduce the 1928 constitution which founded his family's brief dynasty. It is a compulsion. Whether there might have been a more satisfactory way to have spent his life is simply not open to discussion. If he had his time on earth again, he claims, he would do nothing differently. 'It is not everyone who knows what they must do.'

How to untangle the skein of motivations at work? In material terms, were Albania ever to decide to revert to monarchism there would be large tracts of land to be handed back. The trappings of title – even as a pretender – probably provide some pleasure: everybody needs to believe that their life has some purpose. The thought that somehow you are different from, and superior to, those around you is no doubt another source of pleasure. And there probably comes a point where even the self-imposed privations of the role ('it's always lonely at the top, you know') seem to offer a reason to live.

But how would Albania be different if you were on the throne? I ask the king.

'This country *needs* a hereditary monarchy, for at least three or four generations. My father did not seize power. It was the will of the National Assembly, because they were sick of revolutions. His title – my title – is King of the Albanians. Note that: King of the Albanians, not King of Albania. It's a very high king, because every Albanian considers himself a king.'

The lights go out for the second time.

'The constitution of 1928 would need very little updating – it was well in advance of its time, you know. It guaranteed protection for minorities, because this country is rather like Scotland in the

Middle Ages. It is organized around clans. Every village has an elder: the title is usually inherited, so you can see the principle at work.' It made a superficial sort of sense. Many houses in Albania had straw men hung outside their front doors, supposed to ward off evil. The king obviously saw himself in a similarly apotropaic light.

And then he said, 'Look at my son. He's a Muslim, with a Catholic mother and a wife who's Church of England. That's typically Albanian.' I was a little baffled by this, then recalled that his father had once told a journalist that he was a republican: 'When I was made king, I was the only one to protest.'[29]

At this point, one of the dogs seemed to discover the electric cable again, shot out from under the coffee table, rose three feet vertically in the air and landed on the king. Queen Susan got up from her seat, walked to a cupboard and reappeared with a four-foot leather whip.

And, er, how would life be different if you were on the throne?

'Well, for one thing, you wouldn't have so many useless fights in parliament.' (He means this literally as well as figuratively – there had been a punch-up in parliament the previous evening.) 'Under our constitution, the king would have executive powers, so he could put forth laws.'

'You know,' interjected Queen Susan, 'we have people in this country selling their organs. We've got gangsters, massive drug-running, girls being abducted and sold into prostitution.'

All of which was true. But how could a monarchy bring law and order when a democratically elected government cannot?

'Because', said the king, 'it would have the people behind it.'

At which moment, before the lights went out again, or the boxer dogs launched one of their joint throat-and-thigh attacks, I left.

2. Next, Produce an Heir

They give birth astride of a grave, the light gleams an instant, then it's night once more.

Samuel Beckett, *Waiting for Godot*, Act II

Having established your monarchy, the next thing is to ensure the succession. For the first, inescapable duty of the founder of a dynasty is to produce someone who will take over the job when you die. To achieve this it is necessary merely to be capable of reproduction. But a number of factors make the business of providing an heir more troublesome for royalty. Celibacy would be an obvious problem, to start with: the public explanation for the fact that King Edward the Confessor of England died in 1066 without an heir was that he never consummated his marriage. In countries like France, where Salic Law prevented a female from inheriting the throne, the chances of natural dynastic succession would be cut by half. The business of producing an heir was not helped if, like King Richard the Lionheart, you spent most of your reign away fighting wars.[1] And chances were further restricted by the limited number of prospective partners. The rest of society operated to a list of people they were *not* allowed to marry, but royalty worked to a system of endogamy which decreed inbreeding and a shallow gene pool. In some dynasties, like those of ancient Egypt or Hawaii, incest was positively encouraged, as it reduced the number of people who might have a claim on the throne.

The need to find a bride with a fertile womb yet spotless reputation led to some extraordinary matches – children marrying cousins or uncles and seedy old men becoming engaged to young women. The sometimes disastrous consequences of restricting possession of the crown to a tiny group of often loosely related and sometimes interbred individuals are well known. If you're not careful you end up with a succession of gibbering idiots basking in epithets like 'the bewitched', 'the sickly', 'the impotent' or 'the mad'.[2]

Still, the first duty of any queen is to ensure the dynasty lives on, and to bang out a healthy heir. All courts know that history is replete with examples of dynasties which collapsed because no such figure existed. In Russia, the Romanovs only achieved power after the 'Time of Troubles' at the turn of the seventeenth century, during which the throne was fought for by everyone from court officials like Boris Godunov to a Polish adventurer who claimed to be an illegitimate son of the dead tsar. The struggle had been triggered by Ivan the Terrible leaving the throne to his mentally feeble son, Feodor I, whose only discernible skill was to travel the country ringing church bells.

One of the most notorious examples of the political dangers of reproductive failure came with the accession to the Spanish throne of Carlos II in 1665. The product of a union between the Spanish king and his own niece, Marina, daughter of the Holy Roman Emperor, Carlos was a catastrophic example of the dangers of trying to keep the bloodline pure. His enormous, misshapen head looked as if he had been hit by a sledgehammer. His jaw protruded so far that his teeth did not meet and he was unable to chew. His tongue was so large that he could hardly speak coherently. He was wet-nursed until the age of five or six, by which time he had inherited the throne. Afflicted by suppurating blisters, diseased bones and fits, Carlos was not a particularly beguiling marriage prospect, even for the most passionate day-dreamer. A victim was found in Marie Louise of Orleans, who soon discovered that among his other disabilities Carlos was unable to reproduce, probably due to premature ejaculation (although examination of his underwear by doctors procured by the French Ambassador failed to come to any very definite conclusion on this). Marie Louise took refuge in eating and drinking, and expired. A second marriage was then contracted, with the bride this time exorcized, to promote her fertility. But, again, Carlos failed to produce an heir. His fits became worse. His hair and teeth fell out, despite the frenetic efforts of court doctors applying freshly killed pigeons to his head and the entrails of animals to his stomach. Finally, lame, epileptic and partially deaf, he died. His death without an heir triggered the War of the Spanish Succession, which gave the throne to the Bourbons.

That the court did all it could to keep upon the throne a man who was so pitifully incapable ('Many people tell me I am bewitched,' the poor man once said, 'and I well believe it, such are the things I suffer') demonstrates the first essential thing about kings. This is that what they do is less important than the fact that they exist at all. Kings may be good or bad, saintly, lecherous, wise, stupid, athletic or indolent. All will be tolerated because those who believe in the hereditary principle necessarily accept that their head of state will not be there by election, talent or ambition. No other area of human activity is so easily reduced to the three essential transactions of birth, marriage and death.

But eminence is no protection against biology and it is one of the more striking ironies of royalty that the most elevated person in the land lives a life that can be so brutally reduced to the mechanical facts of life. All monarchies require a clear line of succession, and the clearest one of all is the succession of healthy children. The question of succession has been so important that much of English history is dominated by the ovaries and testes of the country's rulers. Neither the Tudors of the sixteenth century nor the Stuarts of the seventeenth, for example, were particularly good at producing healthy heirs to the throne. Henry VIII's frantic search for a male heir led him not only to divorce two wives and behead another two, but also to create the Church of England. Elizabeth I's decision not to breed enabled the union of England and Scotland in 1603, when the crown passed to her Scottish cousin James. And the Stuarts were feeble breeders, too.

Fortunately, by the time the last Stuart queen, Anne, expired, heirless, in 1714, the political class was more concerned with power than with mere heredity. The arrangements it enacted –

specifically, the Act of Settlement of 1701 – which gave the throne to the descendants of Sophia of Hanover, a granddaughter of James, were designed to keep out Roman Catholics. Under the Act of Settlement (a piece of legislation still in force at the start of the twenty-first century) the throne was to be reserved for those good Protestants who would maintain the Church of England.[3] But Sophia's marriage had come about only because her intended husband was unable to face up to the duties of producing an heir. In an extraordinary document, he announced that he planned to spend the rest of his life living 'in coelibatu', and renounced the responsibility in favour of 'his other self', his brother Duke Ernest Augustus of Hanover. He signed a contract declaring that he was 'both unable and unwilling in my own person to engage in any marriage contract', but that his brother would 'soon bestow the blessing of heirs on people and country'.[4] The two dukes and Sophia then proceeded to live in a sort of *ménage à trois*.

Even Hanoverian kings who went about the business of producing an heir with gusto could still be defeated by events. Take the case of George III. The court painter, John Zoffany, was commissioned to produce a family portrait. When he began the project, the king and queen had nine living children. Zoffany approached the task in the spirit of those builders who give an estimate for a job, start work, remove half the roof of your house and then disappear for months. By the time he returned to complete the work, a tenth child, Prince Adolphus, had been born. Zoffany managed to work him into the picture, as a baby being dandled on Queen Charlotte's lap. Then he made the mistake of letting his attention wander. By the time he resumed the task two years later in 1776, Princess Mary had arrived. He sucked his teeth and decided this necessitated major structural work: several of the existing children were painted out of the picture and a new composition begun. But just as he was about to finish the job the following year, Princess Sophia was born. 'Oh, God bless my soul,' he is supposed to have exclaimed, 'this is too much!'[5]

Yet even these industrial labours could not ensure an untroubled succession. As the king succumbed to the ravages of porphyria, there were seven sons and five daughters available to ensure the continuation of the line. His eldest son, the chump who was to reign as George IV, managed to produce one legitimate daughter, but she died giving birth to a stillborn son. On her death, the debt-ridden fifty-year-old Edward, Duke of Kent offered the British people a deal. For the sake of the succession (and in exchange for a decent annuity) he would jettison his mistress of twenty-seven years, Julie de St Laurent, and marry. 'God only knows the sacrifice it will be to make, whenever I shall think it my duty to become a married man,' he said.[6] The sacrifice was made palatable by a doubling of the allowance he received from the public purse and a promise to write off his debts. He duly got rid of Mme St Laurent and married himself off to a widowed princess of Saxe-Coburg-Saalfeld, who bore him one child, Princess Alexandrina Victoria, the future Queen Victoria.[7]

That solution to the precariousness of the succession was not uncommon. Germany abounded with gruff-sounding dynasties with children available for marriage. As Bismarck observed, the Coburgs were 'the stud farm of Europe'. The marriage of the young Queen Victoria to Prince Albert of Saxe-Coburg and Gotha alone produced children, grandchildren and great-grandchildren who would later live in the palaces of Greece, Norway, Russia, Germany, Romania, Sweden, Yugoslavia, Denmark and Spain.

On the night of 16–17 July 1918, Nicholas II, Tsar of All the Russias, was taken down to a basement in the city of Ekaterinburg and there, with his immediate family, butchered. The circumstances of the killing – how the Bolsheviks first shot at them, then chased their victims around the room, stabbing them with their bayonets, finally bludgeoning the survivors with their rifle butts – form one of the best-known episodes in the revolution which began the Russian people's unhappy experience of the dictatorship of the proletariat. The women were said to have been particularly hard to kill because they had sewn most of their jewellery collection into their underclothes, which deflected the bullets and blades of the assassins. But the deed was done and the institution of monarchy dispatched. Murdered alongside 'Citizen Romanov' were his wife, their son and heir Alexei and their five Grand Duchess daughters, together with the family physician, their maid, cook and valet. The bodies were loaded on to a cart and thrown down a mineshaft, from which they were later retrieved, before being set on fire, covered in acid and buried at the roadside in the middle of a forest. Or, at least, some of them were.

The massacre was the twentieth century's most dramatic example of the destruction of an ancient system of government. But it set off a minor epidemic of people claiming to be members of the Russian imperial family who had miraculously survived the event. Even before their deaths, a woman had arrived in America claiming to be the Grand Duchess Tatiana: Sydney Gibbes, the tsarevich's English tutor, had amused the real Tatiana with an account from the *Daily Graphic*, while the family were in exile in Siberia. But when news of the killings began to emerge, there was an explosion in claimants. In 1919 an American 'secret agent' published a diary in which he claimed to have smuggled the tsar out of Ekaterinburg and taken him through Tibet, the two of them disguised as pilgrims. If we are to believe the various published sightings in the following years, the Emperor of All the Russias had a fraught life (or resurrection) thereafter, spotted everywhere – Paris, London, Malta, Poland and, disguised as a Swedish band-leader, in the Crimea.

The most famous of the Romanov claimants, though, was 'Anna Anderson', a woman who insisted she was the Grand Duchess Anastasia Nikolaievna. In 1920, the woman had been admitted to a Berlin asylum under the name 'Fräulein Unbekannt' (Miss Unknown), having thrown herself off a bridge. She spoke poor German, in a foreign accent. A fellow inmate who had been reading a magazine article about the Russian imperial family identified her as one of them, an assertion which consumed the rest of her life. Anna Anderson claimed to have survived the massacre which took her family because she was rescued by one of the guards. Although some denounced her as a fraud, others, including distant members of the tsar's family, became utterly convinced that she was who she claimed to be, and supported her financially (as did the pianist Sergei Rachmaninov, who had a romantic attachment to her cause). Certainly, there were some remarkable physical similarities between her and Anastasia, and not just a resemblance in photographs. She had the same bone deformity in her feet, for example, had a scar on her right shoulder-blade – where the Grand Duchess had had a mole cauterized – and another on her forehead which matched the one which had caused the real Anastasia to wear her hair in a fringe. There were said to be scars on her body consistent with bullet wounds, and even with the triangular shapes of Russian bayonets. Perhaps most startlingly of all, scientific comparisons of Anna Anderson's ears with Anastasia's – considered the most accurate test of identity in the absence of fingerprints and before DNA – showed a pretty precise match, with over three times the number of points of similarity usually required for positive identification under German law.

Anna Anderson died in 1984 and was cremated. If someone made a similar claim in the twenty-first century, science might have resolved the matter definitively. As it was, DNA tests on tissue samples from a biopsy conducted before her death showed that she was almost certainly not the daughter of the tsar and almost certainly was a Polish factory girl with a history of dementia who had disappeared at the time she had first been 'discovered'. The intriguing question is why anyone – and, while Anna Anderson may be the most celebrated, she is a very long way from being unique – should spend their life claiming to be someone else. Some, like 'Princess Caraboo' (a Devon cobbler's daughter in a black turban) who deceived the elite of Bristol in 1817, were simply tricksters. Others are undoubtedly in the grip of a mental illness. In some cases, there may, perhaps, be a fortune to be claimed. But it often seems that the individual wishes merely to be acknowledged as the person they believe themselves to be.

This theme of concealed identity and unrecognized greatness is, of course, a staple of fairytales, from *The Princess and the Pea*, through *The Man in the Iron Mask* to *Star Wars*. Perhaps we should not be surprised that in the world of royalty – an institution based upon belief rather than logic – fiction easily elides into real life. There are, for example, several cases where feral children, who had been abandoned or lost as babies and then grew up wild, have been taken to be discarded royalty. Victor, 'the Wild Boy of Aveyron', who was captured in 1800, was widely said to be the lost Louis XVII. The most famous case of modern times, Kaspar Hauser (who was possibly a feral child, possibly a lunatic, or possibly the victim of a terrible crime of abuse), turned up as an apparent teenager in Nuremberg in the early nineteenth century, virtually unable to speak and completely unsocialized. He was said to be the heir to the throne of Baden.

It is, of course, the eminence of royalty which gave these cases of hidden identity their romantic resonance. People may have wandered the world claiming to be unrecognized farmers or blacksmiths. But every village had its own farmers and blacksmiths. Most of all, you did not enter such trades by virtue of your birth. In the days when kings exercised real power, merely to assert royal parentage might threaten the foundations of the state. If they were lucky, like Lambert Simnel, the child proclaimed as a fifteenth-century English 'Edward VI', such pretenders might be treated comparatively charitably by the kings they sought to supplant (Henry VII employed Simnel as a scullion in the royal kitchens). Others, like the seventeenth-century Russian 'False Dmitri', could find themselves shot to death, incinerated, mixed with gunpowder and fired from a cannon. You cannot take too many precautions in these matters.

Because the birth of an heir affects the whole nation, it cannot be a private affair. Queen Elizabeth II's governess, Marion ('Crawfie') Crawford – one of the first modern royal servants to kiss and tell – once remarked that the only truly private period in the life of a member of the royal family is the time spent in the womb.[8] The moment the foetus shows any sign of travelling down the birth canal, it becomes public property.

What sort of emotions must pass through the already anxious mind of a mother as she prepares for that moment, knowing that her country waits upon her performing successfully a task over which she has almost no control? What can it have been like to be Mary of Modena, wife of James II, as she gave birth to a stillborn child in the spring of 1674? To be followed by a daughter a year later who lived for only nine months? Then by another stillborn child? And then a daughter who died at the age of five? And a son taken off by smallpox after one month of life? And then another daughter who would live only a matter of months? And another stillborn baby? Then to see another infant die of convulsions when less than two months old? To have a further two stillborn children?

Eventually, at the eleventh attempt, in 1688, she brought forth James Francis Edward, who would later become the Old Pretender, father of Bonnie Prince Charlie. The succession was a genuine Matter of State, and the queen gave birth before an audience of sixty-seven people, including the Lord Chancellor gawping at the end of the bed.[9] Even so, after such a long history of obstetric misfortunes, there were immediate rumours that this Catholic heir to the throne was a changeling, perhaps the natural son of Sir Theophilus Oglethorpe, smuggled into the bedroom in a warming pan. (It was claimed that the curtains around the bed prevented any but the Catholics present seeing the most intimate details.) The stories were almost certainly politically motivated lies, but the warming-pan anxiety was still being cited (wrongly, because the custom of having witnesses predated the birth of the Old Pretender) by British government advisers in the middle of the twentieth century. In 1779, there had been so many people crammed around the bed of Marie Antoinette, wife of Louis XVI of France, for the birth of her first child, including several men who had clambered on top of the furniture to get a better view, that she fainted from the heat.[10] When the future Queen Victoria was born to the Duke and Duchess of Kent, the *Morning Post* reported the group of witnesses (all of them male) called to the house to attest the birth. Out of consideration for the duchess, their numbers had been reduced, but they nonetheless included: the Duchess's brother-in-law, the Duke of Sussex; the Archbishop of Canterbury; the Bishop of London; the Chancellor of the Exchequer; the Secretary for War; the President of the Board of Control; the Duke of Wellington; and the former Home Secretary and Chancellor of the Exchequer, the Marquess of Lansdowne.[11]

In time, the number of witnesses was further diminished, but the custom survived in Britain well into the twentieth century. In 1926, the Home Secretary, Sir William Joynson-Hicks, was summoned to certify the arrival of the baby girl who would later become Queen Elizabeth II, even though at the time the chances of her taking the throne seemed remote. Four years later, the Labour Home Secretary of the day, the former millworker J. R. Clynes, was obliged to spend sixteen days waiting at a hotel in Perth for the call to Glamis Castle to validate the birth of Elizabeth's sister Margaret. Small wonder that when, many years later, a young soldier congratulated her on the birth of a grandson, Elizabeth was reported as replying, 'Thank you . . . I am very pleased that we have another heir.'[12] You begin to understand the abiding interest of much of royalty in horse-racing and bloodstock lines.

But the obsession with birth and parentage is not exclusive to starchy officialdom. The legions of witnesses to royal births might be expected to prevent any warming-pan infiltration. But they were not, of course, present at the moment of conception, and history is littered with rumours and accusations that while the identity of the royal baby's mother might not be in doubt, paternity was another matter. Among English kings, Edward IV was said to have been conceived when his mother and father were 160 miles apart: his alleged illegitimacy was used to justify Richard III's seizure of the throne. And in the eighteenth century, Tsar Paul I of Russia claimed to be the product of an affair between his mother, Catherine the Great, and a king of Poland. In the normal course of events, biological parentage does not matter. But scuttlebutt about royal adultery justifies itself by the fact that the baby is given special status by virtue of its presumed ancestry. In questioning the bloodline, the aspersions do more than throw mud, for blood is what determines who sits upon the throne.

These allegations are most easily made against those who do not occupy the position of heir apparent. Perhaps the lesson to be drawn is merely that first children are assumed to be the product of a marriage which has not yet run into trouble. But they are also the blows of people 'willing', in Alexander Pope's telling words, 'to damn with faint praise, assent with civil leer . . . Willing to wound, and yet afraid to strike.'

The role of 'spare' to the heir is thankless enough without having to put up with this sort of thing. Yet it is worth noticing how often the spare has succeeded to the throne. Many of Britain's most famous monarchs have been second (or even third or fourth) children – the list includes the crusader king Richard Coeur-de-Lion, John, Richard III, Henry VIII, Elizabeth I, Charles I and Queen Anne, to pick a few at random. Fifteen of forty-one monarchs – 37 per cent – have been 'spares' of one sort or another. In modern times, the proportion has been even higher: of the five monarchs who took the British throne during the twentieth century, two were second sons. That is a proportion of 40 per cent. In a grown-up world, ancestry need not matter. But monarchy belongs to some earlier, pre-scientific pattern of social organization.

In the end, the important consideration is not so much the biological facts about an individual as the collective delusion of a society. The important thing is that people believe. Which is why, once safely delivered, the royal infant is displayed to his subjects. Kings and queens and heirs and spares are required, therefore, to present their child to its probable, or possible, future subjects. This is now accomplished through television and press photographs. In previous times it was more elaborate: even as the 'spare' second son, the future Henry VIII was anointed with olive oil, sprinkled with rosewater and swaddled in blue velvet and cloth-of-gold.[13] In some European courts, the custom of displaying the new baby to his subjects in similar style lasted to the cusp of the twentieth century. In Spain in 1885 the newborn child arrived as a fully fledged king, his father Alfonso XII having died during the pregnancy. The scene enacted was positively medieval. 'As the cannon triumphantly crashed out a twenty-one-gun salute, the Prime Minister appeared before the assembled court carrying a silver tray on which lay naked the new King of Spain. Five days later the baby was carried in solemn procession, with the golden fleece around his neck, to be baptised in the Royal Chapel with water brought specially from the River Jordan.'[14] Treated so unusually from its earliest days it requires a quite remarkable discernment to recognize that a man's a man for all that.

3. Learning to be Regal

Remember, to be a King, all you need to know is how to sign your name, read a manuscript and mount a horse.

The advice of King Umberto I of Italy to his son, Vittorio Emmanuele

In late June 1894, at White Lodge, Richmond Park, a new heir to the British throne was brought forth. There followed the usual celebrations. A marquee was erected to accommodate the hundreds of people who arrived to sign a book of congratulations. Queen Victoria was cheered through the streets as she travelled to Richmond to inspect her new great-grandson. A dozen – mainly German – godparents were invited to the baptism, which was to be carried out with water brought from the River Jordan, and attended by the Prime Minister.

Other parents might be free to choose the name under which their child is to be introduced to the world. But the naming of royal children is another matter. In 1819 the infant Victoria's father had been planning to call her Elizabeth. But then the prince regent got to hear of it, and turned up at the christening, announcing that as the Emperor Alexander of Russia was to be one of her godfathers he ought to be properly rewarded. When the Archbishop of Canterbury asked by what name he was to christen the child, one man said Alexandrina, the other spluttered alternatives – 'Georgina? Elizabeth?' – until they compromised and she was baptized as Alexandrina Victoria. More than a century later it was considered strikingly radical for Elizabeth and Philip to choose Prince Charles's name for themselves.

Queen Victoria in 1894 was equally proprietorial. She was

dismayed to learn that the Duke of York proposed to name her great-grandson Edward, after 'darling Eddy', the duke's elder brother, who had died of pneumonia two years before. She had imagined herself the author of a dynasty in which male heirs would all be named after her dead husband Albert and females after her.[1] The child was eventually saddled with the names Edward Albert Christian George Andrew Patrick David. The last four names, of the patron saints of England, Scotland, Ireland and Wales, were intended to demonstrate the child's dedication to the peoples of the United Kingdom. The family just called him David.

But there was one notable catcall amid all the fawning on this uniquely privileged and uniquely burdened child. When the House of Commons assembled to pass a motion congratulating the royal parents, the bearded figure of Keir Hardie rose to speak. Hardie was the illegitimate son of a farm servant in the Scottish lowlands, and sat in parliament as the Independent Labour member for West Ham. As a former miner he was outraged that hysteria over the royal birth had driven out all thought of the deaths of almost 290 men and boys in a disaster at the Albion colliery, in the little mining village of Cilfynnid, South Wales. One politician after another rose to shower sugar on the newborn prince, but Hardie was acidic. He wondered what particular blessing the royal family had conferred on the nation that the House of Commons was spending a day celebrating the birth of this child. He was scathing about the circumstances in which he would grow up. 'From his childhood onward,' he told fellow MPs, 'this boy will be surrounded by sycophants and flatterers by the score and will be taught to believe himself as of a superior creation. A line will be drawn between him and the people he will be called upon some day to reign over.'

The House exploded. Other MPs, a reporter wrote, 'howled and yelled and screamed'.[2] But Hardie battled on, denouncing the parasitic nature of the royal family, and claiming that when he grew older the young prince would be sent off 'on a tour round the world, and probably rumours of a morganatic alliance will follow and at the end of it, the country will be called upon to pay the bill'.[3] Since the child in question would later become the calamitous Edward VIII, much of this proved uncannily prophetic. Keir Hardie's disdain expressed the convictions of a class warrior. But it might also stand as a broader warning about the dangers inherent in being born in the purple.

The guiding principle of monarchy is also its greatest folly. We do not have hereditary brain surgeons, nor even hereditary road-sweepers. Although, in a modern constitutional arrangement – with the king or queen little more than a figurehead – it matters less, historically the behaviour of these uniquely indulged individuals might determine the fates of nations. The moral hazards of extreme privilege are obvious. When you are told you have no equals, how do you develop any sense of social obligation? If you stand at the top of the mountain, without having made the slightest effort to climb, what can prevent vainglory and self-indulgence? No parental threat that, if you don't work hard or have some consideration for others, nothing will become of you, can have any force, because it doesn't matter whether you are industrious or indolent, thoughtful or boorish, considerate or selfish, the job is yours for life.

Set alongside this must be added two significant considerations. First, the laws of probability decree that the heir to the throne is no more likely to be congenitally talented than the rest of us. Indeed, bloodlines which have been constructed largely for reasons of state are not necessarily likely to produce children of any great ability. They might avoid the awful warning held out by the misshapen Carlos in Spain, but other Habsburgs were hardly intellectuals. The historian A. J. P. Taylor remarked that the Emperor Ferdinand I of Austria's only sensible remark was 'I'm the Emperor and I want dumplings!'[4] The future Edward VIII's great-grandfather, Prince Albert, had clearly been a talented man. But his late uncle, Albert Victor, Duke of Clarence – who would have inherited the throne had he not been carried off by pneumonia – had been so dim that his tutor decided he hardly knew the meaning of the words 'to read'. His speech was littered with sentences which had an apparently coherent beginning but no ending of any kind, while a letter the prince wrote to Gladstone 'admitted of no possible grammatical construction', according to his private secretary.

Secondly, as Keir Hardie noticed, the especially privileged are especially vulnerable to temptation. The Victorian journalist Walter Bagehot summed it up thus in *The English Constitution*: 'All the world and all the glory of it, whatever is most attractive, whatever is most seductive, has always been offered to the Prince of Wales of the day, and always will be. It is not rational to expect the best virtue where temptation is applied in the most trying form at the frailest time of human life.'[5] Or, as Alan Bennett put it a century later, 'To be heir to the throne is not a position; it is a predicament.'[6] In *The Madness of George III*, Bennett gives the words to the man who eventually became George IV, after nearly sixty years of waiting. At the age of eight his mother had handed him a booklet filled with sentences like 'Abhor all vice' and 'Disdain all flattery', and telling him that his main objective should be to offer 'the highest love, affection and duty towards the King'.[7] It was a doomed mission: he hardly saw a temptation without giving in to it.

Many young people are saved from the self-destruction which can accompany extreme privilege by their friends. But true friendship is a relationship of equals, and to those who believe in the system – as any prince must – the heir to the throne has no equals. There is no peer pressure because there are no peers. The opposite danger exists: because all the fleshy pleasures of the world are offered to the prince, he can find himself surrounded by people who are there to make the most of what is on offer. The danger that people will merely tell you what you want to hear is of such long standing that the saintly Erasmus toyed with the idea of deterring sycophancy by taking a man who had already been convicted of a capital offence and putting it about that he was being executed for the crime of flattery.

The purpose of the education of princes is to save them from themselves and to fit them for the role. Usually this seems to involve the acquisition of religious belief. It has been a long time since a king or queen was canonized as a saint, although the honour was given to a number of medieval monarchs, including the English King Edward the Confessor, Louis IX of France and Hungary's grimy Princess Margaret.[8] In more modern times, it has been sufficient that princes acquire a degree of religious respectability. Most monarchical societies are still not ready for the atheistic king, perhaps because if the king does not believe in God, then his citizens may begin to ask why they should believe in him. Is it simply coincidence that the greatest crisis of modern monarchy occurred when the throne was occupied by a man whom his Prime Minister, Stanley Baldwin, felt was the most spiritually and morally vacuous man he had ever met?[9] Baldwin believed that, as a result, Edward lacked the capacity to understand that, in a democracy, respect for the Crown depended upon its being seen as a symbol in which duty took precedence over personal pleasure and choice.

Shortly after the First World War, in one of his many letters to his then mistress, Freda Dudley Ward, the future king whined about the frustrations of a royal life. 'I'm afraid I've been dancing again,' he whimpered. But:

> we had to stop at 12.00 on account of the P. of W., not your little boy darling, as there are often occasions when he & his name are two different things . . . but Christ it does infuriate me, not because I want to carry on dancing but because of the childishness of all this religious camouflage; they are taking me to church in the morning & they won't let me play golf in the afternoon!![10]

The idea that the royal family should 'set an example' is easy enough to grasp. But the language of the letter hints at more than the frustration of a young man who would rather be enjoying himself. He was obliged to stop dancing 'on account of the P. of W.', he wrote. He had touched upon one of the central peculiarities of the belief in royalty, that any individual king or heir is, simultaneously, two people.

Deep in the theology of kingship is the idea that while individual kings may sicken, age and die, the monarchy is immortal. Shaped by the belief that God had become man through a virgin birth, medieval minds seem to have found it possible to believe that a person could be at one and the same time two things.* Thus a monarchy could be like the mythical phoenix of Arabia, which in dying gave birth to itself: Elizabeth I even used the word 'phoenix' on some of her coins. The conviction made it possible to believe in the sanctity of the institution, even when the throne was occupied by someone as dissolute and incompetent as Edward II, who was eventually dispatched, probably by having a red-hot poker thrust up his backside. In Elizabeth I's reign, a law apprentice at the Middle Temple summarized the distinction between the physical and symbolic bodies in this way. There was a mortal body, 'subject to all infirmities that come by nature or Accident, to the Imbecility of Infancy or Old Age'. And there was another being, the 'Body politic, that cannot be seen or handled, consisting of Policy and Government, and constituted for the Direction of the People and the Management of the public weal, and this body is utterly void of Infancy, and old Age and other natural Defects and Imbecilities'.[11] Although the mystical body politic was superior, the two bodies were one indivisible being. It is easier to get your head around this idea if, like most European monarchs, you are familiar with the Christian conception of the Trinity. Indeed, the belief is only possible because the 'soul' inside the mystical body can migrate. At the king's death it undergoes a 'demise' or transfer to another human being.[12]

Because the position of king or queen is not merely a job but the vehicle through which some higher purpose is expressed, the option is not available – as it is to the chief executive of Mercedes-Benz or whoever – that at the end of the working day they cease to be a boss, and instead become a parent. The king or queen is always the king or queen, awake, asleep, at church, playing golf or having a bath. Once her father had acceded to the throne after the Abdication, the young Princess Elizabeth stopped calling

*Enabling a French nobleman to claim that while he was a bishop he observed strict celibacy, but as a baron he was married.

her parents Mummy and Papa and referred instead to 'the King and Queen'. She discovered that she could make the soldiers on duty outside Buckingham Palace present arms, and walked backwards and forwards for the pleasure of watching them do so.[13] The perceptive Infanta Eulalia, daughter of Isabella II of Spain, and one of the cleverest and most subversive modern royals, found court life very like a prison – 'very gilded, very luxurious, but more guarded than a Bastille'.[14] It was a curious sort of incarceration, in which the inmates seemed to lock the doors themselves. 'They cannot forget that they are Royal, and therefore obliged to mask their feelings more rigorously than is necessary for ordinary people,' she wrote. 'Most princesses I know are reduced by this inexorable discipline to nonentities whose mouths are twisted in an eternal smile.'[15]

Perhaps it is this extraordinary business, of having children who 'belong' not merely to their blood relations but to some mystical entity, which has made so many monarchs bad parents. No recent kings or queens have been as dysfunctional as the Hanoverians in the eighteenth century. None has been heard saying, for example, as Queen Caroline, wife of George II, was reputed to have said, that 'My dear first-born is the greatest ass, and the greatest liar, and the greatest *canaille*, and the greatest beast in the whole world, and I heartily wish he was out of it.'[16] (Her wish was granted antithetically when she herself died, murmuring, 'At least, I shall have one comfort in having my eyes eternally closed. I shall never see that monster again.')[17] Princess Augusta, another unfortunate Hanoverian, who raised the future George III and his eight siblings with her supposed lover, the Earl of Bute, once saw one of her children sitting miserably and asked what he was doing. 'I am thinking,' said the boy. 'Thinking, sir! and of what?' she asked. 'I am thinking if I ever have a son I will not make him so unhappy as you make me.'[18]

No royal parents of the modern era have quite matched that level of indifference, although even his admirers admitted that the future King George V's rigid ideas, chaffing manner and explosive temper terrified his children. His wife Mary was another distant figure, who seems to have lacked the maternal gene, remarking of her eldest son at the age of two that he was 'most civil to her' one day, and utterly unaware that her children were being tortured by a demented nanny. (The nanny would take the young Prince Edward down for tea with his parents, and outside the door pinch and twist his arm, so that when presented to them he was bawling. Not unsurprisingly, it did nothing to improve family relations.)[19] Queen Mary's reserve lasted all her life: while researching a biography of her many years later, James Pope-Hennessy interviewed Prince Axel of Denmark. Axel recalled being in London for a business meeting, during which news was released of the death of George VI. He took himself off to Marlborough House that afternoon to pay his respects to the dowager queen. 'And there was May [as Mary was known to her family], just sitting there, like *this*,' said Prince Axel, folding his hands in his lap, 'quite calm and natural. And do you know what she said? She said: "Axel – this is the third time this has happened to me – the third of my sons to die unexpectedly – curious, isn't it?"' The Danish prince was much impressed by her sang-froid, but it is the most extraordinary way for a parent to talk of the death of a child.[20]

In most families children grow up as they make their way through school – and perhaps university – before beginning independent lives. But members of a monarch's family never truly leave home. Whatever apparent job they may have, it is always just an occupation: their true career is being a member of the family, which is why senior members of the House of Windsor started talking about themselves as belonging to The Firm. But, unlike other firms, this one does not solicit recruits (except for marriage) and it thrives on being seen to be a vital and dignified part of the constitution – otherwise, it must take its chances with the rest of celebrity pond-life. This is perhaps why royal parents take such a censorious view of what their children get up to. Hence George V's distaste for his son's liking for nightclubs. To the selfish and self-indulgent man that the future Edward VIII had become, the censoriousness was intolerable. 'Christ! how

I loathe & despise my bloody family,' he squealed to his mistress, after discovering that the king had criticized his choice of companion.

If H.M. thinks he's going to alter me by insulting you he's making just about the biggest mistake of his silly useless life . . . I'll have whatever friends I wish & what is more I won't have them insulted or I'll bloody well insult him!! . . . words could never describe my hatred & contempt for my father tonight & it's going to be lasting.[21]

Clashes of some sort are inevitable in any animal environment where old and young males are confined together – the old leader of the pack constantly having to fight off the challenges of the young buck. In the annals of bad relations between kings and their sons, Edward's self-pitying outrage is small beer. For the best part of two centuries after his death in 1568 it was widely rumoured that Don Carlos, the mad Spanish heir to the throne, had been murdered by his own father. Tsar Ivan IV of Russia, 'Ivan the Terrible', killed his own son with an iron-tipped cane for protesting when his father struck the young man's heavily pregnant wife because she was improperly dressed. Peter the Great had his son whipped so badly that he died.[22] Frederick the Great of Prussia was almost sentenced to death by his own father, and was forced to watch his best friend (and possibly his lover) being beheaded.

Admittedly, the demands of the job do not make for an easy home life. There are the public engagements, to start with. When their four eldest children were aged between one and seven, the future George V and Queen Mary disappeared on a seven-month tour of the empire. The future George VI and his wife vanished for six months' travelling when Princess Elizabeth was a baby. During their absence, the nanny taught the child to speak the word 'mummy'. Unfortunately, since there was no mummy to hand, she greeted everyone she came across with the words 'Mummy! Mummy!'[23] When Elizabeth became a mother herself, the infant Charles was left at home while she visited her husband, then stationed in Malta as a naval officer. After five weeks away she was in no rush to see her son again on her return. Instead, she spent four days at Clarence House attending to engagements and, the newspapers reported, dealing with 'a backlog of correspondence', and then going to the races to watch her horse Monaveen win at 10–1. Only after all of that was she reintroduced to her son.[24] Later, when she had become queen and the nine-year-old Charles was attending Cheam school, she decided it was time to give him the title of Prince of Wales. Charles learned about it only when he was watching the television, with a group of other boys, in the headmaster's study. No one had thought to tell the boy in advance, just as no one told him when, nine years later, he learned from a news bulletin that he was now old enough to rule without a regent, and that he, rather than his father, would become regent if the queen became incapable.[25]

The royal librarian and close friend of Queens Mary and Elizabeth, Sir Owen Morshead, once remarked that 'The House of Hanover, like ducks, produce bad parents. They trample on their young.'[26] No one would cite the House of Windsor as an example of how to raise children successfully. Precisely how many of the claims of dysfunctionality made by former employees we should believe is anyone's guess, although the great lesson of recent years has been that many of the most outlandish claims about royal marriages have turned out often to be true. But then, how many of us could claim that we have raised our children perfectly? All parents bring up their children in the shadow of their own upbringing. In the case of royalty there is something more. The feminist writer Beatrix Campbell wondered, 'What did a boy know about *how* to be a parent when he had a mother before whom adults bowed and a father to whom a sovereign deferred?'[27]

One of the reasons that her followers supported 'Anna Anderson' in her claim to be the Grand Duchess Anastasia, youngest daughter of the murdered Russian Tsar Nicholas II, was the way she walked. She could, they said, have acquired the deportment of a princess only by being brought up at court. This royal gait has an unmistakable, unfakable serenity. It is not merely a question of deportment (although that, too, is taught). The majestic walk is the product of a lifetime of having doors opened and a footman to ensure that the seat is always placed at the perfect distance when they sit down. It enables kings and queens to walk and talk with their eyes straight ahead, and to cast not even the slightest glance behind to see that a chair is awaiting the royal backside. The writer Harold Nicolson once gushed, 'I have never forgotten once, in the regal palace in Madrid, seeing King Alfonso XIII and his lovely Queen walking hand in hand together through a double row of ambassadors and grandees without looking either to right or left. "This," I thought to myself, "is authentic grandeur."'[28]

But what else does a future king need to know? The expectations are high and contradictory. The ideal product of a royal education is someone who embodies an extraordinary diversity of talents – cultured and intellectually agile, yet fit and brave; capable of making a good speech, yet ready to use it to mouth platitudes; sympathetic but dignified; as ready to turn out to share a football match with tens of thousands as to appreciate a chamber concert; a voice of the nation who has taken a personal vow of silence. Is it any wonder that so few of them are entirely satisfactory?

'Who is that evil-looking Dago?' asked an Australian spectator at the funeral of Edward VII. 'He looks as though he has never been astride a horse in his life.'[29] The funeral was perhaps the grandest gathering of royalty of all time. Eight kings and an emperor rode in the procession, all of them – to the fury of the French Foreign Minister – given precedence over the representatives of republics.[30] The obvious distinction between the kings and the mere politicians was that, while the latter were driven in carriages, royalty rode, three by three, through the streets of London. Five heirs apparent followed. Forty imperial, royal and serene highnesses completed the royal pomp. The Dago was a solid man wearing an astrakhan hat and coat, despite it being a warm early-summer day: the sweat ran in rivulets down his fleshy face.

But he did not get much sympathy from other monarchs. King Ferdinand of Bulgaria was a relative parvenu in royal circles, but now he rode beside King Frederick VII of Denmark. Ferdinand had learned enough about the symbolic significance of horsemanship since his recruitment in a Viennese billiard hall that he attempted to ride into the ancient capital of his country to declare its independence from the Turkish empire. The theatre of the event had been somewhat undermined by his falling from his horse in the process. Now, at the funeral, he sat in the saddle like a sack of onions, glistening. But what excited the contempt of his fellow kings, particularly Kaiser Wilhelm II of Germany, was not so much his posture as that his magnificent horse, of which he was clearly terrified, was being *led*. The Kaiser once explained to an astonished visitor who came upon him at his desk sitting on a military saddle placed across a wooden block that 'he was so accustomed to sitting on a horse he found a saddle more conducive to clear, concise thinking'.[31]

This was taking to heart the judgement of King Umberto, who reigned in Italy at the end of the nineteenth century, and who believed that all that was really required of the education of a prince was that he learn to read the occasional official document, to sign his own name and to ride a horse. That the last requirement should have survived into the age of the internal-combustion engine is interesting. Machiavelli argued that a prince should go hunting because it was the form of activity which most resembled war, 'for it teaches him to surprise his enemy, to select quarters, to lead armies, to array the battle, to besiege towns to advantage'.[32] But learning to ride is rather different. It is hard to resist the conclusion that royalty likes to be able to ride because being on a horse really does elevate you above the herd of humanity. With a few exceptions, such as the ancient Jews – who apparently thought more highly of the donkey or mule[33] – the horse has been seen as the most aristocratic of domestic animals. Riding is about bending it to your will, and public riding is to demonstrate that authority.

Certainly, the association between royalty and horseflesh – breeding, training and racing – is long-standing. It was sufficiently well recognized for Oliver Cromwell to ban horse-racing after the English revolution, not so much to deprive people of pleasure as because he feared that any large gathering of horsey types could turn into a royalist rally. Not for nothing is horse-racing called 'the sport of kings'. After all, on the morning of her coronation, a lady-in-waiting is said to have remarked to Queen Elizabeth II, 'You must be feeling nervous, Ma'am,' and got the reply, 'Of course I am, but I really do think Aureole will win,' referring to a horse she owned that was running in the Derby.[34]

In earlier times, kings might demonstrate their fitness for power by displays of dominance over other sorts of animals. In second-century Rome the people would be summoned to the amphitheatre to watch the deranged Roman emperor Commodus shoot arrows at elephants, hippopotamuses, rhinoceroses and giraffes. In the space of fourteen days, he once slew a hundred lions and had the heads severed from ostriches with semi-circular blades, so that for a few moments the birds could run around headless. The seventeenth-century King Augustus III of Poland was so indolent and fat that his Lithuanian hosts arranged to collect wild animals and fire them from the tops of trees over a canal, which 'gave the king the opportunity of shooting wolves, boars and bears in full flight'.[35]

In more modern times, country sports have retained their hold on royalty, whether it be shooting pheasants at Sandringham, catching salmon in the Scottish Highlands or riding to hounds. Enemies of fox-hunting have generally chosen to ignore the fact that it can be a highly dangerous sport, with broken bones and the occasional fatality. A nineteenth-century editorial suggested that Queen Victoria's consort might be able to overcome the innate disadvantage of being born foreign and having an interest in intellectual things by spending more time on the hunting field. He had been taken out recently, and the upper classes were thrilled to learn that he had ridden passably well. 'His essay at the chase did him great credit; he rode boldly', and, the writer added enthusiastically, 'The Prince has an abundance of *pluck*.'[36]

But the intellectual demands put on the modern monarch are pretty minimal. Historically, much more was expected: a king needed to exercise wise judgement, to understand how economies work, to lead his troops in battle, and, at least in post-Reformation England, to have sufficient theological self-confidence to be able to function as Supreme Governor of the established Church. In the modern king or queen, though, too much learning can be a dangerous thing, for they may develop a mind of their own, and who knows what they might then decide to say or do?

Instead, a good royal education is built around a perverse priority. It seeks not to develop exceptional talent so much as to turn a uniquely privileged individual into the expression of the common man or woman. The chances of the future monarch being naturally gifted are slim. But, if we were to draw up a list of what is demanded of a royal education, scholastic accomplishments would not necessarily be a priority. If anything so crude as a formal set of instructions were to be sent from the palace to a head teacher or tutor, it might include the expectation that the child should emerge able to deliver (but not necessarily to write) a speech, to appear dignified and to have some sense of their nation's history. They should have sufficient knowledge of the constitution to understand the limits of their competence. Morally, they should have developed a sense of empathy and an awareness of duty. It would be a great help to them if, in addition, they could develop a solid enough religious or spiritual base to help sustain them in what is a very lonely job.

The most famous set of instructions for the education of a future monarch was written by Niccolò Machiavelli in 1513, and published almost thirty years later. But it was not the only text on the subject: in the nine hundred years leading up to 1700 there were available about one thousand books and other tracts, each telling the king how to do his job. It was more or less common ground among them that monarchy was preferable to any other system – including democracy – because it was the best defence against tyranny. Many of the writers liked to talk of the king being the 'head' and his state being a 'body'. The English author John of Salisbury drew out the analogy, so that the senate was the heart; the judges and governors the eyes, ears and tongue; the officials and soldiers the hands; the attendants of the prince the sides; the officers of the Treasury the stomach; the farmers the feet.[37]

Machiavelli's *The Prince* is the best known of them all because it took such a worldly view of the ethics of kingship. For him, 'a prince ought to have no other aim or thought, nor select anything else for his study, than war and its rules and discipline'.[38] All other education was to be subordinated to that objective, so that history was merely to be studied for what it told of the lessons of war and the deeds of great men. Doing the right thing was not necessarily the right thing to do, and there was no need for a ruler to be generous. He should promote the arts through his patronage, but keep his nobles cowed. In one of his more notorious passages, Machiavelli advises that a ruler who has seized control of a state should quickly think about 'all the injuries it is necessary for him to inflict', and then 'do them all in one stroke, so as not to have to repeat them daily'.[39] The goal was not affection, but respect, 'to inspire fear in such a way that, if he does not win love, he avoids hatred'.[40]

But there is another, less well-known, yet altogether more humane tract on the subject, which was produced by the great theologian Desiderius Erasmus at much the same time. In *The Education of a Christian Prince*, Erasmus started from the perfectly sensible point that 'On board ship, we do not give the helm to the one who has the noblest ancestry of the company, the greatest wealth, or the best looks, but to him who is most skilled in steering, most alert, and most reliable.'[41] In a kingdom, therefore, it was best to entrust the state to someone better endowed than the rest with the kingly qualities of wisdom, a sense of justice, personal restraint, foresight and concern for the public well-being. Since they were stuck with the hereditary principle, the citizenry should take the greatest care in choosing the person to whom they entrusted the king's education. Erasmus believed that the process should start as early as possible – even Aesop's fables were vehicles of moral instruction – and great thought should be given to the children who were to be his playmates and to the adults who were to work as nursemaids. The prince should learn history and geography, and tour his kingdom, so that he understood his people. The purpose of this education was to turn out a person who was above the common temptations of man. The prince should not tax the people unfairly or waste money on unnecessary wars, elaborate courts or foreign tours. The practice of forcing princesses into foreign marriages for strategic advantage should be abandoned: it was a deplorable way to treat them, and anyway disconnected royal families from their peoples.

Erasmus' benevolent view of human nature is a great deal less well known than the ideas of Machiavelli, whose propositions could be reduced to 'We're all bad: princes need to be badder.' Where Machiavelli believed that almost anyone might become king if only they learned the arts of war, Erasmus agreed with Plato that the only person fit to be a prince was someone who did not seek the post. 'For whoever covets the position of prince must necessarily either be a fool who does not realise how stressful and dangerous a task it is to carry out a ruler's duties properly; or he must be so wicked a man that he plans to use the royal power for his own benefit.'[42] Where Machiavelli proposed settling disputes by war, Erasmus believed a good prince would never go to war unless all other avenues had been exhausted. 'If you want to compete with other princes,' he wrote, 'do not consider yourself superior to them if you take away part of their realm or rout their troops, but only if you have been less corrupt than they, less greedy, less arrogant, less irascible, and less impulsive.'[43] No prizes will be awarded for deducing whether the citizen would be happier in a state governed by Erasmus or by Machiavelli.

Though any student essayist can cite Machiavelli, a conscientious monarch in a constitutional democracy ought to recognize Erasmus as a far superior text. When the future Edward VII reached the age of seventeen in 1858, his mother Queen Victoria wrote to him, explaining how he should behave. He would now have his own suite of rooms and an increased allowance, he would become a colonel in the army and he would wear the insignia of the Order of the Garter. In exchange, he must study to be a proper gentleman and accept that 'Life is composed of duties, and in the due, punctual, and cheerful performance of them the true Christian, true soldier, and true gentleman is recognized.' The prince had had a rigorous schooling for the job, according to rules drawn up by his father, who engaged tutors, set tests and demanded constant reports of progress. Occasionally, he might be allowed to play with other boys, but he was to remember how different he was from them. Victoria evidently had anxieties about whether it had had the desired effect, and admitted that she found her son vain, dull and thoughtless.[44] Citing the Golden Rule of the New Testament, she gave one practical example of how to behave:

> To the servants and those below you you will always be courteous and kind, remembering that by having engaged to serve you in return for certain money payments, they have not surrendered their dignity which belongs to them as brother men and brother Christians. You will try to emancipate yourself as much as possible from the thraldom of abject dependence for your daily wants of life on your servants. The more you can do for yourself and the less you need their help, the greater will be your independence and real comfort.[45]

On receiving the letter the prince is said to have burst into tears, although whether because he was moved by the sentiments or depressed by them depends upon your prejudice.

In the end, the requirements for the education of a modern prince can be distilled pretty simply. Although there have been several monarchs who could claim to be intellectually distinguished – Henry VIII, Mary I and Elizabeth I were all accomplished linguists, while the Stuart king James I was acknowledged to be not just the 'most learned monarch in Europe',[46] but probably one of the most educated of Europeans – cleverness is not necessarily any great asset. In fact, in some circumstances it might be a positive disadvantage. Certainly, as their political powers have died away, so have the demands upon their intellect. George IV may have been a foolish man, but he was educated and cultivated. The next George to take the throne, a century later (1910), had not the slightest interest in books, ideas or art (unless postage stamps count as art), preferring to spend his time blasting away with his shotgun and accumulating a mountain of dead pheasants and partridges. He was forty-four at the time of his accession, yet even his most respectful biographer commented that he had not yet managed 'the normal educational standard of the average public schoolboy at leaving age'.[47] When the writer Thomas Hardy reached his seventieth birthday that year the king was asked to send a congratulatory telegram. 'It shall be done,' he said. The following day, a telegram arrived at the office of Thomas Hardy of Alnwick, Northumberland, who made the king's fishing rods.[48]*

Throughout the twentieth century, the British royal family went for a muscular approach to education. Towards the end of his life, George V recalled the 'hidings' he used to get as an adolescent on the naval training ship *Britannia*, where 'the other boys made a point of taking it out of us on the grounds that they'd never be able to do it later on'.[49] As so often in the British ruling class, he later concluded that if that sort of education had been good – or bad – enough for him, it would do for his sons too. True, he did intervene to engage a new mathematics teacher when, to his horror, he discovered that the boys were unable to calculate the average weight of stags he had shot while out stalking one day in Scotland.[50] But in May 1907 his heir was dispatched to the naval college at Osborne, where, unsurprisingly, he was treated no better than his father had been. Within days of his arrival he was grabbed by a group of senior boys who dyed his hair red: the prince did not report the incident, he said, because to do so would have resulted in a 'tanning'.[51] On another occasion he had his head thrust through a window and the sash slammed down on his neck, to re-enact the beheading of his predecessor Charles I.

Service colleges are not designed to turn out flower-arrangers, and no doubt other boys were also persecuted. But being so readily

*Poor Thomas Hardy (the writer) must have felt particularly unloved in royal circles. The future Edward VIII once asked him to settle an argument he had been having with his mother. Had he really written a book called *Tess of the D'Urbervilles*?

singled out does not make it easier to accomplish the one ambition shared by most teenagers, which is to be the same as everyone else. When George came to the conclusion that the heir needed to know a little more about the world, he was sent to Oxford ('Why is he to be an undergraduate? Surely this cannot be true! it is too democratic,' exclaimed his great-aunt, the Grand Duchess Augusta of Mecklenburg-Strelitz).[52] But university was not a success. The prince carped in later years that it had not been democratic enough: his rooms in the Magdalen College cloisters had their own bathroom and were furnished by the queen with Sheraton furniture, and he was accompanied both by a personal tutor and by his valet.[53] He lasted two years, although he cannot be said to have emerged from the process a cultured man. When his mistress, Freda Dudley Ward, gave him a copy of *Wuthering Heights*, he looked at it suspiciously and asked, 'Who is this woman Bront?'[54]*

The education of Edward's younger brother, later to become George VI, had followed a similar pattern. After naval college (where his trial was being trussed up in his hammock and abandoned in a gangway) he spent a year at Cambridge. Again, higher education did not turn him into an aesthete. In 1942 his wife, Queen Elizabeth, commissioned the artist John Piper to produce twenty-eight watercolours of Windsor Castle, in case it was bombed. Piper painted the castle standing defiant against stormy wartime skies. In what was either a wonderfully deadpan joke, or evidence of his blindness to symbolism, the king remarked, 'You have been unfortunate with the weather, haven't you Mr Piper?'[55]†

When the time came for him to decide upon the education of his daughters Elizabeth and Margaret, he discussed with his wife sending them to school. But George V, the girls' grandfather, would have none of it. 'For goodness' sake,' he exclaimed, 'teach Margaret and Lilibet to write a decent hand, that's all I ask of you.

*On another occasion, it was explained to him that someone was a great authority on Lamb. 'On *lamb*?' he asked in bafflement.

†They were not a cultured lot: Edward VIII once remarked that the only reason a third brother, Harry, Duke of Gloucester, could recognize the national anthem was because everybody stood up for it.

Not one of my children can write properly . . .'[56] So it was decreed that the two girls should learn manners and deportment, some French and how to play a bit of sport. This was supplemented in the future queen's case by private tutorials with Henry Marten, a distinguished history teacher who ambled up to Windsor Castle from Eton College.[57] Precisely what the queen was taught in these lessons is not recorded in the Eton archives – it is assumed to have included advice on the evolution and powers of constitutional monarchy.

But private tuition made for an isolated existence. The young princess would gaze out of the window at Buckingham Palace, watching the cars coming and going in the Mall. 'They all seemed so busy,' she recalled later. 'I used to wonder what they were doing and where they were all going, and what they thought about outside the palace.'[58] Would a broader education, spent among contemporaries, have produced a better queen? It probably would have given her a greater awareness of the lives that her subjects led. But, given the persecution that her father and grandfather had suffered when they were exposed to the attentions of their contemporaries, it is understandable if her family sought to protect her. It might, however, have been kinder to the queen to make her feel less isolated so early in life. When it came to deciding the education of her own expected successor, the queen went along with Prince Philip's misguided enthusiasm for packing the boy off to boarding school, first at Cheam, and then at Gordonstoun.

That Prince Charles loathed both places is common knowledge.[59] Gordonstoun, which had, by mild irony, been modelled on a school established by a Hohenzollern prince[60] to produce leaders who would ensure that Germany never again suffer the humiliating defeat of the First World War, was, to say the least, remote and robust. Many children suffer homesickness when sent away to boarding school. The fact that Charles's junior school did not send any other boy to Gordonstoun aggravated a sense of loneliness. The torments visited upon a shy and sensitive child dumped by his parents in the Scottish Highlands were made much worse by the persecution which enveloped him precisely because of who he was. His jug-handle ears were a come-on to the bullies. But the real provocation came from his status. Any boy who tried to befriend him would be pursued around the grounds by gaggles of others making slurping sounds, indicating that they felt he was 'sucking up' to the heir to the throne. The writer William Boyd, who also endured the place, overheard a gang of school oafs boasting, 'We did him over. We just punched the future King of England.'[61]

The decision to send the prince to this miserable place had been taken because his father felt he needed a more worldly education than the queen had had. It may not have been an intrinsically bad idea. But no thought had been given to whether it was suitable for the boy in question. Had Charles been sent to a school like Eton he would at least have been mixing with boys rather closer to his own home background (and, having met their sisters, might not later have come to the crisis of finding a 'suitable' bride). Prince Philip, a product of Gordonstoun himself, embraced the hearty mentality of the place, which was not that far removed from the naval academies which had nourished previous heirs to the throne. But Philip had attended the school only as an obscure foreigner. It was unreasonable to expect not particularly sophisticated teenage boys to treat normally a contemporary whose mother's face was on every coin in their grubby trouser pockets. At night, they came out to torment him. 'I don't get any sleep practically at all nowadays,' the prince wrote in a letter. 'The people in my dormitory are foul . . . They throw slippers all night long or hit me with pillows or rush across the room and hit me as hard as they can, then beetle back again as fast as they can, waking up everyone else in the dormitory at the same time. Last night was hell, literal hell . . . I still wish I could come home. It's such a HOLE this place!'[62] How any parents could have ignored such letters is a mystery. But ignore them they did.

Eric Anderson, who was one of the few teachers at Gordonstoun with whom Charles developed a good relationship (he produced the school plays in which the prince acted with some ability), confirms how unhappy he was. 'I have no idea why they sent him there. Of course, it wasn't helped by the fact that he was very shy. It was noticeable that Charles was really only friendly with the art master, and with Poppy [Anderson's wife] and myself. Friendship with adults is usually a sign of trouble in a boy.'[63] As it happened, Anderson was headmaster, and then Provost, at Eton when Charles had to think about the education of his own sons. Officials say Charles and Diana were insistent the two boys receive as 'normal' an education as possible. In other families this might have meant attending the local comprehensive. To the palace that would not have been normal at all. They chose Eton, where, according to Anderson, unlike their father at Gordonstoun, the two boys made good friendships, helped by the fact that both were rather hearty and loved sport. Interestingly, the heir, William, received no additional coaching in constitutional matters. Presumably, his A-levels in geography, art history and biology were thought sufficient preparation for his future role. It was expected, anyway, to be a long time before he assumed the throne.

When it came to determining what should become of Charles after Gordonstoun (and six months at Timbertops in Australia) his parents invited to dinner 'as solemn a gathering as had ever met to discuss the future of one not very gifted boy'.[64] The Prime Minister, the Archbishop of Canterbury, the Dean of Windsor, the Chairman of the Committee of University Vice Chancellors, and Charles's 'Uncle Dickie', Lord Mountbatten, talked for two hours before agreeing that that the prince should go to Cambridge before following the usual path to Dartmouth naval college and the Royal Navy. Now, for the first time, an heir to the throne completed a degree course. By the time the next heir apparent, William, left school, the proportion of young people attending university had grown so substantially that it would have seemed 'abnormal' for him not to have followed a similar path.

William's studies of art history and geography at St Andrews University did not earn him the tabloid fiction which had beset the university career of his uncle, Prince Edward, that attendance at university defined him as 'the intellectual of the family'. The thoughtless monicker fell instead upon his younger brother, Harry, whose decision to join the army meant that he was, inevitably, dubbed 'Action Man'. (His role of 'spare' is even less attractive than that of being heir apparent: he is expected to lead as exemplary a life as possible, while knowing that his only chance of becoming king depends upon something dreadful happening to his elder brother. Prince Andrew emerged from his education the sort of person whose idea of humour is bread-roll marksmanship.)

You could argue that what an heir to the throne needs from an education is breadth rather than depth: it is not, after all, as if they are going to pursue a career in any specific discipline, or even to compete for a job in the professions. I had been mildly surprised to notice a shelf at Sandringham holding the most eclectic collection of books, from a leather-bound edition of the sixth-century philosopher Boethius through Dick Francis, P. G. Wodehouse and Frederick Forsyth to a leather-bound collection of poems by Keats. Then I discovered that while all the thrillers had the bookplate 'THE QUEEN'S BOOK' inside their front cover, the leather editions could not be opened: they were bookends. The sort of schooling favoured by twentieth-century British royalty, with its emphasis on hearty activities and disdain for more brainy achievements, at least had the advantage of giving them much in common with their people, who tend to consider intellectuals in much the same way as they regard people who claim they can levitate. The long series of speeches and lectures given by Prince Charles during his time as Prince of Wales perhaps shows how hazardous it is to encourage the conviction that a little learning makes an intellectual.

In many ways, the expectations of a prince are more burdensome than the demands made of those who have a special intellectual, artistic or sporting talent. Anyone lucky enough to be so endowed can follow their star. The rest of us emerge from education to begin a career. But a prince, who is likely to be as ordinarily able as his ordinary subjects, is in the extraordinary position of being unable to begin the job he is destined for until someone else dies.

In a series of announcements, photo-calls and interviews when he left university Prince William discharged one of the essential requirements of royalty: he was said to be 'looking forward' to all sorts of things, from training with a mountain rescue team to taking on the presidency of the Football Association. Enthusiasm – or the appearance of enthusiasm – for every duty is a prerequisite. The trumpeting of the fact that he had passed the entrance test for officer training at Sandhurst needs to be balanced against the caveat that the royal household would have been unlikely to risk putting itself in the position of announcing that the second in line to the throne had failed to qualify to serve in the forces he is expected one day to head. His three weeks' 'work experience' in the financial institutions of the City of London in 2005 did not include the collecting of cups of coffee and operating the photocopier which would have been the reality for other unqualified young people. But other young people would not be expected to be able to give media interviews which sound coherent but signify nothing very much. Nor would they have to be photographed at university buying 'semi-skimmed milk, a packet of crisps, some chocolates and a puzzle book' which he paid for, the breathless reporter added, 'with cash from his own pocket'. Or to have his twenty-first birthday party crashed by someone in a false beard, dark glasses and pink dress, who, for some reason, was said to be 'dressed as Osama bin Laden'.

And other less privileged and less oppressed young people would not find that every time they went out with a girl they would have to gamble upon whether the mass media, in their guise of guardians of the public good, will approve of their choice.

4. Now Find a Consort

What's love got to do with it?

Tina Turner, 1993

There is a large cardboard box stored on the shelves of the British National Archives, stamped with the inscription 'Closed for 100 years'. If you untie the ribbon which holds the box shut you discover it contains documents from a law case of 1866. A north London woman, Lavinia Ryves, was attempting to prove that she was descended from Frederick, Duke of Cumberland, the scandal-mired younger brother of King George III. The woman was clearly obsessed. She wrote a pamphlet appealing to Queen Victoria for support, from 'Lavinia, Princess of Cumberland and Duchess of Lancaster'. Subpoenas were issued and statements taken. An elderly clergyman was tracked down in Honfleur, France, to give evidence from his period as a royal chaplain. Records of baptisms and burials were copied from parish registers by certified clerks, as Lavinia Ryves tried to demonstrate that her grandmother's father and mother had been of royal blood (the Duke of Cumberland having married Olive, the daughter, another fragment of document claimed, of 'the princess of Poland'). As you thumb through the yellowing documents, most of them copies of originals said to be held somewhere else, suddenly you come across a scrap of paper, less than six inches across and about three inches deep, which seems to expose an entirely different royal scandal. It reads:

> This is to solemnly certify that I married George, Prince of Wales, to Princess Hannah, his First Consort, April 17th 1759 and that two princes and a princess were the offspring of such marriage.[1]

What is this? Search the family tree of the eighteenth-century British royal family and nowhere is there a 'Princess Hannah' to be found. But if the Prince of Wales – the man who became King George III the following year – had really married this woman, their sons would have had first claim to the throne. In the question of succession, legitimacy is all. Charles II was said to have had fifty-six bastards, George IV twenty or so, William IV eleven (although none compares to the eighteenth-century King Augustus 'the Strong' of Saxony and Poland, who was reputed to have had 354 bastards). But those born out of wedlock have no title to the throne. If the marriage of George and Princess Hannah were genuine, it follows that every king or queen to have sat on the British throne since George's death in 1820 has been a usurper. Queen Victoria had no entitlement to the crown, and neither did George V or Elizabeth II.

The scrap of paper is signed 'Wilmot, London, April 2nd 176—' – the remainder of the date having been torn off. (Lavinia Ryves's great-uncle was a Rev. Dr James Wilmot.) Deeper in the bundle of documents are two further certificates signed by this Wilmot, in one of which the 'Princess Hannah' is described as 'Hannah Wheeler, alias Lightfoot'. Later there is even a piece of paper signed, in a wavering hand, 'Hannah, Regina'. A quick trawl through the available information about this Hannah Lightfoot discloses a story that at the age of nineteen a 'fair quakeress', the daughter of a Wapping shoemaker, had caught the eye of the future king as he travelled in his coach to the theatre. Aware of the prince's infatuation, the court pressed the girl's family to have her married off to someone else as speedily as possible. But she was spirited away from the door of the chapel and married to the prince instead. When George came to inherit the throne the poor young woman was cast aside, for reasons of state, and he was obliged to marry Princess Charlotte from the German stud-farm of Mecklenburg-Strelitz. In letters, Hannah is said to have referred to 'a certain person', but never disclosed his identity. In her will, the children of the relationship – one of whom took himself off to South Africa, where he rejoiced in the name of 'George Rex'

– were commended to the protection of their father, George III. George Rex was said to have a striking resemblance to the king.

Then, in September 2000, during restoration work in the vaults of St Peter's, the great parish church of Carmarthen, west Wales, a tomb was discovered. Inscribed upon it was the legend that it contained the remains of Charlotte Augusta Catherine Dalton and her niece. The slab of black stone is a great deal less impressive than the nearby memorial to one of the heroes of the battle of Bosworth Field, or indeed than many others in the church. But, according to the churchwarden, the occupant of the tomb was a granddaughter of the unacknowledged union between George and Hannah Lightfoot. 'That's what we believe,' says the churchwarden, daring you to doubt, for locally the story of the secret marriage of George to the 'fair quakeress' seems now to be taken as fact. (By strange coincidence the church has a magnificent organ: it had originally been built for Windsor Castle, but was given to Carmarthen by George III.) When opened up the tomb proved to contain not the advertised two coffins, but four, two of them being those of children. Requests to the vicar for permission to perform DNA analysis on samples from the tomb have been refused, either for reasons of common decency or, perhaps, for fear of destroying a myth.

The tale is the stuff of romantic fiction.[2] Which is probably what it is. As we have seen, the world is full of people who believe they are the unacknowledged heirs to kingdoms. Most are deluded. To a layman, the marriage certificates look a little too conveniently torn, the signatures rather too rambling, to be entirely plausible, like the parental sick-note a teenager might counterfeit to escape games at school. Modern scholars who have examined the story in detail have pooh-poohed it.[3] The Lord Chief Justice at the time declared the documents 'treasonable', and after three days of cross-examination by the Attorney General, the jury found against Mrs Ryves. We can wonder why, if the documents were such seditious forgeries, no action was taken against their perpetrator, for then, as now, the Treason Act (on the statute book since 1351) laid down death as the punishment for the crime.[4] If the documents were harmless forgeries, why were they kept under lock and key for a century? But it is a long time ago and the story looks destined to remain no more than a minor, unprovable historical yarn. What it really points up is the overwhelming importance of marriage in any claim to the throne.

The dining table in the Amalienborg Palace in Copenhagen has been laid for one: being king or queen can be lonely. In the octagonal courtyard outside (the palace is comprised of four near-identical buildings with a public road running between them) are stationed oddly unmilitary soldiers. Dressed in duck-egg-blue trousers, dark tunics, bearskins and white gloves, they do not march so much as amble, occasionally looking at their watches or chatting with the duty policemen. They saunter to no recognizable pattern, pausing to scratch themselves from time to time.

On the first floor, the table is laid with silver plate, crystal glasses and thin white bone china. I am ushered between sideboard and table and into a small, book-lined room, curtains drawn against the winter sunlight.

'I do apologize for the curtains, they're working on the windows,' says the Queen of Denmark.

She is slim, of above average height, her grey hair piled elegantly tight on her head. She wears large, shiny black earrings and almost invisible rimless glasses. In a purple tweed suit, she looks slightly bookish, a librarian or university professor, perhaps, although significantly more expensively dressed. She seats herself on a straight-backed chair (she has had surgery on her back) and lifts a silver canister from the table, from which she extracts an untipped oval-shaped cigarette: like many Danes she smokes as conscientiously as laboratory beagles once did. In half an hour's time there will be three butt-ends stubbed out on the previously gleaming silver ashtray.

Of all the crowned heads of Europe, the Queen of Denmark is the most intellectually accomplished. As we have seen, academic achievement has not generally been the goal of modern monarchy. The British royal family survived the century which split the atom by maintaining a hearty enthusiasm for country pursuits, and Prince Philip is said to have remarked of Queen Elizabeth II, that 'Unless it eats grass and farts, she isn't interested.'[5] It is not entirely fair – the queen certainly takes an active interest in the large Royal Collection of paintings (although that interest is more administrative than aesthetic), personally approving which pictures are loaned where. But, overall, the atmosphere of the court in her reign has been unsophisticated, and her son Charles certainly felt that his own enthusiasms for music, books and paintings were not sufficiently appreciated by his family. On the other hand, ignorance has the merit usually of being uncontroversial.[6]

Of the other courts in Europe, those which are not trivial are generally dull. For intellectual snobs, the only vaguely acceptable modern monarch is Queen Victoria's great-great-granddaughter Margrethe II of Denmark, who studied history, political science and economics at five of the great European universities, is a competent painter, has illustrated the Danish edition of Tolkien's *Lord of the Rings*, designed sets and costumes for the ballet, and co-translated Simone de Beauvoir from the French. Each New Year she broadcasts a speech she has written herself on a subject of her own choosing: it is the most heard and seen speech in the country and not without substance. It might have been otherwise: her father was more noted for being an enthusiastic and jovial sailor than anything else. But the desire to be recognized for achieving something rather than for being something can be one of the great frustrations of life as a constitutional monarch. Kings and queens have to be seen doing things. But they cannot be seen doing anything which amounts to much.

I wanted to ask her about the first responsibility of a monarch, which requires little education. It is simply to ensure that the dynasty continues. No one wants to be known as the last of the line. But while princes make little girls swoon, kings make them quake. And being a single queen is perhaps the most difficult position of all. Margrethe was careful to marry before she inherited the throne. Her husband was a French diplomat she had met while studying at the London School of Economics. Had she been conscious, as a princess, of the need to marry and produce children? She had been a fairly traditional young woman, so had wanted to do it anyway. But it would not necessarily be as easy for her as it can be for others. 'The idea of having to marry as a queen was, I thought, really terrifying. How the hell was anybody ever going to dare to take on a person like that? How would one meet anyone likely to be the right sort of person? But being the *future* Queen of Denmark was probably not quite as terrifying to any candidate as being the actual queen.' And she laughs a throaty laugh.

It takes an unusual combination of qualities – a strong sense of self-confidence allied to a readiness to walk a pace behind – for a man to go courting a queen. Much more common is a sort of refined romanticism, erotic and yet not physical, closer to the medieval idea of courtly love than anything else. You see it in the reign of the Virgin Queen, Elizabeth I, when young men would dedicate love songs and poems to her, or have themselves painted languishing in bowers filled with eglantine roses. All manner of older men fell under the spell of the eighteen-year-old Victoria when she became queen in 1837, the *Spectator* complaining that 'Reginamania' had swept the governing class. Lord Melbourne, in particular, was overcome with solicitude. As she advanced into middle age, Disraeli cynically admitted that when dealing with the queen he laid his flattery on 'with a trowel', telling her that her husband represented the ideal of maleness. When the queen empress (a title he invented for her) sent him a bunch of snowdrops, Disraeli thanked her by saying that he wore them over his heart. The primroses she sent on another occasion were 'more precious than rubies'. A genuine intoxication overcame men who dealt with the young Elizabeth II, of whom her first Prime Minister Winston Churchill gushed that even if film directors 'had scoured the globe, they could not have found anyone so suited to the part'.[7] Her private secretary, Sir Martin Charteris, freely admitted he had been a little in love with her. This capacity to inspire a sexless devotion is perhaps one of the elements which make royal households so attractive to homosexuals. ('Mummy's on the Fabergé,' the queen mother's favourite butler used to twitter when she rang the bell to summon him.)

But devotion does not make it any easier for a queen to find a suitable husband. You can see why Margrethe was anxious to be married before she took the throne. As it turned out, the marriage added a third hazard to the social dangers facing those who entertained the Great Dane, as she is known among the British aristocracy. Her back trouble meant that she preferred to spend long periods standing rather than sitting. A guest at a dinner party to which she was invited described it as 'What Lord Palmerston would have called "a very perpendicular evening" – even the old Duchess of Gloucester, who must have been nearly one hundred at the time, could not sit down because she was only a duchess, and a queen's a queen.' The second hazard was to die of passive smoking. The third was that her husband fancied himself a wine-maker. 'He has an alarming habit of presenting you with bottles of the most disgusting liquid. It's almost black,' says the guest.[8] Nonetheless, the French husband had done his duty and engendered an heir, which was, after all, what he was chosen for.

It is important to understand that, in making arrangements for royal marriages, love is not necessarily the prime consideration. If the couple happen to enjoy each other's company, that is a bonus, not a prerequisite. In the world of cheap novels there is no greater proof of devotion than for a prince to surrender his throne for the woman he loves. In the real world, it is much more common that love gets sacrificed for the sake of the throne. It is true that there are examples of Austrian archdukes who married actresses, Swedish princes who ran off with maids of honour, Spanish queens who contracted secret marriages with soldiers. But those who insisted upon marrying the woman of their choice could find the state capable of tremendous spite. Often, the best they could hope for was a 'morganatic' or 'left-handed' marriage, by which the wife and any offspring were denied any of the husband's inheritance. This was mainly a continental practice. When Franz Ferdinand, the Archduke of Austria (whose assassination sparked the First World War), married for love in 1900 he accepted that his wife would never become empress. The state exacted its revenge in a hundred exquisitely petty ways, forbidding her to act as hostess if her husband was entertaining visiting royalty and denying access to the royal box at the opera. She found that while footmen flung open both sets of double doors at court even for the most junior archduchess, they opened only one side for her.[9] At their joint funeral (she was killed with him), their two coffins lay side by side. But that of the archduke was placed on a higher plinth.

Classically, proper royal marriages were contracted to dignify, glamorize or expand the state. In these arrangements, not only was personal feeling irrelevant, so too was age. When he disappeared, aged ten, in 1483 Richard, Duke of York, the younger of the two princes to be murdered in the Tower of London, had already been married – and was a widower. At the time of his betrothal to the immensely rich heiress Anne Mowbray, he had been four and his bride five.[10] As the prosperity of a dynasty might depend upon the formation of strategic alliances and the production of heirs, kings could go to extraordinary lengths to engineer suitable marriages. On hearing that the Queen of Hungary was expecting a child in 1506, the Holy Roman Emperor, Maximilian I, promised his infant granddaughter Mary to this still-unborn 'son'.[11] In 1515, the 57-year-old Maximilian went through a ceremony with Princess Anna of Hungary (aged all of twelve), promising that he would deliver one of his grandsons as a husband, and pledging that if the boy proved incapable of consummating the marriage, he would do it himself.

Sexual orientation was irrelevant, too, just so long as the individual concerned was prepared to perform the task of begetting an heir. Britain has had several kings and queens – Richard I, Edward II, James I, Mary II and Anne – who are claimed by gay history, and others – William II, Richard II and William III – who may well have been homosexual. (It rather depends upon how you interpret the language of their correspondence.) Yet most proved ready to attempt the production of successors. Some even did so enthusiastically. Bulgaria's attempt to found a dynasty through 'Foxy' Ferdinand's marriage in 1893 seems inauspicious when you read that Lady Paget, wife of the British Ambassador in Vienna, observed that 'He wears bracelets and powders his face. He sleeps in pink surah nightgowns trimmed with Valenciennes lace. His constitution is so delicate and his nerves so finely strung, that he only consults ladies' doctors.'[12] But even though he preferred soldiers for pleasure, Ferdinand did his duty and produced four children.

The way in which England's Henry VIII discarded wife after wife through the first half of the sixteenth century is sufficient evidence of the imperative that the female member of these arrangements should possess a productive womb: it is well enough known not to need retelling. The beautiful Christina of Milan, who was invited to become his fourth wife, is said to have replied that if she had two heads, she might risk the role, but as she did not, she would prefer to stay out of the game. Her replacement, Anne of Cleves, is said in children's history books to have been so much less attractive than the artist's impression Henry had been shown before her arrival in England that he exclaimed that they had brought him a 'mare from Flanders'. This has usually been taken as one of his many less than gallant observations about his wives, because the portrait painter had failed to show the smallpox scars which disfigured her face. But recent research has shown that at the time there was a healthy trade importing horses from the Low Countries, where they had bred a strain prized for being strong, steady and manageable. They were being brought to England to improve the quality of the bloodstock. Rather than being offensive to the poor woman he may well just have been recognizing her role in breeding an heir to the throne.[13]

Like the Tudors, the Hanoverians were conscientious about these alliances. Despite his alleged 'marriage' to Hannah Lightfoot, George III dutifully went through with a wedding to Princess Charlotte of Mecklenburg-Strelitz by whom he had fifteen children. The depth of this devotion led her chamberlain to remark of her after a few years, 'I do think the *bloom* of her ugliness is going off.'[14] The king's father, Frederick, Prince of Wales ('poor Fred'), had been intended for Princess Wilhelmina of Prussia. In a scene which truly resembled something from a livestock market his grandfather George I had travelled to inspect the merchandise himself, approaching the princess with a candle which he held under her nose, looking her up and down without saying a word. 'He embraced me,' the princess recalled later, 'and said nothing further than "She is very tall: how old is she?"'[15] George I died before negotiations for the marriage could be brought to a conclusion, but Frederick managed to convince himself that he was in love with the princess, despite never having met her, and planned an elopement – with which, remarkably, the Queen of Prussia was happy to go along, even though her daughter took the unsurprising view that it was odd to run off with someone you had never met.

On the morning of the wedding of Prince Charles and Lady Diana Spencer a short letter appeared on the correspondence page of *The Times*. The writer Jan Morris wanted to put on the record 'one citizen's sense of revulsion and foreboding at the ostentation, the extravagance and the sycophancy surrounding today's wedding of the heir to the British throne'.[16] Prophetic though it was in some ways, this batsqueak of reproach was drowned in the hysterical cheering which surrounded the event. The bride herself was sick the night before the wedding, telling a friend, 'I felt I was the lamb to the slaughter.'[17] During the ceremony, both were so nervous that Diana muddled up Charles's names, while he promised to share all her own worldly goods with her. But the show had to go on. Alarmed by the level of marital breakdown in the country, the Archbishop of Canterbury declared that when they took their vows the couple would be doing so 'as representative figures for the nation'.[18]

In the event, the wedding turned out highly representative: like four in every ten British marriages, it ended in divorce. But these grand occasions, with their flags, drums, carriages and cuirasses, bearskins, bishops, choirs and fanfares, are representative in another sense, too. Protest though they might, rational democrats are powerless against the collective inebriation of such occasions. The bands play. The crowds cheer. The presents pour in. These tend to be from the very wealthy, the self-important or, most interestingly, from the genuinely generous-hearted. When Princess Elizabeth married Prince Philip in 1947 there was a gold tiara from the Emperor of Ethiopia and a 175-piece porcelain dinner service from Chiang Kai-shek, a piece of cloth spun by Mahatma Gandhi on his own spinning wheel which Queen Mary is famously said to have thought was his loincloth ('Such an indelicate gift,' she muttered), and a further 2,469 other gifts, ranging from books signed by their authors, through many pairs of silk and nylon stockings – and a monogrammed pink satin suspender belt from a Mrs S. Pick – through to a South Moravian peasant-girl costume from a school in Prague. When Charles and Diana married, the treasure chest extended through four thousand items, from a diamond and sapphire jewellery set in a green malachite case given by the Crown Prince of Saudi Arabia to a slightly withered, heart-shaped potato given by two young sisters from Cheshire.

People do not normally send wedding gifts to people they have not met, and the presents signified the extent to which the mass media creates the illusion of familiarity. They also demonstrate the way in which the events drew much of the nation together (just as the subsequent divorce polarized much of the nation). The most famous observation about the function of these ceremonies was made by Walter Bagehot. The occasion might be politically insignificant, but women in particular, he said, 'care fifty times more for a marriage than a ministry . . . A princely marriage is the brilliant edition of a universal fact, and as such, it rivets mankind.'[19] It is, in short, a party to which everyone is invited. Bagehot's observations were prompted by the pairing of the Prince of Wales, the future Edward VII, to Princess Alexandra of Denmark in March 1863. The crowds which turned out to watch the wedding procession through London en route to the service at Windsor were so vast that the police had to force a way through for the carriages, and the *Morning Post* reported that it required the entire staff of St Bartholomew's Hospital to treat the injured. Seven people were said to have been trampled to death. (The poor crowd control reflected generally inept planning: Palmerston had to travel back from Windsor in the third-class carriage of the special train, while Disraeli had to sit on his wife's lap.)

Bagehot was right about the appeal of royal weddings. Few of us have any notion of what is involved in running a government. But we all know what the promises of a wedding are supposed to signify. They are a celebration of hope and devotion. But in the end royal weddings – like other weddings – are only ceremonies, while marriages are relationships, which are much more difficult. Royal couplings suffer from the additional burden of being acted out by people who are the corporeal expression of the nation. A subfusc wedding will not do for the heir to the throne (well, not the first time, at least). The trumpets must sound, the soldiers present arms and the bride descend from her carriage to meet her brilliantly uniformed groom. But, without a solid relationship, these ornate occasions are like an elaborately wrapped parcel which has no present within.

The problem is obvious. Marriage is a decision for the two people involved. But the creation of Mr and Mrs Britain has rarely been a purely private matter. The most notorious of these marriages of inconvenience was that forced upon the future George IV to Caroline of Brunswick. Their loathing for each other was instantaneous and ferocious and continued until she died. Indeed, when told of the death of Napoleon in 1821 with the words 'Your greatest enemy is dead,' the king is said to have replied instantly, 'Is she, by God!'[20] This miserable union had been forced upon the couple because George's existing marriage with Mrs Maria Fitzherbert was illegal. First, Mrs Fitzherbert had the misfortune to be Roman Catholic, and under the Act of Settlement of 1701 the heir to the throne could not be married to a Catholic. Secondly, the Royal Marriages Act had been passed by parliament only a decade or so earlier, after two of George's uncles had married women more at home in beds than in church pews. The legislation – which still applies to those in the immediate line of succession – decrees that no member of the royal family under the age of twenty-five may wed without the consent of the monarch. George had been twenty-three when he persuaded a curate just released from debtors' prison to marry him to Mrs Fitzberbert.

The wedding, ten years later, to Princess Caroline of Brunswick-Wolfenbüttel was a very different affair. The prince was, admittedly, by now on the flabby side. But his debts were big and growing, and the king promised him relief if he married 'suitably'. *The Times* reported the couple's meeting in extravagant terms.

> Both the PRINCE and PRINCESS were extremely affected on their first interview on Sunday, but particularly the former. The Princess on approaching the Prince bent her knee; his Royal Highness snatched her up and embraced her, but it was some minutes before he could give utterance to his feelings. We speak from the best authority when we say, that his Royal Highness is extremely happy and pleased with his lovely Cousin.[21]

As so often with royal reporting, the account did not quite match the reality. The royal bride-to-be was not exactly ugly. But she had been brought up in a small, second-rate German state with very lax standards of personal hygiene. She smelt like a farmyard. The prince immediately crossed the room and turned to Sir James Harris, the first Baron Malmesbury, and muttered, 'Harris, I am not well; pray get me a glass of brandy.' Malmesbury suggested water instead, but the prince was insistent and left the room announcing that he was going to have a word with his mother. Not surprisingly, Caroline exclaimed in French, 'My God!', and asked Malmesbury, 'Does the Prince always act like this?' She added, 'I think he's very fat, and he's nothing like as handsome as his portrait.'[22] The courtier reassured her that the prince would be altogether nicer at dinner. This was something of an exaggeration too: the prince said he found Caroline's conversation ribald and sarcastic.

But the show had to go on, and three days after her arrival in England in 1795 came the most famously awful royal wedding for centuries. On the journey to the Chapel Royal George had told his two companions of his undying love for Mrs Fitzherbert. As he staggered up the aisle he resembled a condemned man being led to his execution (at one point, when he looked as if he was going to attempt an escape, only a sharp look from the king kept him at the altar). He was drunk and almost passed out twice. He slurred and hiccupped his way through his marriage vows while staring meaningfully at his mistress, Lady Jersey, and appeared to weep when the Archbishop asked if anyone knew of 'any just cause or impediment' to the marriage.

According to Caroline, her new husband spent much of the wedding night in the fireplace. For his part, George's occasional foraging in the matrimonial bed left him convinced that he was not the first to explore his bride,[23] although the coupling was enough to produce a daughter. A year later, when a baffled Caroline wrote to him inquiring about their future life, he replied that he would not be sleeping with her again, 'even in the event of any accident happening to my daughter'.[24] In exchange for a mighty allowance, Caroline took herself off abroad. In words which found an echo in the lamentations of another Princess of Wales, she told a mistress of the King of France that she had done the best she could with the British royal family, but that 'they sacrifice friendship, gratitude, everything, to some vain reason of state. There is no heart but in the middle ranks. Were I to marry again, I should take care not to give my hand to a prince.'[25]

Inevitably, love affairs followed. There was a good-looking young man from Milan appointed first as Caroline's equerry and then as her chamberlain. There was, according to the Hanoverian Ambassador to the Vatican, the 'rape' of the King of Naples, Napoleon's former marshal, Murat. Even for 'a town where chastity has never had much of a ministry', her behaviour, he claimed, 'was quite unguarded'.[26] George's attempts to divorce Caroline, though, were seriously hampered by the fact that he had become so hugely unpopular himself. His own womanizing was so widely known that across the country thousands signed petitions in support of his wife,[27] and when plans to divorce her came before parliament, a howling mob gathered outside.

The scandal prefigured the calamity which overtook the

marriage of Charles and Diana two centuries later. Again, a Prince of Wales was required to make a marriage which would satisfy the demands of the state that an heir be produced. Charles himself was flattered by the attention of a pretty younger woman, but the deference customary in court circles meant that there was no one to tell him things he did not particularly want to hear. There was the added complication that the royal family was still attempting to live by the rules of behaviour laid down by earlier generations. Critically, in the field of sex there were entirely different standards for men and women. The bride was to be genteel, faithful, devoted and motherly. Above all, she was to be 'pure', uncontaminated by anything as sordid as physical love. (No such conditions applied to her future husband, whose subjects expected him to have appetites which showed that he was, underneath it all, one of them.) One part of this marriage was, therefore, expected to be almost ethereal, while the other was solidly material.

It had been like this for a very long time. An American resident in Britain during the Abdication Crisis of 1936 had concluded that 'the worst cant, moral hypocrisy and sanctimoniousness of the period flowed from this fundamental conception of woman as a genteel creature, "purer" than man, with a higher standard of morality, but at the same time the chattel of her lord and master, with no character, will, or even legal rights of her own'.[28] And so it remained forty-five years later. The royal household was prepared to abandon the demand that this refined creature also have royal blood in her veins, and had done so with the marriage of the future George VI to Elizabeth Bowes-Lyon. But the 'purity' was not negotiable. Diana was a well-liked, attractive and blameless teenager who fulfilled the essential requirements of being a virgin, a Protestant and an aristocrat. Indeed, members of her family were going out of their way to testify about the state of her hymen. 'Diana, I can assure you, has never had a lover,' said her uncle, the 5th Baron Fermoy. 'To my knowledge she has never been involved in that way with anyone.'[29] No such considerations applied to the prince, who had the good fortune that his human appetites and failings were supposedly offset by the notion that he was anointed for some greater purpose that was beyond the ken of his subjects. The obvious unfairness of the relationship was thus compounded. Not only was the bride expected to live by different standards, they were standards she had to impose upon herself by self-discipline or belief, while the prince could, essentially, do as he pleased because his qualities were simply there by virtue of his birth.

In the famous television interview at the time of his engagement, Prince Charles notoriously responded to the entirely predictable question 'Are you in love?' with the oblique 'Whatever love means.' Perhaps the answer may have reflected no more than understandable discomfort at having to share his private feelings with the world at large. In hindsight, it can be seen as expressing his profound confusion about what he was doing. The remark was later used to tear him to shreds: in the mythology of the worship of Diana it indicated that he had never loved her and had merely used her to further the grand designs of the House of Windsor. In truth, for all their privileges, they were both victims: it was a marriage in which he acquiesced because he recognized that Diana was one of the very few people he would be allowed to marry.

So the ill-matched couple faced their wedding in a cloud of self-delusion. The illusions each nurtured about the other – he in his need to produce an heir, she in her ambition to become Princess of Wales – were apparent in another exchange in the interview, in which Charles described Diana as 'a great outdoor-loving person', which she was not, while she said, 'We both love music and dancing and we both have the same sense of humour,' which was also untrue. As she ticked off the days to the wedding, Diana told a friend, 'In 12 days' time, I shall no longer be me.'[30] She was right: in becoming a princess she was transformed from a citizen into an ornament of the state.

There is a terrible poignancy about the thoughts of young members of the royal family, before the whole ghastly business has been put upon them. As a callow youth Prince Charles had once held forth on the subject. 'My marriage has to be for ever. It's sad, in a way, that some people should feel that there is every opportunity to just break it off when you feel like it. I mean, the whole point about the marriage contract was that it was for life . . . Marriage is something you ought to work at.'[31] There was, of course, no reason to take these opinions more seriously than those of any other unworldly, inexperienced young man, and more than anything else they reflect the views instilled in him by his parents. When the time came to get married, he felt (he said later,) 'ill-used but impotent'.[32] His father had told him, in the language of the Victorians, that unless he married Diana, her reputation would suffer.

Philip himself was made of sterner stuff than his son. No one can ever know what passes between two people in the intimacy of a relationship and judgement is redundant. Marriage to Elizabeth certainly offered escape from penury. But those close to the royal couple speak admiringly of his support for and influence upon the queen. For Elizabeth, the only alternative to marrying the prince had been what became known in court circles as 'the dim Duke scenario'. It was not particularly attractive.

Royal marriages are not inevitably destined to be unhappy. When, for example, Philip ('the handsome', as he became known), son of the Holy Roman Emperor Maximilian I, was introduced to his future wife, Joan of Castile, he demanded that the nearest bishop marry them that afternoon, so they could consummate the relationship at once. When Philip died in 1506, his distraught wife refused to allow his body to be buried, trailing his coffin with her from castle to castle, looking at the corpse every day on the off-chance of a resurrection. But historically it has been understood that weddings contracted for reasons of state cannot necessarily be expected to be models of domestic bliss. The assumption has always been that, once duty had been done and an heir produced, the poor queen might often find consolation in her children, or perhaps in religion, while the king amused himself elsewhere. The sister of the Spanish king Alfonso XII had it right when she declared in 1915, 'If people will not allow a king to enjoy even the ordinary temptations to be virtuous, why should they exclaim if he seeks, outside of marriage, the happinesses of personal intercourse that are denied him in a wife? The fault is not in the kings. It is in the conditions that have required kings to be more than human beings . . . [yet] content with being less than human beings.'[33]

When Princess Louise of Battenberg, daughter of a British admiral of the fleet, rejected the suit of the King of Portugal, Manuel II, in the early twentieth century, she was admonished by Edward VII. She should have taken 'a more patriotic approach to marriage', as it would have been a great thing if the Queen of Portugal had been English.[34] From a personal point of view, Louise chose more wisely and accepted the King of Sweden instead. (She thereby avoided the outer-London exile which awaited Manuel after revolution swept Portugal in 1910: her main claim to fame would then have been to be the wife of the president of the Twickenham Piscatorial Society.) But the English king's advice represents the principles which have governed many royal marriages. Historically, the normal impulses – love, sexual attraction, considerations of whether someone will make a good father or mother – have had little or no part in the business of forming royal alliances. No wonder they take lovers or mistresses.

Once women were allowed to perform on stage, actresses became a ready source of comfort for kings and princes. In the middle of the nineteenth century the (very bad) Irish exotic dancer, Lola Montez, for example, had the sixty-year-old Ludwig I of Bavaria completely under her thumb, until he discovered that he was not alone in this distinction. Edward VII himself enjoyed the company of a series of entertaining and talented women like Lillie Langtry and Daisy, Countess of Warwick – even, it was said, the actress Sarah Bernhardt – to say nothing of Camilla Parker Bowles's great-grandmother Alice Keppel, who was known as 'La Favorita'. In Lillie Langtry's case, her fame as Edward's mistress laid the foundations of her stage career, indicating the historic tolerance of public opinion, such as it was, when it came to royal mistresses. It seemed to recognize a distinction between affairs of state and those of the heart or loins. Nell Gwyn, mistress to perhaps the greatest philanderer of them all, Charles II, understood the limits. Once, it was said, the mob saw a carriage with a pretty young woman inside being driven to an assignation with the king. Convinced the woman was his French, and Catholic, mistress, they besieged the vehicle, rocking it to and fro, until Nell Gwyn leaned out of the window and calmed the crowd by shouting, 'Pray, good people, be civil. I am the *Protestant* whore.'

Courts have always had courtesans. Being a royal mistress might not quite have fulfilled the girlish fantasy of becoming a princess. But if the king was permanently unavailable, it was the next best thing. What other explanation can there be for the capacity of a short, fat, not particularly attractive, not particularly intelligent, man like the future Edward VII to attract mistresses? The more enigmatic figure was the husband of the mistress. Back in the 1820s the satirical magazine *Black Dwarf* suggested a new decoration be created for them, the 'Order of the Golden Horns'. The author Theo Aronson painted a picture of this unappealing corps in the first half of the twentieth century, characterizing them as:

> silent, long-suffering, stiff-upper-lipped gentlemen whose reverence towards the monarchy forbids them to make a fuss. They bow their heads in deferential greeting while their royal guest's gaze shifts to their wife's décolletage; they eat lonely meals in the club dining room while she sips Moët et Chandon in some candle-lit supper alcove; they go on business trips to New York or Chicago while she is whisked off to Biarritz or Dubrovnik. Poor George Keppel [husband of Alice] was forced to go into 'trade' to earn enough to keep his wife in a manner to which her royal lover was accustomed. Ernest Simpson was forever having to find himself some work to do in another room while the scintillating Wallis entertained the Prince of Wales in the drawing room of their Bryanston Square flat.[35]

But something changed as the century went on. Tolerance of royal adultery was feasible only when knowledge was confined to a small social group, who could affect a worldly indulgence befitting their membership of an elite. In the course of the twentieth century, as political power spread and readership of newspapers more than trebled, it became unsustainable.

Victoria had set her family up as some sort of model for the nation, and it is noticeable that since then, with one great exception, British kings have seen public uxoriousness as part of their role. Undoubtedly, double standards applied. The future Edward VII was able to get away not only with his mistresses but with a series of embarrassments, including being involved in a gambling scandal and a divorce case (saved, as one commentator wryly put it, by the British public's inability to believe that adultery could take place at tea-time), and to end his days as an avuncular figure. But he had done his duty and produced a 'respectable' heir.

The exception is Edward VIII, whose obsession with Mrs Simpson in 1936 caused the greatest royal crisis of the twentieth century. It did not help that he was full of self-pity. In one of his many syrupy 'little boy' letters to an earlier mistress, Freda Dudley Ward, from 'your vewy vewy own Yes! your very very own little David', he confessed, 'it would be a d—d shame to even ask you to take on the job of wife to the P. of W. In fact I don't think I could ever summon up the courage to ask you to & I know you would hate it all as much as I should!! It just would not be fair on you sweetheart though who knows how much longer this monarchy stunt is going to last or how much longer I'll be P. of W. . . .'[36] With Wallis Simpson, this infantilizing was even worse. When he asked for a light for his cigarette, she would make him 'sit up and beg' like a dog. The joke went that the couple were 'King Edward the Eighth and Mrs Simpson the Seven-Eighths'.

The political class might have tolerated such behaviour in a prince who was merely behaving as princes always have – indeed, a prince who was desirable to women made the country seem desirable. But they would not stand for it in a king. It was not only that putting away a girlfriend seemed a meagre sacrifice by comparison with the vast numbers who had given their lives in the Great War. There was also a sense in which, by demonstrating the king's weakness, Wallis Simpson showed up something feeble in the country he was said to personify.

The Prime Minister Stanley Baldwin said that Britain was certainly not ready for a 'Queen Wally'. Her supporters have chosen to portray her as the victim of a conspiracy by a circle of upper-class Britons who detested her American nationality almost as much as her status as a multiple divorcee. Certainly, the king was sent thousands of letters from members of the public, most of them offering support. They included one from a man in Glasgow offering to deal with the Bishop of Bradford, whose comments about the king's lack of attention to his religious duties had brought the affair into the open. 'If your Majesty desires that the Bishop of Bradford be bayoneted I shall, if you will so command, be happy to do the needful,' he wrote, 'even though I am at heart a pacifist.'[37] There is some evidence to suggest that, had 'the people' been allowed a say in the matter, they might have accepted the idea of their king marrying a woman he loved. But at this distance, it is almost impossible to disentangle the facts of her unsuitability from the propaganda. Was there really a dossier compiled by MI6 which reported that she had met her first husband in a 'singing house' (brothel) in Hong Kong, where Chinese courtesans entertained with lesbian displays and erotic massage? Did she become pregnant (and have a botched abortion in consequence) by the young man who was later to become Mussolini's Foreign Minister and son-in-law? Could there really have been an affair with Joachim von Ribbentrop, Hitler's Ambassador to London? Had she run guns in the Far East? Did the Metropolitan Police Special Branch really discover that she had a secret lover in the form of a Ford car salesman named Guy Marcus Trundle?

In short, Wallis Simpson had lived too much. Had Edward VIII first contracted a marriage and done his duty of reproducing, the political class might perhaps have tolerated a subsequent affair, even with a woman like Wallis Simpson: the infertile mistress (preferably another man's wife) does not threaten the throne. As it was, only two decades later the unseated king and his wife watched from their exile in Paris with a curious combination of feelings as the British governing class was convulsed by further moral spasms as the daughter of the man who had taken Edward's place announced that she too had fallen in love with someone who was divorced. When told of Princess Margaret's involvement with

Group Captain Peter Townsend, Winston Churchill – who had previously shown his colours (and his touch for popular politics) by supporting Edward in his wish to marry Mrs Simpson – had been enthusiastic. 'What a delightful match!' he exclaimed. 'A lovely young royal lady married to a gallant young airman, safe from the perils and horrors of war!'[38] It fell to Churchill's successor as prime minister, Anthony Eden, to give the princess a cold choice: she could either remain a princess, or she could become plain Mrs Peter Townsend, stripped of royal status, privileges and income. The princess capitulated. For weeks afterwards the press dripped with expressions of sympathy for the woman who had put her duty first. But what was this duty precisely? Margaret's elder sister had already produced an heir to the throne, so the chances of her succeeding were remote. Group Captain Townsend had been, in the language of the day, 'the innocent party' in the divorce and had risked his life for his country.

It was Princess Margaret's misfortune to fall in love at a time when the coterie of people at the heart of the state were still shuddering over the Abdication Crisis. There was still an entity which could be called the 'Establishment', in which the interests of Church, Crown and government coalesced among men in suits in leather armchairs in St James's. For them, royal marriages still carried a residue of the political, religious and diplomatic elements which had been their burden through history. Couples marrying under these circumstances did not expect to have lives of domestic bliss. Happiness was not the prime consideration at all. The successful royal marriage demanded a degree of tolerance: as her biographer puts it, when writing of the alleged affairs of Prince Philip, 'Elizabeth's generation was not brought up to expect fidelity but loyalty.'[39] Hers is one of a number of royal marriages over the last couple of centuries which could be judged reasonably successful. Victoria was, of course, devoted to Albert, and the forty-three-year marriage between George V and Queen Mary and the twenty-nine-year relationship of George VI and Queen Elizabeth were also obviously strong. And, although Edward VII worked his way through mistresses the way others might tackle a box of chocolates (the joke went that when Alexandra saw his coffin she said, 'At least now I know where he is'), the royal couple were both popular and apparently fond of each other to the end.

The arrangements reeked of hypocrisy: Anthony Eden, the Prime Minister who delivered the ultimatum to Princess Margaret, was himself divorced, for example. But somehow this was put to one side, as Eden persuaded himself that he was motivated by weightier matters than personal happiness. As it happened, the princess's later marriage, with the photographer Antony Armstrong-Jones – which was approved by the custodians of public morality – came to a poisonous conclusion (he was said once to have left a note on her desk entitled 'twenty reasons why I hate you').[40] Instead of 'setting an example', the royal family found themselves as much the creatures of social change as many of their subjects. In time three out of Queen Elizabeth II's four children would themselves make marriages which collapsed. The post-war social revolution may not have significantly undermined support for the institution of monarchy. But the royal family could not remain immune to it. The 'respectable' middle classes of late-Victorian society led a life of far greater sexual continence than their Prince of Wales, and everyone understood the idea of 'duty'. A century later, duty had been mislaid somewhere as all social classes chased after some unobtainable utopia of personal happiness. Instead of leading, royalty now reflected the very different society of which it was part. The current British Crown Prince may turn out to have been the last heir to a European throne expected to marry a woman with 'no past'. In recent years, Crown Prince Haakon of Norway has married a single mother, the Crown Prince of the Netherlands an Argentine banker, and Crown Prince Felipe of Spain a divorced television anchorwoman. Modern monarchy survives not by any will of its own, but by the collective delirium of its citizens, and in choosing brides who reflect reality they could be said to be paying their subjects a compliment.

5. Marshals and Mannequins

And what have kings that privates have not too,
Save ceremony, save general ceremony?

Shakespeare, *Henry V*, Act IV, scene i

The family speak of Scrivelsby as an 'island' in the wolds of Lincolnshire. On a warm June afternoon, black fallow deer – there is only one other herd in England – graze under the trees in the parkland outside the family house. It is a perfectly English idyll. The Dymoke family, who own the place, are farming folk, which gives them an attachment to their three thousand acres. But what makes them especially rooted in Lincolnshire is that Scrivelsby was a gift in the division of the spoils which followed the Norman invasion of England almost a thousand years ago.

There are many positions in modern British life, from the Lord High Admiral of the Wash on the English east coast to the Captain of Dunstaffnage Castle on the Scottish west coast, which were given to ancient families by kings worried about the security of their realm. It is true that in 1953 the Hereditary Grand Falconer[1] demanded to exercise his right to take a live falcon in the coronation procession for Elizabeth II (he was dissuaded, sadly) but these posts do not tend to be onerous. This is just as well, because the duty of King's Champion, which William I gave to the inhabitants of the manor of Scrivelsby, is to fight anyone who might wish to challenge the king for the throne of England. That responsibility is not so easily discharged when you are over eighty.

Lieutenant Colonel John Dymoke, the Hereditary Champion, is a pleasant, outdoorsy man who has only once been challenged, when, as a young army officer, he took his battalion to Iceland on manoeuvres and a gaggle of local Communists turned up at the camp and said they would fight him if he didn't take his men home. The confrontation was defused without exchanging blows. But it was not always so. 'Edward IV chopped off one of my ancestors' heads,' he says with a smile. 'We also had tremendous trouble with Henry VIII.' And then there was Oliver Cromwell, who – given his enthusiasm for executing kings – might have been expected to make short work of someone whose job was to defend the monarch. Instead Cromwell contented himself with simply fining the family for the glorious crime of having 'a lewd and malicious title'. Dymoke's ancestors were required to ride their horses into the coronation banquet, throw a metal gauntlet to the ground three times and offer to fight anyone who dared gainsay the new monarch's right to rule. Afterwards, the king would drink the Champion's health from a gold goblet, which then became his property: over the generations, the family accumulated an impressive shelf or two beside their drinks cabinet. Since 1821 monarchs have saved themselves money and trouble and have merely obliged the Champion to carry a flag in a procession: thus the young Captain Dymoke had the pleasure of preceding Field Marshal Viscount Montgomery of Alamein.

There is no salary, no uniform; in truth, there is no job. But the existence of the role is a reminder of the historical imperative that the monarch had to be strong enough to see off anyone who wanted to seize the throne. Success in battle was the foundation of many a dynasty, and military impregnability the basis on which all else was built. Even Alfred the Great, who is often seen as the ideal early English king, built his achievements on the valour he showed on the battlefield, fighting to preserve Wessex from Viking invasion. All the rest – the patronage of the arts, town-planning, promotion of religion and education – necessarily depended upon there being a kingdom for him to govern. Later kings, such as Richard I (or Louis IX of France), established their military reputations on the Crusades: it was said that Saracen mothers frightened their children with the mere mention of Richard's name. Shakespeare's Henry V, offering blood brotherhood to his 'happy few' on the eve of the battle of Agincourt, is the dramatic expression of the type. In practice, some were better generals than others. In the sixteenth century Suleiman the Magnificent extended the Ottoman empire to its zenith. His English contemporary Henry VIII not only led his army personally and is credited by many as father of the English navy, he also acquired a reputation as something of a diplomat. In exile the future James II was a jobbing cavalry commander; after the Restoration he was appointed Lord High Admiral by his brother Charles II and reorganized the navy upon lines which lasted for generations.

But the last British monarch to lead his troops into battle was George II at the battle of Dettingen on the banks of the River Main in June 1743, during the War of the Austrian Succession. His 42,000 soldiers were outnumbered by the French. As cannonfire poured down upon George's forces, the king, who was then sixty, dismounted from his frightened horse and, in a thick German accent, cried, 'Now boys, now for the honour of England; fire and behave bravely and the French will soon run.' It may not have the oratorical flair of 'we few, we happy few, we band of brothers', but accounts of the battle (admittedly written by his supporters) spoke of cannonballs passing 'within half a yard of his head'. That his troops were victorious was all that mattered. Afterwards, the king would appear at public festivals in his old military hat and coat 'and', Thackeray wrote, 'the people laughed, but kindly, at the odd garment, for bravery never goes out of fashion'.[2] It was at around this time that the British national anthem became popular.[3] After a request that God grant the king a long life, he is asked to 'send him victorious', a clear recognition that the first duty of a monarch is to win wars.

It is a little-known fact that King George V was wounded in the First World War. In October 1915 he decided to pay a visit to British troops serving on the Western Front. For centuries it has been received wisdom that the appropriate form of transport for the Commander-in-Chief on such occasions is a horse, and an even-tempered chestnut mare was chosen for the task. The final stage of the king's tour was to be an inspection of a Royal Flying

Corps detachment at Hesdigneul. For two weeks, the horse was intensively schooled in sedate, dignified walking and standing to attention while soldiers presented arms and military bands played regimental marches. By the end of the preparation, a senior officer wrote that 'it would rest its head happily all day long against the big drum of a band playing *God Save the King*. Gunfire did not make it even twitch an ear, I think it would have sat in an aeroplane doing stunts.'[4] Unfortunately, the one thing the animal had not been trained for might, perhaps, have been most easily predicted. With the horse only a few yards in front of them, the ranks of soldiers broke into three cheers for his Majesty. The astonished animal reared up on its hind legs in terror and fell over backwards. The king was crushed, to be carried away with torn muscles in back and legs, a broken pelvis and three fractured ribs.

On the whole, one can see why twentieth-century generals might come to the conclusion that the best place for a king in warfare is as far away from the action as possible.[5] Early kings might have depended upon their military skills to retain their hold upon political power. But, as politics became the province of politicians, generalship became the business of generals. The king remained the living emblem of nationhood and – like the standard around which regiments fought – it was foolish to put him in harm's way. By the outbreak of the First World War the future Edward VIII, then Prince of Wales, had already been in uniform for a few years. His letters drip with self-disgust. 'I am the most bum specimen of humanity,' he wrote to his brother Bertie.[6] In his diary he complained, 'I haven't the remotest chance of getting out with the expeditionary force . . . Oh!! God; the whole thing is too big to comprehend!! Oh!! That I had a job.'[7] The prince had been allowed to join the Grenadier Guards (they waived the height requirement), but when his unit was posted overseas, he was transferred and kept busy with ceaseless paperwork. He did occasionally visit the trenches, and found the experience terrifying and disgusting, which seems a perfectly healthy reaction. Towards the end of the war, when posted to Italy, in a letter to his mistress he wrote of the fighting in France, 'How kind fate is to have sent me back to ITALY, so that I am escaping that fearful battle!! It's very unpatriotic of me to say this but still these are my genuine feelings.'[8] When he came to tell his life story later, he made much of this particular frustration as Prince of Wales. He reported a conversation in which the Secretary for War, Lord Kitchener, the man whose face stared out of recruiting posters saying 'Your Country Needs YOU', explained that the country could not take the risk of his being captured by the Germans.[9]

There were similar anxieties at work in Churchill's mind when Bertie, now George VI, told him that he wanted to join the D-Day armada in 1944. The Prime Minister had planned to watch the bombardment of the German defences from the decks of the cruiser HMS *Belfast*. If he had his way, he would tour the beaches soon after the landings. When the king heard of his plan, he was anxious, peevish and jealous: he had been hoping to do much the same thing himself. There ensued a tussle between the two, in which the king accepted that he could not risk placing himself near the action, but begged his Prime Minister likewise to keep out of harm's way: if he couldn't go, he was damned if Churchill would. 'I am a younger man than you,' he wrote to Churchill, 'I am a sailor, & as King I am the head of all three Services. There is nothing I would like to do better than to go to sea but I have agreed to stop at home; is it fair that you should then do exactly what I should have liked to do?'[10] A crabby Churchill eventually did as he was asked – a rare, if slightly unexpected, example of a constitutional monarch getting his way over against his prime minister.

As a second son – and therefore not expected to inherit the throne – the young George VI had been less sheltered from war: he had served, for example, on board HMS *Collingwood* at the battle of Jutland. Now, having unexpectedly taken the throne, he and his queen seemed to understand that their role was different. In the First World War he had also watched his father setting off on visits to military hospitals, an experience the old king had found sufficiently distressing to tell a lady of the court, 'You can't conceive what I suffered going round those hospitals in the War.'[11] In the

Second World War George VI and his queen had refused to allow the princesses Elizabeth and Margaret to be sent to safety in Canada; instead they stayed at home. The king continued to work at Buckingham Palace during the day – the palace was hit by enemy bombs nine times. He visited battle zones, dropped in on the night shift at a munitions factory and visited citizens huddled in their air-raid shelters. The queen learned to handle a revolver, the king said that he kept both a pistol and a rifle with him in his car. Much was made – too much perhaps, since ordinary people had neither the produce of the royal estates to supplement their ration-book allowances nor the opportunity to sleep in the relative safety of Windsor Castle – of the idea that the two of them were sharing the suffering of their people. Had they been killed in the air raids it would not have been a catastrophe: one of the assets of the monarchical system is that there is usually someone on hand to whom the crown can be passed. But had they been captured, there is no doubt the effect upon morale would have been very damaging.

The more difficult position was that of the king or queen whose country was overrun by the Nazis. Perhaps the Norwegian parliament would by itself have rejected German demands for surrender. But it was King Haakon who spoke first in rejecting them outright, adding that he would abdicate if the politicians accepted the German demand. After the invasion, he went on to lead the resistance from London. Similarly, the broadcasts by Queen Wilhelmina to Nazi-occupied Holland on Radio Oranje were the inspiration for Dutch resistance.

The alternative was to follow the example of King Leopold of the Belgians, who comprehensively mishandled the threat of German invasion, refusing to ask for military support against the massing of German troops on his border in 1940 because, he said, to do so would stoke up tensions in the country and violate its neutrality. Only when the violation happened did he put himself at the head of the Belgian army and appeal for help. It was far too late: within eighteen days the invasion was complete. The king now faced a choice. As commander-in-chief he could behave like the Dutch queen or the Norwegian king and continue the fight from exile in London. Or he could capitulate. Leopold chose to stay in Belgium, explaining to George VI that 'I can better aid my people by remaining with them than by trying to act from outside the country, especially against the rigours of foreign occupation, the threat of forced labour or of deportation and food shortages.'[12] The king attempted to justify his decision by saying that exile would have meant a commander-in-chief abandoning his army. However, it looked like collaboration with the Nazis. Yet even Churchill, who denounced Leopold furiously in public, was more understanding in private, telling his cabinet colleagues that while 'it was certainly not heroic', it 'might well be the best that he could do for his country'.[13] There were immediate demands for the king to abdicate for failing to preserve the country he led. Some thought he should be executed. But by 1941 the government-in-exile in London had changed its tune. Belgians, it said, should 'close ranks around the prisoner–King. He personifies the battered Fatherland. Be as faithful to him as we are here.'[14]

This was a tactical position, based among other things upon an awareness of Belgium's inherent tensions. Since its invention in 1830, it has often seemed that the monarchy is all that holds the country together – the formal title is not King of Belgium, but King of the Belgians. After liberation, Leopold hoped he might be treated like the Danish king, Christian X, who had stayed to 'share the suffering' of his people after the German invasion, supported a collaborationist government and discouraged his people from acts of resistance (or 'foolishness' as he persisted in calling it), yet on his death was honoured by having his coffin adorned with the emblem of the resistance. Belgium was incapable of such collective amnesia. When the country was liberated, the decision which Leopold claimed to have taken in the interest of national unity proved so divisive that he was obliged to abdicate in favour of his son.

If we picture royalty in our minds, we see them in palaces guarded by soldiers in splendid uniforms. Of all the social situations in which Elizabeth II has been seen during her long reign, she has often seemed at her most relaxed – laughing, joking, flirting – when she was with military men. Of course, the officers of the elite regiments came – and to an extent still come – from the upper classes, with whom the monarchy is most at ease. In the case of Queen Elizabeth the easiness was also built upon the fact that the military still shared many of the values with which she was brought up. But there is something else at work, too. Historically, the regiments entrusted with the task of protecting the royal household were seen as the elite of the army, because they were closest to the king (and were sought after too, because they offered access to the court). Of course, there are ceremonial soldiers in republican countries, too – like the Garde Républicain in France – and even in funny little city-states, like the Vatican. But the competition among British Household regiments to avoid ceremonial duties is intense, because they are so stupefyingly boring. All commanders expect that a long tour of duty outside Buckingham Palace will significantly increase the speed at which soldiers decide to leave the army.

Yet there is pride in the tedium, because it signifies the closeness of the military's relationship with royalty. The Household Cavalry do not care that soldiers of less grand regiments call them Donkey Wallopers, because they know that the symbolic value of the Crown to the armed forces cannot be exaggerated. Nowhere in British society is royalty taken more seriously. It is not only that the highest awards for valour, the Victoria Cross and the George Cross, are named after monarchs. Nor is it that until 1900 all officers' commissions were personally signed by king or queen – although the modern facsimile usually ends up hanging on the wall of the downstairs loo, the oath still has real force. It is that, to inure themselves to the horror of war, all armies are ritualistic organizations, in which symbols matter. To swear faithfully to defend her Majesty, her heirs and successors speaks to some profound sense of purpose. 'It is like being in love,' one officer told me. 'You don't want to look too closely. This relationship with monarchy is about finding a home for the heart, not a target for the intellect.' Clearly, the feelings are reciprocated. Military dress is the wardrobe of choice for royalty on most grand occasions, and they relish an invitation to become colonel-in-chief. If Prince Charles, for example, were ever to undertake a tour of all the military organizations with which he is associated he would need a truck to carry his uniforms, which range from kilted Highlanders, through cavalry regiments, infantry regiments, parachute regiments and air force bases, to say nothing of military organizations in Australia, Canada, New Zealand and Papua New Guinea. Even his first wife, Diana, Princess of Wales, had her own regiments, nicknamed in the army 'Di's Guys' or 'Squidgy's Own'.

The role of colonel-in-chief is an honorary one (which is just as well, because at the outbreak of the First World War the Colonel-in-Chief of the Royal Dragoons was the Kaiser). But the association with royalty does give regiments friends in high places. The late queen mother used to make a point of sending Christmas puddings to many of the regiments with which she was associated: some of the soldiers were under the impression that she had made them herself. And when the Cheshire Regiment was sent to serve in Bosnia, for example, Prince Charles, the Colonel-in-Chief, asked its commanding officer if the men were short of anything. The CO told the prince that they would rather like to be able to call home at Christmas. Within days, the Ministry of Defence had provided the regiment with six satellite telephones.

A visit to the military academy at Sandhurst brings home the pressing sense of its own history and monarchical connections. It is an institution designed to instil a sense of belonging to a glorious military heritage – the walls are covered in paintings of historic battles and the chapel inscribed with the names of the fallen from campaigns all over the world. But, for all the lectures on tactics and technology, armies work by cultivating emotion – military training is about turning naturally selfish individuals into members of a team. To do so requires the development of an instinctive loyalty.[15] Military organizations act upon commands, so they need a hierarchy, at the top of which will inevitably sit an individual – the monarch. The army seems to like it that its figurehead does not order deployments and yet is part of its history. As a major from a Highland regiment explained, 'All the soldiers like it. It makes them feel special.' An artillery officer recalled the effect of a royal visit. 'It made us all feel better because they'd taken an interest. You never have that feeling about politicians. You just wonder "What are they after?"' The oath sworn to serve king or queen gives soldiers a way of shutting out the knowledge that the people who send them into battle are mere fly-blown politicians. Immensely controversial decisions, such as that to invade Iraq in 2003, excited almost no argument within the army, at least partly because of the belief that they serve not governments but the monarch.

'We know what the queen's views are,' one general barked. 'She doesn't have any views.' In some parts of the British army, notably those regiments which have the most obvious connections, the House of Windsor almost seems a religion, while many soldiers would probably be unable even to guess at the name of the Defence Secretary. The Commandant of Sandhurst claimed that he had 'never, ever heard a soldier say that he is fighting for Britain (whereas you do hear French soldiers saying they're fighting for France). They're fighting for the queen.' It is one of history's oddities that Britain does not have a 'royal' army. That appellation is reserved for the Royal Navy and the Royal Air Force, each of which, strangely, feels rather more 'parliamentary' in temperament.

At first sight, then, it might seem curious that so many members of the House of Windsor have been trained as sailors. George V, Edward VIII, George VI, even the princes Charles and Andrew, all attended naval college. The historian Philip Ziegler explained the thinking. '[The Royal Navy] was a cherished national institution, its officers were recruited largely from the gentry or aristocracy, it offered less opportunities for debauchery or any kind of escapade than its land-based counterpart, it inculcated those virtues which it was felt were above all needed in a future king: sobriety, self-reliance, punctuality, a respect for authority and an instinct to conform.'[16] The comment belongs to the Dreadnought era, when the British navy was the most powerful force on earth. As the twentieth century progressed, the 'senior service' diminished in size and power, and at the same time became as much about guided weapons as about seamanship.

The decision to send the most recent generation of princes, William and Harry, to the military academy at Sandhurst reflects the fact that Britannia no longer rules the waves and that so much of modern warfare at sea (and in the air) is highly demanding technically. But it is small wonder that one or other of the services is still chosen as the setting where so many royal children make a stab at adult life. It is not merely that romantic ideas about princes decree that they should be able to wear a uniform convincingly. Nor is it solely that they will be in a controlled environment where codes of behaviour and loyalty are more entrenched than in most areas of civilian life. It is also that the military provides an occupation without the demands of a career. What else can you do with an heir to the throne – or even the brother held in reserve in case of accidents?

Just occasionally, a member of the family strikes out on his own. Prince George, the fourth son of George V, had spent his youth in the sort of self-indulgence which can easily overtake a young man born to privilege and at no risk of having to inherit the throne.[17] The king forced him into the navy, but though he might have liked sailors, the prince was not cut out for a life on the ocean wave. He escaped and in 1932 found a job as a factory inspector. He seems to have had a genuine interest in the working conditions of the British people, and requests were issued to the press that he be treated no differently from any other inspector. The prince trundled off in sports jacket and grey flannel trousers to a smelting factory, a dairy, a brewery, an insulin manufacturer, a company which made bicycles, and another producing false teeth. He was enthusiastic enough to turn up at the Kensitas cigarette factory one July day when the place was closed. But the king was baffled. Why was the prince so interested in the conditions in which his subjects worked? And what was a member of the royal family doing in paid employment? An instruction was issued: the prince was also to be available for ribbon-cutting duties. This made his position impossible, since he could neither work full-time nor pass himself off as plain 'Mr George', the inspector. But what finished the thing off was the attitude of the employers. No sooner had Mr George arrived for an inspection than he would be dragged away from the assembly line and taken to an office, in order that the management might fawn upon him over a glass of sherry.

By comparison the insulated world of service life offered Prince Charles and his own sons, the princes William and Harry, activity and purpose with comparatively little gawping. But no prince enjoys a 'normal' military career. When Prince Charles joined the navy, for example, junior officers were hand-picked to serve alongside him, and when, with much fanfare, he was given command of his own ship, the Admiralty recognized that the most important person on the vessel was not its captain, but the experienced second-in-command they had appointed to avoid any embarrassing groundings or collisions.

On the morning of the Service of Thanksgiving for the 1991 Gulf War, the Prince of Wales's private secretary, Richard Aylard, turned out in full naval uniform. He was wearing his Falklands campaign medal, issued to those who had served in the campaign to recapture the islands from Argentina. 'How nice to see the medal being worn,' said the prince. 'Yes,' said Diana, as she ran a finger along the row of medals on her husband's chest, 'at least he *earned* his medal.'

Aylard was chilled by the princess's scorn. It was a spiteful remark, but she had a point. The prince's active military service had ended in 1976. Yet for the next twenty-five years decorations were heaped upon him as he rose through the ranks: commander in the Royal Navy; group captain in the RAF; major general in the army, and on, in 2002, to vice admiral in the navy, lieutenant general in the army and marshal of the Royal Air Force. A senior palace official recalls the 'great pride' with which his mother put her signature to a document promoting the middle-aged prince. 'The effect of the promotion was simply to allow him to wear a more decorated uniform. He had done nothing to earn or deserve the new rank. But you could see the queen's satisfaction.' An obsessive preoccupation with uniforms and medals is almost all that is left of the warrior king in the modern world. At the July 2005 celebrations to commemorate the end of the Second World War, for example, the queen's third son, Prince Edward, turned out in the uniform of an honorary colonel of the Royal Wessex Yeomanry, despite the fact that – much to his father's disgust – he had long since abandoned the training course which might have turned him into a Royal Marine.

One of the most celebrated boobies in this field was Kaiser Wilhelm, whose military genius was limited to appointing officers he liked to positions at court and seeing that 'tall chaps', who would look impressive in fancy uniforms, were prominently displayed on parade. Yet an entire suite of rooms was needed to hold his many hundreds of different military outfits – including those of every regiment in the German army, the dozens of foreign decorations he was entitled to wear, the costumes for receiving visiting delegations, or for entertaining at court. The story went that he was discovered one day about to leave the palace wearing the full-dress uniform of an admiral. When asked where he was going he was said to have replied, 'To the Aquarium.'*

This incessant wearing of uniforms and its complementary assumption of grand rank undoubtedly swell the head. But no recent monarch has become quite as unhinged by the experience as George IV, whose military experience as a younger (and much thinner) man had been confined to a very minor, ceremonial role in the army. As William Thackeray put it, he 'had heard so much of the war, knighted so many people, and worn such a prodigious quantity of marshals' uniforms, cocked hats, cock's feathers, scarlet and bullion in general',[18] that he began to imagine he had actually fought in some of the army's campaigns. At dinner parties he would claim to have led a decisive cavalry charge at the battle of

*It was also claimed that he wore his admiral's uniform for a visit to the opera *The Flying Dutchman*. Both stories have the flavour of the old maxim of tabloid journalism of being 'too good to check'.

Waterloo. Since the guests at these dinner parties included the Duke of Wellington, he could appeal to him for confirmation. The Field Marshal would reply 'So you have often told me, Sir,' while muttering privately that, of course, insanity ran in the family.*

Preoccupation with the right dress is an affliction which seems to run through royalty like an inherited disease. The future Edward VII once rebuked the Prime Minister, Lord Salisbury, when he appeared at Buckingham Palace in what the prince immediately spotted as a mixture of uniforms. 'Here is . . . Europe in a turmoil,' he exclaimed, 'twenty ambassadors and ministers looking on. What will they think – what *can* they think of a premier who can't put on his clothes?' Lord Salisbury replied that it was a dark morning when he dressed, and 'I am afraid that at the moment my mind must have been occupied by some subject of less importance.'[19] When George V came across Sir Derek Keppel walking into Buckingham Palace wearing a bowler-hat he attacked him with the words, 'You scoundrel, what do you mean by coming in here in that rat-catcher fashion? You never see me dressing like that in London.' To which Keppel replied, 'Well, Sir, you don't have to go about in 'buses.' ''Buses!' the king exploded. 'Nonsense.'[20]

But it is with military uniforms and decorations that the mania is most obsessive. George V told the Aga Khan that a king looks on a man who fails to wear his decorations properly with the sort of distaste a mere mortal might feel for a man with his shirt-tails hanging out.† His son, the future Edward VIII, was once accosted by his great uncle Prince Arthur, Duke of Connaught, and sent

*The king liked to claim that he had fought under the name of General Bock, who had indeed led the German Legion at the battle of Salamanca. Unfortunately, Bock had died at sea the year before Waterloo. When George talked of leading the charge down a steep hill, Wellington would mutter, 'Very steep, Sir.' In another dinner-party anecdote, George used to describe in vivid detail how he had ridden a winner at Goodwood.

†He was a stickler for convention. If his son, the future Edward VIII, appeared before him wearing trousers with the then fashionable turn-ups, he was in the habit of asking 'Is it raining in here?'

back to change his clothing for the King's Birthday Parade because he had committed the heinous crime of being in 'guard order' when he should have been in 'review order'. The first prescribed a crimson silk sash with white leather sword slings and knot; the other, a gold and crimson net sash, and gold-laced sword slings and knot. The future king, whose delicate sensibilities do seem to have been genuinely offended by unearned medals,[21] commented:

There were more than a hundred regiments in the British Army, each with its own sacred idiosyncrasy of dress – lacings, badges, buttons, belts, and head-dresses. Uncle Arthur seemed to carry in his head an exact catalogue of every uniform, its history, and how it should be worn. News that he was going to inspect a unit would strike terror into all ranks. He would scrutinize each officer and soldier from head to toe.

'My dear fellow, you're a Grenadier, aren't you?' he was heard to ask sarcastically of an unsuspecting field officer in the guttural accent that was a characteristic of all Queen Victoria's children.

'Sir,' was the officer's affirmative answer.

'Then why the devil', asked Uncle Arthur, 'are you wearing Coldstream spurs?'[22]

Of course, there is a reason for the obsession with proper dress: if the colonel-in-chief can't get it right, why should anybody else bother? But there is also a nagging anxiety that uniforms and decorations may be royalty's equivalent of the British obsession with home improvement, with the significant characteristic that what is being beautified is themselves. There are exquisite gradations. Take the 'Windsor' coat, invented by George III, a dark-blue tailcoat with scarlet facings and cuffs and its own design of gold buttons. It is worn with a white waistcoat, but only for functions at Windsor Castle. In the dress version, the wearer was also festooned in gold braid. William IV abandoned the uniform. Victoria revived it. Edward VII introduced a restriction specifying that it should be worn only in the evenings. George V was painted wearing it. And Prince Philip invented a dinner-jacket version, which he wore with a black bow-tie. When he and Prince Charles appeared for dinner attired in the uniform, a fellow guest felt it 'not a great success. They looked like railway stewards serving kippers on the 8.30 to Manchester.' But Prince Charles seems to like the thing: he even modified the design for use out on the hunting field and wore the evening version for his first public photograph after announcing his engagement to Camilla Parker Bowles.

This obsession with the symbols of rank and organization is the mental equivalent of the coccyx, that little bone at the base of the spine which is assumed to be the vestigial remnant of the tail our species had in some earlier stage of evolution. No doubt these emblems of rank matter in the armed services, which function by command and obedience. But when the task of commanding your troops in battle has been given to others who are more likely to know what they are doing, all that is left is an appreciation of the finer points of military millinery. Perhaps it is also indicative of some deeper worry: once people start disregarding the details of uniform and the symbols of rank they may begin to wonder why they have a king or queen set in authority above them.

6. Being God's Anointed

She will have to walk behind the angels – and she won't like that.

Attributed to Edward VII, on being asked if
Queen Victoria would be happy in heaven

Shortly before the death of Queen Elizabeth the Queen Mother, widow of George VI, the Bishop of Truro was invited to the royal family's country retreat at Sandringham. English kings and queens may no longer rule by Divine Right, but the connection between royalty and religion is profound. An invitation to Sandringham is issued to most bishops at one time or another, and they dare not decline; quite apart from a natural impulse to accept out of curiosity, they all know that the monarch is Supreme Governor of the Church of England. It is a summons to see the Boss. A list arrived of the clothes that the Bishop, Bill Ind, was to take, as if he were a child about to be packed off to boarding school. The list ran from bishop's regalia, through dinner-jacket, to corduroy trousers and a sweater for afternoon walks. He contacted the Bishop of Lincoln for advice. It came in two sentences. Iron your underpants. And don't make the sermon too clever: it'll be wasted on them. (All royal sermons are kept short, but at least today's bishops do not have to suffer Edward VII, who would sit in the church and ostentatiously tap his watch when he thought they had gone on for too long.)

The Bishop arrived at Sandringham in a highly nervous state. He had little idea of what was in store, was uncertain how his sermon would go down, and felt uneasy about what was clearly going to be the smartest social gathering he would ever attend. He now made the customary awkward discovery and so came to understand the advice about ironing his underpants: when he arrived in his room his suitcase had been unpacked and the contents stowed in the chest. Descending in his dinner-jacket he realized that the day's shooting party would also be staying for dinner. There would be two dozen people at the table. 'I'm incredibly nervous,' he muttered to a hovering equerry. He was not reassured to get the reply, 'So am I – every day.' To his further alarm, the queen invited him to sit next to her, explaining, 'Now, Bishop, I'm afraid I can't talk to you for the first course, because I shall be talking to the people on my left. And I need to explain about the napkins. Look over there,' and she nodded across the table, 'they're doing it all wrong. They've got the starched side down. The napkins will slip off their knees. You do it like this, the unstarched side on your lap and then you tuck it under your bottom.'

It was a characteristic encounter: if you're queen you scarcely ever meet anyone who isn't overcome with nerves. Encouraged, the Bishop settled down to dinner, and, when his turn came for conversation, he found the queen an easy dinner companion, with the frustrating butterfly habit of changing the subject if it seems that anything might get a little too interesting. And, at the end of the meal, she did a very unusual thing. She sat at the table and repaired her lipstick. Then she nodded to one of the footmen, the doors flew open and in poured the royal corgis. The queen fed them under the table.

The next morning, the Bishop was dispatched to the Sandringham parish church in the queen's car. 'It was the most extraordinary thing,' he recalls, 'the driver pushed a button, and the floor rose.' Although it was still a couple of hours before the scheduled service, a crowd had already gathered outside the church. The Bishop had carefully turned over in his mind what sort of sermon he should preach. The task would not be made any easier by his awareness that the royal party might well be sitting in the choir-stalls, and so would be watching his back as he spoke. Finally, he had settled on a plan. He invited the congregation to see how many of the characters in the television comedy *Dad's Army* they could remember. It was an inspired idea. The royal family adored the gentle humour of the series (the queen mother in particular had a comprehensive collection of recordings). The Bishop could feel them ticking them off the characters one by one – Captain Mainwaring, Sergeant Wilson, Pike, Frazer, Corporal Jones, the Vicar. And what was the name of the Air-Raid Warden? Then he got to the point: how many of the characters in the second or third row of the platoon could they remember? 'It was', he recalled, 'a pretty effective sermon.' The triumph was complete when, as the congregation filed out, the organist struck up with 'Who Do You Think You Are Kidding, Mr Hitler?'

Afterwards, there was lunch back at the Big House, and in the middle of the afternoon the queen appeared and sat alone at a table, playing a game of patience. 'It was a very odd sight.' That evening there was dinner ('Do you like caviar, Bishop? I don't, but Philip loves it. Don't worry, we're not being extravagant – it's a present from the Sultan of Brunei'), and the next morning he set off home in his car. In the boot was his suitcase, packed for him, with his clothes wrapped in tissue-paper. Alongside nestled a brace of pheasants with a label hanging from their necks, 'From Her Majesty the Queen to the Bishop of Truro'.

When George V decided in 1912 that the heir to the throne of England should have something of a university education, the joy had been unconfined in Magdalen College, Oxford. The Prince of Wales might not have been much of an intellectual ornament. But the president of the college, Sir Herbert Warren, was perhaps the greatest snob in England. His life had been dedicated – with much success – to raising the scholastic achievements of the college. It seems that he then conceived an ambition. Now that he had the future Emperor of India on the books, he would try for the set, and sign up the emperors of China and Japan. A Magdalen man was dispatched to the Forbidden City as tutor to the young Pu Yi.[1] But as the former emperor was kept a virtual prisoner in the imperial palace, tertiary education on the other side of the world was never going to be a realistic possibility. Warren had better luck with the Japanese. Chichibu, the second son of the emperor, arrived at Magdalen in 1925, soon to be followed, Warren hoped, by his elder brother, Hirohito. As it happened, these plans too were dashed by the death of the boys' father in December 1926, when Prince Chichibu had to return to Tokyo to see his brother succeed to the Chrysanthemum Throne. But he had been at Oxford long enough for the story to circulate that he had satisfied Warren's wildest cravings by declaring that, because Japanese emperors were said to be descended from the sun goddess Amaterasu, he was 'the son of God'. Without missing a beat, the Oxford college president is said to have replied, 'Ah yes. Many Magdalen men have distinguished relations.'[2]

However much it would have gratified his ambitions, like any other educated human being Herbert Warren must have instantly recognized the absurdity of the proposition that a king could claim to be a god.[3] In the post-Enlightenment world, monarchy survives only by the political consent of the people. Yet throughout much of its history it has made the claim that it is somehow supernaturally ordained. Even in 1964, a survey is said to have shown that 30 per cent of the British population believed their queen had been chosen by God.[4]

Since monarchies are one of the very earliest forms of social organization, there had of course been kings and queens in Europe long before the arrival of Christianity. Missionaries concentrated their efforts upon them for the obvious reason that, once they had converted a monarch, the people could be expected to follow. One consequence was that the first 'king of the English', the eighth-century Offa, began describing himself as 'by divine controlling grace, king of the Mercians'. By the middle of the tenth century, some English kings were calling themselves Christ's vicar or deputy. The modern British king or queen is said to rule 'by grace of God' and occupies the role of 'Defender of the Faith'. As bishops remind us when they get the chance, the British system of government is described as 'the Queen in parliament under God'.

The ritual which Elizabeth II went through in 1953 – and which is planned for her son and grandson – would have been instantly recognized by a visitor from the South Seas or from Inca history, for almost all coronation ceremonies comprise much the same elements of symbolic combat, promises to rule justly and a religious anointment. The significance of this religious element cannot be exaggerated: it is only after the religious rites have been performed that the king or queen receives the crown and other emblems of office.

The moment that a monarch dies, the Privy Council asks the Archbishop of Canterbury to produce a Christian coronation. After the death of George VI in 1952, it took sixteen months for the preparations to be completed. Finally, on the day of the coronation of Queen Elizabeth, the Archbishop of Canterbury announced to the world that England had been brought closer to the kingdom of heaven. Before the service he had taken himself off to a hotel in Dovedale, Derbyshire, to prepare a book of devotions to make the future queen ready for her anointing. He described the collection of thoughts and prayers which resulted (and of which the Cambridge University Press produced seventeen copies) as 'the most precious thing I ever did, in a kind of way'.[5] The Archbishop maintained the medieval character of the service, settling thorny issues, such as what to do with Prince Philip, by resorting to the example of what had happened when Queen Anne was crowned two and a half centuries earlier. For the first time, the event was to be televised, so that a ritual previously confined to the elite could be shared with the hoi-polloi.[6] But the central act of the service, in which the young queen was anointed with consecrated oil,[7] was hidden from the cameras, and so has never been shown on television. Evidently, the queen believes that at the act of anointment something mystical happens.

In theory it would be quite possible to have a secular ceremony in which neither crown nor religion was present. Arab kings are not crowned. In medieval Spain the kings of Castile and Aragon were so confident of their authority that they simply put the crown on their own heads. And the only time that the kings and queens of Denmark get to wear their crown is when it is placed upon their coffin. A secular procedure, which confined itself to some form of public acclamation, could, with a clever use of trumpet fanfares and the rest, be made to seem impressive. The English coronation service is, after all, based on the idea of a contract: if there was a cry of 'no' when the Archbishop 'presented' the monarch, the service would have to be abandoned. The ceremony's function is to knit together the element of acclamation with the fact that the monarch is already king or queen simply because his or her predecessor has died. For hundreds of years in Britain these potentially contradictory elements have been reconciled by a ritual which is conspicuously and overwhelmingly religious.

The entire rite – the vesting, the enthronement, the priestly robes – struck one perceptive housewife who watched the 1953 coronation on television in Leeds as 'White Magic'.[8] The words are well judged. It is a Christian spectacular, with the elders of the Church pressing in around the new king or queen, and the state allowed access only through the mediation of the clergy. To any king or queen with sincere convictions, the idea that he or she might abdicate after making promises to the supernatural in such a ceremony is simply inconceivable. You might as well expect the Pope to retire. The queen's personal religious beliefs are fiercely held. One of her closest friends explained that they made the position unambiguous. 'Abdication', she told me, 'is quite impossible – read the Coronation Oath. She simply can't do it.' Indeed, as the queen sees it, there has never been an abdication in recent times. What about Edward VIII? I asked. 'You see, Edward ran away before he was crowned. He was never anointed, so he never really became king. So he never abdicated.'[9]

With sublime anthems like Handel's 'Zadok the Priest', the British ceremony is consciously rooted in echoes of the Old Testament. Many cultures of that Biblical region – Babylonian, Assyrian and Hittite – believed that their king was a national high priest. 'The ancient Near East considered kingship the very basis of civilisation,' writes Henri Frankfort,[10] and those who ruled on earth were held to be doing so as agents of some higher power. In Jewish tradition, David – who is generally believed to have ruled the

Israelites around 1000 BC – was chosen as king by God. Forty chapters of the Hebrew Bible are devoted to his reign. His importance is that, in exchange for a commitment to build a permanent temple, God promised that his dynasty would rule the people of Israel for ever. Becoming king was thus a matter not of popular choice, nor of war, nor even of divine intervention, but of birth. This is the explanation for the interminable family trees laid out in two of the four gospels of the New Testament: they demonstrate Jesus' descent from David (a mere twenty-eight generations).

Despite the fact that so much of modern political history has been the story of the struggle to wrest power from the elite, in the British coronation arrangements the people's role in choosing their king or queen is confined to the 'act of recognition' at the start of the service. According to the order of service for Queen Elizabeth's coronation in 1953 'the people signify their willingness and joy, by loud and repeated acclamations, all with one voice crying out GOD SAVE QUEEN ELIZABETH'. With the question of popular endorsement out of the way, the emphasis of the service is then entirely on the relationship between queen and God. On the morning of George VI's coronation, *The Times* attempted to explain: 'he is on his way to be consecrated – to be dedicated. Once that is done, he is no longer an ordinary man. He is a man dedicated . . . The more closely the burden of kingship is looked at, the more impossible does it seem that any man should bear it unless he were sustained and fortified and inspired by the spiritual power conferred on him in Westminster Abbey today.'[11] Reflecting on the ceremony later, the paper remarked of the act of anointment by the Archbishop that 'it seemed that these two men were alone with God, performing an act greater than they knew, more solemn than any person present could hope to understand'.[12] This was no mere journalistic hyperbole, apparently, for in a private paper the king later told the Archbishop 'that he felt throughout that Some One Else was with him'.[13]

The same newspaper returned to the subject when George's daughter came to be crowned as Elizabeth II. In the person of the monarch was represented something greater. 'The Queen stands for the soul as well as the body of the Commonwealth,' *The Times* explained. 'In her is incarnate on her Coronation day the whole of society, of which the state is no more than a political manifestation. She represents the life of her people . . . as men and women, and not in their limited capacity as Lords and Commons and electors. It is the glory of the social monarchy that it sets the human above the institutional.'[14] The echoes of the Christ story are not merely implied but explicit, which is why the only appropriate setting for the ritual is a religious one. Without it, the coronation would be a meaningless piece of civic theatre.

The appearance of enormous antiquity is essential, for the central premise is that the person being crowned is merely the latest custodian of a role which has lasted for centuries. The symbols employed – jewel-encrusted crowns (the crown symbol dates back at least as far as the pharaohs), orb, the robes modelled on those of Byzantine or Roman emperors, the three sceptres and five swords, the 'Wedding Ring of England' to signify the marriage between monarch and people – are consciously anachronistic. In the 1953 ritual, the Archbishop even reinvented the wearing of gold bracelets to signify sincerity, a custom which had not been employed since the coronation of Elizabeth I. Other elements of the service were genuinely ancient. The young queen sat upon a throne enclosing the Stone of Scone, upon which Pictish and Scottish kings had been crowned, until it was removed to London by Edward I in 1296.[15] The crown placed upon her head contained the St Edward the Confessor sapphire and a ruby worn by Henry V at the battle of Agincourt.

The crowning was often a great deal more dignified than the conduct of those being crowned. In 955, King Eadwy left his anointing to seek 'the caresses of loose women'. At the coronation of William the Conqueror in Westminster Abbey a group of Norman cavalry outside the building mistook the shout of acclamation for a riot and massacred a nearby group of Saxons. King John giggled his way through his coronation. The ten-year-old Richard II fell asleep during his. George IV, ludicrous in curls of false hair designed to hide his age, adorned with plumes and diamonds, spent much of the ceremony ogling his mistress, while hired prize-fighters kept his wife Caroline outside banging on the door for admission. In an effort to avoid accusations of profligacy, his successor, William IV, declared that he would have preferred simply to have sworn an oath in parliament. He was rewarded by having the ceremony nicknamed the 'half Crownation'. Even after a grander ritual had been restored, it had moments of slapstick. The Archbishop of Canterbury shoved a ring on to the wrong finger of the young Queen Victoria, making her want to scream in pain. Lord Rolle tripped on his robes and slid down the stairs, and the Bishop of Exeter fell over. When the young queen was taken into a side-chapel she discovered the altar covered in sandwiches and bottles of wine. 'Pray tell me what I am to do,' she begged the Dean of Westminster, 'for they don't know.'[16]

The consolation was that the blunders were witnessed by only a few people. But the festivities which accompanied Victoria's coronation involved enormous numbers. The *Spectator* decided that the nation had succumbed to hallucination. It sniffed that 'John Bull seized on the present occasion – the weak part of his cranium is still the crown – to give himself a holyday; and he set to work in his usual dogged style.'[17] The streets were crammed with cheering crowds. An enormous fair was staged in Hyde Park, with freak shows, 'rotatory air-sailing ships', fireworks, and stalls selling gingerbread men decorated to look like various European kings. There were feasts across the country, and guests of the state – children at charity schools and in workhouses, even the inmates of prisons – were given extra beef and pudding. We cannot, at this distance, separate the elements at work in this party. Did the people genuinely want to celebrate the arrival of a new monarch, whom the vast majority of them would never clap eyes upon? Or did the Establishment – politicians, Church, landowners and captains of industry – recognize that encouraging a mild bacchanalia would consolidate the new monarch's position, and thus their own? All we can say with certainty is that later occasions – the 2002 celebrations of fifty years of the rule of Queen Elizabeth II, for example

– were kick-started by committees of wealthy men. When the festivities to celebrate Victoria's coronation had finished, the *Northern Star* showed that not everyone had succumbed.

> The farce is over – the 'idle and useless pageant' has gone by – the doll has been dressed, dizened, and exhibited – a host of gaping idlers have been gratified with a spectacle . . . Now that we have time to breathe, let us enquire 'why was the waste made?' What single benefit is likely to accrue, either to the Queen or to the country, from this idle shew – this obstruction of public and private business – and this palpable waste of the national resources, at the precise moment when we are up to the very neck in the mire of national bankruptcy?[18]

The paper thought that if the queen really wanted to have a new relationship with her people, she could start by doing something to improve their living conditions. But brimstone-breathing denunciations were rare. As usual, most seemed ready to settle for bread and circuses.

The coronation of Victoria's successor, Edward VII, was a much bigger challenge. While it might have been easy to gain public sympathy for an unworldly young woman who was having the trappings of state laid upon her (as was also the case when Elizabeth II took the throne) it was another matter when the recipient was a man who had spent his apprenticeship on the shooting field, at the gaming tables and in the divorce courts. The 2nd Viscount Esher, who played a prominent role in the preparations, wailed in a letter to his son that 'Only young girls or boys should be crowned monarchs . . . After 20 no one should be allowed to come to the throne! Then romance would hold her sway.'[19] The new king was a portly sixty-year-old. Esher set about investing the ceremony with some dignified antiquity. The Archbishop of Canterbury, for example, was something of a relic himself – an octogenarian with very poor eyesight. It was decided that he would navigate his way through the service by reading from enormous scrolls held up by his chaplain, on which had been printed the order of service. The Archbishop (who put the crown on the king's head back to front) hated the arrangement, and accused his chaplain of causing the scrolls to wobble, so that he could not read them. But in the early days of the mass media, the scrolls were a prop which suggested venerability.

Cold reasoning says that there is no reason why a king should not assume office in a ceremony shorn of religious ritual and anachronistic flummery (although even the President of the United States, who assumes office as the result of a process we can all understand, does not do so). An impresario who attempted to stage such an event for a king would find himself having to address some very awkward questions. In wealthy western societies the idea of the sacred has been steadily impoverished ever since the Industrial Revolution. Monarchy is almost the last institution in the land to which any mystique attaches. Indeed, the mystique is the most powerful guarantor of its survival. To remove the element of magic from the ritual of enthronement might well leave the institution so exposed that it would wither and die. The king or queen might feel that they had been denied the great affirming moment of their lives. Kaiser Wilhelm II – who was merely 'acknowledged' by the princes of the federation as *Deutscher Kaiser*, or German Emperor – felt so deprived that he was said to have commissioned an ermine cloak and a plasterwork replica of the crown of Charlemagne, so that he might be photographed as befitted his status. And, perhaps most difficult of all, the producer of the subfusc spectacular would have to explain why a ceremony which so obviously predates modern ideas of democracy was taking place at all.

It is a myth as old as monarchy that kings can cure the sick. Roman historians claimed that the Emperor Vespasian could heal the lame and that Hadrian restored sight to the blind. In nineteenth-century Senegal women brought their sick children to be touched by the queen's foot to be cured of their illnesses. In Polynesia, kings were said not only to be able to cure diseases at will, but – even more mysteriously – to spread them by royal command. From a medical point of view, it is all nonsense, of course, evidence merely – like the idea of the king as rain-maker – of the human hunger to believe that those with authority over us must be there because they have some superior faculties.

In Europe, the disease which monarchs were held to be able to cure by touching became known as the King's Evil. This is generally taken to have been scrofula, or a form of tuberculosis of the lymphatic glands, but the term was frequently applied to any large inflammation on the face. Although it was not usually fatal, left untreated the abscesses would swell until they burst through the skin ('pitiful to the eye, / The mere despair of surgery', as Shakespeare puts it in *Macbeth*).[20] Often, the wounds would cause the face to putrefy and stink, which cannot have made the business of 'touching' the victim to cure the disease particularly enjoyable.

In England, the practice is often thought to have begun with St Edward the Confessor, King of England from 1043 to 1066. Edward's sanctity was based upon his openness to the public, his generosity to the poor, his supposedly unconsummated marriage to Queen Edith and, later, the fact that, thirty-six years after death, his body was said not to have decayed. He was also alleged to have seen visions. Certainly, William of Malmesbury records him restoring a woman with scrofulous sores to 'a happy state of health', by dipping his hands in water and stroking her neck, whereupon 'the tumours that were filled with worms and corrupt blood' burst and disappeared.[21] A twelfth-century witness claimed to have seen King Louis VI of France healing scrofula by his touch. Henry II, who ruled both England and much of France, is the first to be recorded a few decades later as touching large numbers of people. (Late-medieval kings were also in the habit of distributing 'cramp rings', made from coins which had been laid at the foot of a cross, which were said to be able to heal conditions like epilepsy.)[22] Specially minted coins, known as 'touch pieces', hung around the necks of sufferers by the king, were supposed to cure sickness, while others, known as 'angels', were distributed as alms. In time, these coins themselves were ascribed the power to heal, evidence that the king's magic could be carried by things that he had touched. In medieval France, a monk even described how sufferers drank the water in which the king had washed his hands after touching others with scrofula and, nine days later, found that their symptoms had vanished.[23]

The practice belongs in the world of magical stones and curative fountains and was altogether too superstitious to appeal to many of the Tudor monarchs. But in the seventeenth century the Stuarts brought it back enthusiastically: Charles I was invested by his credulous followers with such wondrous powers that at one time a Worcester innkeeper was said to have had his tumours removed and placed in a flask of water by the king without his even being present.[24] In the four years following the Restoration in 1660, Charles II touched over twenty thousand people. James II laid his hands on more than four thousand in a mere ten months in 1685. A form of service for curing the sick by the laying on of royal hands was incorporated in the Book of Common Prayer: Samuel Pepys had an engraving of the ritual hanging on the wall of his library. Another diarist, John Evelyn, watched the service as doctors brought, or guided, the sick to the throne, where they knelt while 'the King strokes their faces or cheekes with both his hands at once, at which instant a Chaplaine in his formalities says, "He put his hands upon them and he healed them,"' after which a coin with the figure of an angel upon it was hung around their necks.[25]

Despite the very deliberate echoes of the Bible, it is noticeable that punctilious kings and queens did not profess to cure people in their own right. They claimed that, since they were divinely ordained, they were acting as a medium. 'Le roi te touche, Dieu te guérit' (the king touches you, God cures you), as the liturgy used by Louis XIV put it.[26] Louis XV, for example, was denied the right to touch people on several occasions, because his hands were too busy with various mistresses. But even illegitimate Stuarts were said to have the power to heal the sick, and Jacobite pretenders to the British throne continued with the laying on of hands until the middle of the eighteenth century.

If any king or queen stood in need of a miracle cure, it was bulbous, pock-marked and pain-riddled Queen Anne, none of whose many conceptions produced a living heir. In what one historian describes as 'a stroke of genius',[27] she revived the practice of touching, sitting in the Banqueting House, the scene of her grandfather's execution, and doing much to recreate the notion that a monarch has magical powers. The infant Dr Samuel Johnson was brought up to London by his mother at the age of two to be touched by her for 'the scrophulous evil', an experience which nonetheless left him hard of hearing, blind in one eye and possessed of a face with 'the aspect of an idiot'. He later claimed to be able to remember 'a lady in diamonds and long black hood'.[28]

How appropriate that it should be the Stuarts who made the most of the practice of touching, for it fits most readily with their conception of kingship. The practice was no less nonsensical than all those fairytales about 'lost' princes and princesses snatched from their families whose royal identity would be confirmed by the discovery of a skin-blemish on their shoulder or chest in the shape of a cross. After the Reformation the later Tudor monarchs had sought more subtle ways to suggest their sanctity. Paintings of Queen Elizabeth I, for example, showed her holding a sieve, the emblem of chastity because Vestal Virgins were supposed to have been able to carry water in them.[29] The image of Elizabeth the Virgin Queen, at a time when the country had so very recently thrown off Roman Catholicism, with its central place for the Virgin Mary, was no accident.

Her successor, James VI of Scotland, took the English throne surrounded by swirling clouds of more explicit conviction. 'The state of monarchy', he told parliament,

> is the supremest thing upon earth; for kings are not only God's lieutenants upon earth, and sit upon God's throne, but even by God himself they are called Gods . . . Kings are justly called Gods, for that they exercise a manner or resemblance of divine power upon earth. For if you consider the attributes of God, you will see how they agree in the person of a king. God has power to create, or destroy, make, or unmake, at his pleasure, to give life, to send death, to judge and to be judged nor accountable to none . . . And the like power have kings.[30]

James was a learned man and his defence of the Divine Right of Kings is sweeping. What is hard to understand, at such a distance, is how sincerely he could have held the belief. A conviction that your position is ordained by the Almighty must certainly have been a comfort, since it removed the capacity for self-doubt. Yet his own mother, Mary Queen of Scots, had been forced to abdicate in favour of her son and later executed. And James's son would certainly discover that the English were more than ready to dispose of weak or politically inconvenient monarchs, however highly placed their friends. In practice, this belief that monarchy is somehow divinely sanctioned is a lop-sided thing. If kings and queens get their authority from God, then is it not a sign of divine disapproval, or perhaps of the withdrawal of the endorsement, when things go wrong?

Yet it is noticeable that many of the public functions of the modern British monarchy remain religious rituals of some kind or other. Whether it be honouring the military dead on Remembrance Sunday, parading at the service for the Order of the Garter at Windsor Castle, or appearing at Christmas at Sandringham parish church, the king's or queen's public role is grounded in an appearance of piety. An atheist might say that it is a case of two inherently implausible belief systems supporting each other: the Church benefits from the attendance of the head of state, and the monarch seems invested with special status because he or she is in direct contact with the supernatural. The connection has been recognized for centuries by rulers who built abbeys and churches, promoted church music, encouraged new liturgies (as in Edward VI's support of Thomas Cranmer), attempted to suppress publication of the Bible in English (Mary) or promoted it (Henry VIII and James I). Even in an age which can so often appear rigorously secular, the great national occasions of grief or celebration are still given religious expression. At these events it would be unthinkable for the king or queen to be absent.

Of course, they appear more authentic today because Queen Elizabeth II's religious belief is authentic and well known. Inevitably, perhaps, the palace seems almost embarrassed by talk of her religious convictions. The author Ian Bradley was so moved by the simple devotion he saw in the royal family at prayer at Crathie parish church, during their annual holiday at Balmoral, that he sat down and wrote an entire book on the subject, *God Save the Queen*. Yet when he attempted to discuss the importance of religion in the lives of the royal family – even with senior figures in the Church – he found a prevailing mood that the monarch really ought not to harp on about God too much. 'I think we've had rather too much of the sacred, don't you?' he quotes a courtier saying of the Prince of Wales. 'He needs to be seen as a good bloke.'[31] Yet, in this area at least, Prince Charles, with his mutterings about being a 'Defender of Faith' in general, has made precisely the sort of 'good bloke' noises required by the Church, and seems to have understood something about the nature of kingship. At a personal level, having a spiritual conviction must make it a great deal easier for an individual to cope with living inside the strait-jacket forced upon the royal heir at birth. Perhaps there is no reason to assume a secular monarchy to be impossible. But in the current constitutional arrangements some profession of belief is essential, because, once you attempt to disentangle the knitting put together by history, there is no pattern by which to put it back together again.

Apart from events such as the coronation, perhaps the most conspicuous occasion on which the religious and the royal are intertwined is the annual service on Maundy Thursday, at the start of Easter. The event recalls the moment at the Last Supper when Jesus washed the feet of his disciples and commanded them to love one another. On the face of it, the significance of the ritual seems obvious enough: abbots washed the feet of their monks, and priests the feet of parishioners, to demonstrate a belief that the first shall be last, or at least that all members of the religious community were in some sense equal. But nothing is quite what it seems in the world of royalty. In a perverse way, emulating the humbling behaviour of Christ has always demonstrated the superiority of the person carrying out the washing – if the gesture did not involve an apparent debasement, it would have no significance at all. In the case of the British royal family, extra precautions have been inserted, just in case anyone should get the wrong idea.

In Liverpool Cathedral (the ceremony takes place in a different city each year), the congregation – a sea of white hair and varifocal glasses – have been in their seats for the best part of an hour, awaiting the arrival of the queen. Each time there is a loud noise, which might signify the royal arrival, the low buzz of conversation dies, and heads turn expectantly towards the door. The congregation is finally stilled by the arrival of a procession of Yeomen of the Guard, halberds aloft and heels clicking sharply. They are led by a distinguished-looking old gentleman with a huge feathered hat and a face of steel, who bears a double-take resemblance to the ageing Duke of Windsor. Now come further processions; clergy, judges and a couple of hunched old chaps in academic gowns. Four children arrive, carrying bunches of flowers. These are the celebrated nosegays, prepared to protect the royal nostrils from the whiff of the public. The modern service is carried off with dignity and consummate professionalism, the queen moving among the elderly beneficiaries, managing to have a personal conversation with each of them, her smile constant, interest apparent, engagement perfectly synchronized to begin and end in time with the choir. Ask them later what they felt about the occasion, and they speak warmly of how friendly the queen seemed, how short, how human.

According to St Augustine, English monarchs have been washing the feet of their chosen subjects since the seventh century, although many, like Elizabeth I, took the precaution of having one of her staff rinse them first. Elizabeth II is still attended by retainers bearing white towels. But no washing takes place: the practice has long since been commuted for cash. The specially minted Maundy coins – one for each year of the monarch's reign – arrive in little red and white bags, tied prettily with satin, on silver salvers borne by another procession of Yeomen Warders. The occasion teeters on the edge of Alice-in-Wonderland absurdity – and tips over into it on the occasions when pikes become entangled with the chandeliers. It is when the Duke of Edinburgh reads St John's account of Christ's washing of his disciples' feet and the choir sings about 'washing me thoroughly from my sin' that the nagging uncertainty of what it all signifies becomes most insistent. The second reading is the parable of the separation of the sheep from the goats in which, at the Last Judgement, humanity is divided into the deserving and the undeserving. If the feet-washing has been replaced by a nominal gift of money, what does the service mean?

Even if nowadays the Maundy coins are purely symbolic and have no commercial value (except later on eBay), the mere distribution of largesse tells us nothing – we already know that kings and queens are wealthy. I puzzled over this and concluded that, first, the service recognized voluntary work, since each of those who receives Maundy Money has been recommended by local clergy for their work for their church or community. Second, that for all its pomp and uniforms, it was really not an occasion of state at all but a religious occasion.

One of the consequences of the Church of England's special relationship with the British royal family is that the monarch is one of the very few people in the land who does not enjoy freedom of belief. If you wish to be king or queen, you are required to profess publicly not merely that there is one true religion, but that divine revelation has only one legitimate interpretation. The Act of Settlement of 1701, which, as we have seen, was designed by parliament to clip the wings of the monarch in matters like making war, also decrees that whoever sits upon the throne must be a communicant member of the Church of England. However much an heir to the throne might talk to the trees or flirt with Sufism, on inheriting the crown he would be obliged to deny on oath that it was possible for bread and wine to be transformed into the body and blood of Jesus and to declare that the worship of the Virgin Mary and the Romish mass were 'superstitious and idolatrous'.

In the twentieth century, the oath was toned down to a declaration that the monarch was merely a faithful Protestant. But it is important to understand how this curious necessity was born. James II had done his utmost to insert Catholics into every powerful position at his disposal. The relatively bloodless coup d'état of the Glorious Revolution of 1688–9, at which his Protestant son-in-law William seized the throne, brought to power a man with a healthy disdain for some of the more credulous aspects of monarchology. When someone tried to touch him for a cure for the King's Evil he turned on him with the words 'God give you better health, and more sense.' The authority of such a king rested not in some covenant with God but in a contract with the people – the Crown in parliament. (Curiously, throughout the eighteenth and nineteenth centuries, while kings and queens accepted that there were limits to their divinely ordained status, their subjects came increasingly to believe that the entire nation had acquired some especial God-given destiny as a 'chosen people'. The feeling is caught well in the first lines of 'Rule Britannia', where the country is said to have risen from the sea 'at heaven's command'.) In the coronation service of 1689, a specially printed and lavishly decorated English Bible was incorporated into the regalia to be carried into Westminster, as demonstration of the relationship between political and religious freedom in this especially blessed island nation. In keeping with the Act of Settlement's decree that anyone who might 'profess the Popish religion' or marry a Papist should be 'for ever incapable to inherit, possess or enjoy the Crown and government of this Realm',[32] the coronation oath was rewritten, to include a promise to uphold 'the Protestant Reformed Religion established by law'.

In this arrangement, the belief that kings ruled because of some right given to them by God was clearly preposterous. The sacred element was still important, to ensure that the office of king had some mystery about it, but it was a very British sort of spirituality – utilitarian, pragmatic and knowing its place. As this new arrangement evolved, instead of acting as a vehicle of divine judgement, the king or queen set an example through good works. George III and his wife, Queen Charlotte, set out to be seen as pious, hard-working and philanthropic and gave away more of their wealth than any previous royal couple.[33] Queen Victoria preferred opening hospitals to opening parliament, and would launch a Bible-study class at the drop of a hat, bolstered in her conviction by her Lutheran husband Albert, who once announced that the function of royalty was to be the 'the headship of philanthropy'. Since then, the sponsorship of good deeds has grown to the point where the promotion of charity has become one of the main functions of monarchy.

The requirement that the monarch be a Protestant seems one of the last formal remnants of the interweaving of religion and monarchy and causes much hand-wringing every time there is the possibility of a royal courtship. In more culturally diverse times it is seen as discriminatory. Obviously it is, and no one would devise such a law if they were inventing a constitution for the twenty-first century. But the abolitionists tend to ignore the circumstances of the time, particularly the very long history of Papal encouragement for plots to overthrow English kings and queens. The guiding principle was that a sovereign who was to reign over a free people had himself to be free: anyone who accepted the authority of the Pope could not be so. The Act is, anyway, only discriminatory against those who wish to sit on the throne. Freedom of worship ought to be a basic human right, but the charter has yet to be drafted which decrees it an entitlement to be king or queen.

A promise to protect the Church in England was a coronation promise centuries before the Reformation, and the title of Defender of the Faith had been given to Henry VIII by the Pope. The tale of how Henry later took the English Church out of the jurisdiction of the Vatican, in order that he might divorce his wife and attempt to produce a male heir to the throne, may be theologically threadbare. But the constitutional arrangements of all mature countries are the product of history, and the relationship between the monarchy and the Church is no different. English kings and queens are often – wrongly – described as head of the Church. (They are not: that job is reserved for God.) But it would clearly be absurd if the Church of England found itself with a Supreme Governor who was not a communicant member. So the relationship is like many marriages in which a couple are yoked together and chafe at the frustrations, but deep down remain convinced that they are stronger together than they would be if they separated. There is certainly a constituency within the Church of England which would like to see its special status as the established Church removed, because, they say, disestablishment would give it freedom of conscience. Abolishing the Act of Settlement would also give the heir to the throne the liberty to marry a Catholic, or to become a Hindu. 'The Church of England is like a goat tethered on a very long chain,' one bishop says. 'It thinks it's free. Until it decides to act for itself.' For such people, the relationship is more than quirky: it is intolerable. The apostles of disestablishment have common sense on their side. But – as defenders of the existing arrangements point out – the requirement that the monarch be an Anglican and the Anglican chaplaincies in the institutions of the state at the very least ensure that there is some religious voice there. Even Sikhs and Jews can be heard arguing that, in defending its own convictions, the Church of England is defending theirs.

The shocking death of Princess Diana demonstrated the degree to which religious feeling still attaches to royalty. All those candles, flowers and handwritten messages were reminiscent of nothing so much as the sort of devotion you find at the shrines dedicated to miracle-working saints. Yet the long caravan of advisers, astrologers, clairvoyants, counsellors, gurus, homeopaths, hypnotherapists, 'lifestyle managers', mystics, New Age therapists, personal trainers, psychotherapists, sleep therapists, soothsayers and tarot-card readers whom she had allowed into her life disclose her own inner vulnerability. They also show what happens when all beliefs have parity of esteem. Those who put their trust in princes and princesses want them to put their own trust in something more than a passing snake-oil salesman.

In any case, in modern times the monarch's role in the Church of England is hardly dramatic, confined as it is mainly to approving the appointment of archbishops, bishops and deans and opening sessions of the Church's governing body, the General Synod.[34]

The queen may not be theologically well read, but she has a native intelligence, a prodigious memory and firm, quietly held low-church spiritual convictions which belong to a more rigorous age. She was uneasy that part of Verdi's Requiem was played at Diana's funeral, for example, because Protestants do not attempt to intercede with God on behalf of the dead. She is not even exclusively Church of England: when she is in Scotland, she is a Presbyterian. Not only does her religious faith give her comfort, it is surely more reassuring to her citizens than the thought that she might at any moment decide to give herself to the Scientologists or Sun Myung Moon's Unification Church.

The Church of England is an undemanding master, but at least you know more or less where you are with it.

7. Killing a King

What subject can give sentence on his king?

Shakespeare, *Richard II*, Act IV, scene i

It is late January, a bitterly cold Thursday in central London. The clouds are leaden and the wind frosty. Occasional flurries of snow whirl down Whitehall, past the enormous Edwardian stone blocks which housed the thousands of civil servants who ran the British empire. On the pavement across from Horse Guards Parade a dozen or so people huddle, shivering in the cold.

Apart from the three old soldiers in the scarlet tunics of Chelsea Pensioners, they are an unremarkable crowd – predominantly male, of all social classes, hair colour tending to grey.

A young priest – short fair hair, round gold-rimmed glasses – emerges in a white surplice. 'Brethren,' he begins, 'we are gathered here in the name of God to commemorate in this place, made sacred by the shedding of his blood, the Martyrdom by beheading of his Majesty King Charles the First on the thirtieth of January in the year of our salvation 1649.'

The building they are standing outside is the Banqueting House, the only remaining part of the great palace in Whitehall, the main residence of British sovereigns from Tudor times until it burned down in 1698. Built on the orders of King James I of England, the Banqueting House was designed by Inigo Jones for the performance of court masques – productions of dance, drama, opera and pageant, intended to mix entertainment with propaganda relating to the authority of the Stuart kings. Often the first half of the performance showed a chaotic and corrupt world, which was brought to order and civilization by the king in the second half.

The evening generally ended with much of the court on their feet, dancing. In the Banqueting House, Inigo Jones wanted to provide the perfect setting for a dainty morality tale. Both James and his son Charles loved the place. But, as it turned out, its main historical significance is as the scene of the most dramatic rejection of kingship.

The trial and execution – or 'martyrdom' – of King Charles was the biggest test of kingship ever to take place in Britain. At its heart was the question of whether power came from God or from the people. In the theology of kingship the trial itself was simply impossible. Kings ruled by God's authority, and because justice was done in the name of the Crown, a monarch could not be judged.[1] King Charles's father, James I, who was probably the most intellectual and certainly the most published of English kings, had explained the contract. It was the duty of the king to administer justice to his people and to protect their liberties. In exchange, they were to give him utter obedience, except in the unlikely event that one of his commands went against the wishes of God. The admission of this surprising possibility raised an obvious question. How were the people to protect themselves against a tyranny? On this, James was firm. Taking up arms against the king would be an evil act, and evil should never be done, even if the intention was that good should result. If a people did find themselves saddled with a tyrant, that was God's judgement, and the solution was not resistance but prayer. A people without a king, he asserted, in an expression which would have a certain irony when his son was brought to the scaffold, was 'a headlesse multitude'. In a society in which people believed their illnesses might be cured by a touch from the king, putting him on trial was so outlandish that it was said that in England one person died of shock.

Having emerged victorious from the bloody convulsions of the Civil War, the parliamentarians did their best to dignify their effrontery. Westminster Hall, the scene of the trial, was draped with scarlet cloth and guarded by soldiers in red coats, and the judges' and defendant's chairs were covered in crimson. The suggestion that the king could not face a jury of his peers, since he had none, was dismissed contemptuously. A jobbing lawyer, John Bradshaw, decked out in a scarlet robe, was persuaded to preside over the court. But an indication of Bradshaw's anxiety is given by the high-topped, broad-brimmed hat he wore for the occasion. It was specially reinforced with steel, and looking at the thing in the Ashmolean Museum in Oxford it seems a wonder he could lift his head.[2]

The army spent three days in prayer at Windsor, and then decided 'to call Charles Stuart, that man of Blood, to an account for that blood he hath shed and the mischief he hath done to his utmost, against the Lord's cause and people'. Against the Stuart interpretation of the Biblical foundations of kingship, a by now highly politicized army could assert the supremacy of its own analysis. Charles was compared with the idolatrous Old Testament kings Ahab and Nebuchadnezzar. Psalm 149 talked of the people of Zion binding kings with chains and the Book of Numbers of how a land on which blood had been shed could be cleansed only by the blood of the person who had shed the blood.

In what amounted to a coup d'état, Colonel Thomas Pride had already marched into the House of Commons and purged it of those politicians who might have dealt with the king leniently, and at around two in the afternoon of Saturday, 20 January 1649, the trial began.

It immediately turned into a contest over jurisdiction. Algernon Sidney had warned Cromwell bluntly that 'First, the king can be tried by no court; second no man can be tried by this court.'[3] Cromwell's position was that the king had power only in trust: if he betrayed that trust, he had to be answerable. The king's master was the law, and the law was made by acts of parliament.

The king, in a sombre suit, with the blue band of the Garter ribbon round his neck and wearing a black hat, faced his accusers.

The clerk read the charge. Charles was accused of high treason, 'out of a wicked design to erect and uphold in himself an unlimited and tyrannical power, to rule according to his will and to overthrow the rights and liberties of his people'. The king sat looking dismissively around the room. He then stood up, only to sit down again. The clerk concluded with an announcement that the court was 'on behalf of the people of England [to] impeach the said Charles as a tyrant, traitor, murderer and implacable enemy to the commonwealth of England'. At this point, the king laughed. Bradshaw demanded to know whether he pleaded guilty or not guilty. The king simply refused to recognize the court. 'I have a trust committed to me by God, by old and lawful descent. I will not betray that trust to answer to a new unlawful authority.'

Bradshaw attempted to explain the authority of the court. It had been constituted by the House of Commons, which represented the people of England, 'by which people you are elected king'. The king sneered at the claim. 'England was never an elective kingdom. It has been an hereditary kingdom for near a thousand years,' he said. Again and again, Bradshaw demanded that the king plead, one way or another, and repeatedly the king refused. Bradshaw was forced to adjourn the court. But when the session reconvened, the king was as implacable as ever. He appeared composed and authoritative. His usual stammer had deserted him and the only time in the proceedings that he seemed at all discomposed was when the gold head broke off the staff on which he was leaning. Finally, his patience exhausted, Bradshaw ordered the king to be taken from the court.

The parliamentarians' confidence came from a straightforward analysis. First, the people, under God, were the fount of all just power. Second, the people chose the House of Commons. Third, whatever was decided by the House of Commons had the force of law, regardless of whether the House of Lords or the king liked it.

The following day the president of the court attempted for a third time to get the king to plead guilty or not guilty. Charles presented an alternative analysis of legitimacy. The king represented the liberties of the English people: he could not set them the example of submitting to arbitrary authority. Bradshaw had no idea how to deal with the king's dogged refusal to engage. For the third time, he ordered soldiers to take him away.

The trial was going nowhere. So now the parliamentarians

decided that, when the court met again at the end of the week, its job would be not to try the king, but to sentence him. Yet it was hard work to gain the necessary signatures on the death warrant. There were 135 'commissioners', but only fifty-nine names appear on the document. Some had signed their names before it was dated, one signature was added over a name that had been erased. It was said that Cromwell coerced one of the signatories, by forcibly guiding his hand. The clerk read the sentence to the king: he was to be put to death by the severing of his head from his body.

The story of Charles's final days has been the subject of a thousand royalist tear-jerkers. The king who had previously enjoyed such privileges now found that his gaolers at St James's Palace went out of their way to insult him. A man so devout that he always said his prayers even before setting out hunting at the crack of dawn, he was denied access to his chaplains. He hated the smell of tobacco, so the guards lounged around gossiping and made a point of smoking in front of him.

On the morning of his execution the king rose two hours before dawn. 'I will get up now,' he said to Colonel Thomas Herbert, 'for I have great work to do today.' For his last public appearance he was determined to appear every inch the king. He insisted that especial care was taken with his barbering – 'though it has not long to stand upon my shoulders, take all the care you can of my head'. He chose his clothes carefully. He put on an extra shirt, in case he shivered from the cold, which might have given the impression that he was afraid. He wore a striped silk waistcoat, black doublet, breeches and cloak adorned with the bright blue ribbon and diamond-encrusted star of the Order of the Garter. In a medallion around his neck hung a miniature of his wife. William Juxon, the Bishop of London, arrived and the two men celebrated holy communion. The Bishop's readings were about the rivers of Egypt turning to blood, and St Matthew's account of the trial and death of Christ.

Next the king said goodbye to his two youngest children, the thirteen-year-old Princess Elizabeth and the eight-year-old Prince

Henry. It was a farewell scene that became the subject of a nineteenth-century tableau, in which the pale-faced king stands at a window, one arm crooked at the elbow, as the faithful Bishop Juxon ushers the two children out of the room. The princess has her arm around the shoulders of her younger brother and looks back pityingly into the room. The king, with his shoulder-length hair and eyes lifted to heaven, is portrayed as some bejewelled Christ figure.

The king's two eldest sons – Prince Charles and James, Duke of York – were already in exile and there had been talk about perhaps installing the young Henry as a puppet king. So the king's words – or such of them as were recorded – were less a farewell than a piece of stern advice. The children fell to their knees, the princess in tears. The king spoke quietly to them, telling his daughter to write down what he had said as soon as she was able. The princess records him as telling her not to grieve, declaring that he had forgiven his enemies, and advising her on which books to read to guard herself against popery. But, in monarchy, succession is everything. The king told the princess to pass on to her absent brothers that it was his last wish that James should regard the eldest child, Charles, not merely as his brother but as his sovereign. Then, seating the eight-year-old Henry upon his knee, the king said, 'Mark, child, what I say. Sweetheart, now they will cut off my head.' The boy looked up as the king continued, 'Heed, my child, what I say; they will cut off my head, and perhaps make thee a king. But mark what I say, you must not be a king so long as your brothers Charles and James do live. For they will cut off your brothers' heads (when they can catch them) and cut off thy head too, at the last: and therefore I charge you, do not be made a king by them.' The little boy is said to have sighed and answered, 'I will be torn in pieces first.'[4]

At ten in the morning a Colonel Francis Hacker knocked on the king's door. The man was trembling, but the king was calm: he dismissed the colonel, turned to the Bishop of London, took him by the hand and said, 'Come, let us go.' Outside, soldiers had lined the sides of the path across St James's Park. A section of halberdiers formed up in front of the king, another behind, their axes across their shoulders. Drums beat so loudly that 'one could hardly hear what another spoke' – the idea was to drown out any shouts of support for the king. According to some versions, a man called Tench, whose brother had been executed as a parliamentary spy during the Civil War, walked alongside, staring at the king. Tench had enthusiastically helped to build the scaffold on which the king was to die. When the Bishop saw the king's discomfort, he brushed the man away. At the other side of the park, the doomed man and his companion were escorted to a private room. At noon the Bishop persuaded the king to eat a bit of bread and to drink a glass of claret to fortify himself against the cold.

The parliamentarians had had enormous difficulty in finding someone prepared to wield the axe that would sever the king's head. Thirty-eight sergeants had been summoned, and £100 and instant promotion promised to any two prepared to carry out the execution. But even in an ideologically driven army which had been through a bitter war there had been no volunteers. The official executioner Richard Brandon and his assistant, a Whitechapel dustman, were sent for, but the latter could not be found at all, and Brandon said he would rather be executed himself than do what was being asked of him. He was offered a reward of £200, and, when he still refused, was threatened with burning at the stake. Even this, he later claimed, had not been enough to change his mind. Precisely who swung the axe will probably always remain a mystery. The executioner and his assistant were dressed in dark, close-fitting woollen smocks – the sort of thing a butcher might wear – with masks over their eyes, and completed their disguises with false beards and wigs, grey for the executioner and black for his assistant. One account claimed that the masks concealed Oliver Cromwell and the commander of his army, Thomas Fairfax. There were many other suspects, too. But the sheer efficiency of the execution seemed to testify to previous experience, which suggests it was, after all, the work of the official executioner, Richard Brandon, a man who prided himself on only ever needing one swing of the blade, and who had already taken off the heads of the Archbishop of Canterbury, the Earl of Strafford, Sir John Hotham and Sir Alexander Carew.

Finally, shortly before two in the afternoon, there was a knock at the king's door. Charles was led from his room, through ranks of soldiers standing shoulder to shoulder, into the Banqueting House. He passed beneath the magnificent ceiling he had commissioned from Sir Peter Paul Rubens. It told a morally uplifting tale of the Divine Right of Kings, the Stuart dynasty's peaceful union of the crowns of England and Scotland, and the prosperity which was said to be the natural consequence of God-ordained government.

Now the hall was crammed with ambassadors, along with soldiers, politicians and members of the public. It was, thought the king's attendant Thomas Herbert – who was a parliamentarian – 'the saddest sight England ever saw'. As Charles walked through the crowd, people muttered prayers for him, unrebuked by any of the soldiers. Then he passed through the first-floor window frame and on to the scaffolding built outside.

On the cold January day more than 350 years later, the small group gathered at the place where Charles's head fell from his body has grown to perhaps thirty or forty people. The Chelsea Pensioners stand alongside a tall, thin man of about forty in a black tailcoat. 'King Charles', the priest says, 'chose to lose his throne and his life to save the Church of England, and in that choice exchanged an earthly crown for an incorruptible crown in the heavens.' The sentence echoes the last words of Bishop Juxon to the king. On arriving at the scaffold, Charles had discovered that the block on which he was to lay his neck was very low. It was described as being 'about eighteen inches long and six inches in height' – so low that the king would have to lie flat on his stomach to allow the executioner a clear swing.[5] Charles, who had imagined himself kneeling to die, protested. But he was told no other block was available. He also saw that the crowd had been kept well back from the scaffold, and that the railing had been draped with cloth, making it impossible for those at ground level to witness what was about to happen. As a consequence, members of the crowd had clambered on to surrounding roof-tops, or hung from upper-storey windows; those further away could see over the screen. Shorthand reporters on the scaffold were ready to take down his last words. They heard the king declare his innocence and ask for the restoration of the Church's glory. He was utterly unapologetic about his absolutism: the people were entitled to liberty and freedom, he said, but that did not mean their having a share in government – 'a subject and a sovereign are clean different things'. Yet he claimed to be dying 'a martyr of the people', for refusing to acquiesce in allowing the laws of the land to be changed at the point of the sword.

Finally, he took off his cloak and the jewelled insignia of the Order of the Garter, and gave them to the faithful Bishop with the one word 'Remember.' The executioner fell to his knees and asked for the king's forgiveness. But Charles could not find absolution in his heart. 'The king cannot pardon a subject who wilfully sheds his blood,' he explained, and matter-of-factly asked, 'Does my hair trouble you?' before tucking it up into his skullcap. The reporters heard the last words of the Bishop to the king, 'You go from a temporal to an eternal crown, a good exchange.'

In case the king struggled, ropes and pulleys had been fastened to the scaffold, to drag him to the block. They were not needed. Charles told the executioner that he would say a short prayer at the block and explained that 'when I put my hands this way' – at which he stretched them out – 'then'. The king laid his head on the block, said a few words to himself, and extended his arms. During his final statement the king had interrupted himself once, when he saw someone touching the axe. Afraid that the blade might be blunted (at Fotheringhay, his grandmother, Mary Queen of Scots, had had to endure several blows of the axe before her head was finally parted from her body), he said, 'Hurt not the axe, that it may not hurt me.' He need not have worried. When it fell, the king's head dropped away. The crowd had been silent. Now, a witness reported, there came 'such a dismal universal groan amongst the thousands of people who were in sight of it as I never heard before and desire I may not hear again'. It was almost 2 p.m.

In conventional beheadings for treason, the executioner's assistant would lift the victim's head and shout, 'Behold the head of a traitor.' But such a declaration on King Charles's scaffold risked revealing the assistant's identity. So he merely lifted the king's head, showed it to the crowd and threw it to the floor so forcibly that the still-warm face was badly bruised.

In the cold of the modern London, a drop has formed at the end of the nose of the man in morning dress and he joins the crowd moving inside the Banqueting House.

Upstairs, a few hundred chairs have been set out in the room through which Charles passed on his last walk to the scaffold. In front of them is a table laid out as a makeshift altar, on which are a crucifix, a couple of candles and some glass frames. One contains a fragment of King Charles's shirt, another a shard from his coffin and a third a hair from his beard. Immediately after the execution, the soldiers had set up a lucrative trade, charging people to dip their handkerchiefs in the king's blood, allowing them to hack hair from his head, or selling bits of the bloodstained execution block. In the spirit of the Stuarts, the bloody handkerchiefs were soon credited with the power to cure the sick: the diarist John Evelyn records the Bishop of Bath and Wells recalling that King Charles's blood had once cured a man of blindness.[6]

The seats begin to fill. Hard to say what the occupants have in common. There are a few anoraks among the overcoats. There is a man with the grimy sheen of the long-term homeless. But there is a mink coat, too. There is a much higher-than-average bow-tie quotient. There are at least five priests in the congregation. On the whole, they seem a quiet, decent, slightly dusty group.

A young man offers me a prayer book. 'You need a pre-1859 edition,' he says. 'Queen Victoria removed the order of service for the commemoration of Charles's martyrdom. Quite illegally, of course.' And indeed, there it is. Other early editions of the Book of Common Prayer also included a service for Touching for the King's Evil.

Three priests process to the altar as the choir of King's College, London sing the story of Charles's execution in Latin:

Traitors shedding blood like water
Filled the land with crime and slaughter . . .
Violent men without compassion
Proudly spurned the ancient fashion
Of the sacred right divine.

There is a recitation of the Ten Commandments, prayers for King Charles and the current queen, a profession of the Nicene Creed, with much crossing of the chest, head-bowing and genuflection. There are prayers that England may be forgiven for the act of 'cruel and bloody men'. The address, given by the Librarian of Trinity Hall, Cambridge, talks of Charles almost as a prisoner of conscience, his life and death a religious text, an example of submission to the will of God and 'faithfulness unto death'.

For anyone with a sense of history, there is something undeniably moving about the sombre, gory memorial mass being celebrated below Rubens's fleshy celebration of the glory of kingship. The whole occasion has a very high-church feel about it – bells are rung, knees are bent. In this version of events, Charles died not because he was a tyrant but because he refused to succumb to Presbyterianism. The echoes of the Christ story are explicit. The hymns have familiar tunes, but the words are another matter.

Oh holy King, whose severed head
the Martyr's Crown doth ray
With gems for every blood-drop shed,
Saint Charles! For England pray.

As I head for the door at the end of the mass, the tall man in the tailcoat introduces himself. He wonders whether I might be able to help with suggestions of names to sit on a committee to raise a memorial to the late Queen Elizabeth, widow of George VI. No problem, I say. I give him my telephone number and ask what he is doing there.

'Oh, I am a direct descendant of King Charles. Ten generations, sir.' And I look at him, and it strikes me that he might well be telling the truth. The colouring, the hair, the long face, the angular nose, all of them are straight from Van Dyck's famous triptych of Charles I.

The king's body was taken from the scaffold for embalming by a Maidstone doctor, Thomas Trappam, an operation reputedly carried out on the kitchen table of the Dean of Westminster. Trappam removed the king's vital organs, then sawed open the severed head to remove the brain, before draining the remaining blood from the body. When he had filled the cavities with powders and myrrh, he sewed the head back on the body.[7] The reconstituted body was laid inside a lead-lined coffin and covered with a black velvet shroud. Mythology claims that late one night a hooded figure entered the room in which the body was laid out, stared at the corpse and muttered, 'Cruel necessity.' The man's voice and walk were said to be those of Oliver Cromwell.

Fearing the capacity of the king to stir dissent even though he was dead, parliament decreed that the body should be taken at night for interment away from the London mob, at Windsor. No monarch had been buried there for over a century. At three on a grey, frosty afternoon, a small procession carried it from St George's Hall to the chapel. A flurry of snow covered the coffin with a white pall – a sign, said the king's followers, that heaven was declaring his innocence.[8] The parliamentary authorities had banned the use of the Book of Common Prayer, so no prayers were spoken. The king's body was simply lowered into the tomb.

That day a book was published in London. Perhaps the Greek title, and Greek lettering *Eikon Basilike* ('The Image of the King'), was designed to give some cover to the anonymous printer, but the subtitle, *The Portraiture of His Sacred Majestie in His Sufferings and Solitude*, explained exactly what it was about. A strange mixture of prayer and political commentary, it purported to have been written by the king himself in the days before his execution.[9] The book was a manifesto from beyond the grave. 'As I have leisure enough, so I have cause more than enough, to meditate upon, and prepare for my death,' it begins, 'for I know there are but few steps between the Prisons and Graves of Princes.' The king conceded that he had perhaps made mistakes, but he had been doing what he believed to be his duty to God and his country. His misfortune was to be a divinely appointed man who had fallen among evil-doers. Though the book is tinged with self-pity, Charles was acute enough to see that he was being put to death not so much because there was a united hunger for his extinction as because it was one of the very few things a disparate group of enemies could agree upon. God would avenge the execution of the king, who had had a duty laid upon him by God which could not be compromised. In being put to death the king was imitating Christ. 'If I must suffer a violent death, with my Saviour, it is but mortality crowned with martyrdome.' Like Christ on the cross, the king forgives his enemies for not knowing what they do and ends with the *nunc dimittis*: 'Lord now lettest thou thy Servant depart in peace, according to thy word, for mine eyes have seen thy salvation.'

The book was a stunning piece of propaganda. Despite the imposition of a Licensing Act, editions poured from the presses. Dozens were produced within a year of the execution, many of them of great elaborateness – embellished with the prayers said by the king, his speech from the scaffold and extracts from his private letters. For those who had eyes to read or ears to listen, the claim made by the king in the book became fact: the king was a martyr, done to death by evil men for refusing to abandon his beliefs. Monarchical tributes from others went further: *A Handkerchief for Loyale Mourners*, for example, explicitly compared the execution of the king to the crucifixion. The Bishop of Rochester's private sermon on the Sunday following the execution was on the subject of 'the hellish murder of Christ's anointed'. When printed, it appeared with the letters 'Ch:' in place of the word 'Christ'.

John Milton, a passionate republican, was chosen to produce a counterblast, which he attempted in *Eikonoklastes* ('Image-breaker'). The king was a tyrant who had had to die. Those 'miserable, credulous and deluded' people who had been taken in by his supposed last meditations were ignorant of the fact that he was worthy of respect only if the people decided he was worthy of it. Law was the property not of the king, but of the people.

In the end, the public – as so often – preferred mystery to reason. In the theory of royalism the throne is never unoccupied. So, despite the acts of parliament which prohibited the declaration of any successor, believers in Scotland and Ireland – and even in the Scilly Isles – proclaimed Charles's eldest son as king.[10] At the Restoration – the consequence not of a sudden rediscovery of enthusiasm for monarchy so much as of a recognition that alternative systems simply would not work properly – those who had opposed the king were pardoned by an Indemnity Act. But for the regicides (or as many as could be brought to Restoration justice) the punishment was ghastly:

> You shall be drawn upon a hurdle to the place of execution, and there you shall be hanged by the neck, and being alive, shall be cut down and your privy members to be cut off, your entrails to be taken out of your body and (you living) the same to be burnt before your eyes; and your head to be cut off, your body to be divided into four quarters, and your head and quarters to be disposed of at the pleasure of the King's Majesty. And the Lord have mercy on your soul.

The executions drew vast crowds. In October 1660 Samuel Pepys wandered down to Charing Cross to see Major General Thomas Harrison being hung, drawn and quartered for his part in the king's execution. Pepys had previously seen the king beheaded in Whitehall. Now he saw the first blood shed in revenge. Harrison had spent the previous night in Newgate prison, where he preached to his fellow inmates about the glories of the world to come. The next morning he was taken up on to the roof of the prison to see the crowd which had gathered to watch him die. At the scaffold, Pepys found the General 'looking as cheerfully as any man could do in that condition'.[11] In fact, Harrison had begun to shake, which the crowd found amusing. He attempted to silence them by explaining that he was shivering not from fear but from the tremors which afflicted him as a result of the wounds he had suffered in battle. As the noose was placed around his neck, he offered his soul to God. But his death was quite as prolonged as the justices desired. The General was cut down from the scaffold almost immediately so that he should be fully conscious as he was castrated and disembowelled. The excruciating pain did not prevent him punching the executioner, who had done such an effective job that, one reporter wrote, Harrison was sufficiently conscious that he 'saw his bowels thrown into the fire'.[12] The crowd's blood-lust was up. When the victim's head and heart were raised for display to the crowd, 'there was great shouts of joy', said Pepys.

In April 1662 the Dutch artist Willem Schellinks went to Tyburn with 'thousands of other people' to see what happened to three other signatories: John Barkstead, a London goldsmith; John Okey, who had started out as a stoker in a Bedfordshire brewery; and Miles Corbet, who came from a landed family in Norfolk. All had been captured while in hiding in Holland. The three men were put upon a cart which stood beneath the gallows, and the nooses were placed around their necks. They were allowed to make final speeches to the crowd and then, as they commended their souls to God, the cart was driven away. Barkstead was the first to be cut down and was quartered on the ground, his heart cut out of his body and shown to the people. This was then thrown on to the fire. The intestines followed. Finally, the heads and assorted limbs of the three men were hung on display around the city as a warning to anyone who might entertain the thought of regicide in the future.

Most of the men who had signed the king's death warrant evaded the ultimate penalty for treachery. But those who escaped Restoration retribution by dying had their corpses dug and defiled. The bodies of Oliver Cromwell, Bradshaw and Ireton were disinterred, dragged through the streets, hanged on the gallows at Tyburn on the anniversary of Charles's execution and then buried. Their heads were cut from their bodies and exhibited on pikes at Westminster. Cromwell's remained there for several years.

The ritualistic exsanguinations which occurred when the monarchy was restored suggest much more than mere revenge. There could have been no more dramatic way to demonstrate that a king was mere flesh and blood than to sever his head from his body and to watch the blood spurt from his neck. Yet in scarcely more than a decade the British abandoned attempts to govern themselves without the use of a king, and invited Charles's son back from exile to rule as Charles II.

The contrast is with France, where, a century and a half later, the king was also beheaded. It is an event the French often seem still not to have got over properly. There were some striking similarities. As in England, the king's last moments were compared to the passion of Christ. While the executioner and his assistants attempted to tie King Louis XVI's hands, his Irish priest Henry Essex Edgeworth remarked, 'Sire, in this further outrage I see only a final resemblance between your Majesty and God who will be his recompense.' As the king climbed slowly up the steep steps to the guillotine the priest exclaimed, 'Son of St Louis, ascend to heaven!' The king began a speech, but, worried that his words might have some influence upon the crowd, the revolutionary General ordered a roll of drums to drown his voice. Louis was seized, strapped to a plank and laid beneath the guillotine. Seconds later the executioner reached into the basket and lifted the king's head by its hair and waved it to the crowd.

The significance of this execution still resonates through French politics and society. 'London killed a king, Paris killed kingship,' wrote Victor Hugo.[13] A procession of philosophers boasted that the act marked the end of an age of magical, divine authority and the birth of an age of reason. As Albert Camus was to put it in *The Rebel*, 'It symbolizes the secularization of our history and the disincarnation of the Christian God. Up to now God was a part of history through the medium of the kings. But His representative in history has been killed, for there is no longer a king. Therefore there is nothing but a semblance of God, relegated to the heaven of principles.'[14] In the birth of the revolutionary state, with its celebration of the rational and consequent elevation of the intellectual we can perhaps see some of the origins of the enthusiastic embraces of existentialism, structuralism, post-modernism and a dozen other fashionable and sometimes nonsensical convictions which have swept that society since.

The English, by contrast, concluded that the execution of their king was no more than a one-act political drama of its time, not much more resonant than the masques which took place in the Banqueting House. Although the Civil War which preceded the execution of the king was bloody, the period following the execution had nothing of the orgiastic slaughter of the Reign of Terror which followed the French beheading. It is true that the division between Cavaliers and Roundheads remains perhaps the most enduring fault-line in British politics. But in the end the British experiment with common sense in government failed, partly for the very reason which the king had identified in his final days. The enemies of kingship were united only in their desire to be rid of Charles. Once he had been dispatched, the alliance of proto-Communists, religious zealots, Levellers and Quakers disintegrated. Now they had only each other with whom to argue. Like the French, the British also discovered that, given the seal of state, the most ferocious republican soon comes to believe that there may be something in the hereditary principle after all. Although he publicly resisted petitions to declare himself king, Cromwell embraced laws to make the Protectorate he had established hereditary in his own family. Napoleon, who had seized power in France, abandoned the infertile Josephine, married the daughter of the Holy Roman Emperor and exulted in the fact that their child was declared the King of Rome.

In England they seemed to look at the alternatives to rule by a king, and to take fright. Even when Charles II was succeeded by his inadequate brother James they did not abandon kingship in principle, merely turning to his son-in-law, William of Orange, to replace him. This innate conservatism may not appear to owe much to the sort of devotion displayed by those commemorating the death of King Charles the Martyr. But for many it undoubtedly has a metaphysical element, a belief that the institution is part of 'deep' England. Part of it perhaps stems from that preference for the practical over the theoretical that so many foreign visitors have commented upon, part of it from inherent suspicion of ideologies, part from sentimentality, part from lack of imagination, part from sheer laziness. Above all, there seemed no need to replace a monarchy when the limits of monarchical power had been demonstrated so apocalyptically. After that monarchs might be heroes or fools. But they could only oppress their subjects as far as their subjects' representatives allowed them to be oppressed.

It helped British monarchy's survival, too, that its greatest challenge came before the country's industrialization: like socialism, republicanism was bred among the smokestacks. Royalism had – and has – deep roots in the countryside. And among the English elite there remained a preference for rural life over the attractions of the city. Ever since Louis XIV insisted that his aristocrats dance attendance upon him at court, fashionable French life had been a metropolitan affair, and where large country estates survived the later upheavals of the revolution, they were seen as sources of income, not as an occupation. In England, by contrast, the upper classes moved between the capital and the countryside with little sense that the former was inherently preferable to the latter. Rather the reverse, if anything.

Take the case of the Stauntons of Staunton Hall, Staunton-in-the-Vale, Nottinghamshire. The family have been there at least since the 1100s, which makes them one of the oldest families in England to inhabit the ancestral estate from which they take their name. The family portraits on the walls bear out the adage that, though a prosperous Venetian wanted his portrait painted while he was on his knees, the wealthy Englishman would rather be shown with horse, dogs and house. The Stauntons are very well off by any national comparison, but they do not consider themselves particularly rich. In a corner of the drawing room stands a harp with most of its strings missing. On the floor is a triggered and baited mousetrap. Generation after generation has produced parsons for the village church, engineers, tea planters and insurance clerks. They are not a grand family – well known in the village maybe, but unheard of twenty miles away. You will not find them in *Who's Who*. When I called upon Edmund Staunton, his most onerous responsibility was as a deputy lieutenant of the county, which involved turning out for the odd royal visit and fitted in easily with looking after his farm and with doing a little work for the country landowners' trade association. In Tory houses like this, for generations after the king's execution, each 30 January the walls or wainscots might be hung with black and all meals forbidden until after midnight, as a mark of remembrance.

Staunton's ancestor, Colonel William Staunton, raised a regiment of foot soldiers to fight for Charles I and took part in the first major battle of the Civil War, at Edgehill. On the 350th anniversary of the outbreak of the war, the present generation of Stauntons got together for a little ceremony in which they unveiled a memorial plaque to the old Colonel on the wall of one of their barns. It seemed a strange thing to do.

'To us, the Civil War doesn't seem far away. Some of us still feel pretty passionately about it,' Edmund Staunton says.

Why?

'Because a certain group of people took the King of England, and killed him in cold blood. It's a sad blot on the history of our country.'

For ardent monarchists like this, the Crown is far more than a constitutional convenience. It seems to speak directly to them, at a level beyond (or below) reason. Staunton conceded that his family had found the sorry spectacle of the failed marriages of Queen Elizabeth's children hard to take. These people care about honour, fidelity and wedding vows. Discovering that most of Princess Diana's artful propaganda against Prince Charles was true, he had felt very, very let down. 'We're a bit dechuffed, we royalists,' was how he put it. But they accept that the principle of hereditary crowns is that you have to take the mediocre with the outstanding. He pointed through the trees to the castle at Belvoir, five miles away. There is a Staunton Tower there, named after the pledge that an earlier member of the family had given to his feudal overlord, that if the place was ever attacked, he would provide troops to defend it. The family has not been called out since the Civil War. 'But we're always at the ready,' he says, without a hint of a wink.

8. Divine Right and Diviner Impotence

Those kings whose names are most firmly fixed in the national memory are those who continually did wrong, whether in a constitutional, political, social, moral or religious sense.

A. P. Herbert, *Misleading Cases*, 1935

In 1998 the leaders of the European Union gathered at one of their frequent conclaves. These occasions do not have quite the grandeur of the Field of the Cloth of Gold in 1520, when Henry VIII of England met Francis I of France in such gilded opulence that the fountains ran with claret. But the host country still attempts to display itself to best advantage and fritters away its citizens' taxes on receptions and souvenir knick-knacks for the attendant bureaucrats and journalists. This time the meeting was taking place in the Netherlands. Each politician arrived like some ancient king – official carriage, train of advisers, ambassadors and attendants. They argued long into the night about matters of state, and periodically sent their servants to fetch them more food and drink. And then the Dutch government, which was acting as host, offered them all a social occasion at which to relax. As the alpha males circled each other beneath the chandeliers, Tony Blair struck up a conversation.

He grinned, baring his teeth. The grin was famous, for he was the most talked-about politician in Europe, the fresh-faced young man who had ended eighteen years of Conservative rule. He grinned The Grin at the woman again.

'Hello. I'm Tony Blair.'

'And I'm Beatrix,' said the woman.

Without catching a breath, Blair slipped into the politician's command of social situations. 'And what do you do, Beatrix?' he asked, with easy interest.

She was the Queen of the Netherlands.

When their politicians wield power, what is left to the kings and queens of constitutional monarchies? At least none has reached the position of kings in the Aztec empire where there was a tradition that each year the most handsome of the prisoners captured in battle should be made king. Protected by guards and dressed in jewels and the most sumptuous robes, his every need was satisfied. There was food, there was music and at night there were voluptuous courtesans. This feast of indulgence lasted for a year. Then the king was led to the top of the temple pyramid. Here, stripped naked, he was stretched out on an altar and had his torso sliced open. His heart was torn out and offered to the gods, his head stuck on a pole and the skin flayed from his body before being laid 'as a sticky dressing gown'[1] on the shoulders of a high priest. The ritual celebrated the return of spring, but a belief that sometimes the king must be killed is common to several early societies.[2]

Those European monarchies that have survived have saved the lives of their kings by sacrificing their freedom to act independently. The arrangement is simple: the people indulge their king and, in exchange, they get his co-operation. All successful European monarchies are based upon an understanding of this kind. An early example is the Scots' Declaration of Arbroath in 1320, which explicitly warned their king, Robert the Bruce, that if he refused to lead them in battle the barons would give the crown to someone else. A century earlier, the English barons had obliged King John to sign the Magna Carta, which for the first time laid down the limits of royal power and which remains on the statute book to this day. By the time Elizabeth I had come to the throne in 1558, the conviction had taken hold that England was a sort of commonwealth, a 'rule mixte', where royal authority was balanced by that of the aristocracy and the people.[3] The first town clerk of Tewkesbury, John Barston, wrote in 1576 that a king 'hath not the rule of lawe, but is only the minister and nothing els'.[4] In this context, the revolution which took the head of King Charles I is not an aberration but part of a process. The revolutionaries' propagandist John Milton quoted Cicero – the execution of a tyrant was merely the amputation of a diseased limb. Thereafter, the British political class were ready to indulge monarchs who did not trouble them too much, and to discard those – like James II – who did. An alternative king, William of Orange, married to James's (Protestant) daughter Mary, was summoned and offered the throne, provided the two of them accepted the 1689 Declaration of Rights, guaranteeing free elections and free speech in parliament and requiring parliamentary approval for raising taxes or maintaining a standing army.

This gradual attrition of royal power was not a constant process. Despite Magna Carta, royal power actually increased during the late Middle Ages, and both Henry VII and Henry VIII exercised greater authority than many of their predecessors. It would have been a brave man who defied Elizabeth I by expressing the thoughts of the town clerk of Tewkesbury. But the mistake of the Stuarts was to believe that they could simply ignore those sorts of ideas altogether, and behave like French autocrats. When the last Stuart monarch, Anne, died without leaving an heir, the decision to offer the throne to the Hanoverians was fortunate for British democracy, largely because the new dynasty was initially more interested in German affairs than in England. It is true that the early Georges had great influence upon foreign policy, and modern scholarship has suggested that the usual explanation for King George I's absences from cabinet – that his English was so bad he could not understand what was being talked about – is an exaggeration.[5] But it is certainly the case that his place was taken with growing frequency by the senior minister (later known as the 'prime minister') and that much of the king's role, when he did attend, was to deal with royal formalities, like considering pardons. During the reigns of the first three Georges, which stretch across most of the eighteenth century, the personal authority of the king diminished. When George III attempted to act conscientiously, by reading the documents put before him, his Lord Chancellor, Lord

Thurlow, told him there was not much point in his doing so because he would not understand them, anyway. And when the North American colonies rebelled, the king was powerless to prevent his trusted Prime Minister, Lord North, from resigning and paving the way for them to be granted their independence. All that his son, George IV, could do to obstruct the government of the day in its bid to recognize the independence of the revolting republics of South America was to claim that he had an attack of gout and couldn't find his false teeth.

The long illness of George III and the inadequacy of his sons, George IV and William IV (the latter memorably described by Lytton Strachey as 'a bursting, bubbling old gentleman, with quarter-deck gestures, round rolling eyes, and a head like a pineapple [whose] sudden elevation to the throne after fifty-six years of utter insignificance had almost sent him crazy')[6] made the transfer of power from king to politicians unstoppable. Thwarted in his opposition to the 1832 Reform Bill's proposals to give more of his citizens the right to vote, William was the last king to attempt to defy parliament in choosing his own prime minister. The young Queen Victoria, who succeeded him, was so upset when her mentor, Lord Melbourne, lost office that their final meeting was awash with tears. 'I really thought my heart would break,' she wrote, when she learned he could not continue as her prime minister.[7] Her reaction to her later Prime Minister William Gladstone could hardly have offered a greater contrast: 'He behaves abominably. I really think he is cracked.'[8] However, outside such matters as the appointment of bishops, Victoria's personal feelings – for all her bluster – became increasingly irrelevant to much of the business of government. You begin to wonder why Disraeli, in his gushing weekly letters to 'a gracious, too indulgent sovereign', went to so much trouble to flatter her.

This ever widening chasm between the right to reign and the right to rule saved the British monarchy from the fate which befell so many others. Chance is inherent in any occupation in which the sole qualification is a matter of inheritance, which is why we do not have hereditary brain surgeons. In a system in which the king wielded real power, he really ought to be the wisest man in the country. If the citizens could not have a wise man as king, the best they could hope for was one who was honest and thoughtful. The unlucky ones would find themselves governed by a tyrant, a poltroon or a fool, about whom any self-respecting citizen would be bound to begin to feel like Cromwell. Leaving the business of government to disposable individuals, who exercised power through ambition and election, therefore protected the throne.[9] Winston Churchill once explained it in a speech thus: 'A great battle is lost: parliament turns out the Government. A great battle is won – crowds cheer the Queen.'[10]

Victory in war is another reason for the survival of the British monarchy: had the outcome in either of the world wars of the twentieth century been otherwise, people might well have come to wonder whether it was worth continuing with such an antique arrangement. Germany and Austria became republics after defeat in the First World War, as did states like Bulgaria after the Second. But even those once mighty European dynasties which survived the two world wars were progressively reduced to a crepuscular existence, in which the most that they could count upon was social deference or indifference. Politically, kings became figures of no importance. Yet those that survived possessed a quality which politicians can pursue for years and still never acquire. They had the vital attribute of legitimacy because they occupied a role they had never striven for – one, furthermore, which would continue when they and their prime ministers were long gone. When Churchill ended his wartime broadcasts with the words 'God Save the King', everyone understood what he was talking about.

In theory, most of the powers that remain with the British king or queen are piffling. Formally, all swans, whales and sturgeons in British waters belong to them. Doubtless, when he accedes to the throne Prince Charles will have his own plans for them. But he will have to fight the prime minister's office. For – like almost all the other responsibilities theoretically reserved to the monarch, from making laws without consulting parliament (through Orders in Council), declaring war or a state of emergency, signing treaties, commanding the armed forces and appointing major public officials to instituting or quashing legal proceedings and recognizing foreign governments – the destinies of sturgeon, swans and whales are usually determined by 10 Downing Street. Indeed, the authority exercised on behalf of the king or queen gives the British prime minister so much unhindered power (probably more than any elected political leader in the western world) that even his own office is unsure precisely how far it extends.[11] What is left to the monarch?

Even some of those closest to the queen admit the utter futility of most of the paperwork. 'Much of my work at Buckingham Palace was a God-awful waste of time,' admits one senior official. 'What came across my desk was an endless succession of pointless pieces of paper for the queen to sign.' The queen herself takes a conscientious interest in most of these documents, although it tends to be more intense in the case of the gazetting of generals or the appointment of bishops than it is in new regulations about vehicle emissions. The relentless tides of paper which wash across the desk are at least less pressing than in the early days of Victoria's reign, when she was expected to put her signature to almost every single military commission: she fell so far behind that sometimes whiskery old gentlemen received their appointments long after they had retired from the service.

But the real triviality of the task is that kings and queens cannot change most of the formal documents to which they are expected to give their assent, and many of those which they may alter are of such unimportance that it is hard to see them as a worthwhile use of anyone's time. Might the monarch not be replaced by some sort of rubber stamp or electronic franking machine? Again, it took the most unsuccessful king of the twentieth century to voice the frustration. 'The rôle of a successful constitutional monarch', wrote Edward VIII, 'consists in no small measure of appearing to be not only above politics but also above life.'[12] It is not a role which would suit anyone who had gone into public life to change the world. But that may not mean the tedious formality has no value.

The inconvenience of requiring a royal signature might one day save the people from the potentially dreadful consequences of a piece of draconian legislation proposed by an over-mighty government. In this long-stop view of things, the king's or queen's importance is largely a negative thing: the possibility that a monarch might refuse to sign a really bad law might deter the politicians from going ahead with it. But it is hard to think of an example in recent history.

In any strictly democratic reading of life it is outrageous that an unelected individual should possess any powers at all to obstruct the wishes of a properly elected government, however power-crazed it might be. But all decent systems of government incorporate checks and balances. In the parliamentary system, in which the people cast their votes for candidates representing different parties, the outcome is generally clear: the government will be formed by the party with the largest number of seats in parliament. But elections do not always end in decisive results, and any growth in multi-party politics in Britain could produce more inconclusive outcomes. In the inevitable bargaining which would follow a close result, the king or queen could find themselves having to make a choice about who might be able to knock together the most convincing coalition. It would be a foolish decision to ignore a potential prime minister with obvious support in favour of one with none. But it is theoretically possible. In theory, too, the king or queen might refuse a request from a prime minister to dissolve parliament. George V was against holding an election in 1916, as the country was in the middle of a war. But if the monarch were to refuse a dissolution of parliament – and the consequent fresh elections – he would have to be absolutely confident that the government would not then call his bluff and resign.

But there is one outstanding twentieth-century example of a king making a government. In 1931, George V personally brokered the creation of the National Government, when Ramsay MacDonald's Labour administration collapsed in the face of economic crisis. MacDonald had lost the confidence of his party on which his position as prime minister depended. He trudged disconsolately to Buckingham Palace to resign, and the king persuaded him not to do so. Three times he tried to quit the job and three times the king talked him out of it. Instead, George V took the chair at meetings with MacDonald and the leaders of the Conservative and Liberal parties. His private secretary recorded that he told the three men that 'they must get together and come to some arrangement'. They did. The first that members of parliament heard of the new National Government was on the radio. The consequence was that MacDonald became a hate figure for the left and George V was accused of meddling in politics (as, of course, he had). But what should the king have done? Someone had to form a government. Gold and foreign currency reserves were draining out of the Bank of England and international bankers were refusing the British government credit. It turned out that all three party leaders were willing to share power to try to get the country out of the hole: if the king had stood idly by, he would surely have been guilty of a dereliction of duty.

But the dangers for a democracy in allowing the king or queen to exercise this sort of power are obvious. First of all, who defines what constitutes a crisis? And secondly, how to ensure that the monarch makes a good choice? The 1931 crisis left Ramsay MacDonald in the absurd position of leading a government but not a party capable of forming a government.

'MacDonald was as much the personal choice of George V', remarked the academic and socialist Harold Laski, 'as Lord Bute was the personal choice of George III.'[13] How did a great modern democracy find itself living under arrangements in which an unelected individual whose main interests in life were collecting stamps and filling the air with lead shot could make or break governments in this way? The problem is that without a written constitution, what is constitutionally feasible is merely what is thought by the panjandrums to be constitutionally feasible. In this Humpty Dumptyist arrangement, the powers are potentially as great as they wish them to be. Both David Lloyd George in 1916 and Winston Churchill in 1940 were invited by the king to form a government without even being leaders of their own parties. In theory these decisions are made on advice. But in 1923 George V was left to his own devices when his Prime Minister, Andrew Bonar Law, succumbed to throat cancer after a lifetime's devotion to pipes and cigars. The king chose Stanley Baldwin to succeed him, on the ground that the former Viceroy of India, Lord Curzon (who was sitting at home in the country waiting for the telegram), could not sit in – and be accountable to – the House of Commons. Yet the contrary instinct seemed to apply when George V's son became king and Baldwin's successor as party leader, Neville Chamberlain, resigned the office of prime minister. George VI initially preferred Lord Halifax to Winston Churchill. Churchill's account of the meeting at which the king invited him to form a government has the two men discussing the names of those who might sit in a government of national unity.

Again, this is the sort of direct interference in political affairs which risks outraging strict parliamentarians. But it is hard to imagine any non-executive head of state – however they were chosen – resisting the impulse to do what they could to ensure that a country in crisis had the best government possible. It would be just as likely to happen had the nation elected a retired fishmonger as its president. Indeed, any head of state who did not consider it his duty to help as far as he could would be unworthy of the post.

The king was powerless, of course, to block the people's choice of Attlee as their prime minister at the end of the Second World War, even though, as a deeply conservative figure, he shared none of the new Labour government's socialist convictions. ('I don't see why people should have false teeth free any more than they have shoes free,' was part of his analysis of the National Health Service.) He did, however, interfere with Attlee's choice of foreign secretary. The new Prime Minister was planning to give the job to Hugh Dalton, and had already advised him to pack a lightweight suit because it was likely to be hot on his first overseas mission to the Potsdam Conference which would determine the division of occupied Germany. The king could not abide Dalton, who, apart from being generally dislikeable, had committed the sin of betraying his class by consorting with the socialists: his father had been a tutor and chaplain at Windsor.* The king much preferred Ernest Bevin, the son of a washerwoman, who had proved himself a formidable minister in the wartime government. In his diary the king noted of Attlee's plan, 'I disagreed with him & said Foreign Affairs was the most important subject at the moment & I hoped that he would make Mr Bevin take it.'[14] The Prime Minister subsequently claimed that his decision to give the job to Ernest Bevin was his own work. But it seems unimaginable that the king, who according to his private secretary had 'begged him to think carefully' and 'suggested that Mr Bevin would be a better choice',[15] had had no influence upon him.

The Conservative Party's reluctance for most of the twentieth century to have a system for choosing a leader based on anything as vulgar as a vote of members or MPs landed the queen with the task on a couple of occasions. In 1957, when sickness and lies forced Anthony Eden out of Downing Street, she might have invited 'Rab' Butler to become prime minister; after all, he had carried out Eden's duties during his illness. Instead she picked Harold Macmillan. It emerged afterwards that she had consulted Eden, his predecessor Churchill and a couple of former cabinet ministers, Lords Chandos and Waverley, at least three of whom recommended Macmillan. When Macmillan resigned the post of prime minister, six years later, the choice was wider. 'Tory democracy in action' was the absurd expression used by Randolph Churchill to describe the muttering, nods and winks which now ensued. At the end of the process, a 'magic circle' declared for the 14th Earl of Home. In an unprecedented scene, the queen then visited Macmillan in hospital, where he was laid low with prostate trouble. He asked whether she would like his advice on who

*Dalton had been disliked in royal circles all his life. It was said that as a child he had been invited to tea with Queen Victoria and spent the occasion stuffing his face. The queen is said to have exclaimed, 'What a horrid little boy!' In later life, Dalton tried to play down the story, claiming that he had merely told the queen that he would prefer to eat the bunch of grapes he had on his plate than to talk to her.

should succeed him, and when she said yes he produced a piece of paper, which made an unanswerable case for Home.

Constitutional experts have spilt much ink in arguing whether or not the former Prime Minister was entitled to tender advice on who should succeed him. But, because the events of 1963 finally persuaded the Conservative Party that there was something mildly idiotic about a process which enabled them to pick their own leader while in opposition, but denied them the same opportunity when they were in government, it is not a problem which is likely to occur again.

The European monarch whose commitment to democracy has been most tested is the King of Spain, Juan Carlos I. His reign was the invention of the dictator Francisco Franco, who had seized power after the Civil War of the 1930s and thereafter held the country together through the usual fascistic combination of force and bombast. Franco divined that, when he died, only a pre-Enlightenment institution like the Bourbon monarchy would be able to exercise a similar unifying hold. The grandson of the last Spanish king was groomed for the task. When he came to take the throne, the new king had a reputation as little more than a shallow playboy who liked fast cars and faster women; convinced that he would not stay the course, the Communists nicknamed him 'Juan Carlos the Brief'.

But five years after he became king, on 23 February 1981, a group of Civil Guards armed with sub-machine guns entered the Spanish parliament, held the politicians hostage and demanded a countrywide military insurrection to restore a military dictatorship. It was to be the most dramatic test of whether Spain had indeed shaken off fascism. The king telephoned his brother-in-law, Constantine, in exile in London after a military coup in his native Greece. Constantine told him that, on the basis of his experience, every army barracks in the land would be alive with argument about whether to join the coup. If there were a couple of battalions in Madrid which were loyal, then he had nothing to fear – the coup would fizzle out. As it happened, the coup did indeed collapse, largely for the reasons the exiled Greek king had suggested. But the event which carried the greatest symbolic force was the appearance on television of the king, dressed as commander-in-chief of the armed forces, declaring his commitment to democracy and ordering the army to resist the coup. It was a public-relations masterstroke. After that, no one talked about Juan Carlos the Brief any more.

Few kings or queens have the opportunity for such dramatic gestures, but the political role of a modern European monarchy is essentially always the same. Politicians spend their lives attempting to make a mark upon history. Kings and queens embody history. Ironically, it has become the function of unelected monarchy to dignify democracy.

In Britain, the only occasion on which most people see the king or queen engaged in politics is the annual State Opening of parliament. This little piece of theatre, played out in its colourful pomp – gilded coaches, cavalrymen in glittering breastplates, the trumpet fanfares and artillery salutes, the ceremonial entrance to the Palace of Westminster surrounded by heralds with incomprehensible titles in pack-of-cards liveries – is a modern reinvention, begun by Edward VII in one of his early acts as king. Edward was widely said to have wanted an opportunity to outshine his cousin, the Kaiser, and the ceremony usually offends some left-wing politician, who protests at the indignity of democratically elected members of parliament being summoned to listen to an unelected monarch reading a speech in the unelected House of Lords. But you might as easily see the humiliation the other way round. George V apparently told his son that he 'knew of few worse ordeals than being obliged to deliver somebody else's speech, at the same time balancing on his head a 2½lb gold crown'.[16] If so, he had a remarkably limited imagination.

But the modern State Opening of parliament is less a display of feudal order than a ritual obeisance by the monarch. Littered with promises, mundanities ('My government will introduce a bill to oblige the railway companies to co-ordinate their engineering work') and half-truths, the speech lays out the laws the government proposes to introduce in the coming session of parliament. In reciting the many things that 'My government' will do, the monarch may glorify what would otherwise be as exciting as an old laundry list. But it is demonstration, too, of the extent to which he or she acts as some extravagantly gowned ventriloquist's dummy. The objectors have got it wrong: the State Opening is a ritual not to aggrandize an unelected head of state but to dignify the noisy, everyday world of politics. In requiring the monarch to be present once a year the message is being sent that parliament matters.

Many of the other functions performed by the occupant of Buckingham Palace are similarly contrived to add lustre to the machinery of state. Newly appointed British ambassadors call on the queen before departing for their overseas postings, and horse-drawn carriages are sent to collect the representatives of foreign governments accredited to Britain. They come in national dress (the Fijian High Commissioner arrives in bare feet and skirt), accompanied by the Marshal of the Diplomatic Corps, in tight tunic and carrying a feathered hat. They are met by an equerry in dress uniform and a senior Foreign Office official in court dress – another beribboned tunic which does not fit him too well and looks as if it is the office suit for such occasions. The ambassador is led past six pages – distinguished from footmen in the precise palace hierarchy by the colour of their waistcoats – into a receiving room. Somewhere down the endless corridors with their red carpets, gilded cornices and marble statuary, a clock chimes midday, double doors are flung open and the diplomat advances – one step, bow, one step, bow again – to meet the queen. A minute or so after the diplomat has left, the Chief of the Defence Staff is ushered in, to explain to the queen what is happening to her much reduced armed forces. After that, there is a delegation from the Privy Council, a relic of the days when kings had real power, but still required to assemble (standing) to authorize orders which bypass the inconvenience of trying to get legislation through the House of Commons. After that, there may be bishops to see or a prime minister to meet.

Any and all of these functions could be changed, delegated to someone else or simply forgotten about. They exist simply because they exist. 'Procedure is all the Constitution the poor Briton has' was the way one historian and Conservative MP put it in the middle of the twentieth century.* In practice, this means that things happen in Britain the way they do because the three grandest figures in the bureaucracy, the Cabinet Secretary, the Clerk of the House of Commons and the queen's private secretary agree that that this is how they ought to happen.

The theory was famously laid out by the Victorian journalist Walter Bagehot, who divided government into two parts, the 'dignified' and the 'efficient'. The efficient section of the machinery was the part that got things done. The monarchy was an adornment which made sure that people gave government the reverence it needed to function. It was a neat piece of analysis. Whether it was 100 per cent accurate – Bagehot was, after all, trying to make sense of a monarchy whose popularity had increased at the very time that its political powers had withered – was less important than the fact that everyone accepted his ideas as if they had been carved in stone. George V and George VI each studied *The English Constitution* closely. Both the young Princess Elizabeth and, later, her son Charles were encouraged to read Bagehot to understand their future job. In the words of one constitutional historian, 'the writings of Bagehot were to attain canonical status'.[17]

But Walter Bagehot was no radical. His patronizing conclusion was that, given a choice between the mystery of monarchy and something more apparently intelligible – like true democracy – the people would choose the former, because:

> Royalty is a government in which the attention of the nation is concentrated on one person doing interesting actions. A Republic is a government in which that attention is divided between many, who are all doing uninteresting actions. Accordingly, so long as the human heart is strong

*Sir Kenneth Pickthorn. It was Pickthorn who coined the phrase about the leader of the Gadarene swine claiming to be 'in the van of progress'.

and the human reason weak, Royalty will be strong because it appeals to diffused feelings and Republics weak because they appeal to the understanding.[18]

The assertion has all the bustling, superficial confidence of a clever journalist writing for a country publicly proclaiming that it was the most blessed on earth, while inwardly anxious about the state of its own uncultured masses. Later, the author was explicit: 'the masses of Englishmen are not fit for an elective government; if they knew how near they were to it, they would be surprised and almost tremble'.[19] Bagehot accepted the symbolic attributes which had been conferred upon monarchy by religion, superstition and history. But, as for powers available to the monarch, 'to state the matter shortly', he said, 'the sovereign has, under a constitutional monarchy such as ours, three rights – the right to be consulted, the right to encourage, the right to warn. And a king of great sense and sagacity would want no others.'[20]

Consultation, encouragement and warning have become accepted as the only three legitimate political activities of a constitutional king or queen. The most celebrated of the occasions on which these actions can take place is the regular meeting when the prime minister calls on the queen. These meetings are usually said to take place on a weekly basis, but in fact tend to average out at once every two or three weeks. It is almost impossible to find out what is discussed, for no agenda is circulated and no record is kept. They are just private conversations. Some prime ministers have found the meetings more important than others. James Callaghan used to relish them. John Major's office privately described them as a weekly session 'on the psychiatrist's couch'. Major himself felt that the sessions were the oral equivalent of his being able to kick the cat, and he often returned exclaiming, 'She knows so much!' In the early years of his prime ministership Tony Blair attended much more frequently than John Major, although he later preferred to do some of the discussion by telephone.[21]

But no one has rivalled Churchill in his devotion. One of the queen's private secretaries recalled Churchill emerging from his weekly audience thundering, 'That must *never* recur.' Alarmed at what awful confrontation must have taken place, the secretary asked what had troubled the great man. 'The queen told me she had had to sit through an awful film about one of her ancestors,' Churchill explained. (It was the 1954 version of *Beau Brummell* in which Peter Ustinov played the future George IV and Elizabeth Taylor the female lead.) 'This must *never* recur.' By the following morning, the Home Secretary had established a committee to vet the films sent for viewing at Buckingham Palace. It was presided over by Sir Cyril Radcliffe. He had previously been best known as the man who drew the line dividing India from Pakistan.

When Churchill was worrying about the queen's film-viewing, Elizabeth was a young woman. Tony Blair was chewing rusks. As time has passed, the balance of experience has changed. Conspiracy theorists see these Tuesday-evening sessions (they are scheduled to last an hour, but may go on for longer) as a means by which the dark forces of conservatism manipulate and subvert the wishes of the people. Queen Elizabeth II herself once said, with a demotic looseness of grammar, that 'Occasionally you can be able to put one's point of view which, perhaps, they hadn't seen it from that angle.' But mostly, she claimed, the sessions gave the prime ministers an opportunity to unburden themselves. 'I think it's rather nice to feel that one's a sort of sponge and everybody can come and tell one things.'[22] Former prime ministers say much the same thing. 'I don't want to be melodramatic,' one told me, 'but being prime minister is a very lonely job, and you really can't trust anybody, so to have someone to talk to who isn't after your job, who won't leak what you've said to the press and won't use what you've said against you – that's a real relief.'

There may be drinks offered during these conversations, or, in summer, a walk around the garden. 'We discussed all sorts of things,' one former prime minister says, 'from politics to the latest scandal and overseas trade trips. Of course, she's particularly interested in charities, Church matters and the Commonwealth, and sometimes when I told her about some Commonwealth leader who was making trouble she'd say, "Oh yes, I knew his father."'

Apparently she often expresses preferences when it comes to appointments at the top of the armed forces, but on politics the furthest she goes in expressing an opinion is to ask a question like 'And how will that work?' Coupled with a direct stare, it can be enough to give a prime minister pause. It is often said that the queen used her weekly meetings with the then Prime Minister, Anthony Eden, to attempt to forestall the 1956 invasion of the Suez Canal zone. She was certainly receiving pleas for intervention from other governments in the Commonwealth, and two of her private secretaries were passionately against the war, while Lord Mountbatten was blustering around the palace saying that he thought Eden had lost his mind. Some years later Eden himself forcefully denied having come under any pressure from the palace.[23] The proof of the pudding is that, whether the queen tried or not, the invasion went ahead, and ended in shambling failure.

The queen does what she can to set her prime ministers at ease – she has a good sense of humour and is a surprisingly good mimic. Nonetheless, the thought of an elected leader reduced to quivering inconsequentiality by a figure who has never gone to the inconvenience of election offends the heirs of Cromwell. Eddie Mirzoeff, who once filmed (for a BBC documentary) what happened before and after a meeting between the queen and John Major, was astonished by how nervous the Prime Minister was. 'You could almost see him trembling,' he recalled. Afterwards, when the queen suggested that the two of them take a walk around the garden, Major resisted having a microphone fitted to his shirt, until it was pointed out to him that the queen was wearing one. A portion of the soundtrack (which was never broadcast) has the queen describing the garden to him, and him interjecting, 'Oh yes. And it's all the work of Calamity Brown.' The queen does not put him right.

It is often claimed by the supporters of monarchy that 'The royal family is not political.' This is absurd. To be engaged in public life and not to have political views would be a demonstration of fecklessness or profound stupidity. You cannot be a responsible adult without having political views, whether you are a king or a carpenter. Political involvement, or the possession at least of political opinions, is an indication of maturity and engagement. The danger arises only when an individual attempts to impose their views on others without having been given authority – through election – to do so.

Inevitably, given that it represents an archaic institution, royalty has tended to the conservative. In the 1830s William IV vehemently opposed the abolition of slavery, consistently promoted the idea that the French were the most untrustworthy people on earth and believed that Britain should always support legitimate conservative governments abroad against radicalism. Though comparatively liberal on religious and racial matters, Queen Victoria opposed Lord Ashley's Ten Hours Bill because it would deprive industry of seven weeks of child labour each year, resisted reform of the army, distrusted the idea of a civil service based upon competitive entry and ruled that in the navy 'on no account should moustaches be allowed without beards. That must be clearly understood.'[24] She was quite unable to contain herself on 'this mad, wicked folly of "Woman's Rights", with all its attendant horrors'; a woman who had expressed herself in favour of the limited emancipation of women 'ought to get a *good whipping*'.[25] Lloyd George commented of George V that 'the whole atmosphere reeks of Toryism'.[26] Hugh Gaitskell, Labour's second post-war Chancellor of the Exchequer, remarked of George VI that 'he is, of course, a fairly reactionary person'.[27] The adjective is accurate enough, although doubtless the king would have preferred a word like 'traditionalist'. No one would describe Queen Elizabeth II as a radical. But she has been wise enough to keep most of her opinions to herself. For example, despite what was taken to be her unease about the idea of a devolved parliament in Scotland, she was happy enough to turn out a few years later to make a speech applauding its work.

The problem with opinions is that there is always someone else with a different one. Since the function of a modern monarchy is to act as a unifying symbol, it is therefore usually better not to voice them. Reticence is fine when you are young enough for your comments to invite the response that you might think differently when you've grown up. But it is asking an awful lot from someone that they spend most of their adult life in political silence. Yet that is what is required of the Prince of Wales, despite the fact that when he succeeds to the throne he will be expected to be at ease with affairs of state. The vow of silence may be tolerable only if you are content to spend your apprenticeship like Edward VII, eating, shooting and having sex. Prince Charles could not settle for pleasure and has promoted initiatives, in his charitable foundations and his Business Trust, which even his fiercest critics find it impossible to attack. Many have been imitated elsewhere in the world. He has attempted to get around the requirement that he avoid political controversy by holding forth only on subjects that he claims were somehow 'off the political agenda'. But in modern societies there is almost nothing which is not political to some degree or other. No one could argue with his charitable initiatives, which have undoubtedly helped thousands of deprived young people. But when he defended traditional agriculture he waded into rural politics; when he acted as cheerleader for alternative medicine he launched himself into medical politics; when he attacked modern teaching methods he was embroiling himself in educational politics.

Charles's staff learned to get used to his return from periods spent staying with the Orthodox monks of Mount Athos in Greece or communing with nature in his Gloucestershire garden, when he would fire off instructions about how he was going to save the world.

Each intervention has tended to be seen as merely another 'it really is appalling' outburst. But, discounting their often tetchy tone, there has been an underlying unity to his apparently scattered pronouncements. Charles consistently supports the small over the large, the local over the global, the spiritual over the scientific. His comments give voice to unease at the modern world. They are, in short, the anti-scientific utterings of a man who embodies a pre-scientific role. As he reflected on his various campaigns, he summarized it in one monumental sentence:

> I have gradually come to realize that my entire life so far has been motivated by a desire to heal – to heal the dismembered landscape and the poisoned soil; the cruelly shattered townscape, where harmony has been replaced by cacophony; to heal the divisions between intuitive and rational thought, between mind, body and soul, so that the temple of our humanity can once again be lit by a sacred flame; to level the monstrous artificial barrier erected between Tradition and Modernity and, above all, to heal the mortally wounded soul that, alone, can give us warning of the folly of playing God and of believing that knowledge on its own is a substitute for wisdom.[28]

The small number of people who read this manifesto would doubtless have found little to which they could take exception. Despite his living one of the most privileged lives in the land, Charles somehow intuited that his attitudes on the state of the world reflected those of the citizenry: that he was the voice of the Little Person against the Establishment, taking on the professions from architecture to medical science. He had correctly diagnosed a corrosive anxiety about the pace of life, the inhuman scale of much modern architecture, the brutalism of modern planning, the industrialization of the countryside and the deindustrialization of the cities, the moral vacuum at the heart of much corporate culture, the emptiness of a religion of 'consumer choice' and the anomie of the shopping mall and multiplex world. If anyone but a member of the royal family had uttered them, Prince Charles's conclusions might have been fallen upon with enthusiasm. Instead, he got headlines about how he talked to the trees, or 'Who Does He Think He Is?'

For years, on the aircraft on the way home from foreign visits, Charles produced handwritten accounts of what he had seen. Written in his spidery hand, in black ink on crested notepaper, they provide a first-hand account of his views on all manner of subjects. After arriving home, they were photocopied and circulated to a small group of friends, usually with a covering letter telling them to guard the things with their lives, for fear of their falling into the hands of his least favourite newspaper, the *Mail on Sunday*, which he privately described as controlled by Lord Voldemort, villain of the *Harry Potter* books: Britain had become the Prison of Azkaban. But in November 2005 the newspaper published extracts from one of the journals, describing a visit to Hong Kong to watch the end of colonial rule there. The prince sued for breach of copyright and confidentiality and a judge ruled that there was no public interest to be served by disclosing the prince's opinions, despite the fact that the prince's staff had photocopied the journals and circulated them to dozens of people.

According to those who have seen many of the journals, they are largely harmless documents, part holiday diary – the food, the sights, the people – part ambassadorial dispatch and part plaintive rant. There are occasional overtly political outbursts, but they are much outnumbered by complaints about his accommodation and transport, or the tedium of endless speeches and official visits. There is plenty of sub-*Goon Show* wit. An account of a visit to the Baltic states in 2001 is headed 'RIGA MORTIS'. A journal describing a visit to Brazil and Mexico is entitled 'IT'S A LONG WAY TO TIPPERARY, BUT IT'S EVEN FURTHER TO POPOCATEPETL'.

It is hard not to feel a degree of sympathy for someone expected to trail around the world witnessing one display of national dancing after another or to deliver a speech which will simultaneously catch the imagination of an audience including the Community of Cane Rat Breeders of Benin, Chadian caterpillar eaters and Somalian dromedary farmers. Not surprisingly – as emerged from the Hong Kong journal – the prevailing tone is 'The Things I Do for Britain!' But what had most embarrassed the prince was the newspaper's disclosure that he had described the leaders of China as 'appalling old waxworks'. This might have been interpreted as very mild abuse: rude, certainly, but he did not, for example, go into details of the regime's dreadful human rights record, its occupation of foreign lands, or its contempt for principles of true democracy.

But the comment was nonetheless deemed political, and therefore compromising – both for the western politicians who wished to cosy up to the Chinese government and for the royal household, which is, supposedly, above such things as opinions.

The truth is that, over the years, Prince Charles has disclosed how political a figure he really is. He may not have been foolish enough to meddle in domestic politics. But anyone who paid close attention to his speeches, or talked to his friends, would have known what he thinks about all manner of subjects, from global warming (deeply troubled) and globalization (unsustainable) to the decision to go to war in Iraq (an utter mystery). He detests much modern architecture and distrusts much modern medicine. We know that he despaired of George W. Bush and was baffled by Tony Blair's chameleon-like ability to be all things to all people.

None of these opinions was either surprising or unique. In many of them, the prince was doing no more than reflecting the anxieties of his people. His incomprehension of Blair's decision to join the war on Iraq was shared by millions. In his attempts to promote dialogue between religious faiths and in the battle against pollution, vile food and environmental destruction he is clearly on the side of the angels. But that is not the point. The central difficulty for royalty when it comes to political matters is that they are somehow expected to be in the world and yet not of it, to speak for their people and yet to have nothing to say until someone writes it for them. To be, in short, an empty vessel.

9. We are You

A king is a thing men have made for their own sakes, for quietness' sake. Just as in a family, one man is appointed to buy the meat.

John Selden, *Table Talk*, 1689

In August 1929 the highlight of the season of plays at the Festival Theatre, Malvern, was a new offering from George Bernard Shaw. *The Apple Cart* has lasted less well than some of Shaw's other plays, and is rarely performed nowadays. But at the time it caused a minor sensation. It was popular in Poland, where the king at the centre of the action was thought to be based upon the local hero, Marshal Pilsudski, the nationalist hero who occupies much the same role in the country's history as Churchill does in that of Britain. But a production in Dresden was banned, as an affront to democracy.[1] In Britain, the play disappointed figures on the left, because it turned upon the king being something more than a constitutional glove puppet.

The drama was set at some date in the foreseeable future when, Shaw prophesied, politics would have become such a discredited trade that no one of ability or honour would make it his life's work. The true rulers of the nation were neither politicians nor monarch, but the plutocrats who controlled big business. 'Money talks: money prints: money broadcasts: money reigns; and kings and labour leaders alike have to register its decrees, and even, by a staggering paradox, to finance its enterprises and guarantee its profits. Democracy is no longer bought: it is bilked.'[2] In the age of Stalin, Hitler and Mussolini, the play imagined a future in which parliament had become a playground for egotistical lightweights and ruthless charlatans. The drama is a tussle for such scraps of power as remain between King Magnus on one side and, on the other, the Prime Minister, Proteus, and his tribune-of-the-people cabinet colleague Bill Boanerges – an orphan 'picked up from the gutter by a policeman with his eye on the first presidency in an English republic'.

Magnus sees himself as a repository for values that find no expression in the tawdry trade of politics. In a declaration any modern monarch might wish they had made he proclaims:

> I stand for the future and the past, for the posterity that has no vote and the tradition that never had any. I stand for the great abstractions: for conscience and virtue; for the eternal against the expedient; for the evolutionary appetite against the day's gluttony; for intellectual integrity, for humanity, for the rescue of industry from commercialism and of science from professionalism, for everything that you desire as sincerely as I, but which in you is held in leash by the Press, which can organize against you the ignorance and superstition, the timidity and credulity, the gullibility and prudery, the hating and the hunting instinct of the voting mob, and cast you down from power if you utter a word to alarm or displease the adventurers who have the Press in their pockets. Between you and that tyranny stands the throne.[3]

How Prince Charles must dream of speechwriters of Shaw's calibre, for here is precisely what modern kings and queens think to be their role, as some sort of lightning conductor for the unarticulated or obstructed wishes of the people. Even Kaiser Wilhelm II of Germany had the same idea. When Bismarck told him that there was a chance he might have to lead his army against revolutionary socialists, he claimed to have replied that, on the contrary, he would rather be king of the rabble.

But the politicians in Shaw's play are unmoved. They demand that the king yield. As a man who respects the constitution Magnus recognizes he is obliged to do so. But then the king upsets the apple cart suggested in the play's title. He declares that he will abdicate and let his son succeed to the throne. His final act as king will be to dissolve parliament and clear the way for a general election. He will then stand as a candidate in the Windsor constituency. The new king will have to ask someone to form a government who commands the support of the House of Commons. Seeing the relative popularity of king and politicians, it is likely to be Magnus. Collapse of stout party.

This conviction that kings and queens are the expression of something more profound than mere day-to-day politics is the key to their self-esteem. The royal 'we' carries the conviction not only that the individual monarch is too grand to have personal feelings like the rest of us, but that he or she is the embodiment of the nation: 'we' is all of us. It is for this reason that lineage is important. Before Prince Charles had even been born, his bloodline had already been carefully plotted, to demonstrate that he was descended from William the Conqueror and Alfred the Great, was authentically Scottish – ancestors included Robert the Bruce and Mary Queen of Scots – and was descended both from the ancient kings of Ireland and from the Welsh national hero, Owen Glendower. 'From every point of view,' enthused a biographer, 'the baby was truly a prince of the United Kingdom.'[4] If this seems an awfully big burden to be carried by a mortal of a mere 7lb 6oz, it is worth remembering that every one of his future subjects could have demonstrated similarly ancient lineage, had genealogists taken comparable pains to record it. (There was a great deal less emphasis on the fact that, because British royalty has so often found it necessary to replenish itself with continental blood, he might as easily have been shown to be authentically German.)

The question of 'blood' nationality had come to a head during the First World War, for obvious reasons. Privately, David Lloyd George talked of going to Buckingham Palace to consult the king with the words, 'I wonder what my little German friend has got to say to me.'[5] Not unnaturally, whenever George V heard of these mutterings, he was furious. To H. G. Wells's talk of the king's 'alien and uninspiring Court', George retorted, 'I may be dull, but I'm damned if I am an alien.'[6] Bending to public pressure, he first had the banners of his German relatives taken down from their places in St George's Chapel at Windsor Castle, then abandoned the dynastic name of Saxe-Coburg-Gotha, which had been Prince Albert's legacy. Numerous possible alternatives were considered, from Tudor-Stuart, through Plantagenet, York, Lancaster, England and even, oddly, FitzRoy (odd because 'Fitz' signifies illegitimacy) and D'Este – the name taken by the illegitimate family of a son of George III. In the end, George's family became the House of Windsor, with various Teck and Battenberg relatives renamed, like a train of attendant lords in a Shakespearean history play, Mountbatten, Cambridge, Athlone, Milford Haven and Carisbrooke. When told of the gesture, the Kaiser let it be known that he looked forward to attending a performance of *The Merry Wives of Saxe-Coburg-Gotha*.[7]

In the fullness of time, the claim to be the child of the nation matures into a conviction that you are the mother or father of the nation. The belief seems to date back to the second century BC, when the Roman senate accorded the the Emperor Augustus the title *Pater Patriae*. Its convenience is that it suggests natural authority where none may exist, while at the same time sounding friendly, familiar and legitimate. For example, as the British constructed their empire, it was particularly useful in attempting to persuade foreigners, who had nothing in common with the men with red coats and deadly weapons, that everything was just as it should be. Soon after the death of Queen Victoria in 1901, the future George V was sent to Canada. There the government organized a 'Great Pow-wow' with the leaders of the peoples who had been living there for centuries before the prince's ancestors had any idea where Canada was. After the Native American chiefs had declared their loyalty the prince replied that he was well aware of their attachment to Queen Victoria, 'the great mother who loved you so much and whose loss makes your hearts bleed and tears to fill your eyes'. When times had been hard, he reminded them, 'the great mother listened to you and stretched forth her hands to help you'. The new king (Edward VII) felt that he could 'regard you as faithful children of the grand empire of which you form part'.[8]

The contemporary contrast is with King Leopold of the Belgians, the 'king-sovereign' of the Congo, an enormous slave colony (it was over seventy times the size of his own country), from which he extorted vast wealth. He had an army of thugs who cut the arms off men, women and children if they failed to deliver to his agents the quantities of raw rubber they expected. Nobody knows how many millions died to gratify his greed and glorify the monarchy of his invented state. The British had accumulated an empire for the usual combination of motives – greed, political and religious conviction, military and diplomatic necessity, and because they could do so – and it would be foolish to suggest that their administration was entirely altruistic. But one of the differences was in the empire's relationship with royalty.

By the early twentieth century, despite their German origins, British royalty had taken on the conviction that the continent of Europe was a troublesome, complicated and often distasteful place. Queen Elizabeth II speaks good French. But George V refused to learn the language and on one private journey through France instructed the British Ambassador to arrange his programme in a way that would 'avoid all contact with Frenchmen'.[9] His eldest son, who later became Edward VIII, sent his mistress some photographs of a visit to Italy. 'Aren't they an ugly crowd?' he scribbled, '& isn't that a terrible man with the big black beard!! But I'm sorry to say it's a pretty typical crowd of "dagoes"!!!!'[10]

Yet every visit to a Commonwealth country seems to involve a display of 'traditional dancing' or spear-shaking and the British royal family rarely seems bored by it. Perhaps it is no more than their training. But there seems also an instinctive assumption that somehow royalty is better understood in tribal societies than in those with an invented modern constitution. 'Apart from family picnics at Balmoral, the queen always strikes me as at her most relaxed when she's in the company of Commonwealth leaders,' one courtier says. 'She seems genuinely happy and informal.' Without the queen as its champion, that rather dull but worthy organization the Commonwealth would almost certainly have fallen apart long ago. The former Secretary General of the organization, Chief Emeka Anyaoku – himself minor Nigerian royalty – claimed that it was only the direct intervention of Buckingham Palace which prevented a deep rift, and possible disintegration, over the Rhodesia Crisis.[11] If the organization were to fall apart, it would not set off a period of national mourning in Britain, where it is generally seen as a pointless hangover from empire in which third-rate Third World despots presume to hector the properly elected leaders of democracies. An alternative point of view might be to see it as an organization which tries to promote better international relations – if in a low-key and pedestrian style – as a good thing in itself. But it is certainly true that the royal family have a stronger faith in it than their citizens have.

This may be because, in style and tone, the British empire was a *royal* empire. It was hugely hierarchical, festooned with 'royal' decorations, stars and medals of one kind or another, and celebrated in lavish royal rituals, at the grandest of which, Victoria's Golden and Diamond Jubilees, the 'Empress of India' was escorted by legions of troops from all the colonies of the empire. In return, members of the royal family made majestic visits to the dominions (the precursors of today's royal tours) in which the monarch, or a member of the family, 'took possession' of 'their' property.

The British had also understood relatively early that if their empire was to survive and prosper they needed somehow to knit existing social hierarchies into one over-arching system, at the centre of which would sit the king or queen in London. They had learned from the experience of the American colonies the dangers of allowing citizens to think that there were alternative ways of organizing themselves. Henceforth, the plan was to foster 'a due deference and homage to superiors' and the degree of 'subordination necessary to civilized society'.[12] By the late eighteenth century, the notion of binding local social structures into the British empire had taken root in areas of expansion from Africa to Asia. In places like Canada and Australia, which would later become the 'white Commonwealth', there were proposals to create local settler aristocracies, even replica Houses of Lords. But elsewhere a policy of eradicating the natives was neither practicable nor desirable. As the historian David Cannadine has demonstrated, this inevitably involved acknowledging the status of existing rulers.[13] In India, the five hundred maharajas and rajas, nawabs and nizams of the 'princely states' responded to recognition and protection by the British empire – at the minimal inconvenience of the presence of advisers from the Indian political service – by building themselves new palaces, designing new costumes, adorning themselves with new jewellery and staging elaborate 'durbars', or public audiences, to show themselves off to their subjects. By the late nineteenth century, a policy of management through local rulers became the only practicable method for administering the now enormous empire. Where there was no suitable, undisputed princely ruler, the British simply invented one – hence Winston Churchill's claim that the Emir Abdullah, in Jordan, was 'one of my creations'.[14]

Once accepted by the British, these rulers became members of a club or trade union, invited to Windsor or Balmoral, granted audiences and attending coronations. This majestic freemasonry was one of the devices which kept the empire together. Doubtless, had the British been living under another system of government, some alternative would have been invented. But the fact that their colonizers boasted of their queen fed the vanity of local chiefs. Having made the great journey to attend the coronation of Edward VII, King Lewanika of Barotseland, a little British protectorate in southern Africa, remarked grandly, 'When kings are seated together, there is never a lack of things to discuss.'[15] Imperial courtiers might have smiled behind their hands at the comparison. But once you strip away all the other elements – military, religious or political – is the central proposition of a belief in monarchy really any different from tribalism?

Today the tours in which the tribal leaders present themselves to other tribes – and the visited nation displays itself in return – are planned down to the last detail, in a flurry of emails, telephone calls and reconnaissance visits with everything precisely timetabled from the morning departure to the evening firework display. Comprehensive briefing papers are issued, covering everything from autographs (not normally given), through the order in which cars will travel in processions, favourite colours ('Her Majesty has no marked preferences. The Queen, however, does not like magenta'), food ('Neither the Queen nor the Duke of Edinburgh likes oysters') to presents ('live animals are not accepted').[16]

The custom of giving gifts to the person who has everything is deeply ingrained. They range from gestures of fealty to demonstrations of accomplishment ('look at what we've made!'). One of the most famous gifts – from the people of Britain rather than one of the colonies – is the enormous doll's house designed for Queen Mary, with its tiny taps flowing with real water, minuscule linen tablecloths woven in Belfast, miniature books handwritten by authors of the age from Conan Doyle to Somerset Maugham, and a little gramophone in the nursery which played 'God Save the King'. But what was the point of it? The queen was a grown woman at the time. George V's biographer, Kenneth Rose, remarks that 'The Queen was captivated by the diminutive, a taste shared by most of the crowned heads of Europe,'[17] but makes nothing more of the fact. Perhaps there is nothing more to be said. But among children, a delight in the miniature is the most effective demonstration of a sense of superiority or control.[18]

On tours overseas Queen Elizabeth II found herself on various occasions presented with a crocodile in a biscuit tin; a giant tortoise; a boa constrictor; a bear, a baby elephant and a hundred avocado pears; a bale of cotton; bunches of bananas; tins of sugar; a forest by the waters of Lake Galilee; toys; a consignment of one hundred hot dogs (with mustard) and a nylon bikini. But for sheer disparity few exchanges of gifts match that between the then Prince of Wales (later to be Edward VII) and the nine-year-old Prince of Baroda, on a visit to India in 1875–6. Among other presents, the boy gave the British prince a pearl necklace with a huge emerald pendant set in gold (for his mother Queen Victoria), a diamond ring (for himself), a magnificent diamond brooch for Princess Alexandra, a solid silver tea service and three swords with gold scabbards, one set with diamonds. In return, the Prince of Wales produced a gold watch, a medal, a snuff box, a book of engravings of Windsor Castle and a few pictures of the British royal family.

What became of many of the jewels acquired by the British Crown in exchange for the royal family's paltry baubles is a minor mystery. The gifts were given to them not as individuals but in their official capacity as kings, queens and princes of the British people. It therefore follows that they are the property of the people. And yet, apart from a necklace of fourteen large diamonds with emerald, pearl and ruby drops, which has been worn by Elizabeth II, and a necklace of vast rubies which was broken up for use in a crown, most is unaccounted for. No formal inventory was made of the gifts received by the prince, and no one seems to have taken the trouble to record what subsequently became of such things as the priceless emerald pendant. Apart from a dagger and a crown, there is no trace of much of the booty in the Royal Collection. There is evidence from what became of other objects that neither Queen Victoria nor the future King Edward was much troubled by trifling distinctions between what was a personal gift and what was given to them in their capacity as head of state. Both Victoria and Edward's wife Alexandra (to say nothing of George V's wife Queen Mary, whose personal avarice was so great that people worried about having her visit for fear of what she might take away with her), thought little of taking stones from jewellery and having them reset in some other form, often recutting them in the process. The fate of much of the jewellery will probably never be known, but the overwhelming likelihood is that it was broken up and distributed to children, friends and royal mistresses.

For most of her reign, Elizabeth II had the use of the royal yacht, *Britannia*, for her overseas visits, with its crew of three hundred in soft-soled shoes, communicating with each other by hand signal, so as not to disturb the royal peace. Despite the inevitable collection of knick-knacks and 1950s chairs – accumulated either by accident or by Prince Philip – the vessel was maintained to immaculate standards. You could see your face in any surface which could be polished into a shine and no one who ever visited the yacht left unimpressed. Even off-duty, the crew were only allowed ashore in a collar and tie.

Its true significance was in what it represented, for no other mode of conveyance so effectively signalled the specialness of royalty. Kings and queens may ride in carriages. But we know that they are merely making a showy little journey in consciously antique style. Aboard *Britannia* royalty could visit other countries without ever really leaving their own. But the yacht – the very idea of having a royal vessel on such a scale – belonged to another age, when Hohenzollerns and Romanovs tried to outdo each other in grandeur and the British empire was spread across the globe. It was fitting that *Britannia*'s last great international appearance should have been decades later in the harbour at Hong Kong as the base from which Prince Charles could watch the British flag hauled down and the colony returned to Chinese rule.

The culprit, if that is the right word, was John Major, who protested publicly that he had wanted to build a new royal yacht, yet for over two years failed to do anything much about it. As his government clanked its way towards a general election, like a broken-down old car with smoke billowing out of its engine and bits falling off, the question of whether there should be a new royal yacht became a matter of increasing political sensitivity. Sensing an opportunity to wrap themselves in the flag, Major's government eventually came out in favour of a replacement. And, inevitably, when Labour won power in 1997, they cancelled the scheme. Major now privately admits that his failure to act was a mistake, as was the fact that the replacement royal yacht was never built.

Elizabeth thus became the first British monarch since Charles II not to have an official yacht. It was not just that air travel had become a more sensible way of covering the world. Nor was it even an increased preoccupation with value for money: the Labour government which refused to spend £60 million on a replacement for *Britannia* was thrilled to throw £750 million away on a Teflon-coated dome in Greenwich to mark the turn of the millennium. What had really changed was the politicians' perception of how the people felt about their monarchy.

All heads of state cost money. Once the politicians had removed their right to raise their own taxes, they became dependent upon the state. The question which then inevitably arises is 'What are they worth?' The Roman architect Vitruvius explained that emperors needed imposing buildings 'to add lustre to their importance'.[19] The belief holds as much force in modern republics as in constitutional monarchies: the presidents of the United States and France demand millions from their fellow citizens because the grandeur of their lives is claimed to express the dignity of the entire nation. Perhaps so. But it is the citizens who must pay for it. When things are going well, it may be relatively easy to persuade them that they should surrender their taxes to enable the royal family to live a grander life than they themselves could ever aspire to – because, the argument goes, a shabby monarch (or president, come to that) reflects a shabby nation. But, in return, those who pay the taxes expect their royalty to make them feel good about themselves. The Windsors' misfortune when it came to building a replacement for the royal yacht was that the decision had to be taken in the 1990s, which had been the worst decade for British royalty for a century. An assiduously cultivated image of an ideal family had been exploded. The marriages of three of the queen's four children had collapsed and the heir to the throne and his wife had both made televised confessions of adultery. The queen seemed remote and out of touch, the heir callous and selfish. Even her castle at Windsor had caught fire. Only a government as detached from public opinion as that of John Major could have come to believe that promising more public money to the royal family would be a way to the public's heart.

The Emperor Vespasian famously taxed the urine collected at public lavatories and, when his son Titus questioned him, presented him with a coin and asked, 'Does it smell?' Public ignorance about the royal finances in Britain is profound. That has been how the royal household likes it. Occasional issues, like building a replacement for *Britannia*, show how bitterly embarrassing arguments over money can be. There are two questions to be asked of the House of Windsor's finances. How much are they worth? And how much do they cost? It cannot be an accident that neither can be answered easily.

Although they are enormously wealthy by the standards of their citizens, by most international or historical standards the House of Windsor is of comparatively modest means. The really deep pockets belong to kings like the Sultan of Brunei and Kaiser Wilhelm II of Germany, whose property included several dozen palaces and castles – including the 650-room Berlin Palace – three theatres and enormous estates, making him the richest man in Germany. Tsar Nicholas II of Russia was said to own personally 70 per cent of the country's land, which at the time of his abdication an excited *New York Times* estimated to be almost one-tenth of the earth's surface. By contrast, Queen Elizabeth seems a church mouse. She does not feature on the *Forbes* list of the world's richest people. An estimate by the *Sunday Times* put her fortune at £4 billion in the early 1990s. A little over a decade later the paper had reduced the assessment to £250 million, because her supporters had effectively argued that since her palaces and the like were merely 'held in trust for the nation' and not disposable, they therefore had no real monetary value. The proposition has never been tested in the courts, but it is hard to believe that the royal family could not make a claim to legal ownership. The Royal Collection of Old Masters, miniatures, sculpture, gems and other treasures cannot technically be sold or bequeathed to anyone other than the next sovereign. But while it may be true that the art collections and the Crown Jewels are made available (at an admission fee) to the public who theoretically own them, the queen and her family have almost exclusive rights to their enjoyment and use. The list of the queen's 'inalienable' assets produced by Buckingham Palace includes her jewellery, much of it inherited from Queen Mary. There is no proper catalogue of this collection. But a radical could argue – with some justice – that, since much of it has been acquired in the course of royal duty, it is rightly the property of the people. Yet a significant number of these pieces have been seen and photographed on royal mistresses like Wallis Simpson or old retainers like 'Bobo' Macdonald.

By comparison with continental spendthrifts the modern British royal family have been relatively abstemious. The last British monarch to spend truly profligately was George IV, although even with his vast tailors' bills and opulent interior decoration, it is hard to work out quite how he could have spent as much money as he did.[20] No modern British monarch has had the taste for the suffocating opulence of Louis XIV's Versailles, where a clock struck the hours by causing a statue of the king to emerge, on which Fame descended to crown him with laurel, and where the pure white lambs on Marie Antoinette's model farm were sprayed daily with eau de Cologne.

The endless gloomy corridors of Buckingham Palace are another matter altogether. They may be carpeted in red and spotlessly maintained, but, for all that, they have the air of a slightly dingy town hall. Most of the building is offices anyway, and the private quarters on the upper floors, many of them furnished with 1960s tables and chairs, are hardly grand. Walking down one of the corridors at the front of the building you are likely to trip over a giant teddy bear, over a red plastic Porsche left by a grandchild or even over a photocopier. The *Daily Mirror*'s 2003 infiltration of an undercover reporter into a job as a footman revealed a world in which Queen Elizabeth and Prince Philip ate their breakfast from Tupperware containers while listening to a portable radio. None of the royal family likes the place much, which is why they escape whenever they can to the apartments in Windsor Castle, to Sandringham or Balmoral. (They are not the first to find it gloomy: William IV could hardly contain his glee when the Houses of Parliament burned down in 1834, because he believed he might be able to palm Buckingham Palace off on the politicians as a replacement.)

Buckingham Palace does not belong to the royal family. Neither do other royal residences like St James's Palace, Clarence House or Windsor Castle. The Windsors' personal possessions, such as Victoria and Albert's beloved Balmoral and Edward and Alexandra's curious Sandringham, are an acquired taste. The Prime Minister Lord Rosebery once said that he thought the drawing room at Osborne, Victoria and Albert's house on the Isle of Wight, was the ugliest in the world, until he saw its counterpart at

Balmoral.[21] Sandringham was described by the fastidious royal biographer James Pope-Hennessy as 'hotel-like – Pitlochry or Strathpeffer perhaps – tremendously vulgar and emphatically, almost defiantly, hideous and gloomy'.[22] This condescending tone is typical of a certain class of snob: Harold Nicolson thought the rooms of the cottage at Sandringham which was home to George V before he took the throne 'indistinguishable from those of any Surbiton or Upper Norwood terrace house'.[23] Much to his wife's irritation, the king furnished the place by buying a selection of tables and chairs from Maples Store.

The personal thriftiness of Queen Elizabeth II is one of the legends of the House of Windsor. Belonging to a generation which lived through the Depression and the Second World War, she was, we were told, accustomed from childhood to squirrelling away pieces of wrapping paper for future use. She was often reported to wander around her palaces switching off the lights. However embellished they may have become in the telling, these stories had a ring of plausibility about them and helped to disarm republican critics when the question arose of how much taxpayers' money royalty cost. When Buckingham Palace published accounts in the summer of 2006 showing how much public money was spent on the royal family, it claimed that the monarchy cost each citizen 62 pence a year. The figure was duly incorporated into every newspaper account of the finances, usually with the comparison – also supplied by the palace – that this was the equivalent of one minute's worth of a ticket to see one of the World Cup soccer matches then being played in Germany.

But on this second question – the true expense of the monarchy – things are almost as complicated as attempts to establish precisely what the Windsors own. The most transparent of the arrangements is the Civil List, which began in 1689 when the House of Commons resolved that the king should be given a grant to pay for the upkeep of his household. The bulk of the almost £11 million a year now given to the royal household is spent on staff salaries, garden parties, cleaning expenses, uniforms and so on. Friends of the monarchy argue that it is an arrangement which actually benefits the taxpayer, since for the last two and a half centuries the Exchequer has received in exchange the enormous income from the king's or queen's hereditary feudal estates, which in 2005–6 alone was claimed by Buckingham Palace to be worth £190.8 million. But then it all becomes much more labyrinthine. There are the other sources of public money, like the Grants-in-Aid, to pay for the upkeep of numerous palaces,[24] communication and travel expenses (nearly £6 million in 2005–6), the income from the Duchy of Lancaster which funds the Privy Purse, and the parliamentary annuities to other members of the royal family.

There was something of a public relations coup for the palace in 1992 when it was trumpeted that Queen Elizabeth would submit herself to the burden endured by her citizens and pay direct taxes. But the arrangement does not mean quite all it seems. There is, for example, no tax paid on the Civil List or the Grants-in-Aid, because these sources of income are claimed not to be remuneration. The Privy Purse has a sum deducted before tax to cover official spending. Inheritance tax is not charged on bequests from one sovereign to another, or from sovereign's consort to sovereign, so that private property, including Balmoral and Sandringham, can pass from generation to generation. This arrangement is said to be justified because a king or queen cannot start a new business to generate wealth and 'must have, and be seen to have, an appropriate degree of financial independence'.[25] This explanation has a faint whiff of cant about it. It might as well be argued – and was when Queen Anne was prevented from selling Crown lands[26] that financial independence is potentially risky for the state because it frees the monarch from accountability. The profitability of the Prince of Wales's business ventures has demonstrated that the Windsors are not inoculated against commercial success. When it comes to Balmoral and Sandringham, which are privately owned and yet are passed on without the payment of inheritance tax, the arguments expire in tortuousness.[27]

Yet these arguments matter. The political arguments for replacing an unelected head of state with a president are dry and complex. Value for money – how much of their subjects' taxes they should be entitled to – is not. Republicans know that constitutional reform may not be much discussed in the nation's sitting rooms and workplaces. But if the royal family come to be seen as a bunch of wastrels, indulged at the expense of the citizens, they are on the way out.

Even devoted campaigners against monarchy admit that their movement has no fizz and has failed to find any real place in modern Britain. The republican cause may be less marginalized than the Flat Earth Society, but it has much less presence than the battle for animal rights. It has few advocates among the country's politicians, and it features in none of the manifestos of the major parties. Given the well-established political practice of discovering what people would like and then offering it to them, we can be confident that if public opinion were to change, the parties would soon reflect that. As it is, faith in pure democracy, with the king or queen replaced by an elected head of state, remains a minority pursuit. Even during the 1990s, when the British monarchy seemed so embattled, the number of people telling opinion pollsters that they would vote in a referendum in favour of replacing it with a republic was no more than one in five. Three-quarters of those surveyed said they were satisfied with the way the queen was doing her job.[28] 'The level of support for Britain becoming a republic is as constant a trend line as I have ever seen – anywhere in the world,' says the opinion pollster Bob Worcester.

'Republicans are edged into such an absurd cul-de-sac because there is no effective space for them in the public arena,' complained the Marxist Tom Nairn, in his perceptive analysis of monarchy in the late 1980s. 'There is no serious Republican campaign or movement, no Republican press, and no recognized or avowable anti-Monarchic stance in everyday argument and debate. It is this climatic fact that defines Republicanism from its first syllable as posture and wilful eccentricity.'[29] It was, in short, a hobby for cranks. Much the same applies today. One or two national newspapers – notably the *Guardian* – have since adopted the republican creed, but it is noticeable that most of those who profess hair-shirted republican purity at the start of their political careers have abandoned or at least hidden it by the time they reach high office. Few seem to have got to grips with the fact that, for all its inherent absurdity and illegitimacy, monarchy continues to give off what Nairn called 'an apparently inexhaustible electric charge'. They are all big on disdain though.

Why should Britain have remained immune to a more common-sense way of organizing its affairs? It is a question which republicans often answer by talking about the propaganda available to the monarchy ('The keeper of the British conscience is the BBC, which does not permit free speech about religion or monarchy,' said the *New Statesman* editor Kingsley Martin in the early 1960s).[30] But this will not quite do. There are deeper forces at work. At much the same time, after decades studying the Shakespearean theme of kingship, the literary scholar G. Wilson Knight decided that, as it existed in Britain, 'the Crown is not part of our system; it encloses it. It is both heart and aura of the nation's body, at once soul and whole. It belongs to a category, or dimension, notoriously difficult to define, and indeed scarcely susceptible of any but a poetic and dramatic treatment.'[31] One only has to look at monarchy's symbolic role in institutions from parliament, through the law and the Church to the armed services and even the prisons of Britain (where young inmates can be detained 'during her Majesty's pleasure'), to find this picture plausible. The British state was formed by the union of kingdoms, and there is simply no way of understanding it without recognizing the significance of monarchy. But history alone does not quite answer the question of why the monarchy should enjoy apparent stability in the twenty-first century.

It has been this way for a long time. When political unrest swept Europe like a firestorm in 1848, the *Edinburgh Review* talked of 'revolutions which have threatened to subvert the constitution and the relations of every state, except our own'.[32] Set against the mayhem which carried away the monarchies of much of the rest of Europe, with Hungary in revolt and the French, Bavarian and Austrian thrones toppled, the British disturbances were a civilized affair. *The Times* described how a demonstration in central London smashed a few windows of the Reform Club and 'occasionally shouted for a Republic, not knowing what it was'.[33] It did not get much more threatening. The *Court Journal* astutely read the intrinsic, pragmatic conservatism of the people: while 'there can be no doubt of the Republic being the *ideal* of a human government . . . England asks herself what she could gain under a republican form of government, that she may not gain under that which she possesses; and what she may, or rather, what she must lose by the change'.[34] In short, was it worth overthrowing the Crown?

This is not to say that there were not strongly held (and expressed) republican sentiments, as the very widely sold *Reynolds's Newspaper* testified in 1855. The spirit of the 1848 revolutions was still alive. 'Before freedom can smile upon mankind, or justice re-descend from heaven, royalty, root and branch, must be extirpated from the soil . . . The truth is, that monarchs are a perpetual menace to mankind; and as long as royalty exists in any country, the people can have no security that they shall not, in one moment, be plunged into calamities, from which oceans of blood and centuries of toil will not be able to redeem them.'[35] How the writer must have smacked his palms after such a dreadful warning of the coming apocalypse. But three years later he was driven to despair by the stupidity of the British people. The nation was transfixed by the marriage of Queen Victoria's eldest child, the Princess Royal, to the heir to the throne of Prussia. *Reynolds's Newspaper* groaned.

> If the poor people who flock like sheep to do homage to their oppressors . . . knew that their presence in such crowds along the line of the royal wedding procession, would be twisted into an expression of their indifference to reform, and of their approbation of Court robbery and extravagance, it is not surely too much to assume that they would have stayed at home . . . where no such political construction could be put on their presence.[36]

There were better days ahead for republicans, though. By 1869, the economy was in trouble and over one million people were receiving poor relief. At the same time, Victoria's enormous family seemed perpetually to be squawking for more money. There was, for example, a request for a £30,000 dowry to enable her daughter, Princess Louise, to marry the Marquess of Lorne, to be followed by an allowance of £6,000 a year. These demands did not sit happily with widespread poverty, and later spawned the maxim coined by the Scottish radical J. M. Davidson that 'hereditary royalty, at the top of society, necessarily implies hereditary poverty at the base'.[37] Both the princess and her intended husband came from immensely wealthy families, and neither was obliged to perform much in the way of public duties. But the *Spectator* leaped to their defence. There might well be worthwhile arguments against monarchy, but its expense was not one of them. The British was one of the most economical royal families in Europe, and:

> The Princess is a daughter of England, and must have such dowry as befits England to give . . . It is not by false statements as to the cost of the Monarchy or by dirty little snippings at the gold fringe on its robe that the cause of liberalism . . . ought to be promoted. The Throne may be an injury, or a surplusage, or an anachronism, but at least let us sneer down the men who, keeping the Throne as a symbol, would substitute for its covering cotton velvet.[38]

As we shall see, this haughty defence intuited the essential flaw in republican agitation, that while the cost of monarchy might be a useful recruiting sergeant for the cause, it was neither here nor there in the important political argument. Victoria was, anyway, busy building up the fortune which would one day see her successors listed as among the richest people in the world. The Hanoverians were not a wealthy dynasty when she took the throne. But by the time she died she had managed to appropriate for her personal use a substantial sum from the Civil List, and had had the very good fortune to be bequeathed almost the entire estate of John Camden Neild. Mr Neild, a short man in patched and tattered clothes, was a miser of such prodigious commitment that for some time he did not even buy a bed to sleep on in his house in Cheyne

Walk, Chelsea. He built up a large property portfolio across the Home Counties, and travelled to visit his possessions either on foot or on the outside of public stagecoaches. When he died in 1852, he left almost his entire estate of £500,000 (about £35 million at today's values) to her Most Gracious Majesty, who promptly set about investing it well.

After the death of her beloved Albert, Victoria was not only increasingly wealthy, but also increasingly unseen, wrapped in her widow's weeds at Balmoral or Osborne, and untroubled by tiresome duties like opening parliament or entertaining foreign dignitaries. Wealthy eminence and public invisibility were a highly combustible mixture, and the man to set the spark was Sir Charles Wentworth Dilke, one of the most intriguing characters in Victorian politics. Dilke's hatred of Napoleon III and a vague sentiment about the natural affinity between England and Germany had led him and two other MPs to enlist in the ambulance corps attached to the Crown Prince of Prussia during the Franco-Prussian War. Although it was a post he deserted after seeing action in several battles, he survived to see the fall of the French Second Empire and the birth of the Republic. He returned to England wearing a red tie and breathing defiance.

The overthrow of Louis Napoleon and the declaration of a French republic in September 1870 sent shivers down the spines of British royalty. Victoria was horrified, telling her diary that she had 'heard that the mob at Paris had rushed into the Senate and proclaimed the downfall of the dynasty, proclaiming a Republic! . . . Not one voice was raised in favour of the unfortunate Emperor! How ungrateful!'[39] One hundred or so Republican Clubs sprang up in Britain. Although Dilke coined the memorable epigram 'I am of the opinion that a Constitutional Monarchy is a good Government for children, and that a Republic is a good Government for grown men,' by his own admission he was no great orator. Yet his attacks on the British royal family could exploit a widespread sense that they were a tribe of parasites. In the strict sense this may not have been true republicanism, which objects to a hereditary head of state whether they travel by gold-plated

Rolls-Royce or on roller-skates. But it was alarming enough to the Crown.

In the autumn of 1871 Dilke began a series of public meetings arguing for a redistribution of seats in parliament, and then, through an attack on Princess Louise's dowry, to a broader assault on the institution of monarchy. It was, he said, wasteful, corrupt and, insofar as it provided incompetent senior officers for the armed forces, dangerous to the nation. In Newcastle upon Tyne on 6 November, he ended his speech with the words 'If you show me a fair chance that a republic here will be free from the political corruption which hangs about the monarchy, I say, for my part – and I believe that the middle classes in general will say – let it come.'[40] When *The Times* reported this speech, three days later, there was a fit of the vapours across the land. The paper's editorial accused him of 'recklessness bordering on criminality'. The wife of the Master of Trinity Hall, Cambridge disclosed that she had nursed her father on his deathbed, had seen the dying agonies of two sisters, and the death of a brother, but she had never been as distressed as she was by Dilke's remarks. In clubs and country houses they harrumphed that the man should be shot.

None of this was, of course, a reasoned response to Dilke's critique. What saved the institution from further scrutiny was not a reasoned defence but the great ally of monarchy, sentiment. On the very day that *The Times* reported Dilke's speech, the Prince of Wales fell ill at Sandringham with typhoid fever, the disease which had killed his father. The prince's most notable public appearance might have been in the witness box, when he had been cited as a co-respondent in a divorce case, but he *was* the heir to the throne. It became hard for Dilke to stomp around the countryside lambasting the monarchy for its profligacy while a series of reports issued from Sandringham that the queen's eldest son might be at death's door. Dilke's meetings were regularly disrupted by crowds incited by placards which invited them to 'rally to support the throne . . . Let it be seen that you are true-born Englishmen, and refuse a hearing to any man who preaches sedition and treason.'[41] When Dilke appeared in Bolton there was a full-scale riot, with windows smashed, furniture broken and one man dying of his injuries. The announcement on 14 December (the anniversary of his father's death) that the prince was recovering from his illness was sufficient to turn the tide: Edward did more for the monarchy through six weeks of sickness than through thirty years of privileged good health. The monarchists capitalized. On 27 February 1872, a thanksgiving service was organized at St Paul's Cathedral to celebrate his deliverance.

By the time Dilke rose in the House of Commons in March to recite his closely argued but tediously delivered speech (as he put it, thirty-eight 'unutterably dull' columns in Hansard), the die was cast. Gladstone tore into him, but the effort was unnecessary. Dilke's political argument had been swept aside by a torrent of collective emotion. As the *Manchester Guardian* reported, his arguments 'proved so far convincing' that 'he carried with him into the lobby only just so many followers as he could have carried away with him inside a cab'.[42] He was defeated by 276 votes to a paltry 2. Republicanism in parliament was dead. Dilke gave up his campaign, having discovered that attacking the monarchy did nothing to advance radicalism. Later, he reflected that his comments on the cost of the court 'were accurate, though possibly unwise'.[43] Republicanism grew factionalized and withered. Though she had survived the storm (not that there had ever been much chance of her succumbing to it) Queen Victoria nourished her dislike of those places where the republican zephyrs had begun. She declined to open the new town hall in Manchester in 1877, although whether it was because the new mayor had once supported the Chartist campaign to make parliament more representative or because the city had erected a statue to Oliver Cromwell was unclear.

Elsewhere the salvoes from the republicans continued. Whatever the lack of support in parliament, the anonymous author of *Republicanism in England and the Fall of the British Empire* claimed that 1880 'may be regarded as marking the dawn of Republicanism in England'.[44] J. M. Davidson's *New Book of Kings*, a popular (and rather well-researched) 'horrible history', went through edition after edition throughout the 1880s and 1890s. It was full of damning indictments of past monarchs and continued robustly to point out that the queen did nothing to earn either her salary or her status.[45]

These tenants of the State are the worst imaginable. They are about twenty degrees worse than the worst Irish tenants ever known. They not merely pay no rent, but they recklessly destroy their land-lord's property . . . Is there a Socialist working man in Soho or Clerkenwell who ever in his wildest dreams made such heavy demands on the State as these insatiable Guelphs, whose muddy German 'blood' constitutes their sole claim to public consideration?[46]

Radicals like Charles Bradlaugh and Annie Besant kept up the bombardment, by focusing again on the money issue. Bradlaugh's *The Impeachment of the House of Brunswick* battered away at the royal family's wealth: 'Her Majesty is now enormously rich, and – as she is like her Royal grandmother – grows richer daily. She is also generous, and has recently given not quite half a day's income to the starving poor of India. A few months prior to this many thousands of pounds were wasted in formally proclaiming her imperial.'[47] Annie Besant added that the sheer size of the family and their hangers-on meant a fortune was being spent on allowances, pensions and sinecures. The solution was for an act of parliament to remove the royal family from the throne.[48]

In middle age, Annie Besant became a disciple of Madame Blavatsky's Theosophical Society. While republicanism may not have sailed quite as far over the horizon as theosophy, it has hardly become more central to national life. In 1911, Ramsay MacDonald remarked that republican sentiments in socialist tracts were merely 'some interesting survivals of a historic past',[49] and while the left disliked Edward VII's friendship with Tsar Nicholas II, they did not hold him personally responsible for the fact that the Russian revolutionaries of 1905 had been so harshly treated. In the end, of course, it was the tsar who perished, in the great extinguishing of kingship in the twentieth century. The Chinese, German and Austrian emperors went too, as did the kings of Portugal and Italy, to say nothing of the bemedalled martinets of less significant states. Although Edward VII once introduced his son to a guest with the words 'Let me present to you the last King of England,'[50] the intriguing question is why the British monarchy did not suffer a similar fate.

What royalty feared was being found out. If any organization was going to undermine the foundations of precedence in an age of mass democracy, it ought to have been the newly formed Labour Party. People like Charles Dilke had been on shaky ground attacking the hereditary principle when they were themselves hereditary baronets. But a politically powerful working class was another matter. The Russian revolution of 1917 depressed British royalty hugely. 'I am in despair,' George V wrote in his diary when told that his cousin Tsar Nicholas II had been forced to abdicate.[51] The following year his son, the future Edward VIII, confessed to his mistress that he had been introduced to a 'thoroughly revolting . . . coarse trades unionist', whom he much disliked, 'but one must look on this type as the ruling spirit nowadays . . . All this Bolshevism & revolutionary stuff makes me do a lot of straight thinking & puts the wind up me.'[52]

The burgeoning Labour Party showed every sign of justifying royal anxiety. The movement was built upon the principle of equality of opportunity and there was no better example of an institution built upon inequality of opportunity than the monarchy. Keir Hardie, the cloth-capped founder of the Independent Labour Party, had described the 1902 coronation of Edward VII, which he attended, as 'a meaningless ceremony', witnessed by 'whole rows of fantastic nobodies'.[53] George V was, he said, 'destitute of even ordinary ability'.[54] Hardie was not alone. Contempt for the royal symbol was a necessary part of radicalism. At the Independent Labour Party conference in April 1917, Ramsay MacDonald declared of the Russian revolution that 'a spring tide of joy has broken out all over Europe'.[55] A convention was summoned in Leeds to celebrate, and to begin to 'do for this country what the Russian Revolution has accomplished in Russia'.

It never happened. The flush passed, and within a few years, as membership of the Labour Party grew, animosity towards royalty abated. At the annual party conference in 1923 a private resolution 'That the Royal Family is no longer necessary as part of the British Constitution' garnered under four hundred thousand proxy votes, and was overwhelmingly defeated by the 3,694,000 in support of the king. The breakdown of the vote revealed the fact that republican feeling was much weaker within the trade unions than it was among many of the party's intellectuals.

Nonetheless, when Ramsay MacDonald became the first Labour prime minister the following year, King George must have felt a degree of apprehension. The king was an instinctive reactionary, and a dozen years beforehand had protested to Downing Street after learning that the great naturalist Alfred Russel Wallace OM had declared himself a socialist, on the ground that 'the Order of Merit should not be given to Socialists'.[56] But dynasties do not survive for great lengths of time without recognizing the limits of their competence. If they choose to use it, monarchs often also have, in addition, a formidable ability to charm the birds out of the trees.

MacDonald found the king delightful. 'The king has never seen me as a minister without making me feel he was also seeing me as a friend,' said the new Prime Minister.[57] His trade-unionist comrade J. R. Clynes was bowled over by 'the genial, kindly, considerate personality of George V, a truly constitutional monarch who always put the will of the people nearest his heart'.[58] The king was even prepared to bend on testing matters, like questions of dress. When his ministers attended, George expected them to arrive in a gold-encrusted coat and cocked hat and carrying a sword – wearing knee-breeches if it was an evening engagement. The king was sensitive enough to recognize that the first representatives of the working class to live in 10 Downing Street would be unlikely to have all the props in their wardrobe at home. So his private secretary, Lord Stamfordham, wrote to MacDonald, apologizing for troubling him with such things 'when you are dealing with weighty matters of state' and pointing out that the king was not insistent upon knee-breeches, and suggesting that he might like to hire a few suitable court suits from 'Messrs. Moss Bros., which is, I believe, a well-known and dependable firm'.[59] Perhaps because he had more important things on his mind, MacDonald turned out to be remarkably amenable. He did not hesitate to kiss the royal hand and justified his wearing of court dress to himself with the argument that braids and uniforms were 'but part of official pageantry, and as my conscience is not on my back, a gold coat means nothing to me but a form of dress to be worn or rejected as a hat would be in relation to the rest of one's clothes'.[60]

Not everyone saw it this way. The greatest scorn came from the gently born intellectuals who considered themselves the grandest socialists. Beatrice Webb, daughter of a railway magnate and self-appointed keeper of the radical conscience, called MacDonald 'an egotist, a poseur and a snob'. As evidence, she later cut out a report about him in *The Times*: 'The Prime Minister left Dunrobin Castle yesterday, after his visit to the Duke and Duchess of Sutherland, for Loch Choire, near Lairg, where he will be the guest of the Marquess and Marchioness of Londonderry. It is understood that he will go to Lossiemouth today and will go to Balmoral to-morrow.'[61] Beatrice Webb's friend Leon Trotsky was dismissive of the claim that accepting a role for royalty did not interfere with the building of a socialist state. It was pure 'conservative stupidity', as absurd as claiming to believe in materialistic science and then treating toothache with magic incantations. No society could emerge from serfdom while retaining a belief in kings and queens.

> Of course, the form of dress is only a detail, but the masses simply will not understand – and they are right – why the representatives of the working class should submit to the complicated pomp of monarchic masquerade. And the masses are gradually beginning to learn that those who make mistakes in little things will also be undependable in big things.[62]

As it turned out, over the twentieth century, the British monarchy could hardly have had a better defender than the Labour

Party. Before meeting the king or queen there might be paroxysms of anxiety about whether it was more absurd to bow or curtsey or to make a point of not doing so. When it came to the point of introduction, some suddenly swooped low and others stuck awkwardly to their principles, unsure whether they were being resolute or priggish. In truth it hardly mattered (and, in recent years, the person to whom it has mattered least of all has probably been the monarch). The important point was not the physical genuflection but the psychological recognition.

Looking back, it is surprising that the House of Windsor's greatest emergency did not lead to a bigger swelling of republicanism. For if the institution rests on the claim that there is only one person fit to occupy the role, its justification was seriously undermined by a man turning his back on the post. The paroxysms which engulfed the British ruling class in December 1936 are usually referred to as 'the Abdication Crisis'. But they were more a drama than a crisis. Reading the official papers and the private diaries, what is striking is how, in the end, the king's determination to marry his divorced American mistress came to turn simply on the question of how it might be *managed*. Of course it helped that there was a substitute waiting on the sidelines whom the peoples of the British empire might be persuaded was just as plausible a king, since he had the same parentage as his elder brother. With the usual capacity of the Great and Good for hypocrisy – and a Humpty Dumptyish belief that words merely meant whatever they decreed they meant – a vast constitutional issue was reduced to a matter of practicalities. The man born to be king wasn't up to the job. Very well, then, someone else would have it.

But why did it not provide the republican cause with the perfect opportunity to remove the Crown altogether? The Conservative Prime Minister Stanley Baldwin opened the House of Commons debate on the afternoon of 10 December 1936 with a long speech full of words like 'perturbation' and 'anxiety'. He asserted that while the monarchy might have been stripped of many of its powers 'it stands for far more than it ever has done in its history'. It therefore followed that 'no more grave message has ever been received by Parliament' than the king's letter indicating his intention to resign the throne. His task as prime minister was 'difficult, I may almost say repugnant'. He explained that, although the king was a friend of his, he had had to tell him that the marriage he was planning 'would not receive the approbation of the country'. The king had asked whether he might marry Mrs Simpson, without her becoming queen, but after discussing it Baldwin had told him it was quite impossible for the king's wife to be anything other than the queen.[63]

The Labour leader, Clement Attlee, offered sympathy to the feckless king's mother and expressed the hope that his replacement might have a slightly simpler style, to bind him to his people more closely. Sir Archibald Sinclair told of how his little band of Liberal MPs were 'grief-stricken'. But he agreed that a morganatic marriage, in which the king's wife would not become queen, was out of the question. Those politicians who were least bothered about the king's choice of wife – and might even have preferred him to become engaged to someone who might show up the royal charade – found themselves in an impossible position. There was no true King's Party in parliament, and it would, anyway, have been unthinkable to join it if it existed. As the editor of the *New Statesman* pointed out afterwards,

> those who were least puritanical and most hostile to the Prime Minister were compelled to behave like Roundheads. They detested what they regarded as a hypocritical conspiracy engineered by the Prime Minister, the Editor of the Times and the Archbishop of Canterbury. But if the alternative was an alliance with a twentieth-century royalist party, they had to choose to be parliamentarians.[64]

It was left to a tiny handful of radicals to point to the elephant standing in the middle of the room which everyone else was pretending not to notice. To shouts from all sides of 'No! No!' the 'Red Clydesider' James Maxton claimed that the lesson to be drawn from the proposed marriage was that 'the monarchical system had now outlived its usefulness'. Another Scottish left-winger, George Buchanan, taunted the majority by asking why they kept going on about the admirable qualities of the man who was leaving the throne: 'if he is a tenth as good as you say, why are you not keeping him? Because you know he is a weak creature.' The following day Maxton tabled an amendment, arguing that 'this crack-up of a monarch is not merely just the matter of a failure of a man, but is something deeper and something more fundamental than that – the whole break-up of social conceptions, the whole break-up of past ideas of a Royal Family clear of the ordinary taints and weaknesses of ordinary men'. It was time to stop living in a fool's paradise and sweep the whole institution away.

But yet again the apostles of republicanism failed to appreciate that while a fool's paradise may be foolish, it is also paradisial. The oldest politician in the House, Sir Austen Chamberlain, rose to explain. Chamberlain's political career had never scaled the heights imagined for him by his ambitious father ('Poor man,' said Churchill, looking at him, 'he always plays the game, and never wins it'). But he claimed to be able to intuit the feelings of the Birmingham people he represented in parliament. It was, he said, a constituency of 'poor streets and mean houses, the people living in back courts to a very large extent, all of them very near the hardships and sufferings of life in their cruellest form'. Yet they saw the monarchy not as a castle of privilege but as something transcending class. They believed monarchy to be 'their guardian and their supporter . . . Let it go forth that our king is the people's king, their guardian and supporter.' 'Guardian of what?' asked Willie Gallacher, the Communist MP for West Fife. 'Guardian of their poverty; guardian of their suffering.' When MPs asserted that monarchy was 'an idea deeply cherished', what they meant was that it was 'an idea deeply cultivated'.

Gallacher was a voice crying in the wilderness. Confronted with a crisis in the monarchy, the instinct was to ditch not the institution but the person through whom it was expressed. Outside parliament, the largely conservative press banged the same drum. 'Kingship, as an institution, means much in this land,' wrote the *Spectator*, and it would be no trouble simply to change the king. 'Deep as was the reverence and affection King George inspired, the loyalty he commanded was transferred unimpaired to his eldest son, and it will not weaken under the train of another transfer, if another there must be, even in conditions so abnormal.'[65] Pure republicanism was left in the hands of obsessives. Even on the left, there were more pressing battles to fight. Another Labour MP, who claimed to speak as 'a theoretical republican', put it frankly: 'I am much more seized with abolishing the poor than I am with abolishing the monarchy.' Maxton's amendment, suggesting that the crisis demonstrated the need for the country to do away with an antediluvian system, was defeated by 403 votes to a mere 5.

The crucial element that was missing in this and every subsequent debate about monarchy is something for republicans to get really angry about. The very perceptive – and mildly republican – Spanish princess Eulalia drew a comparison in 1915, when she asked what liberty the British people would acquire by casting off royalty. 'They would gain as little as if, by a popular uprising, the citizens of London killed the lions in their Zoo. There may have been a time when lions were dangerous in England, but the sight of them in their cages now can only give a pleasurable holiday-shudder of awe – of which, I think, the nation will not willingly deprive itself.'[66] This does not make the institution itself inherently any more logical or defensible: it just makes you come to much the same conclusion as those Labour MPs who felt there were more pressing concerns on which they might expend their energy.

Against this acceptance, some republicans became bad-tempered. The most splendidly vitriolic outpouring came in 1957, from the playwright John Osborne in the magazine *Encounter*. It did not matter that the Crown had no power. 'My objection to the royal symbol is that it is dead,' he wrote,

> it is the gold filling in a mouthful of decay. While the cross symbol represented *values*, the crown simply represents a *substitute* for values. When the Roman crowds gather outside St Peter's, they are taking part

in a moral *system*, however detestable it may be. When the mobs rush forwards in the Mall they are taking part in the last circus of a civilisation that has lost faith in itself, and sold itself for a splendid triviality, for the 'beauty of the ceremonial' and the 'essential spirituality of the rite'.

But the pointless devotion cultivated by the BBC's 'highly trained palace lackeys with graveyard voices' was also politically objectionable. Because royalty had been shorn of real power it had been absolved of the need ever to make moral decisions. Its tenacious grip on the public imagination had put it 'not merely above criticism [but] above the necessity of having to justify its existence'.[67]

Against Osborne's invective we may set the judgement of Ernest Jones, psychoanalyst and one-time colleague of Sigmund Freud:

> When the sophisticated pass cynical comments on the remarkable interest the majority of people take in the minute doings of royalty, and still more in the cardinal events of their births, loves, and deaths, they are often merely denying and repudiating a hidden part of their own nature rather than giving evidence of having understood and transcended it. With the others there is no trace of envy, since the illustrious personages are in their imagination their actual selves, their brother or sister, father or mother. In the august stateliness and ceremonial pomp their secret daydreams are at last gratified, and for a moment they are released from the inevitable sordidness and harassing exigencies of mundane existence.[68]

This is the Catch 22: if the tribal function has been at all effective, you cannot begin to question the significance of monarchy without starting to wonder about the purpose of your own existence.

And so, like many a bad marriage, the tensions express themselves in repeated and undignified squabbling about money. Once the principle had been conceded that parliament could determine how much money was spent on the Crown, there was an obvious pressure point for those who either detested the entire institution or merely sought to alter its style. The end of the royal yacht *Britannia* may not have reflected any great republican animus in the country. It was just that in a mass-media age it was a focus for more incoherent feelings of disappointment: had the marriage of the Prince of Wales not imploded, had the queen herself seemed more in touch, had the media been handled better, had there been a stronger government in place, a replacement could probably have been built.

But the republican cause has always suffered from a confusion of motives. That it was at its noisiest when times were harsh in the late nineteenth century indicates that it is not concerned solely with arguments about democracy and legitimacy, which are the same whether the citizens are feasting or starving. It flourished when Queen Victoria was invisible, but was finally drowned in sentimentality. Twentieth-century kings and queens have generally been more adroit. When the Depression arrived, monarchy postured as a defender of the unemployed and the hungry. When wartime meant universal conscription, members of the royal family wore khaki. When the relationship between Crown and people soured in the early 1990s, the queen talked publicly of her *annus horribilis*[69] and appealed for public sympathy.

The fact that the Crown has so very little power makes it almost impossible for republicans to demonstrate that anything much would be gained by getting rid of it. We are left with mere gestures. When the Sex Pistols celebrated Queen Elizabeth's Silver Jubilee in 1977 with 'God Save the Queen', it was predictably (and designedly) banned by the BBC, and equally predictably it shot up the charts as a consequence. Identifying – and purporting to rhyme – the queen with a 'fascist regime' and claiming 'she ain't no human being' did not advance the constitutional debate. Nor did later attempts to scandalize by bands like the Smiths ('The Queen is dead') or the Stone Roses' 1989 contribution 'Elizabeth My Dear'. Perversely, what their creation indicated (apart from a desire to posture as 'anti-Establishment' and to make money) was not so much the importance of the monarchy as its harmless familiarity.

10. The Happiness Business

Of more worth is one honest man to society, and in the sight of God, than all the crowned ruffians that ever lived.

Thomas Paine, 'Common sense', 1776

There are flurries of snow blowing across the tracks as the royal train draws into the centre of Bristol. On the platform, the Lord Lieutenant, in boots and spurs, the Lord Mayor in tricorn hat, the High Sheriff dressed like a refugee from an early sitting for *The Laughing Cavalier*, the Chief Constable, the station master and assorted local worthies. A Buckingham Palace press officer gives the huddle of local reporters the essential detail demanded by every news editor: 'She'll be wearing a green coat and fur hat.' On the concourse outside, a royal car with a silver equestrian statue on its bonnet and royal standard flying from its roof waits to collect the queen and takes her at a stately pace through the centre of Bristol. The visit has been mentioned in the local press, so on the streets gaggles of shoppers stop their business to wave. The Kwik-Fit fitters have slipped out on to the pavement to watch. Several primary schools have turned their children out into the freezing cold to wave home-made English and British flags. The bricklayers on a building site down tools as the royal cavalcade passes. From the back of the enormous car the hands of the queen and her husband rise and fall in mechanical, effortless salute.

There are two pieces of advice given to new arrivals at the higher levels of Buckingham Palace. The second is 'Never help out at the Queen's barbecues.' Too many people have suffered a tongue-lashing from Prince Philip as he burns the sausages. The first, coined by the Queen's favourite private secretary, the late

Martin Charteris, is the essential nostrum of modern royalty: 'Never forget you're in the happiness business.'

Today's destination is a community centre in a former school in Knowle West, one of the numberless British suburbs planned by municipal officials who never expected to have to live there. It is one of the most depressed and troubled parts of the city, plagued by high unemployment and a serious drug problem. The local MP says that those who live here can expect to die a decade earlier than those in the prosperous north side of the city, only three miles away. So few children were bothering to turn up for school that the building was closed and reopened as the community centre to be visited by the queen today.

As the royal car approaches, people emerge from their houses to stand at the front door and wave. Several dozen – all ages from a couple of elderly women in their Women's Royal Army Corps uniforms down to young children – have gathered at the gates of the old school. They cheer and clap as the queen emerges from her limousine.

Inside the low-rise building she is taken on a walk from the nursery to the catering course, to a room where they recycle computers, and to another where pasty-faced, wordless teenage boys are being taught bricklaying. She has missed the parenting class, though. In every room the queen asks questions – 'And what do you do in here?', 'How long do people keep their computers before they send them off for recycling?' and so on, and one or more of the participants recites a prepared response. They confess afterwards how nervous they had been that they would forget the sentences they had learned, and many of the speeches have that rote-learned intonation that comes from hours of practice. Finally, there is a very short concert. It is performed by 150 dancers and musicians who might not otherwise set foot inside any school building: they have been rehearsing for two months. After an hour – and precisely on time – the queen leaves. Another ripple of cheering and clapping is set off. Wearing the same fixed but apparently natural smile she walks through the crowd receiving flowers, either in home-made bunches or in supermarket cellophane.

By the time she arrives at her next engagement, there are nearly a dozen bouquets of flowers inside the car. At the university, she will open a new engineering facility, be introduced to 120 of the city's Great and Good and have the opportunity for a 'comfort stop'. The suite of rooms appointed for this purpose has been repainted for the occasion and equipped, at palace request, with a bottle of gin and one of Dubonnet. Then there will be lunch (paid for by the university) for the ten dozen guests, the opportunity for a quick retouching of makeup, and a return to the station, to name a new locomotive and to return home. All told, she has been on public display for about four hours, and has had to seem engaged in everything that has been shown to her. 'This was a good visit,' says the Lord Lieutenant's wife, as she waves off the brown carriages of the royal train: 'she was genuinely interested all day.'

There was nothing unusual about this visit. There is something like it taking place somewhere or other every month, although as the queen has got older an increasing number have been carried out by her children. What did this encounter between the country's most privileged citizen and some of its most deprived achieve? I had asked a dozen or so of those who had been introduced to the queen what it meant to them, and the most frequently used word in response was 'thrilled'. 'I'd expected her to be a snob,' said a youth on the catering course, 'but she wasn't.' The commonest observation was the surprised discovery that she was 'human'. The suggestion that a visit by the Prime Minister might have been just as rewarding (when it did not draw an instant, dismissive 'I don't trust any politicians') elicited the reasonable suspicion that politicians only went to places, trailing camera crews, for their own advantage. This, by contrast, had been a visit from an elderly grandmother which she had had no need to make, and from which she received no discernible benefit. There had, doubtless, been many local people who had chosen to ignore the appearance, and whose indifference was therefore not apparent. But for those who had chosen to be involved – and they included all social classes – it had quite clearly meant something. Perhaps one of the middle-aged women on the housing estate put it best. 'Well, we can't be all bad', she said, 'if the queen came to see us.'

When King George VI and his family paid a visit to the set of the wartime movie *In Which We Serve*, Noël Coward wrote in his diary that he hoped that the studio appreciated the gesture. It was not, he thought, merely that 'the King and Queen and Princesses of England put themselves out to make everyone they met happy and at ease. There are many who might say, "So they should, for it's part of their job." This is perfectly true. It was also part of Pavlova's job to dance perfectly and part of Bernhardt's job to act better than anyone else. I'll settle for anyone who does their job that well, anyhow.'[1] This is the appreciation of the theatrical connoisseur. But, like judging a play by its opening night, it gives only part of the picture. These royal visits are preceded by elaborate preparation, during which officials in well-cut suits will select the things that will be seen and decide many of those who will be presented. They will have reconnoitred convenient bathrooms and, if necessary, persuaded a local institution (like the university in Bristol) to lay on a meal. There is always a briefing paper and it is always read. The homework enables the convention to be followed that any conversation is always initiated by the visiting royal personage. But there is more to it than preparation and training. In fact, the most tedious elements of every visit are the insistence that those who are to meet royalty are there an hour beforehand and the precise organization of presentation lines. You can understand it, perhaps: who wants to be the person who organizes the visit in which a member of the royal family is mooned at by a guest, or is left shifting from one foot to the other with no one to talk to?

But why should anyone want to meet the king or queen? There is a story in ancient history, sometimes told of Philip of Macedon, sometimes of the Roman emperor Hadrian. While travelling on a journey he was approached by a woman who demanded he listen to her. The woman was insistent. But the emperor replied that he had no time, he had to be on his way. To which the woman replied, 'Then do not be a king!' The emperor stopped, turned around, and listened.

At a time when kings and queens exercised real mastery over their country, the citizen could appeal to them to dispense justice and to right wrongs. Yet, even though European monarchs have been stripped of almost all their powers, people continue to beseech them to listen. Every day, the queen receives two to three hundred letters, a very large number of which are appeals, to what the writer clearly feels is a court of last resort. They betray a belief in some other reality, beyond the dreary dejections of small-claims courts, local councillors, benefit offices and national politicians. Sometimes – if the individual seems to have been overlooked or mistreated by the bureaucracy, for example – a letter on Buckingham Palace stationery may yield results. But most of the time the best they can hope for is an acknowledgement.

This appeal to royalty when all else has failed belongs in the world of Greek and Roman drama, where plays would end with a god being lowered on to the stage – a *deus ex machina* – to sort out insoluble problems. There is no *deus ex machina*, of course. But there is another motivation at work, too. In 1861 Queen Victoria paid a visit to a military hospital where she was introduced to a soldier at the point of death. As the queen leaned across, she heard the man's almost-last words: 'Thank God that He has allowed me to live long enough to see your Majesty.'[2] You begin to understand what the nineteenth-century Republican Clubs were up against. But this emotional impetuousness is not unusual, even today. A lady-in-waiting who has accompanied the queen on royal visits for several decades remarks on how often people become completely flustered and say inappropriate things ('The queen deals with it all with her usual serenity – you see it's happened so many times before'). 'People burst into tears,' she says, adding, 'It's always the men.' Often the tears are accompanied by 'verbal diarrhoea', and, if the queen is particularly unfortunate, it is coming from someone who speaks no English. 'Sometimes it's awfully hard,' she says. 'I have to pretend to sneeze,' to disguise a fit of the giggles.

It is often said that people behave in this fashion because they are overcome with nerves in the presence of someone who seems so much grander than themselves. But perhaps there is more to it than that. Maybe the nerves indicate a form of devotion. When the future queen and her husband visited Canada in 1951, Percy Black, at the time a psychologist at the University of New Brunswick, was so baffled by his countrymen's enthusiastic reaction that he sought a psychological explanation. He concluded that when royalty appeared in public it was not merely – as is usually suggested – a case of the king or queen exhibiting themselves, to bask in public adoration. It could just as easily be seen the other way round. 'The public is on display,' he wrote, 'because it desires to be loved. It wants the smile of monarchy, the royal sign of gratitude. It craves to display its ability, its planning, its intelligence, its kind-heartedness and courage. The public in effect says: "Look on us, O monarch. We are your people; we are good!"'[3]

Fifty years later, on a sweltering July afternoon in central London – the sort of weather for shorts and T-shirts and perhaps an aspirin – the gardens of Buckingham Palace are swarming with men in waistcoats, tailcoats and hired top-hats; soldiers, sailors and aviators are in heavy uniforms and spit-and-polished shoes; bishops are in purple cassocks and women in new frocks and best hats. The Burmese Ambassador and his entourage look particularly exotic. The staff at the palace call these sunny, humid days 'the Queen's Weather' – even the rain seems to stand off when she holds one of her garden parties. All told, eight thousand people have been invited this afternoon: by the time of the queen's Golden Jubilee in 2002 Buckingham Palace estimated that well over a million people had attended her garden parties there or at the palace at Holyroodhouse in Edinburgh. The stated aim of the organizers is to invite people 'from every section of society'. Few decline the chance to see what lies behind the high palace walls.

At the stroke of four, Queen Elizabeth emerges on to the terrace. The Duke of Edinburgh is at her side. Prince Charles and Prince Andrew walk a few steps behind. Again, the first impression is her size. She is tiny, dwarfed by the ushers, the soldiers and most of the guests. As she pauses at the top of the steps down to the lawns, one of the three military bands strikes up 'God Save the Queen'. The princes stand basilisk still with top-hats in hand and umbrellas at their side. The moment the band finishes, a ripple of applause suffuses the crowd and the queen descends the steps to mingle with her guests. Thoroughfares are cleared through the crowds by the Corps of Gentlemen Ushers – retired military officers in the black tailcoats and top-hats of morning dress, with tightly furled umbrellas: bouncers with cut-glass accents. (One astonished Chief Constable was recently barked at, 'You there. You're obviously used to crowd control – can you get them to step back?')

As one after another of the military bands plays favourite songs from *Mary Poppins* or top-ten hits from the 1970s, the family fans out. The queen takes the central lane cleared for her by the bossy ushers. Prince Charles takes a branch-line, Prince Andrew another. The queen's cousin Princess Alexandra has appeared from somewhere, attended by her lady-in-waiting, and seems to be free-associating with anyone who wants to chat. Those who have been selected for a few words with the queen or one of her family are mustered. And then she moves off down the endless lines of guests hoping to snatch a few words. Many are almost speechless with anxiety, but away from the royal presence it is not overly formal but fairly relaxed. So relaxed, in fact, that the former mayor of Gloucester has taken himself, his partner and a couple of friends off to a quiet corner, where shoes have been removed. He pronounces the event 'dull'. The others nod in agreement. At one level, he is right. A lot of people have put on uncomfortable clothes to stand in the humid air waiting for the chance to make stilted conversation with someone they don't know. Many of them will have no opportunity to do so. Some have already sloped off to sit on plastic chairs in the shade. Others stand in enormous lines waiting for a cup of tea.

But there are many others, certainly the overwhelming majority, who feel quite differently. Even in noisily republican cultures it seems to apply. At a 1991 garden party at the British Embassy in Washington the desire to meet the queen was so strong – even on the part of people like Jesse Jackson – that she was obliged to walk around protected by a phalanx of naval officers in front and with a couple of ladies-in-waiting with sharp-pointed parasols behind. From past experience, the Duke of Edinburgh has devised a rule-of-thumb that when married couples attend these events, the fifth man will always curtsey: he has been so nervous that he merely repeats what the person next to him has just done. After the Buckingham Palace garden party, a factory foreman from Birmingham stretches his arms and says, awestruck, 'She came *so close* to me . . . and I realized how ordinary they are.' And then he adds the curious comment, 'It made me feel so humble.' This reversal of what one might have expected at the discovery that his ruler was mere flesh and blood takes some thinking about. Perhaps what he means is that they *seemed* normal or ordinary, despite the fact that they are not. Three ladies from north Yorkshire are equally moved. Appalled by the lack of facilities for the mentally handicapped in their area, they have founded a centre for people with learning difficulties. They are now providing a service to hundreds of people. The invitation to stand on the lawn at Buckingham Palace, one of them says, 'makes me feel I've done something worthwhile in my life'.

This, too, is curious. How can she and her friends doubt that they have done something worthwhile with their lives? It seems self-evident. And yet it appears to have taken an invitation to the palace to convince them.

The invention of broadcasting gave the opportunity for the millions who were not – and would never be – invited to the garden parties and receptions to gain a personal impression of royalty. The first head of the BBC, John Reith, was as ardent a monarchist as could be found. During the First World War King George V had visited Reith's unit, the 5th Scottish Rifles, in Flanders. As the king looked up at the tall, craggy officer, Reith thought he read his mind. 'You may be killed – considering the length I've got to look up at you, you'll probably catch it in the head. I represent what you're fighting for. Good luck and a safe return home.'[4] For years after his return from the war, Reith attempted to persuade the king he had served to make a Christmas or New Year broadcast to the nation and empire. Finally, in 1932, he succeeded. Sitting at a desk under the stairs at Sandringham on Christmas Day, the king read the words written for him by the great imperial poet, Rudyard Kipling. 'I speak now from my home and from my heart to you all, to all my peoples throughout the empire,' began 'Grandpa England' in the tones of a country gentleman, 'to men and women so cut off by the snows, the desert or the sea that only voices of the air can reach them, men and women of every race and colour who look to the Crown as the symbol of their unity.'

The function of the broadcasts was apparent in that first sentence, and if the idiom has changed, the purpose has not. Queen Elizabeth's first broadcast, in 1952, talked of 'my people'. While mildly religious in tone (they always wished the worldwide audience a Happy Christmas, despite the fact that very large numbers of those listening were not Christians), they had a political message. The king or queen came across in them as a father or mother figure: in George VI's first broadcast in 1937 he was explicit. 'Many of you', he said, 'will remember the Christmas broadcasts of former years, when my father spoke to his peoples at home and overseas as the head of a great family.' For George VI, with his terrible stammer, the talks must have been a nightmare. People who listened to them willed him the strength to get to the end without collapsing. Even decades later, the king's broadcast on Christmas Day in 1939, when the country had just embarked upon the war which would tear Europe apart and lead to the end of the British empire, still carries an extraordinary resonance. He sat in front of two enormous microphones, dressed in the uniform of an admiral of the fleet and laboured his way through a speech to inspire his people. At times he wavered and seemed about to stop altogether. Once, he halted and repeated the phrase, as his speech therapist had taught him. His wife had come across a poem written by Minnie Louise Haskins, an ageing American teacher living in England, which gave the king words of comfort for his people.[5] 'I said to the man who stood at the gate of the year,' recited the king, '"Give me a light that I may tread safely into the unknown," and he replied,

"Go out into the darkness and put your hand into the hand of God. That shall be better than light and safer than a known way."' In the mood of black apprehension which pervaded the country, the words were understated, elegant and reassuring.

The following October, his fourteen-year-old daughter Elizabeth made her first broadcast, a radio speech to the 'children of the empire'. But it is the broadcasts at three on Christmas afternoon, when, it is assumed, most people are digesting their turkey and pudding, which became the most direct communication between monarch and people. Despite the fact that they have been televised since the 1950s they retain a stately, radio quality: there is something infinitely more dramatic in the imagined picture of a king sitting upright at the microphone in naval uniform than the observable reality of a queen in a quiet dress with a pearl necklace, surrounded by a pretty constant set of props – a couple of Christmas cards, a framed family photograph, a lamp burning to symbolize new light. The same conversational motifs recur every year. Pre-eminently, there are remarks about family. The royal advisers have never abandoned Bagehot and know that the emotional connection which makes a constitutional monarchy viable is the capacity to believe that all families – even this most privileged one – are essentially similar.

Each year's broadcast tends to have a theme, some more coherent than others, although almost none of them ever posed a risk of being controversial. (The Queen of Denmark's speech, by contrast, which is given at the New Year and is the most seen and heard speech in the country, can often – as when she asked recently why people were alarmed by immigration – force politicians to engage with an issue.) Perhaps the most heartfelt, and the most political, of the British queen's broadcasts was the very first that she gave on television. They have all, inevitably, been conservative in tone. But in 1957 the young queen seemed most passionate in her defence of 'traditional values', quoting from *Pilgrim's Progress* and saying that she gave her audience 'my heart'. Overall, their precise content is less significant than the fact that they occur when they do. Because the speech is made on Christmas Day it usually includes some thoughts about the spirit of the occasion or the significance of Christian values – in 2000, for example, the queen talked about her conviction that she would be held accountable before God.

It would be foolish to exaggerate any parallel between the royal family and the holy family. But it is no accident that the British king or queen should speak to the peoples of the Commonwealth on 25 December, instead of, say, on his or her birthday or on the national day of the different parts of the United Kingdom. John Reith gave the royal household a choice between a New Year or Christmas broadcast. By opting for Christmas Day, the palace chose a date when families tend to be together and reinforced an association between monarchy and religion. In France, for example, the elected President of the Republic speaks to the nation on New Year's Eve, and ends his address with the solemn 'Vive la République! Vive la France!' The king or queen of Britain finishes by wishing everyone a merry day, which is a lot more homely. At an intuitive level, it underscores the sense of nation as an extended family.

During the First World War, the redoubtable Queen Mary was forever in and out of hospitals – sometimes three or four in an afternoon – visiting the British wounded. It was on one of these tours that another family member being dragged around in her wake complained, 'I'm tired and I hate hospitals.' The queen's reported response encapsulated the attitude of modern monarchy. 'You are a member of the British Royal Family. We are *never* tired, and we all *love* hospitals!'[6]

As we have seen, it is a long time since a king led his troops into battle. It was because this was a male role that, in her famous speech at Tilbury before the expected Spanish invasion in 1588, Elizabeth I spoke of knowing she had 'the body of a weak and feeble woman, but I have the heart and stomach of a king, and of a king of England too'. Among the most touching parts of the personal writings of the next iconic English queen, Victoria, are her anxieties about whether her gender will prevent her being a 'proper' ruler: the traditional education of a prince was designed to instil both wisdom and courage in battle. But Queen Victoria worried too much. She was fortunate enough to sit upon the throne at a time when the empire's boundaries were in more or less constant expansion, which allowed the monarchy to become a different kind of institution. Whether it would have done so as readily had the throne been occupied by a man is one of those chicken-and-egg questions to which there can never be a satisfactory answer.

But certainly, when we see the qualities demanded of a monarch in the pulpits of the mass media, they tend to be feminine virtues, or virtues which have historically been seen as feminine: piety, continence, fidelity, attractiveness and kindness. Modern monarchy is a feminized institution. When historians advance this argument they do not have in mind the sort of nanny role which Kaiser Wilhelm II saw for himself in Germany, which included, astonishingly, instructions to his people about their table manners; rather they mean that the responsibilities have become increasingly those of giving comfort and nurturing good causes. 'Constitutional monarchy is what results when the sovereign is deprived of those historic male functions of god and governor and general, and this in turn has led – perhaps by default, perhaps by design? – to a greater stress on family, domesticity, maternity and glamour,' is the way the historian David Cannadine puts it.[7] It has even been asserted that Walter Bagehot's celebrated Victorian definition of the political powers of a monarch – the entitlements to be consulted, to encourage and to warn – 'were the rights not of a sovereign but of a wife'. Thus the constitution became 'a perfectly adapted marriage between masculine efficiency and feminine dignity'.[8] This pre-feminist analysis is not really enough. William Kuhn concluded that Bagehot had 'laid the foundations for an enormous increase in [royal] power . . . not political power exactly, but a sort of prestige that commanded the attention and attendance of politicians . . .'.[9] This association with organizations which nurture the sick and the poor is, surely, the area in which royal influence has grown, as royal power has withered.

All kings have been enjoined to be kind to the needy. But from the later Hanoverians onwards, we can trace a growing involvement in public good works. Doubtless George III had been influenced by the fact that his son Octavius died from a botched smallpox inoculation, but when asked to support the work on vaccination begun by Edward Jenner, almost the entire royal family signed up as patrons. George's wife, Queen Charlotte, was estimated to give away £5,000 a year, and was largely responsible for financing a Berkshire charity for distressed needlewomen. George IV, who as a result of his public caricature does not immediately strike one as the sort of man to give money to charity when there were curtains to be bought, nonetheless gave to the arts, education, widows and orphans. The king was a notorious sucker for hard-luck stories, tearfully giving his purse away and later, of course, expecting parliament to replenish it. It was during his reign that we see good causes beginning to capitalize upon the advantages of royal endorsement.[10]

During the reign of Queen Victoria royal patronage acquired real momentum, becoming what one historian of philanthropy likened to 'china eggs planted in a nest to encourage the hen to lay'.[11] Victoria had been trailed around charitable institutions by her parents, and her husband seized upon involvement with good causes as a way of carving out a role for the prince consort. When Britain proved largely unshaken by the wave of revolutions which swept Europe in the middle of the century, Albert declared that it was royal philanthropy which had staved off republicanism and prevented 'the practical adaptation' of socialism.[12]

Her husband's public enthusiasm for charitable institutions allowed Victoria to watch her beloved Albert being clasped to the public bosom. 'I glory in his being seen and loved,' she wrote.[13] Her army of children were encouraged to emulate their father – apart from anything else, it provided them with something to do. Her daughters went about the London slums incognito and were active in organizations which worked with nurses or unmarried mothers. Her son Prince Alfred became the first royal to be wounded while on charitable duty: he was shot by an Irish revolutionary during a picnic to raise money for an Australian sailors' home.[14]

Active involvement with charities also gave the monarchy an opportunity to address the underlying political challenge of the twentieth century: how could the anachronism of a hereditary head of state survive the arrival of proper democracy? The natural allies of monarchy were the nobility, whose role in government was now more or less over. Philanthropy, and royal patronage of organizations whose work was not with the plutocracy but with the poor, offered the possibility of constructing new alliances, notably with the growing middle class who were being enjoined from the pulpit to act philanthropically. Edward VII used his influence to raise money for the King's Fund (originally the Prince of Wales's Hospital Fund for London), while his wife Queen Alexandra became obsessively interested in nursing, especially military nursing, much to the annoyance of the Secretary of State for War, Lord Haldane, who found her 'about the stupidest woman in England'.[15] Their son, the future George V, and his wife processed from mine to colliery to mill to factory, delivering speeches about the importance of the workers and stressing how keenly the royal family felt the need to alleviate their suffering.

'I'm the king, may I come in?' said Edward VIII when he knocked on a door in Glasgow.[16] He had inherited a talent for slum-visiting, even if he lacked the stamina for kingship. He had the knack of appearing genuinely concerned about the social conditions in which so many of his subjects lived. Ten months after his accession he toured the coalfields and furnaces of South Wales which had been rendered idle by the Depression. The visit brought on the second most famous remark of his reign. Standing with his bowler-hat in his hand at the abandoned steelworks at Dowlais on a damp November morning he told the hundreds of unemployed, 'Something must be done.'[17] It sounded emphatic, and the crowds cheered. But what did the comment signify? The king was quite obviously upset by what he had seen – the great majority of men in the village had lost their jobs when the factory closed and families were going hungry. He repeated the remark the following day, on a visit to Blaenavon. The comment endeared him to the unemployed, to many of whom he became a hero. But it also pointed up the impotence of the king's position. He did not sell all he had to give to the poor. He had no executive power. 'Something must be done', by somebody else. Within a few weeks he had quit his post anyway.

But this symbolic engagement in the lives of their people had given the monarchy a new role. Although the capacity for executive action was limited, it certainly had a political purpose. The overthrow and execution of the tsar in 1917 had sent a shudder through the British royal family, and George V's private secretary Lord Stamfordham had cannily seen that a greater apparent interest in the lives of ordinary people would do much to secure their chances of survival. The challenge was to transcend the view that the king was a mere figurehead 'which, as they put it, "don't count",' and instead to enable people to see him as 'a living power for good, with receptive faculties welcoming information affecting the interests and social well-being of all classes, and ready, not only to sympathise with those questions, but anxious to further their solution'.[18] He encouraged the king to get out into the factories, and to talk to working people, so that they would recognize the 'virtues' of the Crown. The new role gave royalty an illusion of involvement in the daily lives of their subjects, while remaining distant from government. And they came rather to enjoy it. After watching George VI's wife open some new buildings at a college in Lambeth, Harold Nicolson marvelled that she possessed 'an astonishing gift for being sincerely interested in dull people and dull occasions'.[19] Her daughter Elizabeth II inherited the talent, and has spent decade after decade travelling the country looking at displays of children's dancing, shaking hands, listening to ineffably tedious speeches and unveiling plaques commemorating her visit. The Reverend Charlie Robertson, a Church of Scotland minister who considers the queen a good friend, says he once asked her how she maintained her enthusiasm – he found it hard enough to keep turning out for yet another of his own children's primary school concerts. 'You must set out to enjoy it,' she told him. It struck him that she had something of the sense of vocation you might find in an Irish nun.[20]

This enthusiasm for voluntarism undoubtedly gave a great deal of help to the charities concerned, for the royal imprimatur persuaded potential supporters that they were worthwhile causes. (It also meant that royalty remained wedded to charitable solutions long after politicians had concluded that only taxation could address the country's deep-seated social problems.) The voluntary sector's enthusiasm for royal patronage reflects the beliefs of a previous age, when kings made things happen: by comparison, the state seems lumbering, bureaucratic and mechanical. Engagement with 'good works' has given monarchy a role in civil life to compensate for its loss of political power.

Royal endorsement continues to be sought after. As a result, the list of hundreds of good causes which have persuaded the queen to become their patron runs to thirty-seven pages of A4 paper, from the Additional Curates Society and the Anglo-Norse Society, through organizations like the Bombay Seamen's Society, the Calgary Highlanders, the Girl Guides, the National Ice-skating Centre and the National Society for Epilepsy, to the Royal Watercolour Society, the Yellow Labrador Club and the Zoological Society of London. The Duke of Edinburgh's list of patronages is longer. Most of these are 'passive' patronages, which merely enable the charity to put an impressive name and title on the letterhead. But a small number involve a more active role, perhaps chairing committees. Minor members of the family may even hire themselves out, promising to attend events in exchange for a donation to one of their charities. It would take a very bleak view of human nature to argue that this promotion of causes which fall between the paving stones of everyday life was anything but a good thing.

But it is quite a distant, dignified engagement. The person who most enthusiastically capitalized on the modern, feminized monarchy was Diana, Princess of Wales. Her visits to AIDS hospices, the cuddling of children who had lost their limbs to landmines, her empathetic solidarity with the victims of eating disorders, were for her journalistic confessor Andrew Morton an echo of another sort of monarchy. There was something genuinely impressive about some of these actions, such as the very public demolition of superstitions that you could somehow catch AIDS by touching those who had the disease, or the private embrace she was said to have given on a visit to Sarajevo to a blind, severely mentally handicapped child lying in her own urine. These incidents explicitly recall the examples not of princesses (apart from St Margaret of Hungary) so much as of saints like Francis of Assisi, who kissed lepers, or Catherine of Siena, the 'holy anorexic', who drank pus from the sores of the sick, and evoke the image of Christ washing the feet of his disciples a great deal more effectively than the distribution of Maundy Money. But they were, of course, for a few moments only. After that, it was back into the car, on to the helicopter and off to the gala dinner.

After her death, Andrew Morton wrote that 'Diana embraced, albeit unconsciously, the monarchy of our dreams and fantasies, her beauty and charisma harking back to the distant days when royal persons were seen as healers, magicians, objects of worship and veneration, even divine beings imbued with supernatural powers.'[21] This was, in short, medieval superstition for the mass-media age. It is hard, reading her explanations of why she did what she did, to escape the feeling that she enjoyed the experiences because they seemed to give direction to an otherwise purposeless life. Her former butler and high priest, Paul Burrell, recalled a hospital visit in which Diana had floated around, giving everyone a box of chocolates. 'It had been her awakening,' he wrote. 'She truly felt that her most rewarding time was when she helped the sick and the dying. She felt "replenished" by doing it.'[22] In the end, this empathetic style was simply too much for the rest of the very buttoned-up House of Windsor to stomach. For them, the charitable world provided a mission which neither diminished their popularity nor demeaned their dignity. In a constitutional arrangement which denied them real power it offered a way of expressing their belief that they stood for human values which did not find expression in everyday slogans or laws. Diana, who had not enjoyed the training which those born into the family had undergone, had watched and, she thought, learned. But it was like a child walking behind an adult, imitating his strides. It was remarkable for its exaggeration.

11. Gilded but Gelded

He who loses support of the people is king no longer.

Aristotle

You can always tell a chap who has a valet. Most men wear their business suits with vertical creases down the front of their trouser legs. But a man with a valet has knife-edge ridges down the arms of his jacket too. The grey suit being worn by the husband of the British queen, father of the heir apparent and grandfather of the second in line to the throne, may be old. But it is well cut and perfectly pressed on both jacket and trousers. Prince Philip, Duke of Edinburgh, wears a folded white handkerchief in his breast pocket. A pale-blue tie seems to be fixed in a symmetrical Windsor knot.[1] His shoes are ancient, but their toecaps have been spit-and-polished to gleam like mirrors. The style of his library matches his clothing. In the 1960s its hexagonal desk, steel and wood bookshelves and fluted armchairs probably looked cutting-edge.

It is still a long way from the picaresque details of his early life – the birth on a kitchen table, the escape from revolution hidden inside an orange box, and the wandering indigence of a youth whose entire worldly goods could be held inside one battered suitcase. Marriage in 1947 to the heir to the most prestigious throne in the world turned his life upside down. 'If I had stayed in the navy I might have become an admiral or something,' Prince Philip admits, 'but I never would have been able to do many of the things I've done, which were possible not because of my personality but because of the position.' But the wealth and status came at a price. 'You have virtually got to say goodbye to innocence and your predilections in life,' he says. 'You haven't got a choice, or not anything like as wide a choice, because it could attract criticism. You have to be careful about friends because people feel jealous about them. You discover that you can't have your cake and eat it.' The words could carry a whiff of self-pity, but that is not how they seem when he utters them – as he concedes, his privileged position is one of great material comfort. But it is one he enjoys simply by marriage, and the role of queen's consort has no formal definition. When his wife reached the throne, 'I did ask various people what I was expected to do,' he says. And? 'They sort of looked down and shuffled their feet.' There was the example of the last man to find himself saddled with the task, Queen Victoria's husband Prince Albert, but it was not a great deal of help. The formal demands of the job were limited ('Any bloody fool can lay a wreath at the thingamy. You don't have to be a genius for that'). Prince Philip may not have had Albert's creative gifts, but he did possess a Teutonic approach to work – even friends sometimes comment upon how much more German than English he often seems – and his involvement in organizations from Cambridge University to the National Playing Fields Association has been much more than nominal. Millions of young people embarked upon the Awards Scheme he established. In the process he earned the acceptance of the British people, even if they never embraced him with great warmth.

The duke's personal style is a disconcerting mixture of bluff affability and utter disdain: although no intellectual himself, he does not suffer fools gladly. He has a blazing temper and appears almost pathologically incapable of saying sorry. But his staff seem devoted to him: even the duke's *retired* private secretary still ambles into Buckingham Palace most weeks. They have had to get used to his sense of humour. On one state visit the duke was showing Queen Beatrix of the Netherlands down the receiving line in Buckingham Palace, introducing her to members of the household. At the end of the line, blinking out from behind the palm fronds, stood his private secretary. 'I've no idea who this is,' said the duke to the visiting queen. 'Must be some gatecrasher.'

In royal circles, the bluff manner would not have struck previous generations as offensive, or even odd. It is rather reminiscent of George VI, whose biographer records a visit to the British colony of Rhodesia. Before setting off for a picnic he teased the Governor's aide-de-camp:

> 'Do ADCs always wear ties for picnics?' [the King] said, giving it a sharp tug; later, at the picnic, when handed an enormous tomato, he remarked, 'What am I to do with this – throw it at you?' With his usual sharp eye for details of dress and decoration he told off the Governor for wearing one of his stars in the wrong place and his miniature medals overlapping the wrong way. The Governor looked down his nose for a minute or two before replying coolly, 'That's funny, Sir, because they are on the same way as yours.' 'Oh,' said the King, 'of course I always look at mine in the mirror' . . . On his return [from another event] the King shouted, 'Off parade at last' and threw his hat at the ceiling, which was caught by the ADC and returned to him; he then threw it on to the floor and the Queen kicked it into the dining-room. The King then seized the gong and went round the house beating it before trying to hang it round one official's neck, saying, 'I'm sure you'd like another one of these!' He then opened the door of the ladies' lavatory and, seeing a fur hanging on a peg, said, 'My God, some woman has left her beard in here.'[2]

But it was Prince Philip's misfortune to live in another age, when almost anything said by royalty was liable to be amplified by the mass media. Before long he had acquired an awesome reputation for putting his foot in it: he coined the term 'dontopedology' to describe it. On a visit to a town where the local mayor was proudly displaying a new housing development, carefully zoned according to price, the duke corrected his description of 'the lower income area' and referred to it as 'the ghetto'. In 1961, he was telling British industry to 'Get your finger out,' without recognizing the obvious pot–kettle comparisons his comments would provoke. Five years later he said he was 'fed up with making excuses for Britain'. He once declared there ought to be a tax on babies. Introduced to a blind girl, he told her a story about a blind man whirling his guide dog around his head to 'have a look around'.

In China he warned a visiting British student not to stay in the country too long, for fear of acquiring 'slitty eyes'. Arriving in Canada on a visit with the queen, he was asked by a friendly Canadian what sort of flight they had had. 'Have you ever flown in a plane?' asked the duke. 'Yes? Well, it was just like that.'[3]

An increasingly civilianized society simply failed to understand this sort of wardroom humour, and every newsroom had a resident moralist ready to sermonize. Indeed, as newspapers found themselves supplanted by television as the main source of news, increasing acreages of newsprint were occupied by columnists whose entire *raison d'être* was to thunder, as controversially as possible. In theory, the columnists were independent-minded. In practice, many shared the same stock of prejudices about the world. Philip was too easy a target, and it clearly makes him very cross. There ought to be a proper mechanism for forcing the press to justify what they've written, he says. The 'slitty eyes' incident, which he calls 'the classic case', was all got up by a journalist on Murdoch's *Times*. His voice gets testy. 'I didn't say it to any Chinese. [But] there was no way I could deny it, and there was no way I could hold him accountable . . . You see the trouble with journalists is that they have no sense of humour. Period.'

It is hardly surprising that the experience has affected the way he behaves towards the mass media. The public incidents are well enough known. A Pakistani photographer falls off a pole while trying to get a high-angle shot during a walkabout in Lahore, and Philip exclaims, 'I hope he breaks his bloody neck.'[4] When shown the apes on Gibraltar he asks, 'Which are the press and which are the bloody apes?' and then pelts them (the photographers, not the apes) with peanuts.[5] At the Chelsea Flower Show he 'mistakenly' turns a hosepipe on reporters.[6] In private, a huffy note enters his voice when he talks about how his family is treated by the mass media. 'On the basis of the way the family have been treated by the media at the moment, I'm surprised people don't chuck it,' he says, his voice rising in exasperation. 'Because it is absolutely extraordinary what has happened in the last thirty years. I mean, before that we were accepted as quite normal sort of people. But *now*, I mean *now* I reckon I have done something right if I *don't* appear in the media. Because I know that any appearance in it will be one of criticism. I will be criticized for doing something. So I've retreated – quite consciously – so as not to be an embarrassment. I don't want to be embarrassing.'

Do you read the papers, then? I ask. He shrugs. 'I don't read the tabloids. I glance at one [one of the broadsheets]. I reckon one's enough. I can't cope with them. But the queen reads every bloody paper she can lay her hands on.' His voice has risen an octave. There is a tone of persecution about these comments. Some of it is justified: any royal connection, however spurious, will give shine to the dullest story. 'People go out of their way to try and find a relationship,' says the duke, 'and someone says, "Oh there's a paedophile, well his great-uncle's nephew used to work in the palace," that sort of thing. Some poor chap gets into trouble and it turns out that he is the third cousin of the queen by marriage or something. It's that picking on you the whole time which is depressing.'

It can't be much fun to have every detail – or the few details that become public property – of your life pored over. 'As far I'm concerned, every time I talk to a woman, they say I've been to bed with her – as if she had no say in the matter.' The duke laughs, in a world-weary way, and then his voice rises again and he is almost wailing. 'I mean, I like carriage driving. And they go and say, "Oh, so and so is his 'driving companion'."' He raises his eyebrows, as if I know what he means. 'Well I'm bloody flattered at my age to think some girl is interested in me. It's absolutely cuckoo!' And he pauses, seems to hear himself, and stops. 'Well, there it is . . .'

In previous ages kings and queens worried about their dealings with the barons, or with parliament. Now, it is the relationship with the mass media which eats them up. There is something unimpressive about the peevishness of Prince Philip (as there is to the moans of his son, Prince Charles): for the monarchy to complain about the media is about as fruitful as the rest of us complaining about the weather. It is not that the newspapers wish to get rid of the royal family and replace it with something more democratic. Apart from anything else, that would be killing the golden goose. But they are a fact of life.

What has gone wrong in the relationship between the newspapers and the royal family? The duke has a predictable cast of villains. 'Something happened in the 1960s, with the permissive society. I mean, it pulled the plug on an awful lot of attitudes and perceptions. You started calling your teachers by their first names for instance – you undermined the whole concept of having respect for people. Respectfulness is not the right answer, I think politeness matters far more. I don't see why you shouldn't be polite to people no matter what position they're in. I mean, why should you be rude to somebody who can't answer back, and polite to somebody who can hit you over the head? You ought to be polite to both.'

But then the pitch of his voice rises again. He has identified the cause of it all. 'It's Murdoch,' he explodes. 'It's the arrival of television, it's the decline of the print media, it's the mentality that thrives in the tabloids. It's Murdoch's anti-Establishment attitude, which has really pulled the plug on an awful lot of things that we considered to be quite reasonable – and sensible – institutions.' He is off now. 'He's succeeded in undermining them all . . . If you attack what people have grown up to accept, suddenly people find that they can be rude to them. I think it gives a lot of tabloid journalists a tremendous buzz to feel that they can say what they like about people in visible public positions.' Although he is evidently exasperated, he believes he understands why they do it. 'It's like an Indian shooting a tiger. I shot a tiger therefore I am as strong as a tiger.'

It is repeatedly claimed – most often by those who consume the stuff most compulsively – that modern royalty is a victim of the mass media. It is hard to see quite how this can be true, given the simpering nature of most royal reporting. Even reporters who affect shock that a young prince might get drunk and fall over at a nightclub are suggesting that higher standards should be expected because royalty are, in some sense, a superior order of being. For the most part, the mass media dance slavishly to the palace's tune. It is true that 'they can't fight back' when untruths are told about royalty. But that has always been the case. It was alleged, for example, that the future George V's wedding to Princess Mary of Teck was bigamous, because he already had a secret wife and three children. The claim was dispatched in a libel trial and, more recently, by a biographer with access to his private diaries, but was still being repeated at the turn of the twenty-first century.[7] George V's brother, 'Prince Eddy', Duke of Clarence, was also alleged to have made a secret marriage, to a shopgirl named Annie Crook, and to have been the real Jack the Ripper. Wallis Simpson, who kept Edward in thrall by deploying sexual skills learned in the brothels of the Far East, was alleged to be a secret agent for the Americans, the Russians and the Germans. Lord Mountbatten attempted to negotiate a peace with the Nazis, in order that he might become king of part of the Rhineland, and later worked for the KGB.[8] According to various websites, Elizabeth II controls the international drugs trade, through an 'international Zionist conspiracy', the rock music industry, Freemasonry, Rosicrucianism, the honours system and the Cult of Isis. In November 2003 the Prince of Wales's private secretary was obliged to take to television to deny the ridiculous fiction that the prince had been caught in bed with his valet. Absurd fantasies are the price that has be paid for being an institution which in many ways still depends for its survival upon mystery.

But it is impossible to imagine a serious newspaper today marking the death of a king or queen in way that *The Times* mourned George IV in 1830. It described the late king as fat, frivolous, grotesque, selfish, lazy, vain, lecherous, spendthrift, corrupt and essentially worthless. Given his over-indulgence, the paper said, it was remarkable that he had lived to the age of nearly seventy. Reliable sources had told the newspaper that all attempts to make him understand money – 'the difference, as it was intimated, between pounds, shillings and pence' – had failed. His treatment of his wife Queen Caroline 'was a stain to manhood. A fashionable strumpet usurped her apartments.' As for George's court, it was like 'the den of Circe', the mythological goddess who lured travellers to her palace, then drugged them and turned them into pigs.[9]

By Victoria's reign it became received wisdom to accept Tennyson's description of 'the fierce light that beats upon a throne'. By now the abuse was directed much more at foreign interlopers. Prince Ernest, future Elector of Hanover, who entertained hopes of the British throne, was described by one periodical as 'a miserable nonentity; an eel-skin stuffed with smoked German sausage-meat'[10] – though he was one of George IV's brothers. The same paper later welcomed Prince Albert to England from his 'half-starved' lice-infested castle in Germany with the disclosure that while he was asleep he was to be fumigated with sulphur and have his head shaved, while his clothes would be baked to kill off the bugs claiming the 'joint tenancy' which was found 'alike in English slums and German "palaces"'.[11]

But the prevailing tone of coverage of British royalty was simpering. When Victoria ascended the throne, the newspapers were full of stories about the delicacy of her ankles and the daintiness of her feet. The first police press pass – formal recognition of the fourth estate – was issued for her coronation, and soon the papers were filled with gibbering about her exquisite qualities. Pre-eminent among the royal reporters of the time was Rumsey Forster of the *Morning Post* (or The Triumphant Toady of the *Fawning Post*, as *Punch* knew him). Forster's reporting ran from the riveting ('Yesterday morning her Majesty and his Royal Highness Prince Albert walked out for a short time on the Terrace,' and 'it is not expected that there will be any music at the Castle for the next three weeks')[12] to the sensational ('Unostentatious benevolence of the sovereign towards the sick poor' – an account of the decision to give away the dregs of the wine cellar).[13] Later in her reign Victoria became accustomed to being followed around the Scottish Highlands by a pack of reporters desperate to satisfy their editors with anything at all. The convention was that they simply stayed out of sight – those who failed to observe the protocol had to face the wrath of her loyal servant John Brown.

By the time of the Diamond Jubilee in 1897 the *Spectator*, which had once been defiantly sceptical, had succumbed. The twelve words uttered by the queen, 'From my heart I thank my beloved people. May God bless them,' had the paper in ecstasies. 'The words are nothing,' it wrote,

the simple thanks of a mother to her children who have been paying her a compliment; but imagine how any other Sovereign in the world would have worded that message, how stilted it would have been, how cautious, or how suggestive of a head slightly turned with adulation. The Queen, whom we have heard defined by Ministers of State as 'the most truthful woman in Europe,' says nothing but what rises in her to say, and in her outburst and her self-restraint, touches her people more nearly than if she had possessed or used any amount of literary skill.[14]

This is not untypical of the swooning fits which overcame – and still overcome – much of the mass media when they are obliged to think about monarchies. The most striking characteristic is the combination of slavish devotion ('the most truthful woman in Europe') and intellectual condescension ('if she had possessed or used any amount of literary skill' – unlike those of us who write this stuff). The style announces the distinctive feature of constitutional monarchies: they are grander than we are, and yet they are also subservient to us.

Victoria was fortunate to have taken the throne at the point at which British military strength, industrial productivity and imperial vision turned much of the map of the world pink. The empire was the greatest the world had ever seen; and it happened to have a queen at its head: monarchy seemed somehow part of the engine of global dominance. Imperial grandeur did nothing to diminish the poverty in which masses of British people struggled, but the greater the number of aboriginal peoples obliged to bend the knee to the Great White Queen, the more the mill-workers and miners at home might be persuaded there was something special about their place in the scheme of things. As we have seen, the British empire was a *royal* empire. Its queen grew older and fatter as the empire grew older and fatter. At a personal level, the queen lived a life of irreproachable domestic dullness, enthusiastically performing the task of providing an heir and plenty of siblings, with no danger of questions being raised about their paternity. In the marriage of public and private the monarchy now came to represent a set of values – conservatism, science, enterprise and empire – which influential newspapers admired. Above all, as the enthusiasts at the *Spectator* expressed it, the relationship with her people seemed to be that of a mother to her children.

But, for the impression to be convincing, the queen had to be seen. After Prince Albert's death from typhoid fever ('My life as a happy one is ended! The world is gone for me!' she wailed to her uncle),[15] she became a distant, shrouded figure. On several occasions she simply refused to conduct the State Opening of parliament. In the summer of 1869, eight years after her bereavement, Gladstone wrote to ask whether she would perform the opening of Blackfriars Bridge. The queen refused: 'the fatigue and excitement would be *far too great*'.[16] Gladstone fumed inwardly and replied, in terms almost as frank, that 'the appearance of the Sovereign in public from time to time upon occasions of great interest, while in exterior it is a mere form, is in reality among the substantial, and even in the long run indispensable, means of maintaining the full influence of the Monarchy'.[17] Without public appearances there would not be enough for the press to write about, and without newspaper reporting, the queen would be invisible.

Fortunately, a large family and a long reign meant that there was a whole caboodle of other royal fiestas. Births were proclaimed as if no human being had ever managed to reproduce before. And at royal weddings all common sense flew out of the window. When the *Daily Telegraph* reported the marriage of the future Edward VII to Princess Alix of Denmark it was quite overcome.

He came at last, young, gallant, confident, with a noble bearing and an upright mien, walking with the assured tread of one who knew himself to be *porphyrogenitus* ['born in the purple', as opposed, presumably, to 'born in the gutter'] yet bowing his comely head from side to side gracefully to those who rose to do him homage. This was the Prince of Wales. It is a wonder that the people did not leap up at him, or cast their garments upon him, as the Athenians did of old to their favourites . . . It was admitted on all sides that he looked handsome and dignified, and that his face beamed with intelligence . . . he looked from top to toe the favourite of fortune and the idol of his countrymen.[18]

At which the *Spectator* exclaimed, 'Why can't a Prince kiss a Princess without all this moral treacle?' The slobbering tone of the coverage evoked a scene 'in richness of colour and design quite equal to the illumination of the National Gallery; only while you don't have the gay effect of the light, you do smell the gas very strongly indeed'.[19]

But fastidious noses were a rarity. No one really minded the smell as long as the imperial project flourished. His wedding duty done, Edward VII could pursue his affairs and flatter himself that he was an international diplomat. George V collected his stamps and shot his pheasants. As long as they turned out for the occasional pageant, the newspaper proprietors would leave them alone with their hobbies and their vanities. Is it only coincidence that the greatest drama of modern British monarchy, the Abdication Crisis of 1936, occurred at the point at which the shadows began to lengthen over the empire?

Yet it was not the mass media which created the Abdication Crisis. At the time, and for much of the twentieth century, kings could count on the support of newspaper proprietors and their editors. There was still, clearly, a British ruling class. Well over a century earlier, when George III's prolonged illness (believed now to be porphyria) made it necessary to appoint his son as regent, William Cobbett had remarked that, even with three hundred newspapers in circulation, for the three years preceding the appointment 'the English people knew no more than the people of China did what was the real situation of the king'.[20] It was little better in 1936. If pointed in the right direction, a conscientious British newspaper reader studying the Court Circular might have worked out what was going on. But it was only foreign – and especially American – newspapers which reported the king's clearly intimate friendship with a divorcee with any openness. At the king's request Lord Beaverbrook scurried around the newspapers, requesting discretion in their coverage of Mrs Simpson's impending divorce case.

The dominant public virtues – honour, restraint, duty – long outlived the Victorians, and would have been as recognizable in 1950 as in 1850. Among those allowed access to the royal presence, discretion was absolute. Sir Philip Hunloke, George V's sailing master, once confided to a colleague that 'there is a blackbird on the lawn. But for God's sake, don't quote me.'[21] When Elizabeth II took the throne she could count upon a similar reticence. Loyalty was still a clearly understood concept. The compulsory military service introduced in wartime was still in force, and the population was therefore well used to the idea of hierarchy and to the figure who sat at its head. But a social revolution occurred during her reign. By the time of Elizabeth's Golden Jubilee, conscription was long gone, and loyalty had been overshadowed by mass emotion, which became perhaps the dominant characteristic of the mass-media age. The most extraordinary demonstration of this new behaviour occurred with the funeral of Diana, Princess of Wales, when something close to collective hysteria seemed to overtake the nation. But the change might also be seen in the different responses to the funerals of Elizabeth II's parents, which were separated by fifty years. When George VI succumbed to lung cancer in 1952 his biographer reported that his funeral expressed 'that quiet dignity he had shown in his life'.[22] When his widow, by now Queen Elizabeth the Queen Mother, died in 2002, more than one million people lined the route of the funeral procession, but they did so showing a great deal less restraint. The first funeral took place among a people who had shared the experience of wartime, worn uniforms together and endured. The mourners at the second were civilians, living in a comfortable consumer society in which television reporters and newspaper editors played the parts once performed by vicars and bishops.

In the period between the two funerals the British empire had evaporated. The Great White Queen no longer sat as the mother of a vast international family but as a distant great-aunt. The grumbling began within a few years of her coronation. In 1957, an article in the *National and English Review* complained that the people who surrounded the queen were 'almost without exception the "tweedy" sort', so out of touch with the times that the speeches they wrote for her made her seem like 'a priggish schoolgirl, captain of the hockey team, a prefect and a recent candidate for confirmation'.[23] The remarks earned the author a mountain of hate-mail, insinuations about his sexuality, an appearance on television and a slap in the face from a member of the League of Empire Loyalists. But the comments were largely justified. It was unusual for the queen's advisers to have been to university. They were more at home in the drawing rooms of country houses and on the shooting field than in the cities in which the vast bulk of the population lived, and their only awareness of middle- or lower-middle-class life was when they visited a house on their or a friend's estate. 'We *were* a tweedy lot,' a senior official of the time happily confessed, many years later. 'In truth, we were hardly paid at all, so you could only afford to work there if you had some private means. I could never have done the job otherwise. You were expected to do it out of loyalty.'[24]

The attack on the royal advisers was accompanied by John Osborne's splutterings of anger the same year about the institution itself being 'the gold filling in a mouthful of decay'.[25] The royal household affected disdain. But if it did not find a way to reinvent itself for the new age in which it found itself, the monarchy would slide from remoteness to irrelevance. The central conundrum of the new mass-media age could be summarized as how to retain a distance while appearing intimate – for distance without intimacy nourishes public hostility, while intimacy without distance destroys respect. The solution, which was actively encouraged by Prince Philip, took another decade to arrive. In 1969 the BBC was allowed to make a documentary which would give its viewers a closer look at the royal family than had ever been possible before.

Royal Family was a pact with the devil. Throughout the early years of the queen's reign there had been a watertight distinction between official functions and what were considered to be private engagements. The line was clearly known and understood and largely respected by the press and the youthful television services. *Royal Family* blew a hole in the dyke. At the time, the film seemed to the queen's new press secretary, William Heseltine, its main advocate at the palace, to be a way of buying the good opinion of the British people. Heseltine, an amiable Australian, was undoubtedly a breath of fresh air. His previous experience as private secretary to the Australian Prime Minister made him acutely aware of how old fashioned and out of touch the palace was. But it had also given him a very different way of looking at the world: one of the main jobs of the staff of a democratic politician is to promote the individual to the electorate, which is not quite the same as promoting an institution. The resulting BBC documentary undoubtedly achieved its purpose of showing people how their queen lived her life. A remarkable two-thirds of the population of the country was estimated to have watched one or other of its two screenings.

The idea behind *Royal Family* had been to present the monarchy to its people as bigger than one person. The 'peg' on which it was hung was the forthcoming investiture of Prince Charles as Prince of Wales, a ritual which had itself been invented only in 1911, as a stunt to proclaim the special authority of the future Edward VIII. Charles's investiture, on a set devised by his aunt's husband Lord Snowdon and the theatre designer Carl Toms, was replete with much bogus medievalism invented for television. But it was the documentary film showing the domestic life of the Windsors which had the lasting impact. Much of what purported to be observational filming was stilted, but in the most famous scene the family were shown at a loch-side barbecue, with Prince Charles mixing a salad dressing while his father grilled some sausages. The natural-history filmmaker David Attenborough gave the producer Richard Cawston a typically anthropological analysis of the damage he thought would be done by letting daylight in. 'You're killing the monarchy, you know, with this film you're making,' he told him. 'The whole institution depends on mystique and the tribal chief in his hut. If any member of the tribe ever sees inside the hut, then the whole system of the tribal chiefdom is damaged and the tribe eventually disintegrates.'[26] But the fault – if fault it was – lay not with the producer, who was only doing what any journalist would want to do. It had not been necessary to break down the door. It had been opened from inside, and it would be very hard to close it again. How could the palace complain about invasions of privacy when, by inviting the cameras to film domestic events, it had invaded its own privacy?

And the very title of the film, *Royal Family*, had promoted the idea that there was something special not merely about the person in whom the office of state was embodied, but about all her immediate relatives – 'The Firm'. There was no constitutional need to promote this fiction, and, given how badly junior members of the royal family have behaved throughout the centuries, anyone with the slightest grasp of history ought to have recognized the hostage which had been surrendered. Now the opportunity to grow up privately had been severely circumscribed.

The public claimed to want to believe that their kings and queens and princes were like them, yet simultaneously seemed to demand evidence that they were not. The sight of royal domestic life gave the satirists a field day, for the film had revealed the great sin, in an age of mass fashion, of clinging to different standards of dress, speech and behaviour. The monarchy looked buttoned up, fusty and slightly absurd. *Private Eye* moved from parodies of the Court Circular ('After breakfast consisting of grapefruit segments, cornflakes, haddocks, eggs, bacon, sausage, fried bread, tomato and mushroom, the Princess mounted a bingo – a cross between an ostrich and a giraffe – and set off on a sogat hunting expedition . . . Later the Princess watched a native display of television in the Maudling Lounge of the Ethiopian Hilton')[27] to marking the collapse of the marriage of Queen Elizabeth's sister, Princess Margaret, in 1976 with a Royal Divorce Souvenir Supplement, beginning 'It was the Fairy-Tale Separation of the century!' When the queen celebrated her Silver Jubilee the following year, the magazine was so nauseated by the obsequious coverage that it published 'Travesty', a parody of Robert Lacey's book of tribute, *Majesty*. It disclosed that 'She once startled Harold Wilson by asking why Arthur Bottomley wore red, white and blue braces,' that 'one of the most closely guarded secrets of the Queen's entire 25-year reign was her brief but tempestuous love affair with Glenn Miller, the legendary American band-leader who later "mysteriously disappeared"', that 'the Queen sleeps in a four-poster bed which she takes round with her wherever she goes. She wears fluffy woollen bedroom slippers, and likes to read for at least an hour before going to bed. Her favourite books are *Black Beauty*, *Murder on the Orient Express*, and *The Jeffrey Bernard Book of the Turf*,' while 'the Royal Corgis sleep in the kitchen along with Lord Weidenfeld, and other members of the Royal Household'.[28]

This was in similar vein to the nineteenth-century satirists describing how Prince Albert was to be fumigated and have his head shaved, to make him ready for the higher sanitary standards of England. The real problem came with the mainstream newspapers. The days when the king's affair with Mrs Simpson could be kept out of the media just by having a word with a few pliant press barons were gone. Many newspapers have been owned by power-crazed, or simply crazy, rich men. But the new generation cared more for commercial success than social acceptance. What mattered to them was what sold. Figures like Beaverbrook and Northcliffe minded about what the court might think of them. Rupert Murdoch was indifferent. And while it might appear much safer for the royal household to be preoccupied with horse-racing and country life, instead of, say, Edward VIII's taste for the louche extravagances of café society, it left them with fewer metropolitan ears in which to whisper. In addition there were currents flowing through society to which the court seemed oblivious. Feminism, for example, would never be reconciled to the principle that male children would always have a prior claim to the throne over girls: when Prince Charles became engaged to Diana Spencer, the feminist magazine *Spare Rib* was giving away badges reading 'Don't Do It, Di'. The end of deference enabled the *Socialist Worker* to enliven its usually dour view of the world with the headline 'A Fairy Tale Comes True: Big Ears Marries Noddy'.

In retrospect, the palace might have wished Diana had taken the feminists' advice, for the eventual collapse of the marriage presented the monarchy with its gravest crisis since the Abdication. Reading the press from the time discloses the remarkable scale of the firestorm. You would have serious trouble in finding a single day between June 1992 and January 1993 in which the royal family did not appear in the tabloid press. Even the once staid broadsheets joined in, although it was noticeable that the staunchly royalist *Daily Telegraph* maintained a dignified distance from the more sordid revelations, while the *Guardian*, which subsequently declared itself republican, luxuriated in every detail of the gossip, under the pretence that it was carrying out a comparative media analysis.

There had been rumours that the royal marriage was in trouble for months, but the storm broke in June 1992, with the publication of Andrew Morton's *Diana: Her True Story*. His timing was perfect: it was the start of the summer 'silly season', when true news is hard to find. Serialization of the book in the *Sunday Times* was accompanied by stories in other Murdoch publications, notably the *Sun*, of how the queen mother had witnessed a suicide attempt by Diana, by publication of photographs of the royal couple's separate bedrooms,[29] by homilies from tabloid agony aunts (which usually ended up blaming the queen) and by telephone votes in which readers were invited to give the nation the benefit of their views on whose fault it was, whether the couple should divorce, and who should have custody of the royal princes. 'The tabloid press has for years suffered from a compulsive eating disorder which leads it to "binge" on royal stories, only to follow them up with enforced vomiting of bile upon the Windsors,' said the *Guardian*, sniffing humbug. Considering the experience of Diana, following on from those of Lord Snowdon, Mark Phillips and Sarah Ferguson, the newspaper wondered whether there was 'something about the condition of Royalty that may be, literally, insufferable to incomers. How much this is due to the media's own role is an irony not addressed.'[30] On 12 June, the *Sun*'s front page was taken up by a picture of Diana bursting into tears, 'overwhelmed by a tidal wave of love'.[31] There were more photographs inside and a helpful checklist headed '10 tell-tale signs of a woman about to crack'. These did not include an estimation of what was likely to happen if newspapers hound someone for weeks, and then revel in watching them collapse. (Just as well, perhaps, since it later turned out that Diana was the source of most of the stories about herself.)

By the middle of June, it was clear that things had gone too far. Someone had to be punished. The newspapers did not blame themselves. They did not blame Diana, who was clearly the 'victim'. None drew the lesson that the institution ought to be abolished. Quite the reverse. The question was not 'How can we get rid of it?' but 'How can we revive it?' The storm found the old lightning-conductor of the royal finances. The *Daily Mail* suggested there was a sense that 'our monarchy is overblown and out of tune with the times'.[32] How cutting the budget of the palace was supposed to make their marriages work was never explained. But Something Must Be Done. The *Daily Mail*'s editorial, 'Why we have a right to know', concluded that 'Those who ask where is the public interest in all of this need look no further. The throne may have been rocked. But on new foundations it can become stronger than ever.'[33]

In August the newspapers were adorned with pictures of the Duchess of York on holiday with her children where she was foolish enough to sunbathe without her bikini top. Her 'financial adviser', John Bryan, was photographed sucking the then-royal toes. The ghost of the *Royal Family* film struck. The editor of the *Daily Mirror*, which published the photographs, declared, 'I do not think that someone in the Duchess's position, as a member of the archetypal family, which the royal family is, is in the position to do the kind of things that she is doing with Mr Bryan.'[34] The duchess – a commoner who had been welcomed into the royal family as 'a breath of fresh air' – was a wonderful target. This time, there did seem a connection to be made between the 'scandal' and the bigger point. The target was again the royal finances, but now the newspapers could reasonably ask why the British taxpayer should support frivolous minor figures now very unlikely to come anywhere near the throne.

No sooner had the Duchess of York been exposed than a tape recording appeared in the *News of the* World which showed her friend Diana in intimate telephone conversation with a lover. The recording was said to have been made by a seventy-year-old retired bank manager who claimed he had merely been listening out for racing tips and happened to have a tape-recorder to hand. Whether, as was claimed, the source was really one of the intelligence services was never established. Transcripts of the 'Squidgy' tape, larded with the terms of endearment and pet names which disclosed the lovers' intimacy, were spread over page after tabloid page and fanned the flames of scandal yet more. After five pages, the *Sun* drew its editorial conclusion. 'The queen does not deserve to be at the centre of such a crisis of confidence. Her 40-year reign has been impeccable,' it said, blithely ignoring its own role in the affair, before going on, inevitably, to settle on the money question. Using calculations which would make the back of an envelope seem like a doctoral thesis, it concluded that the queen could support herself and her immediate family from her own income, and that she should pay taxes.[35] Five days later, the *Daily Telegraph* turned on the whole notion of a royal family – it was 'largely a sentimental Victorian concept, with progressively little basis in reality' – and suggested that the queen abdicate in favour of Prince Charles, to give him something to do.[36] The newspaper had travelled quite some distance, although not as far as the readers of the *Sun*, 63 per cent of whom had come to the conclusion that Britain no longer needed a monarchy at all. (This is not, of course, the same as saying that they would prefer an elected president, and anyway the poll was of a self-selecting sample of a mere six thousand who could be bothered to telephone the newspaper's phone bank.)[37]

By January 1993, Diana had had enough. 'Princess Diana is to divorce Prince Charles, withdraw from the Royal Family and walk away from a bitter "custody" battle over sons William and Harry,' splashed the *Sunday Mirror*.[38]

Nothing like this had happened since the disastrous marriage of the future George IV and Princess Caroline. But at the time of their wedding, in 1795, there was no mass-market press. Now, both sides were laying out their partner's dirty laundry for the benefit of the readers of tabloid newspapers. The royal household attempted to fight back by discrediting the media. Taking the palace at their word, Lord McGregor, the seventy-one-year-old chairman of the Press Complaints Commission, drafted a statement in which he talked in horrified tones about reporters 'dabbling their fingers in the stuff of other people's souls'. He read the statement to the queen's private secretary, Sir Robert Fellowes (Eton, Scots Guards, married to Diana's sister and the son of a man who had also worked for the royal family), who assured him that the princess had not been the source of the stories. When poor Lord McGregor later discovered that Diana had, indeed, been giving reporters the most explosive stories – and that she had arranged the apparently 'intrusive' pictures of herself and her children – he was not a happy man. The invasions of privacy had been perpetrated not by grubby men in cheap suits but by the Princess of Wales herself. The verdict meant that most of what had been reported was true. The question 'Who do you believe, the palace or the tabloid press?' now had a much more ambiguous answer.

But help was at hand for Diana. Just when it looked as if she was in deep trouble, 'Camillagate' broke. By astonishing good luck, coincidence or orchestration, an Australian magazine owned by Rupert Murdoch printed transcripts of a conversation between the Prince of Wales and his mistress, including exquisitely embarrassing intimacies. The tape disclosed an Eeyorish man, prone to seeing the glass half empty, in the grip of a long-lived, intense passion and prone to bad jokes. It left Charles more tarnished than ever, and with a most undignified reputation as a man who dreamed of being reincarnated as a tampon. It was wince-making stuff and left him permanently sullied in the eyes of many of his future subjects. The *Sun* screamed, '6 MIN LOVE TAPE COULD COST CHARLES THE THRONE'.

The *Sun* journalists were troubled by whether the Prince of Wales could inherit the crown – and the position of Defender of the Faith – when he had broken at least two of the Ten Commandments. Only two? There is a long and illustrious tradition of Princes of Wales bedding other men's wives. By comparison with the assiduous adultery of Edward VII, Charles was an innocent abroad. But his predecessor had not had to deal with the media moralists. One member of the Labour shadow cabinet became so exercised about the 'scandal' that he dared to utter the word 'republic' at a meeting in Blackburn, before getting slapped down by his party leader. Rupert Murdoch's *Times* organized a debate on the future of the monarchy with an earnest think-tank at which, to no one's great surprise, the self-invited audience thought it was time for a change. There was a series of fruitless speculations about whether the intelligence services – or rogue elements within them – might have been responsible for the bugging operations. Prince Charles was variously reported to be thinking of giving up the throne, giving up women, or giving up anything but good works. And then, like most fusses, the fuss died away.

But the consequences of what the queen called her 'annus horribilis' were long-lasting. Something snapped in the relationship between the media and the palace when both sides in the failed marriage used television to confess their adultery. It showed itself first in the reaction to a fire which burned down part of the Queen's principal residence at Windsor Castle – an accident which seemed to be a metaphor for the fall of the House of Windsor. A quick announcement by the Major government that repairs would be funded by the taxpayer was followed by a speedy retraction, when the media articulated what they perceived to be the extent of public resistance to the idea. In the event, the work was largely paid for out of the proceeds of admission charges to royal buildings (which the public owned anyway).

But in 1997, before the repairs were complete, the palace faced another test, when Princess Diana was killed in a Paris underpass, pursued by paparazzi. Diana had lived by the mass media and she died by the media. Hidden away in their estate at Balmoral while mountains of flowers piled up outside the gates of the London palaces, the Windsors seemed uncaring and remote. They were unfortunate in having, in Tony Blair, a prime minister with an intuitive understanding of the synapses of the electronic age: his propagandists ensured that the words 'the People's Princess' came tumbling out of his mouth. By contrast, Queen Elizabeth's advisers were struck dumb. The royal family showed how little they had adjusted to the new age by retreating into the dignified silence of previous times. But dignity was no longer enough. For the first time, there was a noticeable anger against the queen: her silence indicated callousness, her refusal to fly the flag above Buckingham Palace at half-mast was presented as a petty act of spite, calculated to insult the memory of a young woman who the palace realized had done them serious damage. Friends of the queen argued that hiding away with your grief was a natural human reaction. But, with the nation in the grip of an emotional spasm, it looked like something worse. A royal family is not just another family, and a public gesture was needed. No words at all came from the queen, until, several days later, she was put on television to deliver a reluctant homily declaring how much Diana was missed. In those days following the death of the princess, the British monarchy confronted its greatest unpopularity in decades. Diana's failings – her petulance, her manipulativeness, her deviousness – were forgotten, in favour of a picture of her as some secular saint. On the day of her funeral, the *Sun* devoted thirty-three of its forty-eight pages to the princess, with headlines like 'The Nation Weeps' and 'Goodnight Angel'. It was reckoned that over ten million people signed the books of condolences which were laid out everywhere from cathedrals to supermarkets. The monarchy discovered that the news media were the repository of an enormous reserve of irrational, pre-modern belief – precisely the sort of instincts upon which they ought to have been able to capitalize, but which they seemed not to comprehend. The opinion pollster Robert Worcester took leave of his trade's usual professed scientism and gothically reflected that at that moment the royal family 'stood on the brink of the abyss, staring down into the chasm of the dismay of a growing number of British subjects'.[39]

In the weeks and months which followed, the palace began to rebuild. In the hysteria of the moment the monarchy's unpopularity was perhaps exaggerated: even when the tide of emotion was at its height, fewer than two people in ten seemed to want to replace it with a republic.[40] But the queen's advisers had been shaken. The House of Windsor had squandered much of the goodwill it had previously enjoyed by first exploiting the press, and then attempting disdainfully to deny doing so. Diana's deviousness had done nothing to tarnish her halo: thirty-two countries issued commemorative stamps within a month of her death. Buckingham Palace now began to wake up to some of the challenges of the mass-media age. A series of private secretaries and assistant private secretaries were hired from other worlds, even occasionally from outside the ranks of government, in an attempt to change the mood of the place. Much of their time was spent in writing thoughtful papers about how to enhance the prestige and popularity of the monarchy, very many of which were quietly dropped into the wastepaper bin. But gradually they had an impact. Some areas of Buckingham Palace life, notably the ceremonial, organizational and catering functions, remain in the hands of individuals who differ little from their predecessors. But by the early twenty-first century the private office, the press office and many of the other areas were increasingly staffed by a new breed. The cosy relationships of clubland which had made it possible to manipulate the press at the time of the Abdication Crisis had largely died. But the new generation of technocrats knew that, if they played their cards cannily, the palace still had a decent hand: in the relationship between royalty and media, the cards had not been dealt evenly, and information was precious. They had also acquired some effective techniques to manage the new relationship.

They showed, for example, a much improved professionalism in handling the death of the queen's mother on a spring Saturday afternoon in 2002. The death was not unexpected (she was, after all, 101) and the machine was well prepared. Whether, as many close to the palace suspect, the announcement was deliberately held back for several hours in order to manipulate the media is speculation. The official time of death was given as 3.15 in the afternoon, with an official statement two and a half hours later. The delay was explained by the need to give time for the family to be informed. While this seems eminently plausible, it is odd, to say the least, that officials in the Cabinet Office, who would have to handle the funeral arrangements, had been called into their offices before midday. 'It's common knowledge', one source claims, 'that she had died much earlier in the day – or perhaps hadn't woken up that morning – and that the news was held back.'

The advantage of holding back the news was that it gave much more opportunity to control the way events were reported. The most unpredictable of the newspapers are the Sunday papers. Had news of the queen mother's death been released early on the Saturday they would have been printing second-wave stories, rather than reporting the fact of her death. The palace feared that these pieces might have included observations about her reactionary political opinions (even, some claimed, 'Nazi sympathies') and tittle-tattle on subjects such as her profligacy and drinking habits. But by releasing the news late in the afternoon, they ensured that the Sunday papers stuck with the comparatively straightforward – and largely sympathetic – story of her death. The claim is never likely to be proved conclusively either way, although there is a probable precedent in the case of George V, who is widely believed to have been helped on his way by his doctor, Lord Dawson of Penn.[41] Having composed on the back of a menu card the immortal line 'The king's life is moving peacefully towards its close,' Dawson is said to have injected morphine and cocaine into his jugular vein in order to ensure that his death met the deadline for reporting in

The Times, instead of the less dignified evening papers. Unusually, the files covering George V's death are closed until the year 2037.

In the case of his daughter-in-law, once the announcement had been made, the palace played the press like a violin. A flag was immediately flown at half-mast over Buckingham Palace. Realizing that the media were a beast which needed to be fed at regular intervals, meals were provided. One announcement followed another, in time for morning or evening deadlines: the lying-in-state, the broad funeral arrangements, followed by detail after detail. There were the traditional artillery salutes, and both Prince Charles and the queen delivered televised statements. Parliament was recalled. The grandsons stood vigil in good time for the television news. None of this was thought up on the spot. The lying-in-state – 'Operation Marquee' – had been planned long in advance, to allow for the coffin to be on display twenty-three hours a day. In fact the opening hours were only gradually extended, to ensure that there was always a healthy line of well-wishers standing in the cold: the last thing the palace wanted was an impression of anything less than multitudinous mourning. The arrangements were an example of the extent to which the queen's advisers had understood the importance of the manipulation of public opinion.

Long-term public relations strategies are now in place, in which television appearances which seem to give an insight into the 'real human being' are incorporated alongside the ceremonial. The Prince of Wales's office recognized that it would take longer to restore any trust with journalists, so used had they become to its habit of denying things which were true. Instead of planted stories there were now brochures produced to talk up his role as a philanthropist. Convinced that once anyone has met the queen or her heir they become a royalist, officials talk freely about 'getting them out working'. At regular meetings they have discussed arrangements for the queen's funeral. The business of the palace is survival.

The monarchy's advisers have their work cut out. The heir to the throne has never been comfortable with the mass media, and in many of his television appearances his contorted body language gives the impression of someone who belongs in another age. As a young man on a visit to Canada he was composing characteristically self-pitying doggerel about the press pack (to be sung to the tune of 'Immortal, invisible, God only wise'):

> Insistent, persistent, the Press never end,
> One day they will drive me right round the bend,
> Recording, rephrasing, every word that I say,
> It's got to be news at the end of the day.[42]

Over the years this contempt had hardened into loathing. The only exceptions were his public excursions on subjects like architecture, organic farming, gardening and the like, in which he dictated and vetoed the content. At his fortieth birthday, he was happily using the mass media to bang the drum for the causes he cared about, for example in a BBC television programme entitled *A Vision of Britain*, in which, while appearing to talk about architecture, he opined on everything from civic capitalism to sustainable farming, by way of meditations on the relationship between God and man. The newspapers loved it. 'God Bless the Prince of Wales!' gushed the *Sunday Express*, and 'Fit to be King NOW!' cried the *Sunday Mirror*. Perhaps he believed there would be some similarly ecstatic response to his decision to summon his friend Jonathan Dimbleby to attempt to regain the initiative when his marriage fell apart. Instead, his confession of adultery merely led Princess Diana to take to television herself and demonstrate how much more effective a performer she was.

Occasionally the mask slips. In the spring of 2005 Prince Charles posed with his sons for photographs on a skiing trip at the Swiss resort of Klosters. The photo-call was a mutually agreed arrangement, in which the royal family posed for pictures instead of being caught unawares on the slopes. The microphones caught the prince asking the boys, 'Do I put my arms around you? . . . What do we do?' 'Keep smiling, keep smiling,' replied Prince William. Charles bared his teeth again, until Nicholas Witchell, a BBC reporter, asked how he was feeling about his forthcoming wedding to Camilla. 'I'm very glad you've heard of it,' he sneered. His sons chuckled and then, forgetting the microphones, the Prince of Wales swore under his breath. 'These bloody people,' he fulminated. 'I can't bear that man. I mean, he's so awful, he really is.'

Any sensitive person caught out being so rude would apologize afterwards. Prince Charles never did so. His contempt seems to stem from a genuine belief that he is above exposure, except on the occasions when he deigns to share with his people his views on the natural world and the built environment. His disdain is hardly original: George V talked of 'these filthy rags of newspapers'.[43] Charles certainly had reason to feel aggrieved: at the height of the Diana débâcle, for example, Camilla Parker Bowles had been besieged in her house and found one photographer, in balaclava and blacked-up face, crawling across a roof. Eventually, she daubed her own face with boot polish, dressed in the darkest clothes she could find, and crawled across two fields in the middle of the night to escape. When citizens are made fugitives for the crime of offending against newspaper editors, one is bound to ask where, precisely, power lies.[44]

Many of the reporters at Klosters were not unhappy about Charles's embarrassment. They felt he had treated them with contempt for such a long time that they were glad to see him reap the whirlwind. The prince had consistently misunderstood or ignored a basic truth at the heart of the relationship between royalty and the people. He seemed to believe that his significance lay in what he believed and did. The truth was simply that his significance lay in who he was.

Royalty and mass media are made for each other. The first is based upon mystery and the second upon disclosure. Courtiers may harrumph at what they claim to be impertinence, but no modern monarchy can survive without the connivance of the newspapers and television. They are the amniotic fluid of royalty.

The emasculation of monarchy coincided not merely with the expansion of empire but with the expansion of the franchise and the explosion of the mass media. Until the invention of television and the arrival of its glossy, apparently friendly inhabitants, the recognizability of royalty made it an ideal vehicle for selling things to the growing mass market. Manufacturers used Victoria's face to sell matchboxes, condensed milk, polish and 'Diamond Queen' cigarettes. What thoughts must have passed through the mind of Bertie, the Prince of Wales who was to become Edward VII, when, halfway through one of his innumerable seductions, he reached for a rubber condom and found the box decorated with the twin likenesses of the most respectable figures the manufacturers could imagine, William Ewart Gladstone and his own mother?[45] Bertie's name endorsed J. J. Matthias's Unrivalled Cherry Toothpaste, Robert Williams's knife powder and Horniman's Pure Tea. Later, his queen would be borrowed to promote 'Alexandra Pomade' and Boisselier's Chocolates, while his mistress Lillie Langtry advertised 'Harlene for the Hair' shampoo, with the cheeky proclamation that it was 'Under Royal Patronage'. His son George V would find his face stuck on to tins of Huntley and Palmers Empire Assorted Biscuits, Camp Coffee and Player's Medium Cut Navy Cigarettes. George's wife was used to advertise 'May Blossom' tobacco.[46]

By the late twentieth century, royalty had been replaced by television celebrities with familiar faces, better teeth and sharper elbows. The new aristocrats are soap-opera stars and musicians. Yet the royal invocation is not dead. Hip-hop stars like Run-DMC call themselves 'the Kings from Queens', and there were other rappers like Queen Latifah, Princess Superstar and Prince Paul.[47] Magazine editors know that if they put a photograph of Prince William on the cover thousands of additional copies will fly off the newsstands. Even Sarah Ferguson, the calamitous former wife of the Duke of York, deployed her nickname ('the Duchess of Pork') to enrich herself promoting Weight Watchers in the United States. Prince Charles used his position to market a brand, Duchy Originals, which traded less on his name than on his holistic convictions about agriculture and manufacture. (He still winces as he tells friends that when he launched the brand he was denounced in one of the newspapers as 'this shop-soiled royal'.) It is noticeable that, as long as the coverage seemed to be benefiting the institution, there were no complaints from the palace and its servants in parliament or the press.

Royal news may no longer be confined to the Court Circular and the *London Gazette*. But most of it comes just as certainly from the Buckingham Palace press office. Royal appearances at public events are treated reverently: the awestruck tone of broadcast commentary was set by Richard Dimbleby ('Gold Microphone-in-Waiting', as he was nicknamed by Malcolm Muggeridge), and it has never really changed. Whenever a member of the family chooses to hold forth on something, they are awarded column-inches which few of their subjects could command.[48] Royal coverage, even in the tabloid press, is rarely directly subversive. Why should it be, when the monarchy is such a productive seam? Conventions have been agreed, deals struck about the limits of legitimate inquiry: much of the domestic media does not need to be muzzled because it has muzzled itself. (The problem is much less with the domestic press than with the paparazzi, who know that while the British media may have entered into agreements with Buckingham Palace, there will be a magazine in Buenos Aires or Moscow which would pay good money for a sensational picture.)

Even when the mass media have dabbled their fingers in the stuff of royal souls, it has been because they have been invited by royalty to do so. No one coerced Charles and Diana to talk about their private lives on television, any more than Prince Philip was forced to barbecue sausages in public, or indeed Queen Victoria to publish her Highland Journal.

It is true that monarchy has to deal with occasional examples of a form of reporting which tries to circumvent the official channels. But that is the nature of journalism. What is remarkable is how few reporters ever really put their shoulders to the task. Despite the foreign trips, the royal beat is not particularly sought after, and – understandably perhaps – there are few enough stories which begin with genuine high-level sources. The problems come elsewhere: in 2005, plans for the wedding of Prince Charles and Camilla Parker Bowles had been kept secret inside Buckingham Palace, the Archbishop of Canterbury's residence Lambeth Palace and the offices of some of the country's most eminent lawyers, but within twenty-four hours of Downing Street receiving the highly confidential discussion document – and with many of the details still to be settled – the news of the wedding plans was splashed all over the newspapers. Newspapers will cultivate servants, pay money for tittle-tattle and, sometimes, acquire genuine scoops in the process. But defining what is in the public interest and what is merely interesting to the public would occasionally have defeated Solomon. On one recent occasion, a senior member of the royal household was obliged to haggle with a newspaper editor who was planning to publish photographs snatched by a visiting builder of one of the queen's lavatories.

It cannot be much fun. But where would the royals be if no one had the slightest interest in them? In a perverse way this need to see that they are just like the rest of us is what feeds the belief that they are not.

12. The End of the Line?

The king never dies

William Blackstone, 1765

As we all know, Diana, Princess of Wales did not die in a car accident in a Paris underpass. She was murdered, on the express instructions of her former husband. According to her one-time butler, she had written a letter prophesying as much, ten months before her death.[1] The elements of the dozens of conspiracy theories – drugs, tampered cars, strange flashes, missing tapes from security cameras, the 'secret service connections' of drivers and bodyguards – lack many vital ingredients, not least a plausible motive. This does not deter the evangelists for the murder hypothesis, among the most eager of whom is a former television presenter named David Icke. He has concocted a plot which links Stonehenge, the Yale University secret society the Skull and Bones, and the Nazis. Icke believes that the world is controlled by and for the benefit of a race of pan-dimensional lizards. He is certain that the accident was truly a murder, planned by Prince Philip and Queen 'El lizard birth' the Queen Mother. 'Does anyone doubt that this was a ritual murder?' he asks authoritatively.[2]

Clearly not, if you believe the world is controlled by giant lizards. But crackpot fantasies are merely the most extreme manifestation of a phenomenon which affects most of us. In the days of mourning which followed Diana's death, millions of perfectly ordinary people behaved in a most extraordinary way. Mountains of flowers were laid spontaneously outside the royal palaces. Handwritten notes were stuck to trees. Men and women wept openly in the street. Thousands lined up to sign books of condolences.

And two and a half billion people were estimated to have watched the funeral on television. But it was noticeable that the great majority of these 'mourners' did not display the usual behaviour of the bereaved. It was, said the writer Ian Jack, 'recreational grieving', promoting the griever from the audience 'to an on-stage part in the final act of the opera . . . It was grief with the pain removed, grief-lite. When people telephoned each other that Sunday morning, they spoke eagerly – "Have you heard that . . . ?" – and not with the dread – "How can I tell him that . . . ?" – familiar to bearers of seriously wounding news, which the hearer may recover from only in months or years or sometimes never at all.'[3] He has a point. No one has ever properly made sense of the spasm which convulsed the country in those September days, and certainly there was a 'Look at me!' element to some of the 'grieving'. The hysteria and the appetite for ludicrous conspiracies show that many people refuse to surrender their royal fantasy, even when the object of it is dead.

But in the end all princes and princesses, kings and queens, succumb to mortality. Although the muffled drumbeats and ornate catafalques of their funerals seek to disguise the fact, the final punctuation point reminds us that, for all their grandeur, they are as frail as the rest of us. It is true that, of the forty monarchs since the Norman Conquest, a higher than average number (a quarter) have died violent deaths, whether disembowelled with a red-hot poker (Edward II), murdered in the Tower (Edward V) or, like Richard I or Richard III, killed in war. But the majority have been taken off by the same mundane, undignified troubles as the rest of us. Stephen died of a blockage in his bowels, Elizabeth I of infected tonsils, Edward VIII and George VI of cancer, others, like Henry III and Victoria, of mere old age or natural causes.

The miles of bombazine, black drapes, books of condolences, lyings-in-state, coffins on gun carriages, are the final expression of a collective devotion. Of course, those who organize these events – if they think about such vulgar things at all – must understand that they are manipulating public feeling. Elaborate funerals are one of the mechanisms by which royalty is recognized as at once human and yet grander than other humans: the public imagination will not tolerate the object of its inebriation being laid away without appropriate pomp and circumstance. The pageantry of modern royal funerals – which began with the immense spectacular arranged on the death of Edward VII in 1910 – is accompanied by a torrent of goo. The silliest royal publication ever written (it is a crowded field) was probably *Where's Master?* of that same year, which purported to have been composed by the dead king's terrier, Caesar. The dog, which took a prominent role in the funeral procession, recalled an ardent churchgoer, keen gardener and loyal husband. His memoirs went through nine editions.

But the deaths of royalty also routinely attract conspiracy theories. Charles I was accused of poisoning James I. Charles II's final illness was said to have been brought on by poison, either in a cup of chocolate administered by the Duchess of Portsmouth or by the queen with a jar of dried pears. When King Ludwig II of Bavaria was found floating in a lake in 1886 the story went that he had been deliberately drowned. Conspiracy theorists were unable to accept that Crown Prince Rudolph of Austria and his mistress Marie Vetsera could have died in a suicide pact in the palace at Mayerling, and assumed that they must have been murdered – the prince's offence apparently being that he had committed journalism. The death of the British Prince George, Duke of Kent, in an air accident in 1942 was still generating conspiracy theories forty years later.[4] But, as the death of Princess Diana demonstrated, it is when the dead member of royalty is a young princess that hysteria really takes over. In 1817, the future George IV's daughter, Princess Charlotte of Wales, died after giving birth to a stillborn potential future king of England.[5] The young woman had been seen as 'a breath of fresh air' in royal circles and her death set off extravagant grief. Lord Byron was so shocked and distressed that he devoted part of the fourth canto of *Childe Harold's Pilgrimage* to the event. His contemporary Leigh Hunt explained that 'If any dreary sceptic in sentiment should ask why the sorrow is so great for this young woman, any more than another, we answer, because this young woman is the representative of *all* the others – because she stood on high, in the eyes of us all, embodying as it were the ideal as well as actual images of youth and promise.'[6] Inevitably, as happened with Diana, the conspiracy theories followed. A writer for a local London newspaper, the *Sun*,[7] published a pamphlet attempting to demonstrate that the official account of the cause of death was full of contradictions and deliberate misrepresentations, in much the same way as happened nearly two centuries later. We will not put away our illusions lightly. Having willed royalty to be higher, grander and better than us, we assume that they cannot have left us by illness or accident, but must have been stolen.

At one end of a walnut side-table in the saloon at Sandringham is a photograph of George V, who loved the house and estate, he said, more than any place on earth. At the other end of the table is a photograph of his cousin, the Tsar and Autocrat of the All the Russias. It is signed, simply, 'Nicky'. One of Queen Victoria's courtiers described the tsar as being exactly like a skinny version of George, and looking at the photographs, with their military uniforms, dark beards and air of comfortable superiority, you could easily take one for the other. George liked Nicholas very much. 'Nicky has been kindness itself to me,' he wrote to his mother; 'he is the same dear boy he has always been to me and talks to me openly on every subject.'[8]

Yet when the tsar found himself engulfed by revolution in 1917, he soon discovered the limits of his cousin's concern. Hearing of the revolution, George sent a telegram – 'My thoughts are constantly with you and I shall always remain your true and devoted friend, as you know I have been in the past.'[9] You might think that, when the 'devoted friend' heard that the Russian authorities had asked the British government to provide a haven for the tsar and his family, George would do all in his power to promote the idea. Yet three times the request was made, and the closer the possibility came, the more King George resisted it. His biographer Kenneth Rose records a series of letters from the king begging his government, in increasingly anxious tones, to refuse Nicholas and

Alexandra exile in Britain, because 'it would be strongly resisted by the public, and would undoubtedly compromise the position of the king and queen'.[10] George's reasons for denying refuge to his cousin were complicated. Like many others, he recognized the unpopularity of the empress – 'not only a Boche by birth but in sentiment',[11] as his Ambassador to France put it. He was aware of fears that offering refuge might damage relations with the new regime in Russia, whom his government hoped to retain as allies in the war against Germany. But, most of all, George seems to have feared for his own skin: sheltering the tsar might invite the suggestion that the British monarchy should be consigned to the same fate as that of his cousin. Dear Nicky was sacrificed.

Having abandoned his cousin to be murdered by the Bolsheviks, George V attended a memorial service at the Russian church in Welbeck Street, Marylebone. He recorded in his diary that his cousin had been the victim of a 'foul murder', and added, 'I was devoted to Nicky, who was the kindest of men and a thorough gentleman.'[12] The strict limits to George's 'devotion' remained unknown until recently. His defenders assert that the first duty of a monarch is to preserve the throne, and he therefore could not take the risk of inciting unrest by giving shelter to the representative of autocracy. Perhaps. But the tale hanging on the two photographs on the Sandringham table illustrates precisely how little freedom is available to the king in a democracy. Shorn even of the capacity to shelter family members in distress and with little real power, royalty is at best able only to give voice to vague expressions, like Edward VIII's comment in South Wales that 'Something must be done.' It remains the most 'political' statement uttered by a twentieth-century king, but it recognizes the limits of the role. Pleading, hectoring and cajoling is one thing. Doing something is someone else's job. In the end Edward was unable even to hold on to the throne if he wanted to marry the woman he loved.

Nonetheless, the House of Windsor endured, while the monarchies of the other great powers in the First World War – Russia, Austria and Germany – tumbled. It is noticeable, worldwide, that the monarchies that have disappeared are the ones which were most autocratic and vainglorious – the Shah of Shahs in Iran, the Chinese and Ethiopian emperors, the Tsar of All the Russias. The Japanese emperor clung on only by abasing himself at the say-so of the conquering Americans. The monarchies that have survived are the ones which were more modest or, like the British, managed to make themselves modest. As George VI surveyed the landscape after the Second World War, he found it hard to remain confident that the institution he embodied had a place any longer. 'Everything is going now,' he said to Vita Sackville-West in 1948, when he heard that her ancestral home was being handed over to the National Trust. 'Before long I shall also have to go.'[13]

The fate that George VI feared has not befallen his family, and Britain entered the third millennium with a queen on the throne and an heir in place. How much longer can the monarchy last?

To be sure, it is a deeply conservative institution. How could it be otherwise given its ancient roots? Radicalism belongs to those who take their bearings from an imagined future rather than from a very public past. If kings and queens represent an institution which has been an almost constant feature of British history, it should not be in the slightest bit surprising that they tend to be conventional or fogeyish in their personal convictions. Does it matter? They have long since ceased to wield real power, and evidence of attempts to interfere directly in day-to-day politics over the last hundred years is, to say the least, limited. In the case of the reign of Elizabeth II, the evidence often suggests that the queen was used by the government of the hour for its own political purpose, which shows not power but impotence. On the rare occasions on which previous twentieth-century monarchs took a political position, as when George V pleaded with his government to restrain its 'cat and mouse' policy of force-feeding suffragettes, it does not seem to have been particularly self-interested.[14]

But republicans object to the whole edifice not because of what it thinks but because of what it represents. The problem is less what they do than the fact that they exist at all. They affront notions of democracy by achieving their eminence simply by privileged birth. They occupy positions at the head of the Church, the armed forces and other institutions of the state without having to earn them. They embody an idea of society in which advancement comes not by merit but by birth. All of this is true. The theoretical case for monarchy is very hard to make, and to any true democrat there is an unanswerable argument for its abolition.

But that is when the difficulties set in. The British monarchy might be got rid of by one of two mechanisms – an act of parliament or a revolution. Each is currently unimaginable. (A third possibility, abdication – which some consider unmentionable – removes only the monarch, not the monarchy.) So, while royalty is part of the scenery, republicanism remains a fringe activity because the discussion exists only in the realm of theory. It defaults immediately into questions of how you would replace the king or queen. Would you wish, for example, to have an executive president, or a figure, like the king or queen, who was there merely for ceremonial purposes? The first would mean that national identity was embodied in a politician. Whether the examples of George Bush or Bill Clinton, François Mitterrand or Jacques Chirac, are appealing is a matter of personal taste. But the post would assuredly become the most glittering prize in politics, and such a president would, necessarily, seek to increase his or her popularity in order to continue as the country's supreme leader. Since politics is all about promising people a better future, a political president would have different priorities to those brought to the post by a king or queen, whose very claim on the title means that the values they express are those of continuity rather than change. Perhaps this would be a good thing. But the unhappy experience of those countries in eastern Europe which were occupied by the Soviet Union after the Second World War – and found that much of their history ceased to exist along with their monarchies – suggests otherwise.[15] As to the suggestion that such figures would be less self-important – or cheaper to maintain – it is worth recalling that the President of the glorious People's Republic of China refused an invitation to stay at Buckingham Palace during his visit to London in 2005, on the ground that it was 'not five-star enough'.

An alternative would be to choose a system in which the functions of a president were confined to the purely symbolic. Such a figure would merely have to turn out for the occasional ceremony, welcome visiting heads of state and put his or her signature to acts of parliament. It would be straightforward enough to devise a way of choosing such a figure – to be truly democratic, you might make it a weekly prize in the National Lottery. But no constitutional theorist would ever settle for something so simple. Instead, the post would be filled by someone elected, either directly by the people or by parliament. To be sufficiently well known to be chosen by direct election, candidates would have to have been in the public eye for some time. But the problem with having a history is that, when you acquire one, you also acquire enemies: would someone chosen in this way be likely to become a unifying figure? If, on the other hand, the choice of president was to be left to parliament it would become a party-political bauble, unless there were some cross-party agreement that the person chosen should be a worthy nonentity. Countries which have taken this latter route often have presidents largely unknown outside their own borders. Does a country feel better about itself for being represented by a nonentity?

Yet the early years of the third millennium saw an increasingly public campaign to abolish the British monarchy. Most of the newspapers marked Queen Elizabeth's eightieth birthday, in April 2006, with good wishes, of a more or less sugary kind. 'Happy Birthday Ma'am' and 'The People's Queen' caught the mood of them. It was left to the *Guardian* to adorn its masthead with the message 'Let's wish the Queen a very happy birthday. And when she goes, let's bury this ludicrous institution.' Paradoxically, the ensuing analysis praised her. 'She has served in a demanding role, that of head of state, for half a century and has made barely a mistake . . . By the usual measures – namely sustained popularity and an ability to avoid trouble – Elizabeth Windsor would have to be judged one of the most accomplished politicians of the modern era, albeit as a non-politician.'[16] But that was not the point. The objection was not to the individual but to what the monarchy represented.

The newspaper's campaign had been gathering steam for a few years. Shortly before Christmas 2000 it had declared its republican convictions by launching an assault on the Act of Settlement, which prevents non-Protestants from taking the throne. No one could deny that the law is archaic and discriminatory. But the paper went further. One of the *Guardian*'s columnists summarized the case. Dispatching the act, wrote Polly Toynbee, was merely the first step. The monarchy had to be consigned to history not because of any temporal power it possessed, but because 'it tyrannizes the imagination'. The paraphernalia of royalty 'trap us in an infantile fairyland of imaginary heritage. Bogus history fuels present national delusion. Look no further than here for the reason why this country breeds small-minded bigotry, Eurosceptic xenophobia, union-flag-painted brutes rampaging at foreign football matches.' There was more. Monarchy had prevented the country reinventing itself after the Second World War, lay behind its difficulties with Europe and was an insuperable obstacle to reform. 'Year by year it is crippling us,' she wrote. 'It is not the ornamental cherry but the rotten core of Britain's decrepit democracy.'[17]

That day's paper was an entertaining piece of polemics, supported by some amusing stunts (the *Guardian* placed advertisements in Germany, for example, to try to flush out Habsburgs or Saxe-Coburgs who might feel entitled to the throne). Before publication, the editor wrote to the Attorney General, asking if he would be open to prosecution under the Treason Felony Act of 1848, which made it a crime punishable by transportation for life to call for the overthrow of the Crown. This antique piece of legislation, passed in panic after the revolutions which swept continental Europe, had not been used for over a hundred years. But the editor felt that it ran counter to guarantees of free speech enshrined in the more recently passed Human Rights Act. The Attorney General declined to humour him with a promise that he would not be prosecuted. In the names of its columnist Polly Toynbee and editor Alan Rusbridger, the paper thereupon mounted a legal challenge in the High Court. They argued that the Treason Act had no place in a modern state (as was surely demonstrated by the fact that no one had been prosecuted under it for more than a century). But the case was really no more than a squib. The legal Establishment has been around long enough not to watch people digging a hole and then accept their invitation to jump into it. The legislation might still be on the statute book, but there is no practical danger of anyone being prosecuted for advocating a republic.

No one devising a constitution for the twenty-first century would come up with the idea of a hereditary head of state. But there seems little doubt that no national newspaper would have gone to the trouble of mounting such a campaign had the House of Windsor not taken such a battering in the last decade of the twentieth century. Serious-minded republicans make a point of saying that they would still be arguing their case even if the streets were jammed with millions waving flags, singing the national anthem and proclaiming their devotion to the Crown. The issue, they assert, is bigger than individuals. But the two are inseparable. Victoria's consort, Prince Albert, understood. 'The exaltation of Royalty is possible', he once said, 'only through the personal character of the Sovereign.'[18]

The problem is a Prince Charles problem. Even devoted monarchists have their anxieties. 'I do rather dread it when the queen dies,' one told me. 'I mean, how many people will Charles have on his side?' But if you're a monarchist, I said, you must accept that there will be popular kings and unpopular kings, just as there are good ones and bad ones. 'Ah,' she replied, 'if it became very unpopular, and there was a government with members with strong Roundhead convictions, who knows what might happen?'

Forty years earlier, as the young prince entered his teenage years, the diplomat, politician and writer Harold Nicolson considered the sort of task that he faced. His education, he felt, should equip him to understand his duty. This was to obey the government of the day, endure ceremony without looking bored, be discreet, tolerant of fools and humble under grandeur. Nicolson went on, in words which carry a horribly ironic resonance:

> Realizing that for the vast majority of his subjects he represents the enhancement and idealization of the national character, his domestic life will be an example of constancy, austerity and self-denial. Subjected as he will be to 'that fierce light which beats upon a throne', he will be aware that the slightest indiscretion, the momentary display of petulance or exhaustion, will be observed, reported and magnified. He will know that he is condemned, under the glare of arc-lights, to a life-sentence of hard labour; if he possesses the required reservoirs and aqueducts of duty, he will bow his head obediently to this cruel fate. He must be careful even not to take overt pleasure in pastimes that do not appeal to the common man; he must never indulge in irony or in the facile jokes that serve as the lubricants of social intercourse; he must laugh loudly when not amused and never laugh at some incident that would not be regarded by his subjects as a fit subject for hilarity. In fact he must surrender his personality to the exigencies of his task. He is bound in the process to become something of an automaton.[19]

Nicolson concluded that he gave the heir 'my reverence and compassion'.

According to this prospectus, Charles failed, and failed very publicly, and in his inability to meet so many of the requirements lie the origins of his later unpopularity. He certainly learned many of the necessary social skills. It is received wisdom at Buckingham Palace that, if the Prince of Wales is carrying out an Investiture, it will be more drawn out than one conducted by his mother: he talks to people for longer. But in his comments on architecture, food production, medicine and education he has set out to embroil himself in controversy. He has not bothered about whether his pastimes appeal to the common man (or, more accurately, the common man's self-appointed spokespeople in the mass media). When the queen's private secretaries tried to persuade him that playing polo with rich playboys was doing nothing to persuade the public that the royal family understood what it was like to live through an economic recession, he just refused and told them, 'Without polo I'd go stark, staring mad.'[20] He has shown occasional petulance and has decidedly not surrendered his personality to the exigencies of his task. He has moaned about occupying a uniquely privileged position and he has, both by accident and by design, let his anger and frustration become public.

Most spectacularly, his domestic life was no model of 'constancy, austerity and self-denial'. In marrying Diana he was unfortunate in taking on someone who seemed in many ways the ideal vehicle for monarchy in an age when the light that beat upon the throne was far, far fiercer than anything Tennyson might have imagined, even at his most visionary. She was glamorous. She was attractive. She was attentive (everyone who met her commented on the unnerving intensity of her gaze). She seemed most engaged with the most marginalized members of society. But the chasm between her understanding of the world and the Windsors' reading of it was bottomless. On a visit to Balmoral, they tried build a bridge. But, as the Duke of Edinburgh claimed later, 'It was just impossible. She didn't appear for breakfast. At lunch, she sat with her head-phones on, listening to music. And then she would disappear for a walk or a run. Believe me, we tried.' Charles and Diana seemed to express the distance between the last vestiges of nineteenth-century royalty and some avatar of the media age. Supporters of monarchy can look on the bright side by imagining how much more damage might have been done to the institution had the marriage collapsed after the prince had inherited the throne. But it is scant comfort. By comparison with his wife he seemed cold, stuffy, selfish, peevish and callous.

Prince Charles's offences, from his vanity and self-pity to his adultery, were no greater than those of legions of his subjects. But he committed them very publicly. History may well judge him more kindly than easily censorious headline-writers, because the more you discover about the human beings at the heart of the institution of monarchy, the more you realize how very few of them have ever been in any sense remarkable. It is the degree of exposure which has changed. George V may have been considered a dolt among the small circle who knew what he was like. But he was a private dolt. Prince Charles is an eccentric, and a very public eccentric. By his behaviour his enemies claimed that he had squandered not merely goodwill but the moral authority of the Crown. His parents and grandparents may have been dull by comparison, but their dutiful performance at least kept the good name of the institution safe. As a young man, even the prince himself had seemed to acknowledge the importance of the personal. 'There isn't any power,' he said of his role, and continued, in words which later carried an ironic ring, 'But there can be influence. The influence is in direct proportion to the respect people have for you.'[21] He did not set out to have an unsuccessful marriage, but its failure seriously aggravated the readiness of many people to believe the worst of him. A decade or more after the scandal people had still not got over the toe-curling intimacies which had been disclosed.

One of the most extraordinary stories that I came upon while researching this book was unutterably trivial. It was that the prince liked to have a boiled egg after a day's hunting. But because his staff were never quite sure whether the egg would be precisely to the satisfactory hardness, a series of eggs was cooked, and laid out in an ascending row of numbers. If the prince felt that number five was too runny, he could knock the top off number six or seven.

Although the story came from one of the prince's friends, it seems so preposterously extravagant as to be unbelievable. And yet so many jaw-dropping stories have emerged of the way in which his household is run that it can sound credible. 'The queen has nothing so grand as Prince Charles,' says someone who has been a guest of both. Where his mother has been unintellectual, sensible and modest, he has been intellectually pretentious, eccentric and indulged. The former butler Paul Burrell listed examples of the way that he communicates with his staff by memo.

Did someone pick up the seeds for the garden?
Is there a bottle bank in Tetbury?
Can you get someone to look at my telephone?
Could the china dish be mended, please?

And, most absurdly, 'A letter from the Queen must have fallen by accident into the wastepaper basket beside the table in the library. Please look for it.'[22] The testimony of Charles's valet in 1983 was that he was the most popular royal to work for, because he was so easygoing and genuinely cared about his staff.[23] Yet according to Burrell, who started working for the prince three years later, he would throw things when he was angry, screaming at him on one occasion when the butler had failed to cover up for a meeting he had had with Mrs Parker Bowles. The butler asked whether Charles was telling him to lie, and received the reply, 'Yes, I am! I am the Prince of Wales . . . and I will be king! So Yes. YES!' The prince was overcome with remorse a few minutes later and summoned the butler back so that he could apologize. As he bent to pick up the book Charles had thrown (his remorse did not extend as far as retrieving it himself), the butler meekly replied that if the prince could not vent his feelings on his staff, who could he vent them on?[24]

Bad temper is part of the human condition, and there must be millions of his future subjects who have also thrown tantrums, without the embarrassment of their words being laid out in cold print afterwards. But stories of this kind show that a life of extreme privilege merely seems to have produced a character in which the petulance is offset by self-pity. In fairness we should have to acknowledge that any innate character flaws have been magnified by the curious role in which Prince Charles has been obliged to spend most of his adult life. There is, for a start, no job description – the last Prince of Wales with a clearly defined 'proper job' was Edward I, whose father thrust a load of responsibilities on his shoulders in 1254. Deprived of an obvious purpose, Charles invented one. On many issues on which he has spoken out he has shown himself to be ahead of both government and public opinion.

Any fair-minded audit would have to conclude that he has done a lot of good. It is true that he held forth on climate change while driving around in an Aston Martin: like many of his fellow citizens, he enjoys the benefits of prosperity while being troubled by the damage it causes. But his businesses have raised millions of pounds for schemes he believes in and his inner-city projects have helped thousands of young people. He cares. But he cares too much and about too many things. Every phrase has a deliberative intensity about it, whether he's talking about securing a scholarship for a student or the end of civilization.

His comments are not uninformed: he does plenty of homework. (A piece on homeopathy and 'complementary' medicine provoked a flood of letters from people asking for a diagnosis of their complaint. One read, 'My son, who is eleven, has a persistent headache. What should I do?') But he is not a professional. Indeed, if anything, his advocacy on behalf of what he perceives to be 'ordinary people' against entrenched hierarchies is a sort of all-purpose anti-professionalism. It certainly irritates those who have spent their lives in the fields into which he wanders: his enthusiasm for alternative therapies led to heartfelt pleas from conventional doctors that the best therapy he could prescribe himself would be a vow of silence. After the prince had used his position to advance the suggestion that drinking carrot juice and having coffee-bean enemas might help fight cancer, a distinguished breast-cancer specialist, Professor Michael Baum, wrote an open letter in the *British Medical Journal* daring to suggest that his forty years of study and twenty-five years' involvement in cancer research might perhaps be as solid a basis for holding forth on the subject as 'your power and authority [which] rest on an accident of birth'.[25] One can imagine the agonized wince passing across the prince's face if one of his staff dared to bring that July 2004 edition of the *BMJ* to his attention. But it was not enough to deter him. A year later a report he had commissioned claimed that the National Health Service could save itself millions of pounds each year if only it would take his advice and prescribe more complementary therapies like homeopathy. The year after that he was lecturing the World

Health Organization about the need for medicine to incorporate alternative therapies into the treatments of disease.

One of his former aides once revealed that the prince felt himself to be a 'dissident working against the prevailing political consensus'.[26] As a member of the most privileged family in the land, 'dissident' seemed a strange term to use, and some of his own staff sometimes privately wondered whether such an approach was strictly constitutional. But there is nothing unusual about princes of Wales being at odds with the government of the day. Contests between father and son – and especially between the father who will not cede his position to a mature son in full command of his faculties – can be found as far back in history as one may choose to look. Once the idea of a formal Opposition to the government of the day was no longer considered treasonous, politicians could exploit this natural tension and congregate around the Prince of Wales, in hope of patronage when he succeeded his father. The Hanoverian kings of the eighteenth century – just about every one of whom was on appalling terms with his heir – are an obvious example. Cultivating the heir, and creating a court-in-waiting, was known as the 'reversionary interest', a bet on the future.

Charles has not been foolish enough to let his discontent at the state of the world take crudely party-political expression. He seems pained by much bigger questions which, he claims, get far too little attention from politicians of any party. It is no accident that these concerns – about medicine, agriculture, architecture and education – convey a profound anxiety about the modern world and its fate. Since he represents an institution which predates anything as déclassé as universal suffrage, we should not be surprised that his solutions are traditional. Perhaps, as he claims, he speaks on behalf of a massive constituency of people who share his unease and distrust their rulers. But the difficulty is not whether we find his ideas congenial. If we look for a one-sentence definition of a monarch's job, we should have to conclude that it is to unite. But, because of his pronouncements, the prince does not unite: everyone knows what he thinks on all sorts of subjects. And many disagree with him. So, instead of uniting, he divides.

As the queen's reign drew towards its close, the palace began a propaganda offensive in favour of the heir. He married his mistress. The ceremony was less elaborate – and less enthusiastically celebrated – than his first wedding. The couple began to undertake royal visits together. These did not draw the ecstatic crowds which had turned out for Diana, but they were not abject failures, and his new wife showed herself to have a straightforward charm. His public relations staff trumpeted his charitable work. With his private office in the hands of a rather nimble former accountant, an 'annual review' was produced, as if the prince was a corporation reporting to its shareholders. 'During the year the Prince of Wales undertook 501 official engagements. He visited 82 towns and 35 counties in the UK, and carried out 103 official engagements abroad . . . attended over 191 formal briefings and meetings, and received over 47,000 letters . . . He wrote over 2,300 letters personally, with a further 18,000 written on His Royal Highness's behalf,' all of this illustrated with numerous photographs of the prince chatting to people as varied as taxi-drivers and artists, or playing dominoes in a country pub.[27]

The prince's staff understood that it would take time for his reputation to recover from the damage done by the Diana débâcle and by his image as a spoilt, talking-to-the-trees grumbler. But he has time on his side – in the world of monarchy nothing succeeds like the succession. And his own position has been made a great deal easier by the fact that he has produced a viable heir: it is noticeable that those kings who have suffered the most serious vilification in the last couple of centuries have been those – like George IV or Edward VIII – who did not do so. Increasingly, public attention and the lenses of the paparazzi are trained on Charles's sons, who are younger and more glamorous and hold the great fascination of unfulfilled promise. Charles has always been no more than one link in a chain. Now it is obvious.

One of the attractions of monarchy – its intuitive comprehensibility – is that it replicates the human condition in a way that politics does not. Politicians make promises and deal in the short-term. Kings and queens are human beings with whose births, lives and deaths we all gradually become familiar. But it is noticeable that the British people seem most to like their kings and queens either young or old. Queen Elizabeth has been lucky enough to be both. Prince Charles will never have that opportunity – the best he can hope for is to sit on the throne as a grandfather. Prince Charles decided some time ago that, if he was to make a mark upon history, it would be as Prince of Wales. The public have not made the same imaginative leap, unsure quite what sort of a figure they would like to occupy the role. Prince Charles's predicament is not unique: both George IV and Edward VII were nearly sixty by the time they inherited the throne. With their reputations for gluttony and loose living, neither provided a happy precedent, although there is consolation in Edward VII, who on becoming king metamorphosed from dissolute apprentice into likeable enough 'grandfather to the nation'.

Because the queen believes she has made a promise to God, her close associates say there is no prospect of her abdicating. Perhaps, if she became very ill, she might reconsider her position. More likely is that her son would be asked to discharge the role of regent – as the future George IV did. Periodically it is suggested that Prince Charles might get sick of waiting for that moment, and decide to retire from the succession. As the law stands, when the monarch dies, the heir succeeds to the throne. There is no more to it than that. For him to 'retire', therefore, would require a bill to pass through parliament beforehand. To be sure of doing so, it would need the support of the British government. Relevant Commonwealth governments would also have to give their consent. The bill would then have to be signed into law by the queen. Is it really credible? Even if the Prince of Wales wanted to cut himself out of the succession – and his mother agreed – there are obvious problems. If the crown was not going to be passed on through a politically neutral process like boring old inheritance, why assume that it could merely skip a generation and be given to Prince William? Why should not politicians and people express an opinion on who else might get the position instead?[28] Of course, if Prince Charles's wife were to decide to become a Roman

Catholic, that would save everyone a lot of trouble because he would be automatically disqualified from the succession. But in neither case would it finish the monarchy. Whatever becomes of the immediate succession, it looks as if the institution is here to stay.

But, for all its comforts, who would want the position? Of course Prince Charles is indulged. But then so are many other people, and they live neither in the public eye nor in the knowledge that any one of their staff might earn large sums of money by exposing their all too human failings to the newspapers. If the same level of life-long fascination were to attach to a presidency (which of course it would not, for obvious reasons) there would be few candidates for the job.

Looked at from a distance, the royal spectacular – from the Lord Chamberlain and the private secretaries down to the Royal Bargemaster, the Keeper of the Queen's Swans, the Yeoman Bed Hangers, the Backstairs Sauce Chef, the Yeoman of the Glass and China Pantry and all the other flunkeys – looks hardly changed from the days when kings made war and law and had bishops burned at the stake.

But it is something of an illusion. Not only does royalty not have the power it once had, it does not live as high off the hog. The royal yacht is gone. Further economies will follow. Buckingham Palace believes it has undergone a wholesale modernization. In its own terms, this is true. But even members of the Prince of Wales's staff affect a shudder at the continuing formality of the place. It does employ a broader range of people than was the case when the roles of private secretary to Queen Victoria, George V, Elizabeth II and Prince Charles were all performed by men from the same family. But, for outsiders from business who were engaged to work there, the experience was like travelling back in time. It was well into the 1960s before more radical members of staff suggested that an internal telephone might be a better means of communication than sending a footman with a written message. Even at the turn of the millennium, staff still communicated with each other by handwritten notes, and the press secretary was able to connect to the internet only by taking in his personal laptop and plugging it into a telephone socket himself. But – perhaps it is inevitable in an organization whose entire existence is based upon precedence – the place is obsessed with hierarchy. While the queen may eat scrambled eggs off a tray in front of her beloved *Songs of Praise* or watching (and voting in) *Pop Idol*, there are separate dining rooms in the royal palaces, reserved for a particular grade of staff. The food is much the same in each of them with your position at the table determined not by anything as personal as length of service but by the grandeur of your employer.[29] The lucky functionaries entitled to entertain an occasional guest can find the rules enforced with astonishing small-mindedness. When one senior official took his secretary to lunch there not long ago he was rebuked by a testy Master of the Household: she really should not have been taken as a guest, as she had last eaten there only three years previously.

But how the palace organizes itself is its own business. It might help its public relations if there was more public access to much more of the royal estate – to see, for example, more of the royal art collection or to visit Buckingham Palace for most of the year. More importantly, a ruthless pruning of those entitled to royal status would help – reverence for the institution diminishes in direct proportion to the number of people to be reverenced. But these are relatively minor changes. The monarchy's survival does not depend upon how it organizes itself. It hangs upon whether people want the thing at all.

The basic conundrum is this: why do the majority of the population go along with an arrangement from which they are almost certain to be excluded by virtue of their birth? In an aside in *Capital*, Karl Marx put it thus: 'one man is king only because other men stand in the relation of subjects to him. They, on the other hand, imagine that they are subjects because he is king.'[30] It has baffled rational beings ever since. Writing in the year of the forced abdication of King Edward VIII, Ernest Jones – arguably the key figure in bringing psychoanalysis to the English-speaking world –

felt that there was a sense in which kings and queens were as much the product of popular choice as any politician. 'Is this ruler of his people, at the same time their highest representative, chosen by the people to fulfil his exalted office, or does he reign by virtue of some innate and transcendent excellence resident in him from birth? Do the people express freedom in choice or do they submit to something imposed on them?' Jones concluded that the arrangements for declaring the succession, in which members of the Privy Council and 'prominent Gentlemen of Quality' meet to proclaim the new monarch, are 'as near the truth as the people's supposed free choice of their functional ruler, the prime minister. In neither case do they actively select a particular individual; what happens is that in certain definite circumstances they *allow* him to become their ruler. Their freedom lies in their reserving the right to reject him whenever he no longer plays the part allotted to him.'[31] You can see how Jones came to this conclusion. But what he suggested was popular choice might as easily be described as inertia. In the theology of monarchy the throne is never empty – the strange idea of the king's two bodies means that the office passes from one to another at the moment of death. Can we really imagine the Privy Council gathering to declare that Prince Charles would not, after all, succeed his mother?

The ancient roles which gave our kings and queens their prominence, like military leadership or the dispensing of justice, have long gone. The Kaiser once sneered that the only warfare in which Edward VII had taken part was the Battle of the Flowers in Monte Carlo. But on the whole that seems preferable to the Kaiser's taste for real war. In modern democracies laws are made by politicians, and in the twenty-first century all that is left to kings and queens is wealth, some social influence and an ability to induce perhaps deference, perhaps indifference. Yet they still have something. There comes a point in any consideration of monarchy when rational thought is drowned out by sentimentality, religiosity and what republicans would dismiss as mere drivel. Yet monarchs stand for something beyond themselves, and in that sense are less political creatures than religious ones. In the 1950s the scholar G. Wilson

Knight concluded from Shakespeare's long meditations on kingship that 'any human system' demanded 'some visible figure of God's majesty'. In offering a connection to both the past and the future, kings and queens belonged to the world of poetry. In a particularly misty-eyed passage Knight decided that the Crown acts as the defender not so much of *the* faith as of faith itself: 'it is a window for ever letting in God's air to the sick room of human politics'.[32] Perhaps it was this idea that Prince Charles was fumbling towards when he talked in his infamous television interview of wishing to be thought a 'defender of faith'. There is certainly an argument for saying that royalty can be properly understood only in religious terms. 'Trying to imagine our society without the monarchy is like trying to imagine the world without Mount Everest' is the way the Reverend Charlie Robertson, one of the queen's chaplains in Scotland, puts it. 'I believe in sacraments, and monarchy is a sacrament: on one side is service – an example of commitment beyond the family – and on the other is devotion. So to advocate republicanism when you live in a monarchy is like an atheist arguing against religion while never having had to live in a country – like the Soviet Union – which had no religion.'

This close intertwining of state and Church is at the heart of the Crown's position. The bishopric of Winchester was already two hundred years old when the Bishop stood alongside Alfred the Great – the first man to style himself 'King of England'. The close relationship led the current Bishop of Winchester to wonder whether a secular monarchy – possible though it is in theory – could ever be created in Britain given that 'for twelve or thirteen hundred years the monarchy in this country has been conspicuously religious'.

The rationalism so prized in a secular age ought to be able to sweep the House of Windsor away. If, for example, the hereditary principle is unacceptable in the House of Lords, why should it be tolerated elsewhere? But reason has little part in this discussion. Kings and queens survive not by their own volition but by some greater collective act of will. We ought to have grown out of them, perhaps. But, for good or ill, a monarch still appears to answer the question 'What sort of people are we?' It reflects the ambivalence of a nation caught between a distinct past and an unclear future. Republicanism, for all its commonsensicalness, remains a hobby like campaigning for phonetic spelling. True, as an idea it has had its high points of popularity. It may be intellectually invincible. But it has failed to engage the feelings of most of the population. And in attacking the status quo it faces a formidable enemy, armed not merely with effective weapons of propaganda but with the great, bulldozing power of conformity and indolence.

The secret weapon of monarchy is not secret at all. It is simply its familiarity. Queen Elizabeth went from vulnerable young woman to doughty grandmother of the nation before her subjects' eyes. Her son's progression from gawky schoolboy through student prince to naval commander, to 'callous husband' and then to eccentric middle age has been even more public. The role he vacated as dashing prince is now taken by his sons, who as already noted have become the focus of attention and emotional engagement. It is quite a show upon which to draw down the curtain.

For most of the time the British royal family is not now, nor has it been for generations, spectacular. It is hard even to describe it as much fun. It reflects the people of Britain. But that, of course, is its strength. Angry-browed ideologues may scorch their words across the pages of periodicals. But they will not incite the masses to revolution, because in the endlessly dutiful old queen they see nothing to revolt against. People want inspiration, but if they cannot have inspiration, they'll settle for certainty, constancy and devotion.

Queen Elizabeth's long reign is now in its twilight years. (If she lives as long as her mother, it will be a long twilight.) It has seen some of the greatest social changes in the nation's history. Like the nation, the institution of monarchy has emerged with its grandeur diminished. But it is still there. Those who seek a more democratically legitimate form of government recognized long ago that challenging Elizabeth II was a waste of time. Hers may not have been the most dramatic or glorious reign in the life of Britain. But no one can question her dedication or conviction. If she has made mistakes, they have been minor ones, and mistakes are anyway part of being human. And she can record real achievements, too: without her personal commitment it is doubtful, for example, whether the Commonwealth would still exist. Most of all, she has endured. Had the British been on the losing side in either of the world wars, people might well have cast around for new symbols for their country. Instead, Queen Elizabeth's reign has seen a steady improvement in the living standards of her subjects; and when people are prosperous they do not seek change.

Behind the façade, the reality of royalty is utterly changed. What began with a primitive belief that one man was a god developed into a belief that he had been chosen *by* God. From this came an emphasis on the saintly virtues of piety and wisdom. As the citizenry grew stronger, the king was judged less on his spiritual values or his ability to lead into battle, and more upon his capacity to rule fairly. Once that idea of a contractual relationship had been established, the rights of monarchy were in a more or less steady decline. By comparison not merely with absolute monarchy, but even with the monarchies of the eighteenth century, Queen Elizabeth is a powerless creature. Queen Victoria found compensation for the loss of executive freedom in being figurehead of the most powerful empire the world had seen. Throughout the twentieth century, with its enormously draining world wars and the loss of imperial possessions, the attention and imagination of the citizen transferred itself to the monarch as head of an ideal family, which, through reflecting the citizens' own families, fostered some sense of the entire nation as a family. Although it was definitely not what was intended, in an unexpected way the fact that so many of the marriages of Elizabeth's family have not worked may have brought it closer to the people, since so many of them have had a similar experience. Her Golden Jubilee in 2002 brought millions on to the streets. Of course it is not surprising that people turn out for a party. But in marking the queen's survival they were also celebrating something bigger: they saw in her continued rule the endurance of the nation. The end of her reign will, in the cliché, mark the end of an era. She belongs to the generation who lived through the Second World War, since when British society has changed – in some respects changed almost out of recognition. The end of the reign of Elizabeth II could provide a natural break-point. The governments of several Commonwealth countries have certainly indicated privately that she will be their last monarch. They have too much respect for the queen to cast her aside. But they are underwhelmed by Prince Charles and feel that choosing their own head of state is a long overdue mark of maturity.

It will not happen in Britain. Conspiracy theorists say that it will be impossible because the dark forces of the Establishment will move immediately to declare a new king and extinguish dissent. In truth, there is not – and there has not been for generations – a sufficient head of steam for change. The experience of Andreas Whittam Smith, the first editor of the *Independent* newspaper, is instructive. As a committed republican, he strove heroically to downplay or exclude from the paper stories about royalty. He failed. When he stood in front of student debating societies to propose that the country become a republic he routinely lost the argument – against what he calls 'low-grade royalist opponents'. If the case could not be made to intelligent, well-educated young people it was unwinnable anywhere. The lesson Whittam Smith drew was that, while the royal family might have been recognized as dysfunctional, the public sensed that they had them under control. It is quite the reverse of the usual republican analysis, with its age-old complaints about the outrageousness of dynastic power. Perhaps people are comfortable with monarchies in western democracies because they know that if they chose to do so, they *might* one day decide to get rid of them. Everyone knows where they stand.

In societies which have increasingly little sense of their own history, kings and queens provide some connection with the past. They are easily understood. They keep the position of head of state out of the hands of those who want it just to gratify their ambition. Merely because they occupy the role for the whole of their lives, the individuals become more familiar to us than here-today-gone-tomorrow politicians, and, unlike politicians, they do not try to force their views upon us. They allow the notion of the state to be expressed through a clearly fallible individual instead of binding it up in flags, anthems, ideologies and simple-minded slogans about national destiny.

Certainly, if we were devising a system of government for the twenty-first century we should not come up with what we have now. The arrangements are antique, undemocratic and illogical. But monarchies do not function by logic. If they work, they do so by appealing to other instincts, of history, emotion, imagination and mythology, and we have to acknowledge that many of the most stable societies in Europe are monarchies, while some of the most unstable and corrupt have presidents. It would theoretically be possible to pull one thread out of the rug woven by history (although we do not know what other threads might then unravel). We could easily pack all of them off to live out their lives in harmless eccentricity on some organically managed rural estate. But why bother?

Acknowledgements

Soon after I began research for this book a *Sunday Telegraph* reporter called. 'I gather you're writing about the royal family,' he said. My heart sank. The reporter explained that he just wanted to have a bit of fun. And, appearing under the decidedly unhelpful headline 'Jeremy Paxman ready to storm Buckingham Palace', that was what he did. I have no complaints about the story he produced, but a day or so later the following letter appeared in the correspondence columns of the *Daily Telegraph*:

> Sir,
>
> I read with great anxiety that Jeremy Paxman is planning to write a new book on the Royal Family and is hoping to be granted 'inside' access. As a former Guardsman and a fervent royalist, I hesitate to give my sovereign and colonel-in-chief advice in the matter, but the only place Paxman should be allowed inside is the corgis' kennels.
>
> Alan Shutt
> York

Fortunately, in the early stages of my research at least, Buckingham Palace ignored his advice. I wrote to Prince Charles, and received no reply (something I discovered later that was not untypical of the then chaos of his office and which can still be characteristic of some parts of Buckingham Palace). But a few weeks later the queen's press secretary wrote to suggest an interview with her private secretary, and listed, over a couple of pages, some of the events she and other members of the royal family would be attending over the coming months. I was, the press secretary said, welcome to come along to any of them. I have to say that the invitation was honoured throughout. When I asked to see palace officials, in most cases the request was granted. Although by and large the British royal family loathes the mass media, the usual response of courtiers was, I think, one of curiosity. When I explained that I wanted to discover how such an ancient institution survived in a modern country their usual response was 'Well, I shall be interested to read what you find out.'

I went through the motions of requesting an interview with Queen Elizabeth, but without any conviction. I was, however, able to talk to the Duke of Edinburgh, to the Prince of Wales, to some of the queen's closest friends and to numerous courtiers, officials and dissidents. I spoke at length to intimates of other European royal families, and to the Queen of Denmark, Margrethe.

Early on, one of Prince Charles's friends had cautioned me: 'Have you any idea what you're getting into? This is much more political than anything to do with politics.' Perhaps so. But I fear that much of the politicking was above my head. One day I did receive a call from Prince Charles's office, inviting me to spend a few days at Sandringham. I assumed this was in connection with a request to interview him, but was told it was just a social matter – every year the prince gathers a group from the arts world. I pointed out that there would be something of a conflict of interest – if I came along and then wrote something, it would surely be a breach of trust. 'Oh don't worry about it,' said the social secretary. But anything I saw and heard would be bound to figure in what I wrote, I protested. 'We're really not concerned,' she said. Well, I eventually thought to myself, you may not be bothered about it, but I am. Even though she repeated the invitation, I decided not to go.

Then, to my amazement, a year later, the same thing happened. You do realize that I'm still working on this book, don't you, I said. 'We know all about that,' she said. But the same considerations apply, I replied. 'Don't worry about it. Do come.' And so I did, and some of what occurred is recounted in the Introduction. Other aspects of the visit – the swimming expedition which involved a group of us processing with the Duchess of Cornwall through a nudist colony, the expression on David Hockney's face when the Prince of Wales asked him to look at his watercolours, Charles's recitation of a monologue taught him by, if I recall correctly – it was late at night after dinner – Barry Humphries, or the bizarre spectacle of one of the country's best-known character-actresses and apparent lefties suddenly erupting into 'Three cheers for the Prince of Wales' over dinner – will have to wait.

The *Telegraph* article also brought a letter from the author Tim Heald, offering sight of his unpublished manuscript on the significance of monarchy, 'Of Life, Of Crown, Of Queen'. This was a comprehensive survey of how attitudes to the British royal family had changed during the reign of Queen Elizabeth II, and had even been read for accuracy by the Duke of Edinburgh – the manuscript was spattered with his pencil comments in the margin. 'Rubbish' he had scribbled on one page, where Heald reported – using the caveat 'it is said' – that in 1952 he had felt he was being treated as if he was no more than a 'a bloody amoeba'. 'It was generally known that at the Palace the Royal couple had separate bedrooms,' wrote Heald on page 111, at which point the duke had scrawled the word 'wrongly'. By contrast with many, perhaps most, books on British royalty, it was clearly authoritative and accurate. But unfortunately Heald had made the mistake of subtitling his work 'A Sensible Book about the Royal Family'. This was not what the publishing industry likes: it is really only comfortable with books which either cringe or spit. One editor even wrote to him to say that his was the most sane thing she had ever read on the British royal family, which was why she would never buy it in a million years. I found the manuscript useful, illuminating and, yes, sensible. Tim was also generous with both advice and contact suggestions.

At Sandhurst, General Andrew Ritchie kindly got together a dozen of the officers and teaching staff to kick around what serving a queen rather than an elected figure meant to them and their regiments. My visit to Albania in search of the pretender to the throne was made much more comfortable by the hospitality of the then British Ambassador and his wife, David and Catherine Landsman, who were immensely helpful, while retaining a strict disengagement from the project. Arlene Boath and Parul Naran at the Embassy and the archaeologist Louise Schofield made a difficult place enjoyable: they are all innocent of my reporting. Soren Dyssegaard was highly instrumental in arranging a meeting with the Queen of Denmark, even, at one point, investigating whether the Danish air force might be able to assist with complicated transport arrangements. The biographer Michael Holroyd kindly tracked down a couple of elusive Shaw epigrams.

Rodney Brazier at Manchester University and Vernon Bogdanor at Oxford were kindness itself in helping with complicated constitutional questions, especially on complex issues such as whether Prince Charles could 'retire' from the succession.

As ever, the staff at two of the great unsung institutions of Britain, the British Library and the National Archives, gave enormous assistance. It is a pity that so little recognition is given to the two places: they are models of efficiency and helpfulness. I also much enjoyed using the London Library. The book was commissioned by Tom Weldon, who has given encouragement throughout, and the manuscript was laboured over by Peter James, who must be one of the best copy-editors in Britain. I was again fortunate to have Alex von Tunzelmann to help with the research. Her industriousness, clear-sightedness and cool judgement saved me from many a pratfall. My thanks to Douglas Matthews, who compiled the index.

Some of those who helped with their time and advice preferred to do so anonymously. But among the rest, to whom I am very grateful, are the following: Andrew Alderson; Graham Allen MP; Sir Eric Anderson; Charles Anson; Chief Emeka Anyaoku; Richard Aylard; Mark Bolland; Sarah Bradford; Ian Bradley; Craig Brown; the Rt Rev. Colin Buchanan; Lord Butler of Brockwell; Lord Camoys; Alastair Campbell; Professor David Cannadine; the Rt Rev. Richard Chartres, Bishop of London; Julia Cleverdon; Samantha Cohen; Michael Colborne; King Constantine; Geoffrey Crawford; Lieutenant Colonel John Dymoke; Sebastian Faulks; Lord Fellowes; Jonathan Fenby; Jim Fitzpatrick MP; Sir Edward Ford; Mary Francis; Timothy Garton Ash; Roy Greenslade;

Belinda Harley; Robert Harris; Sir William Heseltine; Professor Eric Hobsbawm; Anthony Holden; Professor Richard Holmes; Geoff Hoon MP; Coos Huijsen; Mark Humphrys; Peter Hunt; Sir Miles Hunt-Davis; the Rt Rev. Bill Ind, Bishop of Truro; Sir Robin Janvrin; Professor Lisa Jardine; the Rt Rev. James Jones, Bishop of Liverpool; Penny Junor; Alan Kilkenny; Steffen Kretz; Sir Stephen Lamport; Simon Lewis; Lord Luce; Sir Brian McGrath; Don McKinnon; Mike Macleod; Sir John Major; Sir Christopher Meyer; Paul Minet; Eddie Mirzoeff; Prince Michael, Duke of Albany; Jim Moir; Charles Moore; the Rt Rev. Michael Nazir-Ali, Bishop of Rochester; Sebastian Olden-Jorgensen; the Earl of Onslow; Lord Parmoor; Sir Michael Peat; Dr Raj Persaud; Hella Pick; the late Professor Ben Pimlott; Sir Jonathon Porritt; Jonathan Powell; Declan Quigley; General Sir David Ramsbotham; Sir Hugh Roberts; the Rev. Charles Robertson; Byron Rogers; Kenneth Rose; Sir Malcolm Ross; Alan Rusbridger; the late Professor the Earl Russell; Penny Russell-Smith; James Sanders; the Rt Rev. Michael Scott-Joynt, Bishop of Winchester; Ingrid Seward; Sir Tom Shebbeare; Indarjit Singh; Anthony Smith; Lord Sterling; Baroness Symons; Ann Thomas, of the Sealed Knot Society; Professor Caroline Tisdall; Count Nikolai Tolstoy; Graham Turner; Nick Vaughan-Barratt; Paul Van Vlissingen; Hugo Vickers; Simon Walker; Major General Evelyn Webb-Carter; Alison Weir; Frances Welch; Brigadier Barney White-Spunner; Andreas Whittam Smith; Jean-Louis Wolzfeld; Sir Robert Worcester; Philip Ziegler.

I was lucky enough to have the manuscript read by two authorities in the field. Bill Purdue, Reader in British History at the Open University, began his exhaustive commentary with the words, 'I enjoyed reading this manuscript, even though I am largely in disagreement with the author's sentiments and thesis.' Hugh Massingberd, the former obituaries editor of the *Daily Telegraph*, has an encyclopaedic knowledge of royal matters, right down to the occupants of such vital roles in British national life as the Hereditary Grand Falconer. I thank both men, and absolve them of all responsibility for what appears in the final manuscript.

Notes

Introduction

1 The historian Sarah Bradford, who lists the tea ingredients, notes that 'He was relatively abstemious, however, where alcohol was concerned, drinking only a few glasses of champagne with dinner, rarely anything else, and sometimes a glass of brandy afterwards, port almost never.' (Bradford, *George VI*, p. 10.)

2 Woolf, *After the Deluge*, pp. 71–2.

3 Quoted in Thompson, 'Labour and the Modern British Monarchy', p. 345.

4 His talent for picking pockets had earned him the nickname 'The Thief of Cairo'. He finally ate himself to death, collapsing at the dinner table.

5 'An essay for the use of new republicans in their opposition to monarchy' (1792), in Paine, *Thomas Paine Reader*, p. 387.

6 Masters, *Dreams about H.M. The Queen*, p. 21.

7 *Ibid.*, p. 28.

8 Amis, 'My Imagination and I', in Barnett, ed., *Power and the Throne*, p. 79.

9 'When the process is interrupted by adversity at a critical age, as in the case of Charles II, the subject becomes sane and never completely recovers his kingliness.' 'Maxims for Revolutionists', in *Man and Superman*.

10 *Hello!*, 2 June 2004. The magazine's assembly-line clichés had another appearance in September, when Princess Elizabeth of Bavaria married a businessman in what was, inevitably, 'the society wedding of the year'. Undeterred by the fact that the House of Wittelsbach had not ruled Bavaria since 1918, five hundred guests turned out to watch. The bride had met her husband while she was working at 'one of the world-famous cafés in Vienna'. (*Hello!*, 27 September 2004.)

11 Nicolson, *Monarchy*, p. 167.
12 See, for example, Richards, Wilson and Woodhead, *Diana*, p. 48.
13 *Ibid.*, pp. 10 and 59.
14 Nicolson, *Monarchy*, pp. 167–8.

1 First, Find a Throne

1 Gibbon, *Decline and Fall of the Roman Empire*, vol. I, pp. 93–4.
2 See Adam Zamoyski, *The Polish Way: A Thousand-Year History of the Poles and their Culture* (1987; John Murray, London, 1989), pp. 95–8.
3 Voltaire, *Lion of the North*, p. 59.
4 'Royal confusion over Estonian role for prince', *Daily Telegraph*, 11 July 1994.
5 Anonymous, *Ferdinand of Bulgaria*, p. 19.
6 Tsar Ferdinand of Bulgaria quoted in *ibid.*, p. 23.
7 Fitzherbert, *The Man Who was Greenmantle*, p. 46.
8 Quoted in *ibid.*, p. 1.
9 *Ibid.*, p. 123.
10 *Ibid.*
11 *Ibid.*, p. 229.
12 Quoted in Bolitho, *James Lyle Mackay, First Earl of Inchcape*, p. 162.
13 Fry, *Life Worth Living*, p. 296.
14 McColl, *Dateline and Deadine*, p. 75.
15 Quoted in *ibid.*, p. 78.
16 Quoted in Tomes, *King Zog*, p. 2.
17 *Daily Express*, 12 July 1930.
18 Hocart, *Kingship*, p. 7.
19 Quoted in Nicolson, *Monarchy*, p. 72.
20 *Ibid.*
21 Paul Johnson, 'What Edward II, Diana and Russia's last tsar had in common', *Spectator*, 29 August 1998, p. 21.
22 James I to Prince Charles, *Basilikon Doron*, Book I, ed. MacIlwain (Harvard Political Classics, I) 1918, p. 12.
23 'No one should judge the career of the Emperor William II without

asking the question, "What should I have done in his position?" Imagine yourself brought up from childhood to believe that you were appointed by God to be the ruler of a mighty nation and that the inherent value of your blood raised you far above ordinary mortals. Imagine succeeding in the twenties to the garnered prizes, in provinces, in power and in pride, of Bismarck's three successive victorious wars. Imagine feeling the magnificent German race bounding beneath you in ever-swelling numbers, strength, wealth and ambition, and imagine on every side the thunderous tributes of crowd-loyalty and the skilled unceasing flattery of courtierly adulation' (Churchill, *Great Contemporaries*, p. 17).

24 Eulalia, *Court Life from Within*, pp. 135–6.

25 Haslip, *Imperial Adventurer*, p. 212.

26 Lees-Milne, *Diaries, 1942–45*, p. 55.

27 Among the unpaid bills were several for repairs to the Mercedes given to Zog by Hitler. Some of Zog's entourage found the Chilterns sufficiently congenial to give up being royal: one of his nephews took a job as a farm labourer, married a nurse and settled in the village of Frieth.

28 *Daily Telegraph*, 22 July 2004.

29 *Daily Sketch*, 11 December 1945, quoted in Tomes, *King Zog*, p. 267.

2 Next, Produce an Heir

1 Richard was so long away on Crusades that he spent only ten months of his ten-year reign in England.

2 It would clearly have been preferable to have been one of the Spanish Alfonsos ('the Chaste' or 'the Learned'), one of the Sanchos ('the Strong', 'the Desired' or 'the Fierce') or a Philip ('the Handsome') rather than Ordono the Bad, Vermudo the Gouty, Henry the Sickly, Henry the Impotent or Joan the Crazy (the latter held to be the origin of much of the genetic spaghetti which finally did for Habsburg rule in Spain).

3 And also, after the 1707 Treaty of Union, the Church of Scotland.

4 Declaration of George Wilhelm, Duke of Brunswick and Lüneburg,

Duke of Hanover, 11–21 April 1658. Quoted in Sophia, *Memoirs*, pp. 73–4.

5 Ziegler, *William IV*, p. 19.

6 Thomas Creevey, *The Creevey Papers* (1904), vol. I, pp. 267–71. Quoted in Strachey, *Victoria*, p. 16.

7 It was a busy summer for marriages contracted in a bid to ensure the succession. Prince Edward's elder brother, the Duke of Clarence – who had previously had eleven illegitimate children with Caroline von Linsingen (though she claimed to be his wife) and the actress Mrs Jordan – married Adelaide, daughter of the Duke of Saxe-Meiningen, for similar reasons. In 1830, he took the throne as William IV.

8 Crawford, *Queen Elizabeth II*, p. 12.

9 Barwick, *The Royal Baby*, p. 7; Aronson, *Kings over the Water*, p. 27.

10 Bernier, *Imperial Mother, Royal Daughter*, p. 268.

11 *Morning Post*, 25 May 1819, p. 3.

12 Pimlott, *The Queen*, p. 488.

13 Barwick, *The Royal Baby*, p. 8.

14 Judd, *Eclipse of Kings*, p. 97.

3 Learning to be Regal

1 When the future George II named his fifth child without consulting his father, the king simply ordered his children removed from their father's care.

2 Benn, *Keir Hardie*, p. 122.

3 Hansard, 28 June 1894.

4 Taylor conceded that he had misquoted him – strictly speaking it should have been 'noodles'; 'but for a noodle to ask for noodles would be in English an intolerable pun' (Taylor, *The Habsburg Monarchy*, p. 47n).

5 Bagehot, *The English Constitution*, p. 50.

6 Bennett, *The Madness of George III*, p. 63.

7 Parissien, *George IV*; pp. 22–3.

8 Her humility, and appetite for the most revolting jobs in the house-

hold, was so great that other nuns were afraid to sit beside her. Other notable royal saints include St Elizabeth, Princess Elizabeth of Hungary, Queen (Landgravine) of Thuringia, 1207–31; St Hedwig, Duchess of Silesia 1174–1243; St Henry, Duke Heinrich II of Bavaria and Holy Roman Emperor Henry II, 973–1024, and his wife St Kunigund (Cunegund), Holy Roman Empress, 978–1033; St Ladislas, King Laszlo I of Hungary, reigned 1077–95; the Anglo-Hungarian St Margaret, queen of 'Bighead' Malcolm III of Scotland, 1045–93; St Stephen, King Istvan I of Hungary, 975–1038; and his son St Henry, Prince Imre of Hungary; St Wenceslaus, Duke of Bohemia, the 'Good King Wenceslaus' of Christmas-carol fame, 907–29.

9 In despair at the behaviour of the then Prince of Wales, in 1927 his assistant private secretary, Alan 'Tommy' Lascelles, had asked for an interview with the Prime Minister. He told Baldwin that 'the Heir Apparent, in his unbridled pursuit of wine and women, and whatever selfish whim preoccupied him at the moment, was rapidly going to the devil, and unless he mended his ways would soon become no fit wearer of the British Crown'. He confessed that when he saw the prince riding in a point-to-point he sometimes felt the best thing that could happen to him – and the country – would be for him to fall and break his neck. Baldwin replied, 'God forgive me. I have often thought the same.' (Bradford, *George VI*, pp. 166–7.)

10 Edward, Prince of Wales to Freda Dudley Ward, 31 August 1919. In Godfrey, ed., *Letters from a Prince*, pp. 222–3.

11 Plowden, cited in Kantorowicz, *The King's Two Bodies*, p. 7. The reconciliation of the two forms of kingship is a persistent theme in Shakespeare, particularly in plays like *Richard II*, and it is noticeable that, apart perhaps from the young Henry V, there is no perfect king in any of his works.

12 Curiously, the theory that the king had two bodies helped the revolutionaries in the English Civil War. Ernst Kantorowicz points out that it enabled parliament to summon an army in the name of the king's body politic to fight against forces loyal to the king's natural body.

These kinds of beliefs are all the more essential when you consider the undignified ways in which – like all human beings – so many monarchs have met their ends. Few suffer the grotesque explosion that characterized the death of Queen Caroline in 1737, after bungled attempts to fix a strangulated hernia. But several, including her husband, George II, and Catherine the Great, died 'on the throne'.

13 Pimlott, *The Queen*, p. 42.
14 Eulalia, *Court Life from Within*, p. 3.
15 *Ibid.*, p. 146.
16 Marples, *Poor Fred and the Butcher*, pp. 37–8.
17 Quoted in Gordon and Lawton, *Royal Education*, pp. 102–3.
18 Thackeray, *The Four Georges*, p. 74.
19 See Bradford, *George VI*, p. 20; Gordon and Lawton, *Royal Education*, p. 176; Forbes, *My Darling Buffy*, p. 167.
20 Pope-Hennessy, *A Lonely Business*, p. 247.
21 Edward, Prince of Wales to Freda Dudley Ward, 21 May 1920. In Godfrey, ed., *Letters from a Prince*, pp. 373–4.
22 See Green, *The Madness of Kings*, pp. 99, 145, 151; Ashdown, *Royal Murders*, pp. 109–11; Röhl, Warren and Hunt, *Purple Secret*, p. 91.
23 Pimlott, *The Queen*, p. 10.
24 *Ibid.*, p. 162.
25 Bradford, *Elizabeth*, pp. 275–6.
26 Quoted in Ziegler, *Edward VIII*, p. 8.
27 Campbell, *Diana*, p. 146.
28 Nicolson, *Monarchy*, p. 218.
29 Anonymous, *Ferdinand of Bulgaria*, p. 9.
30 There were also twenty-nine princes, five grand dukes, seven royal dukes, one non-royal duke (of Fife) and the Comte d'Eu. All took precedence over the republican leaders, even pretenders like the princes Pierre and Louis d'Orléans and complete nonentities such as his Serene Highness Prince Wolrad of Waldeck. A similar sense of exclusivity was discernible even at the funeral of Prince Rainier of Monaco in April 2005, with royalty – including obscure German princelings – marshalled separately from mere politicians, such as the President of the French Republic. Kings and queens are perfectly willing to be civil to such people. But they are only truly at ease in the company of fellow royals.

31 Windsor, *A King's Story*, p. 100.
32 Machiavelli, *The Prince*, pp. 112–13.
33 Quite why this should be is not known. But the great sociologist Max Weber theorized that an anti-monarchical tradition in ancient Israel identified the horse with kingship, while judges and ordinary people rode donkeys.
34 Pimlott, *The Queen*, p. 209.
35 Stanislaw Augustus Poniatowski, *Mémoires*, vol. I, pp. 59–60. Quoted in Zamoyski, *The Last King of Poland*, p. 36.
36 *Court Journal*, no. 575, 2 May 1840, p. 299. He could rather spoil the impression, though, by wearing a German hunting coat and insisting upon stopping for a cooked lunch. The queen did not much appreciate it either, when he shot tame stags out of the drawing-room window at Balmoral.
37 *Policraticus* (1159).
38 Machiavelli, *The Prince*, p. 111.
39 *Ibid.*, p. 68.
40 *Ibid.*, p. 131.
41 Erasmus, *The Education of a Christian Prince*, p. 5.
42 *Ibid.*, p. 25.
43 *Ibid.*, p. 16.
44 'Poor Bertie! He vexes us much. There is not a particle of reflection, or even attention to anything but dress! Not the slightest desire to learn, on the contrary, il se bouche les oreilles, the moment anything of interest is being talked of! I only hope he will meet with some severe lesson to shame him out of his ignorance and dullness' (Queen Victoria to Princess Victoria, Princess Friedrich Wilhelm of Prussia, 17 November 1858. In Victoria, *Letters and Journals*, pp. 107–8).
45 Quoted in Esher, *The Influence of King Edward*, pp. 13, 14, 15.
46 Gordon and Lawton, *Royal Education*, p. 52. As a child he read Plutarch and the Bible before breakfast and Livy and Cicero afterwards, to be followed by cosmography, arithmetic, logic, rhetoric and Greek.
47 Quoted in Aronson, *Crowns in Conflict*, p. 33. George V had been suspicious of 'highbrow' activities ever since he first heard the word. What eyebrows had to do with intellect he simply could not understand.

48 Tomlinson, *Divine Right*, p. 110.
49 Quoted in Gore, *King George V*, p. 32.
50 Gordon and Lawton, *Royal Education*, p. 177.
51 Windsor, *A King's Story*, pp. 59–60.
52 Grand Duchess Augusta, quoted in Mosley, *The Duchess of Windsor*, p. 41.
53 Windsor, *A King's Story*, pp. 92–3.
54 Ziegler, *Edward VIII*, pp. 96–7. In June 1936, the great pianist Artur Rubinstein was invited to play for the king at Argyll House in London. The king grew increasingly fidgety during the Chopin recital. Finally, he could stand it no more. As Rubinstein finished the final bars of an étude, the king crossed the room in front of everyone and brought the concert to a close by barking, 'We enjoyed that very much, Mr Rubinstein.' The pianist left in a fury. Edward then asked Noël Coward, who had been in the audience, to take over at the keyboard, and they all laughed and clapped as he knocked out 'Mad Dogs and Englishmen' and 'Don't Put your Daughter on the Stage, Mrs Worthington'. Quoted in Higham, *Wallis*, p. 126.
55 Quoted in Morton, *The Wealth of the Windsors*, p. 78, and Pearson, *The Ultimate Family*, p. 68.
56 Gordon and Lawton, *Royal Education*, p. 202.
57 A task for which he was rewarded in 1945 by being knighted by the king in front of the entire school, on the steps of the college chapel.
58 Annigoni, *An Artist's Life*, p. 82.
59 The Arundel Herald of Arms Extraordinary, Dermot Morrah, evidently writing with the approval of the queen, says as much in *To be a King*, while Jonathan Dimbleby's biography, *The Prince of Wales*, which was fact-checked by Charles's then private secretary, talks of Gordonstoun as 'the most miserable few years he had yet to encounter' (p. 58).
60 Prince Max of Baden.
61 Bradford, *Elizabeth*, pp. 321–2.
62 Charles, private letter, quoted in Dimbleby, *The Prince of Wales*, p. 65.
63 Eric Anderson, interview.
64 Pimlott, *The Queen*, p. 358.

4 Now Find a Consort

1 National Archives, J 77/44.

2 And, indeed, formed the basis for a novel, *The King and the Quakeress*, by Jean Plaidy.

3 In 1867 William Thoms dismissed it in *Notes and Queries* because, among other things, he could find no reference to the story during the king's lifetime. An inquiry published in the same periodical a century later (Ian Christie, 'The Family Origins of George Rex of Knysna', January 1975) declared that there was 'not a scrap of real evidence' to link George III with 'George Rex'.

4 Until 1814, the convicted man would be dragged through the streets to the place of execution, hanged, have his entrails torn out and burned, then be beheaded, and finally be cut into quarters. Until 1790, women convicted of treason were treated to the more compassionate punishment of merely being burned at the stake.

5 Bradford, *Elizabeth*, p. 493.

6 The first King Charles was said by Rubens to be 'the greatest amateur of painting among the princes of the world', acted in dramas, supported Ben Jonson, and amassed the finest art collection ever seen in Britain. But it did not improve his judgement.

7 Pimlott, *The Queen*, p. 181. Among later prime ministers, both Harold Macmillan and Jim Callaghan had lively relationships with the queen that combined chivalry with a suggestion of flirtatiousness. The sexual element was even more apparent in the case of Diana, Princess of Wales. At one point when she was on a tour of Canada with Prince Charles, the Premier of New Brunswick made a speech of such gushing enthusiasm for the princess that he was asked afterwards whether he had been drunk at the time. Yes, he confessed, he had been, 'totally drunk on her charm'.

8 Private information. In May 2006 the Prince Consort also disclosed a liking for dog-meat. 'It tastes like rabbit,' he said, 'like dried baby goat. Or perhaps – I know! Like veal. Like the veal of a baby suckling calf, only drier.' At the time he was honorary president of the Danish

Dachshund Club. 'The dog-lover Prince and a question of good taste', *The Times*, 3 May 2006.

9 Aronson, *Crowns in Conflict*, pp. 69–70. By Habsburg standards, she escaped lightly. When Franz Ferdinand's younger brother insisted upon marrying the daughter of a university professor he found himself deprived first of his military rank, then of his income, then of his position in the official genealogy of the Habsburgs. He died a habs-been in Munich as plain 'Mr Burg'.

10 She died, aged eight, in 1481, and was given a full state funeral with a river procession and interment in Westminster Abbey. Bland, *The Royal Way of Death*, pp. 18–19.

11 He had a 50 per cent chance of being right, and, as luck would have it, the betrothed foetus did turn out to be a boy, Lajos.

12 Aronson, *Crowns in Conflict*, pp. 82–3.

13 See Hyland, *The Warhorse*, pp. 2–3; Jardine and Brotton, *Global Interests*, pp. 169–70.

14 Bird, *The Damnable Duke of Cumberland*, p. 18.

15 Marples, *Poor Fred and the Butcher*, pp. 7–8.

16 *The Times*, 29 July 1981.

17 Morton, *Diana*, pp. 63–4.

18 *The Times*, 28 June 1981.

19 Bagehot, *The English Constitution*, p. 41.

20 Parissien, *George IV*, p. 224.

21 *The Times*, 7 April 1795, p. 2.

22 David, *Prince of Pleasure*, p. 165.

23 The prince said that she exclaimed, 'Ah mon dieu qu'il est gros!', a comment which he felt showed she was no stranger to male members, while, of course, feeding the male obsession. According to David, *Prince of Pleasure*, pp. 167–70, she attempted to simulate the loss of virginity by smearing her nightdress with toothpowder and water.

24 George, Prince of Wales to Caroline, Princess of Wales, 30 April 1796. Quoted in *Court Journal*, no. 62, 3 July 1830, p. 426. Publication of the letter generated a horrified response. William Cobbett, a contemporary journalist, railed against George's letter and actions on the ground that the British people were not getting value for money from their monarch. If they paid for a family, he implied, they should

get one – virtuous, stable and decorative. For all his skills as an advocate, it is an early example of the way in which Victorian (and subsequent) radicals lost the plot when they attacked monarchy: once you start to argue about what the money is spent upon, you have surrendered on the key argument. (See Chapter 9.)

25 *Court Journal*, no. 2, 9 May 1829, p. 68.

26 Parissien, *George IV*, p. 217.

27 '14,000 Bristol women, more than 9,000 women from Edinburgh, 11,000 women from Sheffield, 17,600 married women from London, 3,700 "ladies" from Halifax, 7,800 from Nottingham, 9,000 from Exeter and tens of thousands more signed addresses in support of the queen. In Newcastle-upon-Tyne, where the pro-Caroline address was confined to men, one woman brought along her five sons and made them all sign, complaining to the organisers at the same time about her own exclusion: "for it was a woman's cause"' (Linda Colley, *Britons* (Yale University Press, New Haven and London, 1992), p. 265. Quoted in Parissien, *George IV*, p. 219).

28 Anonymous, *The Twilight of the British Monarchy*, pp. 19–20.

29 Maureen Johnson, 'Prince's bride-to-be "fits the bill" as future queen', Associated Press, 24 February 1981.

30 Lily Snipp cited in Morton, *Diana*, p. 128.

31 Charles, *In his own Words*, pp. 85–7.

32 Dimbleby, *The Prince of Wales*, p. 283.

33 Eulalia, *Court Life from Within*, pp. 100–1.

34 Brook-Shepherd, *Uncle of Europe*, p. 276.

35 Aronson, *The King in Love*, p. 50.

36 Edward, Prince of Wales to Freda Dudley Ward, 10 April 1920. In Godfrey, ed., *Letters from a Prince*, pp. 346–7.

37 Quoted in Williams, *The People's King*, p. 135.

38 Aronson, *Princess Margaret*, p. 131.

39 Bradford, *Elizabeth*, p. 392.

40 Aronson, *Princess Margaret*, p. 234.

5 Marshals and Mannequins

1 The eccentric 12th Duke of St Albans, who was a descendant of Nell Gwyn.

2 Thackeray, *The Four Georges*, p. 38.

3 The precise date on which the anthem was composed is unknown. Some accounts claim that parts belong to a commemoration of the discovery of the Gunpowder Plot. 'God Save the King' is said to have been sung before Louis XIV in 1686. But the words of the 1745 version, including prayers for General Wade, who had been sent 'rebellious Scots to crush', indicate a connection with the Jacobite rising.

4 Charteris, *At GHQ*, 29 October 1915, p. 120.

5 The Germans' last big push of the First World War was named the 'Kaiserschlacht', or Emperor's Battle. As his army made initial advances, the Kaiser declared, 'The battle is won, the English are totally defeated!' After this early optimism, his generals kept him in the dark. As division after division was sent into battle, he continued to sound off about the impending victory. It never came. When the terrible losses in the Kaiserschlacht offensive became known, they did nothing to enhance his standing among his people. He abdicated in November 1918. (Lawrence Wilson, *The Incredible Kaiser: A Portrait of William II*, Robert Hale, London, 1963, pp. 165–6, and Lamar Cecil, *Wilhelm II*, vol. II, University of North Carolina Press, Chapel Hill, NC, 1996, p. 272.)

6 Edward, Prince of Wales to Prince Albert, 5 August 1914. Royal Archives: George V EE 8/94. Quoted in Ziegler, *Edward VIII*, p. 49.

7 Diary of Edward, Prince of Wales (unpublished), cited in Windsor, *A King's Story*, pp. 106–7.

8 Edward, Prince of Wales to Freda Dudley Ward, 1 April 1918. In Godfrey, ed., *Letters from a Prince*, p. 13.

9 Windsor, *A King's Story*, pp. 109, 112. To be fair, the preoccupation with keeping the heir to the throne safe has often not applied to other members of the family, who could be risked more readily. The Duke of Kent was killed in a plane crash in 1942, while flying to

Iceland to inspect RAF bases. Prince Andrew may have been an unpopular officer (many fellow officers thought him spoiled and selfish), but he did serve in the Falklands War as a helicopter pilot.

10 Quoted in Bradford, *George VI*, pp. 475–6.

11 Gore, *King George V*, p. 293n.

12 Quoted in Rémy, *The Eighteenth Day*, p. 215.

13 Gilbert, *Winston S. Churchill*, vol. VI: *Finest Hour, 1939–1941*, p. 415.

14 Quoted in Arango, *Leopold III*, p. 77.

15 That is why barrack-room theft is simply not tolerated. And neither is sleeping with a fellow officer's wife. The latter prohibition of adultery caused some difficulty when it was discovered not only that the Prince of Wales's marriage had collapsed, but that his partner in crime was the wife of a brother officer.

16 Ziegler, *King Edward VIII*, p. 19.

17 These included a drug habit and an alleged affair with Noël Coward.

18 Quoted in Parissien, *George IV*, p. 366.

19 Bradford, *George VI*, p. 4.

20 Gore, *King George V*, p. 368n.

21 When his father wrote to him in September 1915, asking why he had not worn the French Legion of Honour ribbon and another given to him by 'Uncle Nicky' (Tsar Nicholas II), he replied, 'I feel ashamed to wear medals I only have because of my position, when there are so many thousands of gallant officers, who lead a terrible existence in the trenches and have been in battles of the fiercest kind (many severely wounded or sick as a result) who have not been decorated' (letter from Edward, Prince of Wales to George V. Quoted in Windsor, *A King's Story*, pp. 117–18).

22 Windsor, *A King's Story*, pp. 189–90.

6 Being God's Anointed

1 Played by Peter O'Toole, in a Magdalen College tie, in the film *The Last Emperor*.

2 The recent president of Magdalen, Anthony Smith, believes the story may have had another origin. The Theosophists Annie Besant and

Mary, daughter of the architect of imperial India Sir Edwin Lutyens, attempted to persuade Warren to accept as a student Jiddu Krishnamurthi, the Theosophists' prophesied 'World Teacher' who had been discovered on a beach in India. To them, he really was 'the son of God'. Refusing to succumb to the religious fads then sweeping Oxford, Warren politely put them off with the information about the college's impressive parents.

3 The American forces of occupation obliged the Japanese formally to renounce the emperor's divinity at the end of the Second World War, although there are many Japanese who prefer to live in the fantasy world of royal divinity.

4 Brendon, *Our Own Dear Queen*, p. 197

5 Purcell, *Fisher of Lambeth*, p. 264.

6 At the coronation of George VI, his predecessor as archbishop had decreed that pictures should not be shown live on the infant television service, for fear that the king's stammer might get the better of him: it could be edited out of any later cinema release.

7 The oil of anointment contains oils of orange, roses, cinnamon, musk and ambergris.

8 Mass-Observation Archive (University of Sussex): TC 69, 1953 Coronation Directive Replies from Panel, 7/D [housewife from Leeds].

9 While this airbrushing of a king from history clearly suits the House of Windsor, it ignores one of the essential rules of the hereditary principle, that the heir becomes king immediately the previous reign ends, *dei gratia*. Whether kingship starts with accession or coronation is a point of disagreement among those who care about such things. Certainly, plenty of the queen's antecedents fought hard for the alternative view, and won.

10 Frankfort, *Kingship and the Gods*, p. 3.

11 Quoted in Bradley, *God Save the Queen*, pp. 84–5.

12 *The Times*, 13 May 1937.

13 Lambeth MS, Lang Papers, vol. 223, 'Notes on the Coronation of George VI and Queen Elizabeth', quoted in Bradford, *George VI*, p. 280.

14 Quoted in Harris, *The Queen*, p. 145.

15 The Stone was returned to Scotland by the British government in 1996. According to legend, it was the very rock on which Jacob slept when he dreamed of a ladder ascending to heaven, thereby establishing a link between Scottish and British monarchs and the throne of David. Unfortunately, modern geological analysis seems to show that this would have been feasible only had Jacob dreamed his dream in Perthshire.

16 Greville, *A Journal of the Life of Queen Victoria*, vol. I, p. 106.

17 'The coronation', *Spectator*, 30 June 1838, pp. 599–600.

18 'The coronation', *Northern Star*, 30 June 1838, p. 4.

19 Quoted in Kuhn, *Democratic Royalism*, p. 70.

20 *Macbeth*, Act IV, scene iii.

21 William of Malmesbury, quoted in J. S. Billing, 'The King's Touch for Scrofula', *Proceedings of the Charaka Club*, vol. II, 1911, p. 68.

22 Richardson, *Renaissance Monarchy*, p. 23.

23 Etienne de Conty, quoted in Bloch, *The Royal Touch*, p. 53.

24 Bloch, *The Royal Touch*, p. 216. The story is from John Brown, *Adenochoiradelogia* (Sam Lowndes, London, 1684), pp. 133ff., with a letter from the Warden of Winchester College testifying to the veracity of the story.

25 Evelyn, *Diary*, 6 July 1660, p. 266. All spellings *sic*.

26 It would have taken religious conviction or enormous stamina to endure the hardship: on one occasion Louis touched three thousand people (Burke, *The Fabrication of Louis XIV*, p. 43). This power was presumably self-replenishing, like the holy oil in the phial delivered by the Holy Spirit at the baptism of King Clovis of the Franks, with whom the custom originated in France.

27 Kishlansky, *A Monarchy Transformed*, p. 317.

28 Piozzi, *Anecdotes*, pp. 9–10.

29 See Strong, *The Tudor and Stuart Monarchy*, vol. II, pp. 11–12.

30 Quoted in Bradley, *God Save the Queen*, p. 100.

31 *Ibid.*, p. xii.

32 *Ibid.*, p. 111.

33 Prochaska, *Royal Bounty*, ch. 1.

34 Queen Elizabeth II does not meddle in the appointment of bishops as eagerly as Queen Victoria did (with whom it was an obsession);

neither does she presume to lecture them – as Edward VII did Cosmo Gordon Lang, urging him as Archbishop of York to stop the clergy from wearing moustaches.

7 Killing a King

1 A similar, more mundane example of the conundrum arose in 2002, when the former royal butler Paul Burrell was put on trial for theft. The case collapsed when Burrell claimed that the royal family had known of and approved his actions: the bizarre prospect arose of the British queen being required to appear in her own courts as a defence witness in a prosecution brought in her own name. No doubt the theory that the monarch has two bodies – the mystical body politic and the natural body – could have been applied to the Burrell case, just as it was used by the parliamentarians to justify their fight against Charles I. But it would have taken some explaining.

2 In the event, Bradshaw survived the trial, and died one year before the Restoration. He was buried in Westminster Abbey. With the king's return, his remains were dug up and 'executed' for treason.

3 Ross Williamson, *The Day they Killed the King*, p. 17.

4 Quoted in Wedgwood, *The Trial of Charles I*, p. 179, and Bland, *The Royal Way of Death*, pp. 49–50.

5 The block to be used was generally employed to decapitate corpses. Traitors sentenced to be hung, drawn and quartered were in no state to kneel at the conventional block by the time they had already been hanged and disembowelled.

6 Evelyn, *Diary*, 16 September 1685, p. 485.

7 Evidently, the doctor did the best job he could: when the vault was opened in 1813, for the funeral of the Duchess of Brunswick, mother of the Princess of Wales, the coffin was opened. Sir Henry Halford, personal physician to the prince regent, described the appearance of the corpse. 'The complexion of the skin of it [the face] was dark and discoloured. The forehead and temples had lost little or nothing of their muscular substance; the cartilage of the nose was gone; but the left eye, in the first moment of exposure, was open and full, though

it vanished almost immediately: and the pointed beard, so characteristic of the reign of King Charles, was perfect. The shape of the face was a long oval; many of the teeth remained . . . When the head had been entirely disengaged from the attachments which confined it, it was found to be loose, and without any difficulty was taken up and held to view . . . The back of the scalp was perfect, and had a remarkably fresh appearance; the pores of the skin being more distinct, as they usually are when soaked in moisture; and the tendons and filaments of the neck were of considerable substance and firmness. The hair was thick at the back part of the head, and, in appearance, nearly black . . . On holding up the head to examine the place of separation from the body, the muscles of the neck had evidently retracted themselves considerably; and the fourth cervical vertebra was found to be cut through its substance transversely, leaving the surfaces of the divided portions perfectly smooth and even' (*Examiner*, 11 April 1813).

8 White has also been the colour of mourning, specifically royal mourning. Queen Victoria was buried in white – to signify also her reunion with her beloved Albert. George VI's widow, Elizabeth, wore the colour during the mourning period for her own mother, and Prince Charles wore a white naval uniform for the funeral of President Anwar Sadat.

9 After the Restoration, John Gauden, who was made a bishop by Charles II, claimed to have compiled the book, based upon papers given to him by the king.

10 This question of who, precisely, was king at a particular time became a thorny one with the Restoration. When the restored royalists decided to put on trial the people who had executed the king, they were quite unable to agree in whose reign the crime had taken place. As the law did not recognize fractions of days, the question was whether the crime had been committed on the last day of the reign of Charles I or the first day of the reign of Charles II. The problem was solved by charging the victims of revengers' justice not with the execution, which took place on 30 January, but with plotting the crime on 29 January.

11 Pepys, *Diary*, 13 October 1660.

12 Quoted in Ross Williamson, *The Day they Killed the King*, p. 205.
13 Victor Hugo, 'Paris incendié', from *L'Année terrible* (Gallimard, Paris, 1985), 3:399
14 Albert Camus, *The Rebel*, translated by Anthony Bower (Vintage, New York, 1956), p. 120.

8 Divine Right and Diviner Impotence

1 The phrase comes from Nicolson, *Monarchy*, pp. 17–19. The language is colourful, but the ritual more or less accurately described. See Inga Clendinnen, *Aztecs: An Interpretation* (1991; Cambridge University Press, Cambridge, 1995), pp. 104–7.
2 A belief that the king must die for his people to flourish can be found as far back as the cult of Osiris in ancient Egypt. The Old Testament of the Bible abounds with tales of king-killers, like Jehu who was rewarded for double regicide by having his family sit on the throne of Israel for five generations. Even in modern times there were forms of execution reserved especially for royalty: when the King of Siam became embarrassingly mad in the late eighteenth century (he had come to believe that, as a reincarnation of the Buddha, he might be able to fly), he was shackled hand and foot with gold chains, bundled into a velvet sack, so that no royal blood should touch the floor, and beaten to death with a sandalwood club.
3 The phrase comes from John Aylmer, quoted in Markku Peltonen, 'Citizenship and Republicanism in Elizabethan England', in Gelderen and Skinner, *Republicanism*, vol. I, pp. 99–101.
4 John Barston, *Safeguard of Societie*, quoted in Peltonen, *Classical Humanism and Republicanism*, pp. 67–8.
5 See Hatton, *George I*, p. 130.
6 Strachey, *Victoria*, p. 38.
7 Victoria, *Letters and Journals*, 7 May 1839, pp. 45–6.
8 Queen Victoria to Princess Louise of Battenberg, 14 July 1886. In Hough, *Advice to a Grand-daughter*, p. 81.
9 And, contrastingly, countries like the United States, which threw off their monarchies before they were properly enfeebled, created

constitutions which gave their president much the same role as an eighteenth-century king. If George III returned, he would be much more at home in the White House than in Buckingham Palace.

10 Churchill, speech 27 May 1953, quoted in Gilbert, *Winston S. Churchill*, vol. VIII: *Never Despair, 1945–1965*, p. 835.

11 Asked in parliament to explain the extent of his powers, Tony Blair could only come up with the feeble formula that they 'have evolved over many years, drawing on convention and usage, and it is not possible precisely to define them' (Hansard, 15 October 2001).

12 Windsor, *A King's Story*, p. 321.

13 Laski, *Parliamentary Government in England*, p. 403.

14 Quoted in Bradford, *George VI*, p. 506.

15 Pimlott, *Hugh Dalton*, p. 414.

16 Windsor, *A King's Story*, p. 323.

17 Bogdanor, *The Monarchy and the Constitution*, pp. 40–1.

18 Bagehot, *The English Constitution*, p. 35.

19 *Ibid.*, p. 48.

20 *Ibid.*, p. 67.

21 Between 1994 and 1996 John Major saw the queen in prime ministerial audiences an average of sixteen times per year. Between Tony Blair's election victory in 1997 and 2000 he attended an average of twenty-two audiences a year.

22 Hennessy, 'Searching for the "Great Ghost"', p. 223, quoting the BBC documentary, *Elizabeth R.*

23 See Pimlott, *The Queen*, p. 255. The Royal Archives contain no correspondence with Commonwealth governments on the subject.

24 Quoted in Strachey, *Victoria*, pp. 196–7.

25 *Ibid.*, pp. 237–8.

26 Quoted in Brendon, *Our Own Dear Queen*, p. 93.

27 Williams, ed., *Diary of Hugh Gaitskell, 1945–1956*, p. 244.

28 The Prince of Wales, 'A Time to Heal', *Temenos* 5, Spring 2003, p. 15, quoted in Lorimer, *Radical Prince*, p. 357.

9 We are You

1 Years later, the former Kaiser claimed that it demonstrated Shaw was 'the best democratic brain in Europe'.

2 Shaw, Preface, *The Apple Cart*, in *The Bodley Head Bernard Shaw Collected Plays*, vol. VI, p. 273.

3 Shaw, *The Apple Cart*, Act I, pp. 325–6.

4 Bradford, *Elizabeth*, p. 139.

5 Stevenson, *Lloyd George: A Diary*, 25 January 1915.

6 Nicolson, *George V*, p. 308.

7 The First World War finally destroyed the old idea that peace between European nations could be assured through regal marriages and a sort of royal trade union. At the outbreak of hostilities, the Kaiser's brother had had to cut short his holiday at Cowes, as European royalty caught trains back to the countries they reigned over. Almost all of them adopted a loyalty to state above family. The Belgian queen, a member of the Bavarian royal house, had a brother-in-law commanding the German Sixth and Seventh Armies, fighting Belgium's ally France; later she would declare that 'an iron curtain' now separated her from her German relations. The British-born Duke of Coburg fought with the German army on the Russian front, while in Britain Prince Louis Battenberg was forced to resign as First Sea Lord, partly because he had a German name. The Russian tsaritsa, Alexandra, had a brother, the Grand Duke of Hesse, serving in the German army. Romanian troops carried in their kitbags copies of *The Country I Love* written by Marie, formerly Princess of Edinburgh. The book was in fact a translation, as she spoke no Romanian, and indeed before meeting her husband she had thought Romania was a town in Hungary.

8 Quoted in Henry, 'Imagining the Great White Mother and the Great King', p. 100.

9 Hoey, *Mountbatten*, pp. 62–3. Even so, there was something reasonably pacific about his dislike of foreigners. His cousin Kaiser Wilhelm II was another matter altogether. Obsessed by the 'Yellow Peril', he sent German troops off to China in 1900 telling them to take no

prisoners and that he wanted the name 'German' to be stamped on China for a thousand years; he predicted that Japanese soldiers would soon parade through Moscow and Poznan and, later, would seize the Panama Canal. He called the French national anthem a celebration of regicide and referred to the King of Italy as 'the dwarf' and to his queen as the 'daughter of a cattle thief'.

10 Edward, Prince of Wales to Freda Dudley Ward, 26 July 1918. In Godfrey, ed., *Letters from a Prince*, p. 77.

11 In 1979, at the height of the Rhodesia Crisis, the Commonwealth conference was due to be held in Lusaka, a city which had been bombed by the Rhodesian air force. Margaret Thatcher, who was either loathed or distrusted by much of the Commonwealth for her perceived softness towards the illegal white minority government in Rhodesia, was wondering openly, and through allies, whether it was safe for the queen, the head of the organization, to attend. Had the queen not been present, the Commonwealth could have fallen apart. Certainly there would have been very vigorous disagreement. A swift statement from Buckingham Palace that it was the queen's 'firm intention' to travel to Lusaka nailed the device, and even Margaret Thatcher then changed her mind and decided to attend in person. According to two witnesses, it was only because the queen was there that the organization not only survived but produced the declaration which paved the way for the conference that eventually ended white minority rule. 'Generally the queen leaves the reception she gives at about 10.30 p.m. In Lusaka she stayed until almost midnight, quartering the room and talking to the various heads of governments. I am convinced that that intervention spurred the organization – which was on the point of possibly splitting up – on to compromise,' says Anyaoku.

12 Quoted in Cannadine, *Ornamentalism*, p. 16.

13 *Ibid., passim.*

14 *Ibid.*, p. 79.

15 Quoted in *ibid.*, p. 113.

16 The examples are taken from a Colonial Office file of 1965 in the National Archives, WIS680/20/021 and 2WID20/317/1/A.

17 Rose, *George V*, p. 285.

18 George's wife was a notorious snaffler of other people's possessions, often telling the owners of objects she desired that 'I am caressing it with my eyes,' and waiting for them to suggest that she must, therefore, have it as a gift. If that failed, she might hesitate on their doorstep at the end of a visit and tell them she was going back to 'say goodbye' to the piece of furniture she lusted after. If that failed to persuade her hosts to surrender the piece, she might later write and ask to buy it.

19 Vitruvius, *De architecturibus*. Quoted in Millar, *The Emperor in the Roman World*, p. 18.

20 When he appealed to his father for financial help, in 1786, it was disclosed that he was spending three times his income, or the equivalent of about £170,000 a year (approximately £17 million at current values). The average wage of an agricultural worker was £21 per annum, or £88 for a doctor.

21 The walls of Balmoral were coated in a dark ginger paint; the curtains, chair covers and even linoleums were in various designs of tartan. The queen's passion for fresh air (she preferred to eat her breakfast outdoors, unless there was snow on the ground) meant that arctic draughts blew through the place.

22 Quoted in Tomlinson, *Divine Right*, p. 123.

23 Quoted in McLeod, *Battle Royal*, p. 8.

24 These are Buckingham Palace, St James's Palace, Clarence House, Marlborough House Mews, the residential, office and general areas of Kensington Palace, Windsor Castle and related areas, Frogmore House, Hampton Court Mews and Paddocks and, since 1999, the maintenance of Marlborough House (home of the Commonwealth Secretariat). There are 285 apartments and houses on the Occupied Royal Palaces Estate. Holyroodhouse Palace in Edinburgh is maintained by direct government vote. The 'Historic Royal Palaces' or 'Unoccupied Palaces' are administered by the Historic Royal Palaces Agency. These comprise the Tower of London, Hampton Court, the state apartments at Kensington Palace, the Banqueting House at Whitehall, Kew Palace and Queen Charlotte's Cottage.

25 *Royal Finances* (2nd edition, London, 1995), p. 33.

26 The 1702 Civil List Act prohibited the monarch from selling Crown

lands, to ensure that he or she was kept under parliamentary control.

27 The argument is that they are sometimes used for official as well as private business. On this basis, a pair of earrings might be exempt.

28 *British Public Opinion*, Winter 2002–3, p. 15.

29 Nairn, *The Enchanted Glass*, pp. 53–4.

30 Martin, *The Crown and the Establishment*, p. 12.

31 Knight, *The Sovereign Flower*, p. 274.

32 Quoted in Leslie Mitchell, 'Britain's Reaction to the Revolutions', in Evans and Pogge von Strandmann, *The Revolutions in Europe*, pp. 87–8.

33 Quoted in *ibid.*, pp. 92–3.

34 *Court Journal*, new series, vol. I, no. 4, 15 April 1848, p. 84.

35 'Monarchs and their rights – divine or diabolical? which?', *Reynolds's Newspaper*, 9 September 1855, p. 8.

36 'The Royal Wedding and the Working Classes', *Reynolds's Newspaper*, 31 January 1858, p. 1. Quoted in Plunkett, *Queen Victoria*, p. 59.

37 Davidson, *The New Book of Kings*, p. 102.

38 'The princess and the people', *Spectator*, 28 January 1871, p. 98.

39 Quoted in Buckle, ed., *The Letters of Queen Victoria*, vol. II, p. 58.

40 *The Times*, 9 November 1871.

41 Quoted in Nicholls, *The Lost Prime Minister*, p. 53.

42 Quoted in *ibid.*, p. 56.

43 Quoted in Jenkins, *Sir Charles Dilke*, p. 77.

44 Anon, *Republicanism in England*, p. 6.

45 'Mr Henry George generously proposed in a memorable speech in St James's Hall to allow the Queen, as a widow woman, £100 per annum out of the rent or revenue of the national soil. Her services to the State as a Queen he correctly estimated at *nil*' (Davidson, *The New Book of Kings*, p. 99).

46 *Ibid.*, pp. 106–7.

47 Bradlaugh, *The Impeachment of the House of Brunswick*, p. 99.

48 Besant, *English Republicanism*, pp. 6–8.

49 Quoted in '"Some Interesting Survivals of a Historic Past"?: Republicanism, Monarchism, and the Militant Edwardian Left', in Nash and Taylor, eds, *Republicanism in Victorian Society*, p. 90.

50 Quoted in Duncan, *The Reality of Monarchy*, p. 3n.
51 George V, *Diary*, 15 March, 1917, quoted in Rose, *George V*, p. 209.
52 Edward, Prince of Wales to Freda Dudley Ward, 9 December 1918. In Godfrey, ed., *Letters from a Prince*, p. 143.
53 Benn, *Keir Hardie*, p. 207.
54 *Labour Leader*, July 1914.
55 Quoted in Marquand, *Ramsay MacDonald*, p. 208.
56 Rose, *George V*, p. 328.
57 *Ibid.*, p. 329.
58 *Ibid.*
59 *Ibid.*, p. 331.
60 MacDonald, *Diary*, p. 314, quoted in *ibid.*
61 Tomlinson, *Divine Right*, p. 47.
62 Trotsky, 'Where is Britain Going?', pp. 62–3.
63 Almost seventy years later, when Prince Charles also decided that he could not carry the burdens of office without being married to the divorcee he loved, the government of the day happily acquiesced in the fiction that Camilla Parker Bowles could become his wife without, in time, becoming queen. Baldwin was right and Blair was wrong. The debate from which these quotations come is recorded in Hansard, 10 and 11 December 1936.
64 Martin, *The Crown and the Establishment*, p. 107.
65 *Spectator*, 11 December 1936, p. 1026.
66 Eulalia, *Court Life from Within*, p. 113.
67 Osborne, 'And they Call it Cricket', pp. 25–6.
68 Jones, 'The Psychology of Constitutional Monarchy', p. 232.
69 The phrase – referring to a year which saw the separation of the Prince and Princess of Wales, the separation of Prince Andrew and his wife, the divorce of Princess Anne, and a catastrophic fire at Windsor Castle – had been coined in a letter to the queen by her former assistant private secretary, Sir Edward Ford.

10 The Happiness Business

1 Coward, *Diaries*, 8 April 1942, p. 16.

2 *Illustrated London News*, Supplement, 'In memoriam, Queen Victoria', 30 January 1901, p. 40.

3 Black, *The Mystique of Modern Monarchy*, p. 28.

4 Reith was right about the dangers of being tall: the following October a German sniper shot him in the face. Western Front quotation from Boyle, *Only the Wind Will Listen*, p. 70.

5 Elizabeth so liked the poem that it was read at her funeral, six decades later.

6 Pearson, *The Ultimate Family*, p. 20.

7 Cannadine, 'From Biography to History: Writing the Modern British Monarchy'.

8 Kuhn, *Democratic Royalism*, p. 29.

9 *Ibid.*, p. 31.

10 It was, for example, instrumental in enabling the organization which developed into the Royal National Lifeboat Institution to take to the seas.

11 Owen, *English Philanthropy*, p. 166.

12 Prochaska, *Royal Bounty*, p. 86.

13 Letter to Baron Stockmar, quoted in Martin, *The Life of the Prince Consort*, vol. I, p. 335.

14 He had earlier arrived at a lunatic asylum in Melbourne, to be greeted with the banner 'Welcome to our Royal Guest'.

15 Quoted in Prochaska, *Royal Bounty*, p. 126.

16 Quoted in Williams, *The People's King*, p. 15.

17 There is some disagreement about whether he said something 'must' be done, 'will' be done or 'ought to' be done. He repeated one version or another throughout his tour of South Wales.

18 Stamfordham, quoted in Nicolson, *George V*, p. 308.

19 Quoted in Prochaska, *Royal Bounty*, p. 216.

20 It must require something of the sort. In 1996, when a man with a gun ran amok in a primary school in Dunblane, indiscriminately murdering and wounding children, the queen was expected to visit

the grieving families of his victims. 'The parents were all in tears,' recalls a member of her staff who accompanied her to the town. 'It took three-quarters of an hour for her to meet all of them. The queen was in tears herself. It seemed an awful lot to ask of anyone.'

21 Morton, *Diana*, pp. 308–9.

22 Burrell, *A Royal Duty*, p. 265.

11 Gilded but Gelded

1 Developed by the Duke of Windsor, it is wider than the conventional knot and is still considered vulgar in some corners. Ian Fleming has James Bond describe it as 'the mark of a cad'.

2 Bradford, *Elizabeth*, pp. 118–19.

3 *Ibid.*, p. 267; Parker, *Prince Philip*, pp. 223, 225, 229.

4 Parker, *Prince Philip*, p. 229.

5 Davies, *Elizabeth*, p. 153.

6 Bradford, *Elizabeth*, p. 267.

7 See Shaw, *Royal Babylon*, pp. 242–3.

8 He was, therefore, murdered not by the IRA, as was supposed when his boat was blown up, but by either Russian or American intelligence, to prevent him continuing his evil work.

9 *The Times*, 28 June 1830. Opinions had been just as fiercely held on the other side of the fence. *John Bull* (motto: 'For God, the King and the People!'), which had taken the king's side in the horribly public spat with Queen Caroline, was beside itself at the tone of *The Times*. 'Never was such heartlessness exhibited as has been displayed in some of the newspapers during the week. We cannot descend to quote the liberals with which these wretched sycophants have thought fit to insult the memory of a KING whose heart was the kindest, whose qualities were most princely, and whose talents and accomplishments were universal. If these crawling animals hope to ingratiate themselves with his present MAJESTY by vituperating a fond and favourite brother, within one day of his death, they achieve the double merit of inflicting a double insult, and will, we are quite certain, meet the

just reward of their abject baseness and their contemptible meanness' (*John Bull*, 4 July 1830).

10 *Satirist*, 16 February 1840, p. 54.

11 'Preparations for the royal nuptials', *Satirist*, 2 February 1840, p. 34.

12 'Fashionable World', *Morning Post*, 12 February 1844, p. 6.

13 'Fashionable World', *Morning Post*, 24 February 1844, p. 6.

14 'News of the week', *Spectator*, 26 June 1897, p. 901.

15 King Leopold of the Belgians. Buckle, ed., *The Letters of Queen Victoria*, vol. III, pp. 474–5.

16 Victoria R to W. E. Gladstone, 7 June 1869. Quoted in Guedalla, *The Queen and Mr Gladstone*, vol. I, pp. 179–80.

17 W. E. Gladstone to Victoria R, 9 June 1869. Quoted in Guedalla, *The Queen and Mr Gladstone*, vol. I, pp. 181–2.

18 *Daily Telegraph*, March 1863, cited in 'Hysteria of the press', *Spectator*, 14 March 1863, p. 1750.

19 'Hysteria of the press', *Spectator*, 14 March 1863, p. 1750.

20 Cobbett, *George the Fourth*, paragraph 93.

21 Quoted in Prochaska, ed., *Royal Lives*, p. vi.

22 H. C. G. Matthew, 'George VI (1895–1952)', *Oxford Dictionary of National Biography* (Oxford University Press, Oxford, 2004).

23 Lord Altrincham (John Grigg), *National and English Review*, August 1957.

24 Private information.

25 Osborne, 'And they Call it Cricket', p. 25.

26 David Attenborough quoted in Bradford, *Elizabeth*, p. 345.

27 'Anne sees giant vole', *Private Eye*, 23 February 1973, p. 12.

28 'Travesty', *Private Eye*, 18 February 1977, p. 13.

29 Less significant than it might have appeared. Separate bedrooms might seem odd to many others, but were common among the upper classes.

30 Alan Rusbridger and Henry Porter, 'Newspapers cry for attention', *Guardian*, 8 June 1992, p. 25.

31 'The Love that moved Diana to tears', *Sun*, Friday, 12 June 1992, p. 1.

32 'Why we have a right to know', *Daily Mail*, 14 June 1992, p. 18.

33 *Ibid.*

34 Quoted in the *Guardian*, 'Events by a pool in St Tropez', 21 August 1992, p. 16.

35 'The real world and the royals', *Sun*, 24 August 1992, p. 6.

36 *Daily Telegraph*, 29 August 1992.

37 Almost three thousand called in to say whether 'Fergie' should be sent to live abroad, of whom 72 per cent thought she should. Seventy-four per cent of readers calling another line delivered themselves of the view that they would not marry a royal, which must have been a devastating blow to the queen. 'Royal poll sensation', *Sun*, 31 August 1992, p. 4.

38 *Sunday Mirror*, 10 January 1993, p. 2.

39 Robert Worcester, 'The Power of Public Opinion: Princess Diana, 1961–1997', *Journal of the Market Research Society*, vol. 39, no. 4 (October 1997).

40 *Ibid.*, p. 12.

41 As another member of the House of Lords put it:

Lord Dawson of Penn
Has killed lots of men
So that's why we sing
God Save the King.

42 Prince Charles, Prince of Wales, 'Ode to the Press', in Charles, *In his own Words*, pp. 125–6.

43 Quoted in Rose, *George V*, p. 225.

44 Later, there was an attempt by a tabloid newspaper to use an attractive young woman to entrap Mrs Parker Bowles's son into confessing to drug use, by bugging a dinner-table. The only possible reason for choosing him as a target was that he was his mother's son.

45 The custom dies hard. When the Dutch heir to the throne married, Durex published a full-page advertisement in a number of dailies in which it described itself proudly as 'likely supplier to the court'.

46 Given the prominent role that tobacco played in the deaths of twentieth-century British royalty, perhaps they should also have endorsed the manufacturers of surgical instruments.

47 There was even a Deep South street-battler called King James III, who bore strangely little resemblance to previous Stuart claimants to the throne.

48 How many of them could expect an invitation to lecture the World Health Organization on complementary medicine, as Prince Charles did in May 2006?

12 The End of the Line?

1 'I am sitting here at my desk today in October, longing for someone to hug me and encourage me to keep strong and hold my head high. This particular phase in my life is the most dangerous. [The princess then identified where she felt the threat and danger would come from] is planning "an accident" in my car, brake failure and serious head injury in order to make the path clear for Charles to marry' (Burrell, *A Royal Duty*, p. 322). It was later revealed that the blank section should read 'Charles is planning "an accident" in my car, brake failure and serious head injury in order to make the path clear for him to marry.'

2 David Icke, *The Biggest Secret*, p. 451.

3 Ian Jack, 'Those who felt differently', *Granta*, no. 60, 'Unbelievable', Winter 1997, pp. 16–17.

4 'all documentation pertaining to the official Court of Inquiry has apparently vanished into thin air. The Public Record Office, the RAF Historical Branch, and the Royal Archives at Windsor Castle all deny having possession of the key records that relate directly to the death of the Duke of Kent, brother of the King, and at that time fifth in line to the throne' (Warwick, *George and Marina*, p. 134).

5 The princess was married to Prince Leopold of Saxe-Coburg-Saalfeld, who was invited, many years later, to become the first King of the Belgians.

6 Leigh Hunt, in the *Examiner*, 9 November 1817. Quoted in Behrendt, *Royal Mourning and Regency Culture*, p. 78.

7 Jesse Foot, quoted in Behrendt, *Royal Mourning and Regency Culture*, pp. 184–5.

8 Rose, *George V*, p. 209.
9 Quoted in *ibid.*
10 *Ibid.*, p. 212.
11 *Ibid.*, p. 215.
12 *Ibid.*, p. 216.
13 Comment to Vita Sackville-West, quoted in Bradford, *George VI*, p. 511.
14 Even though the king was faced with what his biographer calls 'constant demonstrations, scenes and even outrages' by suffragettes, in 1913 he had his private secretary write to the Home Secretary to say how disgusting he found the practice of force-feeding. 'His Majesty cannot help feeling that there is something shocking, if not almost cruel, in the operation to which these insensate women are subjected through their refusal to take necessary nourishment . . . The King asks whether, in your "Temporary Discharge of Prisons Bill", it would not be possible to abolish forcible feeding' (Nicolson, *George V*, p. 212).
15 As the twenty-first century began there was even a plan to rebuild the Imperial Palace in the centre of Berlin, which had been dynamited by the Communists and replaced with a hideous 'palace of the people'. Without some part of the constitutional architecture of a nation expressing its history, you can begin to doubt who you are.
16 Jonathan Freedland, 'Elizabeth the Last', *Guardian*, 21 April 2006, 'G2', pp. 6–9.
17 Polly Toynbee, 'The need to modernise our country', *Guardian*, 6 December 2000.
18 Rhodes James, *Albert, Prince Consort*, p. 268.
19 Nicolson, *Monarchy*, p. 170.
20 Bradford, *Elizabeth*, p. 456. In 1995, as part of a campaign to repair his tarnished image, he was persuaded to attend the FA Cup Final. That he nearly presented the trophy to the losing side did little to convince people of his close interest in the game.
21 Charles, *In his own Words*, p. 99.
22 Burrell, *A Royal Duty*, p. 112.
23 Barry, *Royal Service*, pp. 100–101. 'I never heard him utter a four-

letter word in the twelve years I worked for him. Nor does he go around kicking the furniture or throwing things. That sort of behaviour is simply not his style' (*ibid.*, p. 103).

24 Burrell, *A Royal Duty*, pp. 156–7.

25 Professor Michael Baum, 'An open letter to the Prince of Wales: with respect, your royal highness, you've got it wrong', *British Medical Journal*, 10 July 2004.

26 'Charles the political dissident, as revealed by his former aide', *Guardian*, 22 February 2006, p. 1.

27 *HRH The Prince of Wales, Annual Review 2005*, pp. 2–3.

28 See Brazier, 'Skipping a generation in the line of succession'.

29 So when Mountbatten was on a private visit to Windsor, 'I would usually find myself at the head of the table, next to the Duke of Edinburgh's staff. But during Garter Weekend at Windsor Castle, when most of the family came to stay, I would gradually be moved some eight places further down the table as the weekend progressed and more and more royal visitors arrived for the Ascot house party which followed the Garter Ceremony . . . This sense of hierarchy was very jealously preserved as much among the Royal Household as among the royals themselves. We all remained most respectful towards the senior members of the Household, notably the Queen Mother's staff, most of whom had been in service for many years and were shown the courtesy and attention that befitted their seniority.' (Evans, *My Mountbatten Years*, p. 96.)

30 Marx, *Capital*, vol. I, p. 149n.

31 Jones, 'The Psychology of Constitutional Monarchy', pp. 232–3.

32 Knight, *The Sovereign Flower*, p. 278.

Bibliography

Books, articles, lectures

Abels, Richard. *Alfred the Great: War, Kingship and Culture in Anglo-Saxon England* (Longman, Harlow, 1998)

Al-Azmeh, Aziz. *Muslim Kingship: Power and the Sacred in Muslim, Christian and Pagan Polities* (I. B. Tauris, London, 1997)

Aldrich, Robert and Garry Wotherspoon, eds. *Who's Who in Gay and Lesbian History* (2001; second edition, Routledge, London, 2002)

Alexander, John T. *Catherine the Great: Life and Legend* (Oxford University Press, Oxford & New York, 1989)

Alexandra Feodorovna, Empress of Russia. *Letters of the Tsaritsa to the Tsar, 1914–1916* (Duckworth, London, 1923)

Allan, J., Sir T. Wolseley Haig and H. H. Dodwell. *The Cambridge Shorter History of India*. Edited by H. H. Dodwell (Cambridge University Press, Cambridge, 1934)

Allen, Graham. *The Last Prime Minister: Being Honest about the UK Presidency* (Politico's, London, 2001)

Allison, Ronald and Sarah Riddell, *The Royal Encyclopaedia* (Macmillan, London, 1991)

Andersen, Christopher. *Diana's Boys: William and Harry and the Mother they Loved* (2001; updated edition, Avon Books, New York, 2002)

Annigoni, Pietro. *An Artist's Life* (W. H. Allen, London, 1977)

Anonymous. *Memoirs of the Most Christian Brute; or, the History of the Late Exploits of a Certain Great K—g* (Richard James, London & Dublin, 1747)

——. *The British Tocsin; or, Proofs of National Ruin* (Daniel Isaac Eaton, London, 1795)

——. ('A Republican'). *The Happy Reign of George the Last: An Address to the Little Tradesmen, and the Labouring Poor of England* (Citizen Lee, London, n.d. [1795?])

——. ('The Author of "A month in town", "General Post Bag", &c. &c.'). *The Secret Memoirs of a Prince; or, a Peep behind the Scenes* (London, 1816)

——. *The Authentic Records of the Court of England, for the Last Seventy Years* (Josiah Phillips, London, 1832)

——. *Republicanism in England and Fall of the British Empire* (Wyman & Sons, London, 1880)

——. ('One of Her Majesty's Servants'). *The Private Life of the Queen* (1897; Gresham Books, Old Woking, Surrey, 1979)

——. *The Real Kaiser* (Andrew Melrose, London, 1914)

——. ('The Author of *The Real Kaiser*'). *Ferdinand of Bulgaria: The Amazing Career of a Shoddy Czar* (Andrew Melrose, London, 1916)

—— ('An American Resident'). *The Twilight of the British Monarchy* (Martin Secker & Warburg, London, 1937)

—— ('SMC'). *Margaret, Princess of Hungary* (1945; Blackfriars Publications, London, 1954)

Arango, E. Ramon. *Leopold III and the Belgian Royal Question* (Johns Hopkins University Press, Baltimore, 1961)

Aronson, Theo. *Kings over the Water: The Saga of the Stuart Pretenders* (1979; Cassell, London, 1988)

——. *Crowns in Conflict: The Triumph and the Tragedy of European Monarchy, 1910–1918* (John Murray, London, 1986)

——. *The King in Love: Edward VII's Mistresses* (John Murray, London, 1988)

——. *Heart of a Queen: Queen Victoria's Romantic Attachments* (John Murray, London, 1991)

——. *Princess Margaret: A Biography* (1997; enlarged edition, Michael O'Mara Books, London, 2001)

Ascherson, Neal. *The King Incorporated: Leopold the Second and the Congo* (1963; Granta Books, London, 1999)

Ashdown, Dulcie M. *Royal Murders: Hatred, Revenge and the Seizing of Power* (Sutton Publishing, Stroud, 1998)

Bagehot, Walter. *The English Constitution* (second edition, London, 1872)

Bahlman, Dudley W. R. 'The Queen, Mr Gladstone, and Church Patronage'. *Victorian Studies*, vol. iii, no. 3, March 1980

Balassa, Imre. *Death of an Empire* (Hutchinson, London, 1936)

Barber, Sarah. 'Charles I: Regicide and Republicanism'. *History Today*, vol. 46, no. 1, January 1996

Barker, Brian. *The Symbols of Sovereignty* (Westbridge Books, Newton Abbot, 1979)

Barnett, Anthony, ed. *Power and the Throne: The Monarchy Debate* (Vintage, London, 1994)

Barratt, John, with Jean Ritchie. *With the Greatest Respect: The Private Lives of Earl Mountbatten of Burma and Prince & Princess Michael of Kent* (Sidgwick & Jackson, London, 1991)

Barry, Stephen P. *Royal Service: My Twelve Years as a Valet to Prince Charles* (Macmillan, New York, 1983)

Barwick, Sandra. *The Royal Baby: HRH Prince William of Wales* (Pitkin Pictorials, London, 1982)

Beaverbrook, Max, Lord. *The Abdication of King Edward VIII*. Edited by A. J. P. Taylor (Hamish Hamilton, London, 1966)

Beeston, David. *A Strange Accident of State: Henry VII and the Lambert Simnel Conspiracy* (Birchwood Publications, Somercotes, 1987)

Behrendt, Stephen C. *Royal Mourning and Regency Culture: Elegies and Memorials of Princess Charlotte* (Macmillan, Basingstoke & London, 1997)

Beller, Steven. *Francis Joseph*. Profiles in Power series (Longman, Harlow, 1996)

Belloc, Hilaire. *Monarchy: A Study of Louis XIV* (Cassell, London, 1938)

Benedict, Ruth. *The Chrysanthemum and the Sword: Patterns of Japanese Culture* (1946; Redwood Burn, Trowbridge & Esher, 1977)

Bennett, Alan. *The Madness of George III* (Faber & Faber, London, 1992)

Bentley, Tom and James Wilsdon. *Monarchies: What are Kings and Queens For?* (Demos, London, 2002)

Bernier, Olivier, ed. *Imperial Mother, Royal Daughter: The Correspondence of Marie Antoinette and Maria Theresa* (Sidgwick & Jackson, London, 1986)

Berry, Wendy. *The Housekeeper's Diary: Charles and Diana before the Breakup* (Barricade Books, New York, 1995)

Besant, Annie. *English Republicanism* (Freethought Publishing, London, 1878)

Betjeman, John. *Collected Poems*. Compiled and introduced by the Earl of Birkenhead (John Murray, London, 2001)

Bird, Anthony. *The Damnable Duke of Cumberland: A Character Study and Vindication of Ernest Augustus, Duke of Cumberland and King of Hanover* (Barrie & Rockliff, London, 1966)

Black, Percy. *The Mystique of Modern Monarchy: With Special Reference to the British Commonwealth* (Watts, London, 1953)

Blain, Neil and Hugh O'Donnell. *Media, Monarchy and Power* (Intellect Books, Bristol & Portland, Oreg., 2003)

Blair Lovell, James. *Anastasia: The Lost Princess* (Robson Books, London, 1992)

Bland, Olivia. *The Royal Way of Death* (Constable, London, 1986)

Blaxland, Gregory. *J. H. Thomas: A Life for Unity* (Frederick Muller, London, 1964)

Bloch, Marc. *The Royal Touch: Sacred Monarchy and Scrofula in England and France*. Translated by J. E. Anderson (1961; Routledge & Kegan Paul, London; McGill-Queen's University Press, Montreal, 1973)

Bloch, Michael. *Wallis & Edward: Letters 1931–1937: The Intimate Correspondence of the Duke and Duchess of Windsor* (Weidenfeld & Nicolson, London, 1986)

——. *The Secret File of the Duke of Windsor* (Bantam Press, London, 1988)

——. *The Duchess of Windsor* (Weidenfeld & Nicolson, London, 1996)

Boehrer, Bruce Thomas. *Monarchy and Incest in Renaissance England: Literature, Culture, Kinship, and Kingship* (University of Pennsylvania Press, Philadelphia, 1992)

Bogdanor, Vernon. *The Monarchy and the Constitution* (Clarendon Press, Oxford, 1995)

Bolitho, Hector. *James Lyle Mackay, First Earl of Inchcape* (John Murray, London, 1936)

Born, Lester Kruger. 'The Perfect Prince: A Study in Thirteenth- and Fourteenth-century Ideals'. *Speculum*, vol. 3, 1928

Boyle, Andrew. *Only the Wind Will Listen: Reith of the BBC* (Hutchinson, London, 1972)

Bradford, Sarah. *Princess Grace* (Weidenfeld & Nicolson, London, 1984)

——. *King George VI* (Weidenfeld & Nicolson, London, 1989)

——. *Elizabeth: A Biography of Her Majesty the Queen* (revised edition, Penguin Books, London, 2002)

Bradlaugh, Charles. *The Impeachment of the House of Brunswick* (Freethought Publishing, London, n.d. [1870s?])

Bradley, Ian. *God Save the Queen: The Spiritual Dimension of Monarchy* (Darton, Longman & Todd, London, 2002)

Brazier, Rodney. 'Skipping a generation in the line of succession'. *Public Law*, Winter 2000, pp. 568–72

Brendon, Piers. *Our Own Dear Queen* (London, 1986)

Brendon, Piers and Philip Whitehead. *The Windsors: A Dynasty Revealed, 1917–2000* (Pimlico, London, 2000)

Brook-Shepherd, Gordon. *The Last Habsburg* (Weidenfeld & Nicolson, London, 1968)

——. *Uncle of Europe: The Social and Diplomatic Life of Edward VII*, (Collins, London, 1975)

——. *Uncrowned Emperor: The Life and Times of Otto von Habsburg* (Hambledon & London, London & New York, 2003)

Brough, James. *Margaret: The Tragic Princess* (W. H. Allen, London, 1978)

Brunt, Rosalind. 'A "Divine Gift to Inspire"? Popular Culture and Representation, Nationhood and the British Monarchy'. In Dominic Strinati and Stephen Wagg, eds. *Come On Down? Popular Media Culture in Post-war Britain* (Routledge, London & New York, 1992)

Buckle, George Earle, ed. *The Letters of Queen Victoria* (John Murray, London, 1926–8)

Burchill, Julie. 'Di Hard: The Pop Princess'. In *Sex and Sensibility* (Grafton, London, 1992)

——. *Diana* (Weidenfeld & Nicolson, London, 1998)

Burke, Edmund. *Reflections on the Revolution in France*. Edited with an introduction by L. G. Mitchell (1790; Oxford University Press, Oxford & New York, 1993)

Burke, Peter. *The Fabrication of Louis XIV* (Yale University Press, New Haven & London, 1992)

Burney, Frances. *Journals and Letters*. Selected and introduced by Peter Sabor and Lars E. Troide (Penguin Books, London, 2001)

Burns, J. H. *The True Law of Kingship: Concepts of Monarchy in Early-Modern Scotland* (Clarendon Press, Oxford, 1996)

Burrell, Paul. *A Royal Duty* (Michael Joseph, London, 2003)

Buruma, Ian, *Voltaire's Coconuts: Anglomania in Europe* (Weidenfeld & Nicolson, London, 1999)

Cadbury, Deborah. *The Lost King of France: Revolution, Revenge and the Search for Louis XVII* (Fourth Estate, London, 2002)

Caesar. *Where's Master?* (Hodder & Stoughton, London, 1910)

Campbell, Beatrix. *Diana, Princess of Wales: How Sexual Politics Shook the Monarchy* (The Women's Press, London, 1998)

Campbell, Lady Colin. *The Royal Marriages: Private Lives of the Queen and her Children* (Smith Gryphon, London, 1993)

Cannadine, David. 'The Context, Performance and Meaning of Ritual: The British Monarchy and the "Invention of Tradition", c. 1820–1977'. In Eric Hobsbawm and Terence Ranger, eds. *The Invention of Tradition* (1983; Canto, Cambridge, 1992)

——. *Ornamentalism: How the British Saw their Empire* (Allen Lane, London, 2001)

——. 'From Biography to History: Writing the Modern British Monarchy', Queen Elizabeth the Queen Mother inaugural lecture, Senate House, University of London, 12 January 2004

Cannadine, David and Simon Price. *Rituals of Royalty* (Cambridge University Press, Cambridge, 1987)

Carlton, Charles. *Royal Mistresses* (Routledge, London & New York, 1990)

Carpenter, Humphrey. *Robert Runcie: The Reluctant Archbishop* (Hodder & Stoughton, London, 1996)

Cartland, Barbara, inspired and helped by Admiral of the Fleet the Earl Mountbatten of Burma. *Love at the Helm* (Weidenfeld & Nicolson, London, 1980)

Chaney, David. 'The Mediated Monarchy'. In David Morley and Kevin Robins, eds. *British Cultural Studies: Geography, Nationality, and Identity* (Oxford University Press, Oxford, 2001)

Channon, Sir Henry. *Chips: The Diaries of Sir Henry Channon.* Edited by Robert Rhodes James (1967; Phoenix, London, 1999)

Charles, Prince of Wales. *Charles in his own Words.* Compiled by Rosemary York (W. H. Allen, London, 1981)

Charles I, King. *Eikon Basilike* (London, 1649)

Charteris, Brigadier General John. *At GHQ* (Cassell, London, 1931)

Childs, John. *The Army, James II, and the Glorious Revolution* (Manchester University Press, Manchester, 1980)

Churchill, Randolph. *The Story of the Coronation* (Derek Verschoyle, London, 1953)

Churchill, Winston S. *Great Contemporaries* (1932; Mandarin, London, 1990)

Cimino, Richard and Don Lattin. *Shopping for Faith: American Religion in the New Millennium* (1998; updated edition, Jossey-Bass, San Francisco, 2002)

Clarke, William. *The Lost Fortune of the Tsars* (Weidenfeld & Nicolson, London, 1994)

Cobbett, William. *History of the Regency and Reign of King George the Fourth* (William Cobbett, London, 1830–4), 2 vols

Colley, Linda. *Britons: Forging the Nation, 1707–1837* (1992; new edition, Pimlico, London, 2003)

Connell, Brian. *Manifest Destiny: A Study in Five Profiles of the Rise and Influence of the Mountbatten Family* (Cassell, London, 1953)

Constant, Stephen. *Foxy Ferdinand, 1861–1948: Tsar of Bulgaria* (Sidgwick & Jackson, London, 1979)

Couldry, Nick. 'Everyday Royal Celebrity'. In David Morley and Kevin Robins, eds. *British Cultural Studies: Geography, Nationality, and Identity* (Oxford University Press, Oxford, 2001)

Court Presentation Dresses, 1898–1939. A leaflet published to accompany the exhibition at the Museum of London, February–September 1978 (London, 1978)

Coward, Noël. *The Noël Coward Diaries*. Edited by Graham Payn and Sheridan Morley (Weidenfeld & Nicolson, London, 1982)

Coward, Rosalind. 'The Royals'. In *Female Desire* (Paladin, London, 1984)

Crawford, Marion. *Queen Elizabeth II* (George Newnes, London, 1952)

Crawford, Patricia. 'Charles Stuart, That Man of Blood'. *Journal of British Studies*, vol. xvi, no. 2, Spring 1977, pp. 41–61

Dante [Alighieri]. *De monarchia*. Translated by F. J. Church (Macmillan, London, 1879)

David, Saul. *Prince of Pleasure: The Prince of Wales and the Making of the Regency* (Little, Brown, London, 1998)

Davidson, J. Morrison. *The New Book of Kings* (1884; The New Temple Press, London, n.d. [1890?])

Davies, Nicholas. *Elizabeth: Behind Palace Doors* (2000; Mainstream Publishing Projects, Edinburgh, 2001)

——. *Diana: Secrets and Lies* (AMI Books, Boca Raton, Fla., 2003)

Davis, Reginald. *Royal Family Album* (Pitkin Pictorials, London, 1979)

Deacon, Richard. *The Greatest Treason: The Bizarre Story of Hollis, Liddell and Mountbatten* (Century, London, 1989)

Dee, John. *General and Rare Memorials Pertayning to the Perfect Arte of Navigation* (Iohn Daye, London, 1577)

Defoe, Daniel. *Of Royall Educacion: A Fragmentary Treatise.* Edited by Karl D. Bülbring (c. 1690; David Nutt, London, 1895)

Devere-Summers, Anthony. *Royal Survivors: The Ten Surviving Monarchies of Europe* (Scribe Printing, Rochester, 1984)

Dimbleby, Jonathan. *The Prince of Wales: A Biography* (Little, Brown, London, 1994)

Donaldson, Frances. *Edward VIII* (Weidenfeld & Nicolson, London, 1974)

Driberg, Tom. *Ruling Passions* (Jonathan Cape, London, 1977)

Dryden, John. *The Poems of John Dryden.* Edited by John Sargeaunt (Oxford University Press, London, 1925)

Duggan, Anne J., ed. *Kings and Kingship in Medieval Europe* (King's College London Centre for Late Antique and Medieval Studies, London, 1993)

Dunbar, Agnes B. C. *A Dictionary of Saintly Women* (George Bell, London, 1905)

Duncan, Andrew. *The Reality of Monarchy*, London, 1970

Dunn, Susan. *The Deaths of Louis XVI: Regicide and the French Political Imagination* (Princeton University Press, Princeton, NJ, 1994)

Edwards, Graham. *The Last Days of Charles I* (Sutton Publishing, Stroud, 1999)

Eilers, Marlene A. *Queen Victoria's Descendants* (Rosvall Royal Books, Falköping, Sweden, 1997)

Emerson, Barbara. *Leopold II of the Belgians: King of Colonialism* (Weidenfeld & Nicolson, London, 1979)

Erasmus, Desiderius. *The Education of a Christian Prince*. Translated by Neil M. Cheshire and Michael J. Heath; edited by Lisa Jardine (1516; Cambridge University Press, Cambridge, 1997)

Esher, Reginald Balliol Brett, Viscount. *The Influence of King Edward, and Essays on Other Subjects* (John Murray, London, 1915)

Eulalia, HRH the Infanta of Spain. *Court Life from Within* (Cassell, London, New York, Toronto & Melbourne, 1915)

Evans, R. J. W. and Hartmut Pogge von Strandmann, eds. *The Revolutions in Europe, 1848–1849: From Reform to Reaction* (Oxford University Press, Oxford, 2000)

Evans, William. *My Mountbatten Years: In the Service of Lord Louis* (Headline, London, 1989)

Evelyn, John. *The Diary of John Evelyn*. Edited by William Bray (1818; Frederick Warne, London, n.d.)

Everdell, William R. *The End of Kings: A History of Republics and Republicanism* (Collier Macmillan/The Free Press, London & New York, 1983)

Executive Intelligence Review, Editors of (Lyndon H. LaRouche Jr *et al.*). *Dope, Inc.: The Book that Drove Henry Kissinger Crazy* (1978; new edition, Executive Intelligence Review, Washington, DC, 1992)

Fairclough, Melvyn. *The Ripper and the Royals*. With a foreword by Joseph Sickert (1991; second edition, Duckworth, London, 2002)

Farmer, David. *The Oxford Dictionary of Saints* (1978; fourth edition, Oxford University Press, Oxford, 1997)

Farrer, James Anson. *The Monarchy in Politics* (T. Fisher Unwin, London, 1917)

Fearon, Peter. *Behind the Palace Walls: The Rise and Fall of Britain's Royal Family* (1993; revised edition, Citadel Stars, Secaucus, NJ, 1996)

Field, Ophelia. *The Favourite: Sarah, Duchess of Marlborough* (Hodder & Stoughton, London, 2002)

Figgis, John Neville. *The Divine Right of Kings* (1896, 1914; Thoemmes Press, Bristol, 1994)

Fisher, H. A. L. *Napoleon* (1912; second edition, Oxford University Press, London, 1967)

Fitzherbert, Margaret. *The Man Who was Greenmantle* (John Murray, London, 1983)

Forbes, Grania. *My Darling Buffy: The Early Life of the Queen Mother* (Richard Cohen Books, London, 1997)

Forman, F. N. *Constitutional Change in the United Kingdom* (Routledge, London & New York, 2002)

Frankfort, Henri. *Kingship and the Gods: A Study of Ancient Near Eastern Religion as the Integration of Society and Nature* (University of Chicago Press, Chicago, 1948)

Fraser, Antonia. *Marie Antoinette: The Journey* (2001; Phoenix, London, 2002)

Frazer, James George. *The Magical Origin of Kings* (Macmillan, London, 1920)

Fry, C. B. *Life Worth Living* (Eyre & Spottiswoode, London, 1939)

Gairdner, James. 'The Story of Perkin Warbeck'. *History of the Life and Reign of Richard III, to which is Added the Story of Perkin Warbeck, from Original Documents* (1898; Cedric Chivers, Bath, 1972)

Gelderen, Martin van, and Quentin Skinner, eds. *Republicanism: A Shared European Heritage*, vol. I: *Republicanism and Constitutionalism in Early Modern Europe* (Cambridge University Press, Cambridge, 2002)

Gibbon, Edward. *The History of the Decline and Fall of the Roman Empire* (1777; Routledge/Thoemmes Press, London, 1997), 6 vols

Gilbert, Allan H. *Machiavelli's Prince and its Forerunners: The Prince as a Typical Book de regimine principum*. (Duke University Press, Durham, NC, 1938)

Gilbert, Jeremy, David Glover, Cora Kaplan, Jenny Bourne Taylor and Wendy Wheeler, eds. *Diana and Democracy*. *New Formations*, no. 36, 1999

Gilbert, Martin. *Winston S. Churchill*, vol. VI: *Finest Hour, 1939–1941*; vol. VIII: *Never Despair, 1945–1965* (William Heinemann, London, 1983, 1988)

Gillingham, John, ed. *Richard III: A Medieval Kingship* (Collins & Brown, London, 1993)

Godfrey, Rupert, ed. *Letters from a Prince: Edward, Prince of Wales to Mrs Freda Dudley Ward, March 1918–January 1921* (1998; Warner Books, London, 1999)

Goodwin, Jason. *Lords of the Horizons: A History of the Ottoman Empire* (Chatto & Windus, London, 1998)

Gordon, Peter and Denis Lawton. *Royal Education: Past, Present and Future* (1999; revised edition, Frank Cass, London; Portland, Oreg., 2003)

Gore, John. *King George V: A Personal Memoir* (John Murray, London, 1941)

Grant, Michael. *The Antonines: The Roman Empire in Transition* (Routledge, London & New York, 1994)

Gray, Michael. *Blood Relative* (Victor Gollancz, London, 1998)

Green, Vivian. *The Madness of Kings: Personal Trauma and the Fate of Nations* (Alan Sutton, Stroud; St Martin's Press, New York, 1993)

Gregson, Jonathan. *Blood against the Snows: The Tragic Story of Nepal's Royal Dynasty* (Fourth Estate, London, 2002)

Greville, C. C. F. *A Journal of the Life of Queen Victoria* (London, 1885)

——. *The Greville Memoirs, 1814–1860*. Edited by Lytton Strachey and Roger Fulford (Macmillan, London, 1938), 8 vols

Grosrichard, Alain. *The Sultan's Court: European Fantasies of the East*. Translated by Liz Heron (1979; Verso, London & New York, 1998)

Guedalla, Philip. *The Queen and Mr Gladstone* (Hodder & Stoughton, London, 1933), 2 vols

Hall, Phillip. *Royal Fortune: Tax, Money and the Monarchy* (Bloomsbury, London, 1992)

Hamilton, Willie. *My Queen and I* (Quartet Books, London, 1975)

Harris, Kenneth. *The Queen* (Weidenfeld & Nicolson, London, 1994)

Harris, Leonard. *Long to Reign over Us?* (William Kimber, London, 1966)

Harrison, Michael. *Clarence: The Life of H.R.H. the Duke of Clarence and Avondale (1864–1892)* (W. H. Allen, London & New York, 1972)

Haseler, Stephen. *The End of the House of Windsor: Birth of a British Republic* (I. B. Tauris, London, 1993)

Haslip, Joan. *Imperial Adventurer: Emperor Maximilian of Mexico* (Weidenfeld & Nicolson, London, 1971)

——. *Marie Antoinette* (1987; Weidenfeld & Nicolson, London, 1989)

Hatch, Alden. *The Mountbattens* (W. H. Allen, London, 1966)

Hatton, Ragnhild. *George I: Elector and King* (Thames & Hudson, London, 1978)

Heald, Tim. *A Peerage for Trade: A History of the Royal Warrant* (Royal Warrant Holders Association in association with Sinclair-Stevenson, London, 2001)

Healey, Edna. *The Queen's House: A Social History of Buckingham Palace* (Michael Joseph, London, 1997)

Heaney, Peter, ed. *Selected Writings of the Laureate Dunces, Nahum Tate (Laureate 1692–1715), Laurence Eusden (1718–1730) and Colley Cibber (1730–1757)* (The Edwin Mellen Press, Lampeter, 1999)

Heaton-Armstrong, Duncan. *The Six Month Kingdom: Albania 1914* (I. B. Tauris, London, 2005)

Hedley, Olwen and Rachel Stewart. *Her Majesty Queen Elizabeth the Queen Mother: An 85th Birthday Album* (Pitkin Pictorials, London, 1985)

Hennessy, Peter. 'Searching for the "Great Ghost": The Palace, the Premiership, the Cabinet and the Constitution in the Post-war Period'. *Journal of Contemporary History*, vol. 30, no. 2, April 1995

Henry, Wade A. 'Imagining the Great White Mother and the Great King: Aboriginal Tradition and Royal Representation at the "Great Pow-wow" of 1901'. *Journal of the Canadian Historical Association*, new series, vol. 11, 2000

Herman, Eleanor. *Sex with Kings* (William Morrow, New York, 2004)

Hewitt, James. *Love and War* (Blake, London, 1999)

Hibbert, Christopher. *Charles I* (1968; Penguin Books, London, 2001)

——. *Edward VII: A Portrait* (Allen Lane, London, 1976)

——. *The Court of St James* (Weidenfeld & Nicolson, London, 1979)

——. *George III: A Personal History* (Viking, London, 1998)

Higham, Charles. *Wallis: Secret Lives of the Duchess of Windsor* (Sidgwick & Jackson, London, 1988)

Hill, Christopher. *God's Englishman: Oliver Cromwell and the English Revolution* (Weidenfeld & Nicolson, London, 1970)

Hitchens, Christopher. *The Monarchy* (Chatto & Windus, London, 1990)

Hobsbawm, Eric and Terence Ranger, eds. *The Invention of Tradition* (Cambridge University Press, Cambridge, 1983)

Hocart, A. M. *Kingship* (Oxford University Press, London, 1927)

Hochschild, Adam. *King Leopold's Ghost: A Story of Greed, Terror and Heroism in Colonial Africa* (1998; Papermac, London, 2000)

Hoey, Brian. *Mountbatten: The Private Story* (Sidgwick & Jackson, London, 1994)

——. *The Royal Yacht Britannia: Inside the Queen's Floating Palace* (1995; third edition, Patrick Stephens, London, 1999)

——. *At Home with the Queen: The Inside Story of the Royal Household* (HarperCollins, London, 2002)

Hoffman, William. *Queen Juliana: The Story of the Richest Woman in the World* (Harcourt Brace Jovanovich, New York & London, 1979)

Holden, Anthony. *The Tarnished Crown* (Bantam Books, London, 1993)

Hone, William. *The Riots in London: Hone's Full and Authentic Account* (William Hone, London, 1816)

Horsley, Peter. *Sounds from Another Room* (Leo Cooper, London, 1997)

Hough, Richard, ed. *Advice to a Grand-daughter: Letters from Queen Victoria to Princess Victoria of Hesse* (Heinemann, London, 1975)

Howard, Philip. *The British Monarchy in the Twentieth Century* (Hamish Hamilton, London, 1977)

Hucker, Charles O. *China's Imperial Past: An Introduction to Chinese History and Culture* (Duckworth, London, 1975)

Hughes, Emrys. *The Prince, the Crown and the Cash* (Housmans, London, 1969)

Hughes, Ted. *Collected Poems*. Edited by Paul Keegan (Faber & Faber, London, 2003)

Hume, Martin A. S. *Spain: Its Greatness and Decay* (1898; third edition, Cambridge University Press, Cambridge, 1913)

Hunt, Alan. *Governance of the Consuming Passions: A History of Sumptuary Law* (Macmillan, London, 1996)

Hyland, Ann. *The Warhorse, 1250–1600* (Sutton Publishing, Stroud, 1998)

Icke, David. *The Biggest Secret* (1999; Bridge of Love Publications USA, Wildwood, Mo., 2001)

The Illustrated London News Record of the Life and Reign of Edward the Seventh (Illustrated London News, London, 1910)

Isocrates. 'Προς Νικοκλεα./To Nicocles'. *Isocrates* [Complete Works], vol. I. With an English translation by George Norlin (William Heinemann, London; G. P. Putnam's Sons, New York, 1928), 3 vols

Jack, Ian. 'Those who Felt Differently'. *Granta*, no. 60, 'Unbelievable', Winter 1997

James I and VI, King of England and Scotland, *et al. The Prince's Cabala: Or Mysteries of State* (London, 1715)

James, Edward. *The Franks* (Basil Blackwell, Oxford & New York, 1988)

James, Paul. *Prince Edward: A Life in the Spotlight* (Piatkus, London, 1992)

Jardine, L. and J. Brotton. *Global Interests: Renaissance Art between East and West* (Reaktion Books, London, 2000)

Jenkins, Roy. *Sir Charles Dilke: A Victorian Tragedy* (1958; revised edition, Collins, London, 1965)

Joinville, John de. 'Chronicle of the Crusade of St Lewis' (1309). In Frank Marzials, trans. and ed., *Chronicles of the Crusades by Villehardouin and de Joinville* (J. M. Dent, London, 1908)

Jones, A. H. M. and Elizabeth Monroe. *A History of Abyssinia* (Clarendon Press, Oxford, 1935)

Jones, Ernest. 'The Psychology of Constitutional Monarchy'. *Essays in Applied Psychoanalysis*, vol. I (The Hogarth Press, London, 1951)

Jones, J. D. F. *Storyteller: The Many Lives of Laurens van der Post* (John Murray, London, 2001)

Judd, Denis. *Eclipse of Kings: European Monarchies in the Twentieth Century* (Macdonald & Jane's, London, 1976)

Junor, Penny. *Charles: Victim or Villain?* (HarperCollins, London, 1998)

Kantorowicz, Ernst H. *The King's Two Bodies: A Study in Medieval Political Theology* (Princeton University Press, Princeton, NJ, 1957)

Kapuscinski, Ryszard. *Shah of Shahs* (Harcourt Brace Jovanovich, New York, 1985)

Keene, Donald. *Emperor of Japan: Meiji and his World, 1852–1912* (Columbia University Press, New York, 2002)

King, Greg. *The Duchess of Windsor. The Uncommon Life of Wallis Simpson* (Aurum Press, London, 1999)

Kinross, John Balfour, Lord. *The Ottoman Centuries: The Rise and Fall of the Turkish Empire* (Jonathan Cape, London, 1977)

Kishlansky, Mark. *A Monarchy Transformed: Britain, 1603–1714* (Allen Lane, London, 1996)

Kiste, John Van der. *George V's Children* (Alan Sutton, Stroud, 1991)

——. *William and Mary* (Sutton Publishing, Stroud, 2003)

Kitchen, Martin. *Kaspar Hauser: Europe's Child* (Palgrave, Basingstoke & New York, 2001)

Klier, John and Helen Mingay. *The Quest for Anastasia* (Smith Gryphon, London, 1995)

Knight, G. Wilson. *Collected Works*, vol. IV: *The Sovereign Flower: On Shakespeare as the Poet of Royalism, Together with Related Essays and Indexes to Earlier Volumes* (1958; Routledge, London & New York, 2002)

Kuhn, Annette *et al.* 'Flowers and Tears: The Death of Diana, Princess of Wales'. *Screen*, vol. 39, no. 1, Spring 1998

Kuhn, William M. *Democratic Royalism: The Transformation of the British Monarchy, 1861–1914* (Macmillan, London, 1996)

Kurth, Peter. *Anastasia: The Life of Anna Anderson* (1983; Pimlico, London, 1995)

Lacey, Robert. *Monarch: The Life and Reign of Elizabeth II* (The Free Press, New York, 2002)

Laird, Dorothy. *How the Queen Reigns* (Hodder & Stoughton, London, 1959)

Laqueur, Thomas W. 'The Queen Caroline Affair: Politics as Art in the Reign of George IV'. *Journal of Modern History*, vol. 54, no. 3, September 1982

Laqueur, Walter, ed. *The Terrorism Reader: A Historical Anthology* (Wildwood House, London, 1979)

Lascelles, Sir Alan. *In Royal Service: The Letters and Journals of Sir Alan Lascelles, 1920–1936*, vol. II. Edited by Duff Hart-Davis (Hamish Hamilton, London, 1989)

Laski, Harold. *Parliamentary Government in England* (George Allen & Unwin, London, 1938)

Latham, Robert and William Matthews. *The Diary of Samuel Pepys: A New and Complete Transcription* (Bell & Hyman, London, 1970–83)

Lees-Milne, James. *The Enigmatic Edwardian: The Life of Reginald, 2nd Viscount Esher* (Sidgwick & Jackson, London, 1986)

——. *Diaries, 1942–45: Ancestral Voices & Prophesying Peace* (new edition, John Murray, London, 1995)

Levick, Barbara. *Vespasian* (Routledge, London & New York, 1999)

Lichtervelde, Comte Louis de. *Léopold First: The Founder of Modern Belgium*. Translated by Thomas H. Reed and H. Russell Reed (The Century Co., New York & London, 1930)

Lorimer, David. *Radical Prince: The Practical Vision of the Prince of Wales* (Floris Books, Edinburgh, 2003

Macalpine, Ida and Hunter, Richard. *George III and the Mad-Business* (Allen Lane, London, 1969)

Macaulay, Thomas Babington, Lord. *The History of England, from the Accession of James II* (1849–61; Oxford University Press/Humphrey Milford, London, 1931), 5 vols

MacCaffrey, Wallace T. *Elizabeth I: War and Politics, 1558–1603* (Princeton University Press, Princeton, NJ, 1992)

McColl, René. *Dateline and Deadline* (Oldbourne Press, London, 1956)

Machiavelli, Niccolò. *The Prince.* Translated by W. K. Marriott (J. M. Dent, London; E. P. Dutton, New York, 1949)

Mackenzie, Compton. *The Windsor Tapestry: Being a Study of the Life, Heritage and Abdication of H. R. H. the Duke of Windsor, K. G.* (Rich & Cowan, London, 1938)

McKibbin, Ross. 'Mass Observation in the Mall'. *London Review of Books*, 2 October 1997

McKusick, Victor A. 'The Royal Hemophilia'. *Scientific American*, vol. 213, no. 2, August 1965

McLeod, Kirsty. *Battle Royal: Edward VIII and George VI, Brother against Brother* (1999; Robinson, London, 2000)

Madariaga, Isabel de. *Catherine the Great: A Short History* (Yale University Press, New Haven & London, 1990)

Marples, Morris. *Poor Fred and the Butcher: Sons of George II* (Michael Joseph, London, 1970)

Marquand, David. *Ramsay MacDonald* (Jonathan Cape, London, 1977)

Martin, Kingsley. *The Crown and the Establishment* (1962; revised edition, Penguin Books, Harmondsworth, 1965)

Martin, Theodore. *The Life of the Prince Consort* (Smith, Elder, London, 1875)

Marx, Karl. *Capital.* Introduced by Ernest Mandel; translated by Ben Fowkes (Penguin Books, Harmondsworth, 1976), 3 vols

Mary II, Queen of Great Britain and Ireland. *Memoirs, together with her Letters and those of Kings James II and William III to the Electress, Sophia of Hanover.* Edited by Dr R. Dobner (D. Nutt, London, 1886)

Masters, Brian. *Dreams about H.M. The Queen* (Mayflower, London, 1973)

Menkes, Suzy. *The Royal Jewels* (1985; third edition, Grafton Books, London, 1988)

——. *The Windsor Style* (Grafton Books, London, 1987)

——. *Queen and Country* (HarperCollins, London, 1992)

Merck, Mandy, ed. *After Diana: Irreverent Elegies* (Verso, London & New York, 1998)

Midelfort, H. C. Erik. *Mad Princes of Renaissance Germany* (University Press of Virginia, Charlottesville & London, 1994)

Millar, Fergus. *The Emperor in the Roman World (31 BC–AD 337)* (Duckworth, London, 1977)

Miller, John. *James II: A Study in Kingship* (1978; Methuen, London, 1989)

Monmouth, Geoffrey of. *The History of the Kings of Britain*. Translated by Lewis Thorpe (Penguin Books, London, 1966)

Morby, John E. *Dynasties of the World: A Chronological and Genealogical Handbook* (1989; new edition, Oxford University Press, Oxford, 2002)

Morrah, Dermot Macgregor. *To be a King* (Hutchinson, London, 1968)

Morton, Andrew. *The Wealth of the Windsors* (1989; updated edition, Michael O'Mara Books, London, 1993)

——. *Diana: Her True Story in her own Words* (1992; Michael O'Mara, London, 1998)

Morton, Andrew and Mick Seamark. *Andrew: The Playboy Prince* (Severn House, London, 1983)

Mosley, Lady Diana, with editorial consultant Jack le Vien. *The Duchess of Windsor* (Sidgwick & Jackson, London, 1980)

Mote, Frederick R. 'The Rise of the Ming Dynasty, 1330–1367'. *Cambridge History of China*, vol. VII (Cambridge University Press, Cambridge, 1988)

Munk, William. *The Life of Sir Henry Halford, Bart* (Longmans, Green, London & New York, 1895)

Murray, Margaret Alice. *The Divine King in England: A Study in Anthropology* (Faber & Faber, London, 1954)

Nada, John. *Carlos the Bewitched* (Jonathan Cape, London, 1962)

Nairn, Tom. *The Enchanted Glass: Britain and its Monarchy* (1988; new edition, Vintage, London, 1994)

Nash, David, and Anthony Taylor, eds. *Republicanism in Victorian Society* (Sutton Publishing, Stroud, 2000)

Nelson, Walter Henry. *The Soldier Kings: The House of Hohenzollern* (J. M. Dent, London, 1971)

Nicholls, David. *The Lost Prime Minister: A Life of Sir Charles Dilke* (The Hambledon Press, London, 1995)

Nicolson, Harold. *King George V* (Constable, London, 1952)

——. *Monarchy* (Weidenfeld & Nicolson, London, 1962)

——. *Diaries and Letters*. Edited by Nigel Nicolson (Collins, London, 1966–8), 3 vols

Nicolson, Nigel. *The Queen and Us* (Weidenfeld & Nicolson, London, 2003)

Nightingale, Joseph. *Memoirs of the Public and Private Life of Queen Caroline*. Edited by Christopher Hibbert (1820; The Folio Society, London, 1978)

Noussanne, Henri de. *The Kaiser as he is; or, the Real William II*. Translated by Walter Littlefield. (G. P. Putnam's Sons, New York & London, 1905)

Ollard, Richard. *The Image of the King: Charles I and Charles II* (Hodder & Stoughton, London, 1979)

Opie, Robert, compiler. *The Royal Scrapbook* (New Cavendish Books, London, 2002)

Osborne, John. 'And they Call it Cricket'. *Encounter*, vol. ix, no. 4, October 1957

Osman, John and Tim Graham (photographer). *The Queen's Visit to China and Hong Kong* (Pitkin Pictorials, London, 1986)

Owen, David. *English Philanthropy, 1660–1960* (Oxford University Press, London, 1964)

Paine, Thomas. *Thomas Paine Reader*. Edited by Michael Foot and Isaac Kramnick (Penguin Books, Harmondsworth, 1987)

Palmer, Alan. *Bernadotte: Napoleon's Marshal, Sweden's King* (John Murray, London, 1990)

——. *Twilight of the Habsburgs: The Life and Times of Emperor Francis Joseph* (Weidenfeld & Nicolson, London, 1994)

Paoli, Xavier. *My Royal Clients*. Translated by Alexander Teixeira de Mattos (Hodder & Stoughton, London, 1911)

Parissien, Steven. *George IV: The Grand Entertainment* (John Murray, London, 2001)

Parker, John. *Prince Philip: A Critical Biography* (Sidgwick & Jackson, London, 1990)

Partridge, Robert. *'O Horrable Murder': The Trial, Execution and Burial of Charles I* (The Rubicon Press, London, 1998)

Pearson, John. *Edward the Rake* (Weidenfeld & Nicolson, London, 1975)

——. *The Ultimate Family: The Making of the Royal House of Windsor* (Michael Joseph, London, 1986)

Pearson, Owen. *Albania and King Zog* (I. B. Tauris, London, 2004)

Peltonen, Markku. *Classical Humanism and Republicanism in English Political Thought, 1570–1640* (Cambridge University Press, Cambridge, 1995)

Pepys, Samuel. *The Diary of Samuel Pepys*. Edited by Robert Latham and William Matthews (1971; HarperCollins, London, 2000), 9 vols

Pimlott, Ben. *Hugh Dalton* (Jonathan Cape, London, 1985)

——. *The Queen: Elizabeth II and the Monarchy*. Golden Jubilee Edition (1996; HarperCollins, London, 2002)

Piozzi, Hester Lynch. *Anecdotes of the Late Dr Samuel Johnson during the Last Twenty Years of his Life*. Edited by S. C. Roberts (1786; Cambridge University Press, Cambridge, 1932)

Pitt, Valerie. *Tennyson Laureate* (Barrie & Rockliff, London, 1962)

Plumptre, George. *Edward VII* (Pavilion, London, 1995)

Plunkett, John. *Queen Victoria: First Media Monarch* (Oxford University Press, Oxford, 2003)

Pollo, Stefanaq and Arben Puto. *The History of Albania* (Routledge & Kegan Paul, London, 1981)

Pope, Alexander. *Poetical Works*. Edited by Herbert Davis (Oxford University Press, London, 1966)

Pope-Hennessy, James. *A Lonely Business: A Self-portrait of James Pope-Hennessy*. Edited by Peter Quennell (Weidenfeld & Nicolson, London, 1981)

Prawer, Joshua. *The Crusaders' Kingdom: European Colonialism in the Middle Ages* (1972; Phoenix Press, London, 2001)

Preston, Paul. *Juan Carlos: A People's King* (HarperCollins, London, 2004)

Price, Munro. *The Fall of the French Monarchy: Louis XVI, Marie Antoinette and the Baron de Breteuil* (2002; Pan Books, London, 2003)

Prochaska, Frank. *Royal Bounty: The Making of a Welfare Monarchy* (Yale University Press, New Haven & London, 1995)

——. *The Republic of Britain* (Allen Lane, London, 2000)

——, ed. *Royal Lives* (Oxford University Press, Oxford, 2002)

Purcell, William Ernest. *Fisher of Lambeth: A Portrait from Life* (Hodder & Stoughton, London, 1969)

Purdue, A. W. *Long to Reign? The Survival of Monarchies in the Modern World* (Sutton Publishing, Stroud, 2005)

Ralph Lewis, Brenda. *Monarchy: The History of an Idea* (Sutton Publishing, Stroud, 2003)

Ratcliffe, Edward. *The Coronation Service of her Majesty Queen Elizabeth II* (SPCK, London, 1953)

Redworth, Glyn. *The Prince and the Infanta: The Cultural Politics of the Spanish Match* (Yale University Press, New Haven & London, 2003)

Reid, Michaela. *Ask Sir James: The Life of James Reid, Personal Physician to Queen Victoria* (1987; Eland, London, 1996)

Rémy. *The Eighteenth Day: The Tragedy of King Leopold III of the Belgians.* Translated by Stanley Rader (Everest House, New York, 1978)

Reynolds, George W. M. *The Mysteries of London* (George Vickers, London, 1846–50), 6 vols

——. *The Mysteries of the Court of London* (John Dicks, London, 1849–56), 8 vols

Rhodes James, Robert. *Albert, Prince Consort: A Biography* (Hamish Hamilton, London, 1983)

Richards, Jeffrey, Scott Wilson and Linda Woodhead, eds. *Diana: The Making of a Media Saint* (I. B. Tauris, London & New York, 1999)

Richards, Thomas. *The Commodity Culture of Victorian England: Advertising and Spectacle, 1851–1914* (Verso, London, 1991)

Richardson, Glenn. *Renaissance Monarchy: The Reigns of Henry VIII, Francis I and Charles V* (Arnold, London, 2002)

Roberts, Andrew. *The Holy Fox* (Weidenfeld & Nicolson, London, 1991)

Robertson, Geoffrey. *The Tyrannicide Brief: The Story of the Man Who Sent Charles I to the Scaffold* (Chatto & Windus, London, 2005)

Röhl, John C. G. *The Kaiser and his Court: Wilhelm II and the Government of Germany*. Translated by Terence F. Cole (1987; English translation, Cambridge University Press, Cambridge, 1994)

Röhl, John C. G., Martin Warren and David Hunt. *Purple Secret: Genes, 'Madness' and the Royal Houses of Europe* (1998; revised edition, Corgi Books, London, 1999)

Roland, Llewelyn ap. *Monarchy: Means to What End?* (The Strickland Press, Glasgow, 1952)

Rose, Kenneth. *King George V* (Weidenfeld & Nicolson, London, 1983)

Ross Williamson, Hugh. *The Day they Killed the King* (Frederick Muller, London, 1957)

Rowse, A. L. *The Regicides* (Duckworth, London, 1994)

Rumsey, Christopher. *The Rise and Fall of British Republican Clubs, 1871–1874* (Quinta Press, Oswestry, 2000)

Russel, Nick. *Poets by Appointment: Britain's Laureates* (Blandford Press, Poole, 1981)

Russell of Liverpool, Lord. *Henry of Navarre: Henry IV of France* (Robert Hale, London, 1969)

Saul, Nigel. *Richard II and Chivalric Kingship: Inaugural Lecture at Royal Holloway College* (Royal Holloway College, University of London, London, 1999)

Seymour, Bruce. *Lola Montez: A Life* (Yale University Press, New Haven & London, 1996)

Seyssel, Claude de. *The Monarchy of France*. Translated by J. H. Hexter, edited by Donald R. Kelley, additional translations by Michael Sherman (1515; Yale University Press, New Haven & London, 1981)

Shakespeare, Nicholas. *The Men Who would be King: A Look at Royalty in Exile* (Sidgwick & Jackson, London, 1984)

Shaw, George Bernard. *The Bodley Head Collected Plays of Bernard Shaw* (The Bodley Head, London, 1973)

Shaw, Karl. *Royal Babylon* (Virgin Books, London, 1999)

Shawcross, William. *Queen and Country* (BBC Books, London, 2002)

Shelley, Percy Bysshe. 'An Address to the People on the Death of the Princess Charlotte'. *Shelley's Prose; or, the Trumpet of a Prophecy*. Edited by David Lee Clark (1954; Fourth Estate, London, 1988)

Shils, Edward and Michael Young. 'The Meaning of the Coronation'. *Sociological Review*, new series, vol. I, no. 2, December 1953, pp 63–81

Simmonds, Diana. *Princess Di: The National Dish* (Pluto Press, London & Sydney, 1984)

Sitwell, Osbert. *Rat Week: An Essay on the Abdication* (Michael Joseph, London, 1986)

Smith, Denis Mack. *Italy and its Monarchy* (Yale University Press, London & New Haven, 1989)

Sophia, Electress of Hanover. *Memoirs, 1630–1680*. Translated by H. Forester (Richard Bentley, London, 1888)

Spellman, W. M. *Monarchies, 1000–2000* (Reaktion Books, London, 2001)

Spencer, Herbert. *The Principles of Sociology* (Williams & Norgate, London, 1898)

Stanhope, Alexander. *Spain under Charles II; or, Extracts from the Correspondence of the Hon. Alexander Stanhope, British Minister at Madrid, 1690–1699* (John Murray, London, 1860)

Stevenson, Frances. *Lloyd George: A Diary*. Edited by A. J. P. Taylor (Hutchinson, London, 1971)

Stowell, T. E. A. '"Jack the Ripper" – A solution?'. *The Criminologist*, vol. 5, no. 18, November 1970

Strachey, Lytton. *Queen Victoria* (1921; Penguin Books, London, 2000)

Strong, Roy. *The Cult of Elizabeth: Elizabethan Portraiture and Pageantry* (Thames & Hudson, London, 1977)

——. *The Tudor and Stuart Monarchy: Pageantry, Painting, Iconography*, vol. II: *Elizabethan* (The Boydell Press, Woodbridge, 1995)

——. *Coronation: A History of Kingship and the British Monarchy* (HarperCollins, London, 2006)

Tanner, Marie. *The Last Descendant of Aeneas. The Hapsburgs and the Mythic Image of the Emperor* (Yale University Press, New Haven & London, 1993)

Taylor. A. J. P. *The Habsburg Monarchy, 1809–1918: A History of the Austrian Empire and Austria-Hungary* (1941; new edition, Hamish Hamilton, London, 1948)

Tennyson, Alfred, Baron. *The Death of the Duke of Clarence and Avondale* (London, n.d. [1892])

Thackeray, W. M. *The Four Georges; and The English Humourists* (1855; Alan Sutton, Stroud, 1995)

Thompson, J. A. 'Labour and the Modern British Monarchy'. *South Atlantic Quarterly*, vol. lxx, no. 3, Summer 1971

Thomson, Rev. Patrick. *Lessons Suggested by the Fall of Greatness!: A Sermon on the Death of his Royal Highness the Prince Consort* (Thomson & Baxter, Manchester, 1861)

Thornton, Michael. *Royal Feud: The Queen Mother and the Duchess of Windsor* (Michael Joseph, London, 1985)

Tomes, Jason. *King Zog, Self-made Monarch of Albania* (Sutton Publishing, Stroud, 2003)

Tomlinson, Richard. *Divine Right: The Inglorious Survival of British Royalty* (1994; updated edition, Abacus, London, 1995)

Trotsky, Leon. *The History of the Russian Revolution*. Translated by Max Eastman (1932–3; Sphere Books, London, 1967), 3 vols

——. 'Where is Britain Going?' In *Leon Trotsky on Britain*, introduced by George Novack (Monad Press, New York, 1973)

Troyat, Henri. *Catherine the Great*. Translated by Emily Read (1977; English translation, Aidan Ellis Publishing, Henley-on-Thames, 1979)

Turk, Edward Baron. *Hollywood Diva: A Biography of Jeanette MacDonald* (University of California Press, Berkeley, Calif., & London, 1998)

Turner, Graham. *Elizabeth: The Woman and the Queen* (Macmillan, London, 2002)

Upward, Allen. *Secrets of the Courts of Europe: The Confidences of an Ex-ambassador* (J. W. Arrowsmith, Bristol; Simpkin, Marshall, Hamilton, Kent, London, 1897)

Vanderbilt, Gloria and Thelma, Lady Furness. *Double Exposure: A Twin Autobiography* (Frederick Muller, London, 1959)

Vansittart, Peter, ed. *Happy and Glorious!* (HarperCollins, London, 1988)

Victoria, Queen of Great Britain and Empress of India. *Queen Victoria's Highland Journals*. Edited by David Duff (Webb & Bower, Exeter, 1980)

——. *Queen Victoria in her Letters and Journals*. Selected and edited by Christopher Hibbert (Penguin Books, Harmondsworth, 1985)

Voltaire. *Lion of the North: Charles XII of Sweden*. Translated by M. F. O. Jenkins (Associated University Presses, London, East Brunswick, NJ, & Toronto, 1981)

Vorres, Ian. *The Last Grand-Duchess: Her Imperial Highness Grand-Duchess Olga Alexandrovna* (Hutchinson, London, 1964)

Waller, Maureen. *Ungrateful Daughters: The Stuart Princesses who Stole their Father's Crown* (Hodder & Stoughton, London, 2002)

Walpole, Horace. *Memoirs of the Reign of King George II.* Edited by Lord Holland (second edition, Henry Colburn, London, 1847), 3 vols

Warwick, Christopher. *George and Marina, Duke and Duchess of Kent* (Weidenfeld & Nicolson, London, 1988)

Wedgwood, C. V. *The Trial of Charles I* (Collins, London, 1964)

Weintraub, Stanley. *The Importance of being Edward: King-in-waiting, 1841–1901* (John Murray, London, 2000)

——. *Victoria: Biography of a Queen* (Unwin Hyman, London, 1987)

Weir, Alison. *Britain's Royal Families: The Complete Genealogy* (1989; Pimlico, London, 2002)

West, Nigel, ed. *The Faber Book of Treachery* (Faber & Faber, London, 1995)

West, Rebecca. *The Meaning of Treason* (1949; revised edition, Penguin Books, London, 1965)

Whatley, Christopher A. 'Royal Day, People's Day: The Monarch's Birthday in Scotland, c. 1660–1860'. In *People and Power in Scotland: Essays in Honour of T. C. Smout*, edited by Roger Mason and Norman Macdougall (John Donald Publishers, Edinburgh, 1992)

Wheatcroft, Andrew. *The Ottomans: Dissolving Images* (1993; Penguin Books, London, 1995)

——. *The Habsburgs: Embodying Empire* (1995; new edition, Penguin Books, London, 1996)

Wheeler Bennett, Sir John. *Friends, Enemies and Sovereigns* (Macmillan, London, 1976)

Wheen, Francis. *How Mumbo-jumbo Conquered the World: A Short History of Modern Delusions* (Fourth Estate, London, 2004)

Whiting, Audrey. *The Kents* (Hutchinson, London, 1985)

Whitworth, Rex. *William Augustus, Duke of Cumberland: A Life* (Leo Cooper, London, 1992)

Wilhelmina, HRH, Princess of the Netherlands. *Lonely but Not Alone.* Translated by John Peereboom (Hutchinson, London, 1960)

William II, Ex-Kaiser. *My Memoirs* (Cassell, London, New York, Toronto & Melbourne, 1922)

Williams, Ann. *Kingship and Government in Pre-conquest England, c. 500–1066* (Macmillan, Basingstoke, 1999)

Williams, Neville. *The Life and Times of Henry VII* (Weidenfeld & Nicolson, London, 1973)

Williams, Philip, ed. *The Diary of Hugh Gaitskell, 1945–1956* (Jonathan Cape, London, 1983)

Williams, Richard. *The Contentious Crown: Public Discussion of the British Monarchy in the Reign of Queen Victoria* (Ashgate, Aldershot, 1997)

Williams, Susan. *The People's King: The True Story of the Abdication* (Allen Lane, London, 2003)

Williamson, Philip. *Stanley Baldwin* (Cambridge University Press, Cambridge, 1999)

Windsor, Bessie Wallis Warfield, Duchess of. *The Heart Has its Reasons: The Memoirs of the Duchess of Windsor* (Michael Joseph, London, 1956)

Windsor, HRH Edward, Duke of. *A King's Story* (1951; Prion Books, London, 1998)

Woolf, Leonard. *After the Deluge: A Study of Communal Psychology* (The Hogarth Press, London, 1931)

Woolf, Virginia. 'Royalty'. *Collected Essays*, vol. 4 (The Hogarth Press, London, 1967)

Worden, Blair. *Roundhead Reputations: The English Civil Wars and the Passions of Posterity* (Allen Lane, London, 2001)

Wynn Jones, Michael. *A Cartoon History of the Monarchy* (Macmillan, London, 1978)

York, Sarah, Duchess of, with Jeff Coplon. *My Story* (Simon & Schuster, London, 1996)

Young, Hugo. *One of Us* (1989; final edition, Pan Books, London, 1993)

Zamoyski, Adam. *The Last King of Poland* (Jonathan Cape, London, 1992)

Zee, Henri and Barbara van der. *William and Mary* (1973; Pan Books, London & Sydney, 1975)

Ziegler, Philip. *Crown and People* (Collins, London, 1978)

——. *King William IV* (1971; Cassell, London, 1989)

——. *Mountbatten: The Official Biography* (1985; new edition, Phoenix Press, London, 2001)

——. *King Edward VIII* (1990; revised edition, Sutton Publishing, Stroud, 2001)

Periodicals

Court Journal; *Hello!*; *Illustrated London News*; *The King*; *The King and his Navy and Army*; *Majesty*; *Young Gentlewoman*; *Royal Gazette* (New York); *The Fascist*; *The Times*; *Guardian*; *Independent*; *Daily Mail*; *Daily Telegraph*; *Daily Express*; *Evening News* (London); *Evening Standard* (London); *New York Times*; *The Tatler*; *Town Talk*; *Penny Satirist*; *The Satirist*; *Working Man's Friend and Political Magazine*; *Cleave's Penny Gazette of Variety and Amusement*; *John Bull*.

Index

JEREMY PAXMAN is a journalist, best known for his work presenting BBC's *Newsnight* and *University Challenge*. His books include *Friends in High Places*, *The English*, and *The Political Animal*. He lives in Oxfordshire, England.

PublicAffairs is a publishing house founded in 1997. It is a tribute to the standards, values, and flair of three persons who have served as mentors to countless reporters, writers, editors, and book people of all kinds, including me.

I. F. Stone, proprietor of *I. F. Stone's Weekly*, combined a commitment to the First Amendment with entrepreneurial zeal and reporting skill and became one of the great independent journalists in American history. At the age of eighty, Izzy published *The Trial of Socrates*, which was a national bestseller. He wrote the book after he taught himself ancient Greek.

Benjamin C. Bradlee was for nearly thirty years the charismatic editorial leader of *The Washington Post*. It was Ben who gave the *Post* the range and courage to pursue such historic issues as Watergate. He supported his reporters with a tenacity that made them fearless and it is no accident that so many became authors of influential, best-selling books.

Robert L. Bernstein, the chief executive of Random House for more than a quarter century, guided one of the nation's premier publishing houses. Bob was personally responsible for many books of political dissent and argument that challenged tyranny around the globe. He is also the founder and longtime chair of Human Rights Watch, one of the most respected human rights organizations in the world.

• • •

For fifty years, the banner of Public Affairs Press was carried by its owner Morris B. Schnapper, who published Gandhi, Nasser, Toynbee, Truman, and about 1,500 other authors. In 1983, Schnapper was described by *The Washington Post* as "a redoubtable gadfly." His legacy will endure in the books to come.

Peter Osnos, *Founder and Editor-at-Large*